Marxist Humanism and Communication Theory

This book outlines and contributes to the foundations of Marxist-humanist communication theory. It analyses the role of communication in capitalist society.

Engaging with the works of critical thinkers such as Erich Fromm, E. P. Thompson, Raymond Williams, Henri Lefebvre, Georg Lukács, Lucien Goldmann, Günther Anders, M. N. Roy, Angela Davis, C. L. R. James, Rosa Luxemburg, Eve Mitchell, and Cedric J. Robinson, the book provides readings of works that inform our understanding of how to critically theorise communication in society. The topics covered include the relationship of capitalism, racism, and patriarchy; communication and alienation; the base/superstructure-problem; the question of how one should best define communication; the political economy of communication; ideology critique; the connection of communication and struggles for alternatives.

Written for a broad audience of students and scholars interested in contemporary critical theory, this book will be useful for courses in media and communication studies, cultural studies, Internet research, sociology, philosophy, political science, and economics.

This is the first of five Media, Communication and Society volumes, each one outlining a particular aspect of the foundations of a critical theory of communication in society.

Christian Fuchs is a critical theorist of media, communication and society. He is co-editor of the journal *tripleC: Communication, Capitalism & Critique*. He is author of many publications, including the books *Social Media: A Critical Introduction* (3rd edition 2021), *Communication and Capitalism: A Critical Theory* (2020), *Marxism: Karl Marx's Fifteen Key Concepts for Cultural & Communication Studies* (2020), *Nationalism on the Internet: Critical Theory and Ideology in the Age of Social Media and Fake News* (2020), *Rereading Marx in the Age of Digital Capitalism* (2019), *Digital Demagogue: Authoritarian Capitalism in the Age of Trump and Twitter* (2016), *Digital Labour and Karl Marx* (2014), *Internet and Society* (2008).

Marxist Humanism and Communication Theory

Media, Communication and Society Volume One

Christian Fuchs

LONDON AND NEW YORK

First published 2021
by Routledge
2 Park Square, Milton Park, Abingdon, Oxon OX14 4RN

and by Routledge
52 Vanderbilt Avenue, New York, NY 10017

Routledge is an imprint of the Taylor & Francis Group, an informa business

© 2021 Christian Fuchs

The right of Christian Fuchs to be identified as author of this work has been asserted by him in accordance with sections 77 and 78 of the Copyright, Designs and Patents Act 1988.

All rights reserved. No part of this book may be reprinted or reproduced or utilised in any form or by any electronic, mechanical, or other means, now known or hereafter invented, including photocopying and recording, or in any information storage or retrieval system, without permission in writing from the publishers.

Trademark notice: Product or corporate names may be trademarks or registered trademarks, and are used only for identification and explanation without intent to infringe.

British Library Cataloguing-in-Publication Data
A catalogue record for this book is available from the British Library

Library of Congress Cataloging-in-Publication Data
Names: Fuchs, Christian, 1976- author.
Title: Marxist humanism and communication theory : media, communication and society volume one / Christian Fuchs.
Description: New York : Routledge, 2021. | Series: Media, communication and society; volume 1 | Includes bibliographical references and index.
Identifiers: LCCN 2020040758 (print) | LCCN 2020040759 (ebook) | ISBN 9780367697136 (hardback) | ISBN 9780367697129 (paperback) | ISBN 9781003142959 (ebook)
Subjects: LCSH: Socialism and culture. | Communication--Social aspects. | Mass media—Social aspects.
Classification: LCC HX523 .F83 2021 (print) | LCC HX523 (ebook) | DDC 302.201--dc23
LC record available at https://lccn.loc.gov/2020040758
LC ebook record available at https://lccn.loc.gov/2020040759

ISBN: 978-0-367-69713-6 (hbk)
ISBN: 978-0-367-69712-9 (pbk)
ISBN: 978-1-003-14295-9 (ebk)

Typeset in Univers
by MPS Limited, Dehradun

Contents

Figures	vii
Tables	ix
Acknowledgements	xi
1 Introduction	1
2 Erich Fromm and the critical theory of communication	19
3 Revisiting the Althusser/E. P. Thompson-controversy: Towards a Marxist theory of communication	49
4 Raymond Williams's communicative materialism	79
5 Henri Lefebvre's theory of the production of space and the critical theory of communication	103
6 Towards a critical theory of communication with Georg Lukács and Lucien Goldmann	129
7 Günther Anders's critical theory of technology	151
8 Jean-Paul Sartre as social theorist of communication. A theoretical engagement with "Critique of Dialectical Reason"	177
9 M. N. Roy, socialist humanism, and the critical analysis of communication	205
10 Capitalism, racism, patriarchy	241
11 Conclusion	279
Index	291

Figures

2.1	Erich Fromm's conceptualisation of the relationship between the economy and ideas (adapted from: Fromm 1965b, 212)	22
2.2	The relationship between the economy and culture	27
2.3	Club 2.0	44
4.1	The relation of the economic and the non-economic in society	87
5.1	The dialectic of humans – social relations – social space	120
6.1	Human interactions in society and with nature	137
6.2	Hegel's dialectic of imagination (visualisation based on Hegel 1830/2007, §§455–459)	138
7.1	Concept of *Club 2.0*	173
8.1	A model of the communication process based on Sartre's critical theory of dialectical reason	185

Tables

1.1	The antagonisms in three forms of alienation	16
1.2	The main actors in alienated and humanist society	17
2.1	The authoritarian and the humanistic character in the economy, politics and culture	28
2.2	The present author's variation of Fromm's general distinction of social character types (based on Fromm 1947/2003, 82)	29
2.3	The present author's typology of authoritarian and humanistic forms of information and communication	30
4.1	Williams's typology of the means of communication (based on Williams, 2005: 53–63; 1981a, chapter 4)	86
5.1	Lefebvre's three levels of social space (based on information from: Lefebvre 1991, 32–33, 38–43, 362, 50, 116, 233, 288)	113
8.1	Examples of two Sartrean forms of direct and indirect social relations	189
8.2	The most viewed YouTube videos of all times (source: https://en.wikipedia.org/wiki/List_of_most-viewed_YouTube_videos, accessed on 16 February 2020)	193
10.1	Income, unemployment and involuntary part-time work in the USA	257
10.2	Occupational structure in the USA, 2018 annual averages	258
10.3	Alienation in the context of capitalism, racism, and patriarchy	263
10.4	The economic, political and cultural-ideological dimensions of capitalism, racism, and patriarchy	264
10.5	The interaction of class, racism, gender oppression	265
10.6	Economic, political and cultural communication in the context of class, racism, and gender-related oppression	266
10.7	Characteristics of four types of labour	271
11.1	Alienation processes and the main actors in alienated and humanist society	280
11.2	The economic, political and cultural-ideological dimensions of capitalism, racism, and patriarchy	280
11.3	The interaction of class, racism, gender oppression	281
11.4	Types of alienated communication(s)	287
11.5	Economic, political and cultural communication in the context of class, racism, and gender-related oppression	288

11.6	Three forms of digital alienation	288
11.7	Three antagonisms of digital alienation	288

Acknowledgements

Section 1.2 (Why Do We Need Marxist Humanism Today?) of the introduction (chapter 1) was first published as a section in the following article: Christian Fuchs. 2020. "Towards a Critical Theory of Communication as Renewal and Update of Marxist Humanism in the Age of Digital Capitalism." *Journal for the Theory of Social Behaviour*. doi:https://doi.org/10.1111/jtsb.12247. The article was published using a Creative Commons CC-BY Licence, which allows reproduction. The section was updated and extended.

Section 1.4 (Alienation) of the introduction (chapter 1) was first published as section 2 in the following article: Christian Fuchs. 2018. "Universal Alienation, Formal and Real Subsumption of Society Under Capital, Ongoing Primitive Accumulation by Dispossession: Reflections on the Marx@200-Contributions by David Harvey and Michael Hardt/Toni Negri." *tripleC: Communication, Capitalism & Critique* 16 (2): 454–467. doi:https://doi.org/10.31269/triplec.v16i2.1028. Reproduced and used by permission of the journal *tripleC*. The original section was updated and extended.

Chapter 2 was first published as the following article: Christian Fuchs. 2020. "Erich Fromm and the Critical Theory of Communication." *Humanity & Society* 44 (3): 298–325. doi:https://doi.org/10.1177/0160597620930157. Reproduced based on SAGE's Author Archiving and Re-Use Guidelines.

Chapter 3 was first published as the following article: Christian Fuchs. 2019. "Revisiting the Althusser/E. P. Thompson-Controversy: Towards a Marxist Theory of Communication." *Communication and the Public* 4 (1): 3–20. doi:https://doi.org/10.1177/2057047319829586. Reproduced based on SAGE's Author Archiving and Re-Use Guidelines.

Chapter 4 was first published as the following article: Christian Fuchs. 2017. "Raymond Williams' Communicative Materialism." *European Journal of Cultural Studies* 20 (6): 744–762. doi:https://doi.org/10.1177%2F1367549417732998. Reproduced based on SAGE's Author Archiving and Re-Use Guidelines.

Chapter 5 was first published as the following article: Christian Fuchs. 2019. "Henri Lefebvre's Theory of the Production of Space and the Critical Theory of Communication." *Communication Theory* 29 (2): 129–150. doi:https://doi.org/10.1093/ct/qty025. Reproduction based on Oxford University Press Author Publication Rights Policy.

Chapter 6 was first published as the following article: Christian Fuchs. 2018. "Towards a Critical Theory of Communication with Georg Lukács and Lucien

Goldmann." *Javnost – The Public* 25 (3): 265–281. doi:https://doi.org/10.1080/13183222.2018.1463032. Reproduction granted based on Routledge-publishing agreement signed by Christian Fuchs on 6 April 2018.

Chapter 7 was first published as sections 1, 2, 3, and 5 in the following article: Christian Fuchs. 2017. "Günther Anders' Undiscovered Critical Theory of Technology in the Age of Big Data Capitalism." *tripleC: Communication, Capitalism & Critique* 15 (2): 582–611. doi:https://doi.org/10.31269/triplec.v15i2.898. Reproduced and used by permission of the journal *tripleC*.

Chapter 9 was first published as sections 1, 2, 3, 4, 6 in the following article: Christian Fuchs. 2019. "M. N. Roy and the Frankfurt School: Socialist Humanism and the Critical Analysis of Communication, Culture, Technology, Fascism and Nationalism." *tripleC: Communication, Capitalism & Critique* 17 (2): 249–286. doi:https://doi.org/10.31269/triplec.v17i2.1118. Reproduced and used by permission of the journal *tripleC*.

Parts of chapter 10 were first published as sections in the following article: Fuchs, Christian. 2018. "Capitalism, Patriarchy, Slavery, and Racism in the Age of Digital Capitalism and Digital Labour." *Critical Sociology* 44 (4–5): 677–702. doi:https://doi.org/10.1177%2F0896920517691108. Reproduced based on SAGE's Author Archiving and Re-Use Guidelines The material from the article was substantially extended by new material.

Chapter One
Introduction

    1.1 What is Marxist humanism?
    1.2 Why do we need Marxist humanism today?
    1.3 The structure of this book
    1.4 Alienation
    Literature

The overall task of this book is to outline elements and some foundations of a Marxist-humanist theory of communication by engaging with the works of some relevant thinkers. Such an approach is inherently a critical theory of society and communication, which means that it analyses how class, exploitation, domination, and power shape communication and how communication processed mediate class, exploitation, domination, and power.

The approach I take in has been further developed in the book *Communication and Capitalism: A Critical Theory* that is available open access (Fuchs 2020). The book at hand documents how I arrived at my own theoretical insights on how to theorise communication and capitalism by reading, engaging with, interpreting a variety of critical theory approaches. *Marxist Humanism & Communication Theory* provides an introduction on how to read specific critical theorists' approaches as critical theories of communication.

The book at hand is the first volume of a series of a book titled *Communication & Society*. The overall aim of *Communication & Society* is to outline foundations of a critical theory of communication and digital communication in society. It is a multi-volume theory social theory book series situated on the intersection of communication theory, sociology, and philosophy. The overall questions the *Communication & Society* deals with are: What is the role of communication in society? What is the role of communication in capitalism? What is the role of communication in digital capitalism?

1.1 What is Marxist humanism?

What is Marxist humanism? It is an analytical approach that has several features:

Hegel and dialectical philosophy

Marxist humanism is a form of Hegelian Marxism, which means that it uses dialectical philosophy for understanding society. It stresses the dialectics of subject/object, practices/structures, labour/capital, economic/non-economic, continuity/discontinuity, chance/necessity, etc. in society.

Practices

Marxist humanism analyses society by taking human beings' practices as foundational dimension. It stresses the role of social production as the material dimension of society.

Praxis

Marxist humanism analyses the role of class and social struggles in class and dominative societies. Praxis is human beings' struggle for a good society where everyone benefits and there is wealth, freedom, and happiness for all.

Human essence

Marxist humanism argues that there is an essence of human beings. It recognises that humans face different living conditions, but stresses that humans as such have common features. The commonalities of human beings are the foundation of practical and ethical universalism that argues for the realisation of common rights of all human beings. The notion of the commons plays an important role in this context.

Alienation

Alienation is one of Marxist humanism's central categories. Alienation denotes conditions of society where humans cannot control the conditions of their own existence. Alienation means that there is a difference in the potentials and actualities of humans and society. In alienated societies, humans and society cannot realise their potentials. Humans are alienated from what they could be, which means they are hindered from developing and realising their full potentials. There are different types of alienation. Alienation is characteristic for dominative societies, societies structured by domination. Domination means that one group benefits at the expense of other groups who have disadvantages and that the dominative group has means of coercion at hand in order to enforce its rule.

Democratic socialism, socialist democracy

Marxist humanism is a type of humanism. It understands humanism as the ethico-political stress on the importance of creating conditions in society that allow humans and society to realise their full potentials. For Marxist humanism, humanism is socialism and socialism is humanism. Socialism denotes a society of the commons, where all humans benefit. Socialism is a realisation of the economic, political and cultural commons: All humans live in wealth (economic commons), have democratic participation rights (political commons), and are respected (cultural commons). Democratic socialism sees socialism as inherently humanist and democratic. It is anti-fascist, anti-Stalinist, and anti-capitalist. It is critical of the anti-democratic potentials and realities of these types of systems. Marxist humanism doesn't limit the understanding of democracy to the political system but argues for the extension of democracy to society at large, including the economy. Marxist/socialist humanism stresses the democratic need for the collective self-management of the economy and society. It understands democracy as a participatory democracy.

Open Marxism

Orthodoxies such as Stalinism turn socialism into a dogmatic, deterministic, mechanistic, reductionist and quasi-religious practice. In contrast, Marxist humanism is a form of open Marxism that stresses the need for the unity in diversity of critical theories, practices, praxis and the need for Marxist theory and practice to be reflexive and develop so that it can take account of how society is changing.

Truth

Marxist humanism rejects relativist assumptions that there is no truth in society. It stresses that truth means a condition where humans and society can realise their full potentials and that falseness of society means the hindrance of the realisation of such potentials.

Ideology critique

Marxist humanism includes ideology critique as a dimension of critical theory. Ideology is understood as worldview, consciousness and practices that present and represent the world in distorted ways that do not correspond to actuality in order to justify and legitimate partial interests of the ruling class and dominant groups and to try to make those who have disadvantages believe that this condition is natural, necessary, unchangeable, or caused by scapegoats. Ideology is reified and false consciousness (Lukács 1971).

Critical ethics

Marxist humanism includes a form of critical ethics. It advances principles of how a good society looks like. Categories such as the commons, socialism, participation, democracy, (in)justice, freedom, exploitation, class, power, domination, etc. are of crucial importance for such critical ethics.

Marx' works

Marxist humanism is interested in advancing the engagement with Marx's works and the tradition of thought building on Marx. It sees the whole body of Marx's works as important and stresses that there is a coherent unity of and the connection of philosophy and political economy in Marx's works. It argues that there is no "epistemological break" in Marx's works. The epistemological break is a term introduced by Louis Althusser (1969), by which this French theorist claims that Marx's early works such as Economic and Philosophic Manuscripts of 1844 are esoteric and unscientific and that one should ignore them.

1.2 Why do we need Marxist humanism today?

Marxist humanism emerged in 20th-century social theory. Its theoretical foundations are Hegel's dialectical philosophical and Marx's *Economic and Philosophic Manuscripts of 1844*. Its axiological and political concern has been the establishment of democratic socialism as an alternative to capitalism, fascism, Stalinism, and other forms of authoritarian statism. Its analyses focused on the human being, human essence, human practices, alienation, political praxis, class struggles, ideology critique, and the dialectics of subject/object, practices/structures, labour/capital, the economic/the non-economic, continuity/discontinuity, etc.

Representatives of Marxist humanism have, among others, included Theodor W. Adorno, Günther Anders, Kevin Anderson, Simone de Beauvoir, Ernst Bloch, Angela Davis, Raya Dunayevskaya, Zillah Eisenstein, Barbara Epstein, Frantz Fanon, Erich

Fromm, Lucien Goldmann, André Gorz, David Harvey, Max Horkheimer, C. L. R. James, Karl Korsch, Karel Kosík, Henri Lefebvre, Georg Lukács, Herbert Marcuse, Maurice Merleau-Ponty, Kwame Nkrumah, Julius Nyerere, Bertell Ollmann, the Praxis Group in Yugoslavia, Sheila Rowbotham, M. N. Roy, Edward Said, Jean-Paul Sartre, Adam Schaff, Kate Soper, E. P. Thompson, Raymond Williams (see Alderson and Spencer 2017; Fromm 1965). Marxist humanism's decline had to do with the general decline of the Marxist theory under neoliberal conditions, the postmodern turn against Marxism, structuralism's attack on the human being that fostered the rise of post-humanism, and the influence of Althusser and Foucault in social theory (Alderson and Spencer 2017).

There are *six reasons* why we need a renewal of Marxist humanism today.

The *first reason* is the emergence of authoritarian capitalism. In critical theory, the concept of authoritarianism goes back to Erich Fromm (1969), who defines it as a social character who submits to those in power and enjoys dominating others. For Fromm, fascism is the most developed form of authoritarian society and authoritarian capitalism. Max Horkheimer (1939/1989, 78) sees authoritarian and therefore also fascist potentials immanent in capitalism itself. But not every form of capitalism fully develops its authoritarian potentials. Adorno et al.'s (1950) F-scale outlines a large number of characteristics of the authoritarian personality. The core of this approach are four features: authoritarianism combines the antidemocratic belief of the necessity of strong, top-down leaders, nationalism, the friend/enemy-scheme and ideological scapegoating, and the belief in law-and-order politics, violence, militancy, and war as the best political means (Fuchs 2018). Authoritarian capitalism is a society that combines capitalism with these principles. New forms of nationalism and authoritarianism have emerged in recent years. They pose dangers to democracy and can result in a new world war, genocide, fascism, etc. Marxist humanism stresses socialism and humanism as opposed to fascism.

Racism has intensified in contemporary authoritarian capitalism. The police killing of George Floyd became a symbol of how racism denies people of colour their humanity. Racist anti-humanism led to the Black Lives Matters movement.

The *second reason* is the limits of postmodernism in contemporary capitalism. Althusser and Foucault have had a major influence on the emergence and development of postmodernism and poststructuralism that have attacked Marxist theory, class politics, the notions of the human being, truth, alienation, commonalities, universalism, etc. While there are postmodern theorists who made productive use of Marx, certain versions of postmodernism have contributed to the decline of Marxist theory in an age when class contradictions have been exploding. Marxist humanism foregrounds praxis as class struggle and Marxist theory. It is a critique of postmodernism. Postmodernism has advanced a relativism and anti-universalism where there is no truth. In an age of fake news, post-truth, new nationalisms/fascism, we need a political concept of truth. Marxist humanism enables us to think critically about what is true and false. Postmodernism has fostered identity politics without class politics and consequently liberal reformism. Humanist Marxism advances democratic socialist politics. Postmodernism has advanced the hatred of Marx. In a time of major capitalist crisis, Marx is urgently needed. Post-colonial theory and thought have advanced forms of reverse orientalism (Chibber 2013; Warren 2017) where everything non-European and non-Western has been automatically considered as being progressive, which partly legitimates authoritarianism. Marxist humanism stresses universalism and human beings' commonality.

Marxist humanism challenges capitalism, imperialism, nationalism, patriarchy, racism, fascism, environmental degradation and these moments' interactions as anti-human forces that threaten and degrade humans and society. Patriarchy, racism, and environmental degradation have been challenged by the feminist, anti-racism and environmental movements. Such movements are not automatically politically progressive. There are, for example, also neoliberal feminisms, neoliberal versions of anti-racism, and fascist environmental groups. The point is that gender-related oppression, racism, and environmental destruction stand in relation to capitalist society, class, and the social question. Feminism, anti-racism, and environmentalism have to be socialist in character in order to be politically progressive.

The *third reason* is the need for dialectical analysis. Posthumanism, the concept of the Anthropocene, Actor Network Theory, New Materialism, etc. are attacks on the human being that collapse the dialectic of unity and differences into structures that eliminate or reduce the importance of humans. Post-humanism collapses the dialectic of human/non-humans and human/technology (robots) into the post-human cyborg. Bruno Latour's Actor Network Theory declares that things and instruments such as machines are just like humans, social actors and together with the latter form actor networks. As a consequence, Latour collapses the differentiation between the human as the social being and the non-human into the actant as the social (see also Fuchs 2020, 20–21). Deep Ecology and animal liberation theory collapse the dialectic of nature/society into an undifferentiated whole. Postmodernism collapses the dialectic of class/non-class into identity and the dialectic of culture/economy into culture. The concept of the Anthropocene blames the human being and not capitalism for the environmental crisis. The result of these developments has been the proliferation of undialectical, reductionist thought. While postmodernism and its various currents have continuously claimed that Marxism is reductionist and economistic, they have themselves advanced new forms of reductionism. In contrast, Marxist humanism is dialectical. It foregrounds the importance of humans in society and the dialectical relations that the human being is part of.

The problems of structuralism constitute *the fourth reason*. (Post-)Structuralism reduces humans to bearers of structures that resemble puppets on a string. It underestimates the importance of human practices, human thought, communication, production, and social struggles in society. In contrast, Marxist humanism stresses practices, praxis and the dialectic of practices/structures in society. For example, Althusser sees humans not as active agents but as bearers and "the 'supports' (Träger) of [...] functions" (Althusser and Balibar 2009, 199) defined by society's articulated structures and the mode of production. In Lacanian theory, humans "interact like puppets" and are "tools in the hands of the big Other" (Žižek 2007, p. 8). Lucien Goldmann in a debate with Foucault and Lacan argued that a famous slogan in the May 1968 Paris protests read that "structures do not take to the streets", which means that "it is never structures that make history, but men, although action of these always have a structured and significant character" (in Foucault 1969, 816, translation from French). Lacan commented that "if there is anything that the May events demonstrate, it is precisely the descent of structures into the street" (in Foucault 1969, 820, translation from French). Structuralist accounts of society fetishize structures that are interpreted as autonomous actors acting on and independently from humans. They disregard Marx's dialectical insight that humans "make their own history, but they do not make it as they please; they do not make it under circumstances chosen by themselves, but under circumstances directly encountered, given and transmitted from the past" (Marx 1852, 103).

The fetishism of difference is *the fifth reason*. Postmodernism's focus on difference has parallels to the ideology of the new right that demands the separation of cultures. The new forms of nationalism that have proliferated in the past 10 years fetishize difference by ascertaining pride in the nation and the hatred of immigrants, refugees, people of colour, etc. Marxist humanism stresses the universality of humanity, humans' common features, and the indivisibility of humanity.

The contradiction between capitalism and nature that has led to the environmental crisis is *the sixth reason*. The dangers of climate change have led to movements such as Extinction Rebellion and Fridays For Future. The oil industry is one of the world's largest and most profitable industry. Capitalism makes a profit out of the destruction of nature. The ecological crisis is a humanist concern because the antagonism between capitalism and nature undermines the livelihood and survival-capacities of humans and society.

The atmospheric chemist Paul J. Crutzen, who won the 1995 Nobel Prize in Chemistry, is one of the key thinkers of the Anthropocene. He uses the term Anthropocene for the present geological epoch that according to him started "in the latter part of the eighteenth century", where the "the effects of humans on the global environment have escalated. Because of these anthropogenic emissions of carbon dioxide, global climate may depart significantly from natural behaviour for many millennia to come" (Crutzen 2016, 211).

There is the danger of the concept of the Anthropocene to blame humans and humanity as such for the environmental crisis. It is an anti-humanist category that abstracts from political economy, the relationship of nature and society, and the capitalist organisation of this relation.

The collective ownership of the means of production is a necessary, but not sufficient condition for overcoming the environmental crisis. Moore (2015) argues that there are Four Cheaps that capital seeks: cheap labour-power, cheap food, cheap energy, cheap natural resources. In capitalism, capital strives to find ways to cheapen and reduce the socially necessary labour time required for the production of labour-power, food, energy, and raw materials/natural resources in order to advance capital accumulation. We do not live in the Anthropocene, but the capitalist age. The Capitalocene is the "Age of Capital" that, among other moments, is based on the "worldwide appropriations of Cheap Nature" (Moore 2016, 81). The Capitalocene has been an "era of fossil energy powering the modern capitalist industrial system" (Altvater 2016, 145). "In the Capitalocene, 'nature' has been transformed into a capital asset. Nature has been reduced to something that can be valued and traded and used up just as any other asset" (Altvater 2016, 145). The class relation between capital and labour is capitalism's first antagonism. Its second antagonism is the one between capitalism and nature (O'Connor 1998)

Marx formulated the capitalist tendency to destroy nature and to thereby undermine the livelihood of humans in the following manner: "Capitalist production, therefore, only develops the techniques and the degree of combination of the social process of production by simultaneously undermining the original sources of all wealth – the soil and the worker" (Marx 1867, 638). The establishment and struggle for red-green socialism is a dimension of Marxist humanism. Red-green socialism is the best foundation for the survival of humans and society, including human nature and external nature.

Marxist humanism is a counter-narrative, counter-theory, and counter-politics to these developments. A critical, dialectical theory of communication can draw on and start from this intellectual tradition. The methodological approach that the present author takes in this context is to make visible, engage with, draw on, start from, use, interpret, and further develop elements from often unknown, hidden, ignored, neglected, and forgotten Marxist-humanist works.

1.3 The structure of this book

Each chapter in this book focuses on (a) particular Marxist humanist theorist(s): Erich Fromm (Chapter 2), Edward P. Thompson (Chapter 3), Raymond Williams (Chapter 4), Henri Lefebvre (Chapter 5), Georg Lukács and Lucien Goldmann (Chapter 6), Günther Anders (Chapter 7), Jean-Paul Sartre (Chapter 8), M. N. Roy (Chapter 9). A reading of particular works of these theorists is presented as well as my own interpretation that situates these approaches in the context of a critical theory of communication and thereby goes beyond the respective original approaches. None of these thinkers established a full-fledged theory of communication. But we can find elements in their thought that can inform the development of a critical theory of communication. Chapter 10 operates on a meta-level. It analyses the relationship of capitalism, racism, and patriarchy in general and in the context of communication. Some conclusions are presented in Chapter 11.

The thinkers whom the reader encounters in this book will now be briefly introduced. The list of thinkers I engage with is incomplete. More work remains to be done. I did some more related work, situating the works of Frankfurt School thinkers in the context of a critical theory of communication (Fuchs 2016). On another occasion, I engaged with the debate between Nancy Fraser and Axel Honneth that focused on the question of how recognition and redistribution are related (Fuchs 2011, Chapter 2, Section 2.3).

Erich Fromm (1900–1980) was a Marxist-humanist philosopher, psychoanalyst, and sociologist. He coined the notion of the authoritarian character. Among his most important books are *Escape from Freedom*, *The Sane Society*, *Marx's Concept of*

Man, *The Anatomy of Human Destructiveness*, and the collected volume *Socialist Humanism*.

Edward P. Thompson (1924–1993) was a Marxist-humanist historian, who analysed the working-class history and the history of working-class culture. His most important books are *The Making of the English Working Class*, *The Poverty of Theory and Other Essays*, *William Morris: Romantic to Revolutionary*. *The Poverty of Theory* is a critique of the approach of the French structuralist and anti-humanist Louis Althusser.

Raymond Williams (1921–1988) was a Marxist-humanist literary and cultural theorist and novelist. He established the approach of cultural materialism. Among his most important works are *Marxism and Literature*, *Communications*, and *Television: Technology and Cultural Form*. As a novelist, he wrote stories that are often set in the working class and the socialist and communist movement.

Henri Lefebvre (1901–1991) was a Marxist-humanist philosopher and sociologist. He can be considered as the most important and most influential French Marxist theorist. He published more than sixty books, including the three-volume *The Critique of Everyday Life* and *The Production of* Space.

Georg/György Lukács (1885–1971) was a philosopher who is often considered as the most influential theorist of the 20th century. In his book *History and Class Consciousness*, he coined based on Marx the notion of reified consciousness that influenced ideology critique and the development of the Frankfurt School's notion of instrumental reason. *Zur Ontologie des gesellschaftlichen Seins* (*The Ontology of Society's Being*) is Lukács' second masterpiece but has been widely forgotten and overlooked.

Lucien Goldmann (1913–1970) was a philosopher and sociologist who was strongly influenced by Lukács' works, which is why Lukács and Goldmann are in the book at hand discussed in one chapter. Among Goldmann's books are *The Human Sciences and Philosophy*, *Cultural Creation in Modern Society*, and *Lukács and Heidegger: Towards a New Philosophy*.

Günther Anders (1902–1992) was a philosopher and critical theorist of technology. He analysed how contemporary technologies are used by capital and bureaucracy for advancing alienation and destroying humans' control of society. Anders's most well-known book is the two-volume *Die Antiquiertheit des Menschen* (*The Outdatedness/Antiquatedness of the Human Being*).

Jean-Paul Sartre (1905–1980) was an existentialist philosopher and novelist. His first main work *Being and Nothingness* that was first published in 1943 has often been criticised as advancing individualism and nihilism. Sartre increasingly turned towards Marxist humanism and communism. His two-volume *Critique of Dialectical Reason* grounded an existentialist Marxist humanism. *Critique of Dialectical Reason* is the focus of the Sartre chapter in the book at hand. Sartre's lifelong partner Simone de Beauvoir (1908–1986) was an important humanist, socialist, feminist writer and theorist.

M. N. Roy (1887–1954) was a philosopher, political theorist, and anti-Stalinist communist activist who founded the Mexican Communist Party and the Communist Party of India. Roy was influenced by both humanism and Marxism. Among his major works are *Reason, Romanticism and Revolution, New Humanism: A Manifesto, Science and Philosophy, Fascism: Its Philosophy, Professions and Practice, Revolution and Counter-Revolution in China*. At the Second Congress of the Comintern in 1920, Roy presented supplementary theses to Lenin's *Theses on the National and Colonial Questions* and convinced Lenin to agree with his position. Roy put the interaction of capitalism, imperialism, and racism on the agenda of the international communist movement.

Chapter 11 theorises the relationship between capitalism, racism, and patriarchy. It engages with the works of a variety of authors, including Vivek Chibber, Mariarosa Dalla Costa, Angela Davis, W. E. B. Du Bois, Zillah Eisenstein, Eric J. Hobsbawm, C. L. R. James, Selma James, Rosa Luxemburg, Karl Marx, Maria Mies, Eve Mitchell, Cedric J. Robinson, David Roediger, Marisol Sandoval, Audrey Smedley, Sylvia Walby, Carter Wilson, and Cornel West.

Vivek Chibber is a Marxist sociologist and critic of anti-humanist versions of postcolonial theory. He is author of the book *Postcolonial Theory and the Specter of Capital*. Mariarosa Dalla Costa is a socialist feminist who together with Selma James authored *The Power of Women and the Subversion of the Community*, a classical work in socialist feminism that analyses the role of housework in capitalism. Selma James started the International Wages Housework Campaign. Angela Davis is a philosopher and a representative of feminist black Marxist theory. Among her books are Women, Race & Class and Are Prisons Obsolete? W. E. B. Du Bois (1868–1963) was a sociologist, historian and civil rights activist campaigning for the rights of Afro-Americans. He was involved in founding the National Association for the Advancement of Colored People. Among his main works are *Black Reconstruction in America: An Essay Toward a History of the Part Which Black Folk Played in the Attempt to Reconstruct Democracy in America, 1860–1880* and *The Souls of Black Folk*.

Zillah Eisenstein is a Marxist-feminist political theorist. She edited and contributed the major essays in the influential collected volume *Capitalist Patriarchy and the Case for Socialist Feminism*. Eric J. Hobsbawm (1917–2012) was a historian of the modern age. He is best known for his trilogy *The Age of Revolution: Europe 1789–1848*, *The Age of Capital: 1848–1875*, and *The Age of Empire: 1875–1914*. C. L. R. James (1901–1989) was a Marxist-humanist philosopher and anti-Stalinist socialist activist. Among his writings are *Notes on Dialectics: Hegel, Marx and Lenin*, *The Black Jacobins: Toussaint L'Ouverture and the San Domingo Revolution*, *State Capitalism and World Revolution*, *Modern Politics*, and *World Revolution, 1917–1936: The Rise and Fall of the Communist International*. James' wife Selma James was already mentioned. Rosa Luxemburg (1871–1919) was a political economist, political theorist, and politician who was involved in the founding of the Communist Party of Germany. Her major political-economic work is *The Accumulation of Capital*. Luxemburg gave attention to the roles of imperialism, war, nationalism, and women in capitalism. Karl Marx needs no further introduction.

Maria Mies is a sociologist and socialist-feminist theorist. She is the author of the book *Patriarchy and Accumulation On A World Scale: Women in the International Division of Labour*. Together with Vandana Shiva, she wrote the book *Ecofeminism*. Together with Veronika Bennholdt-Thomsen and Claudia Von Werlhof, she wrote the book *Women: The Last Colony*. Eve Mitchell is a Marxist-feminist and critic of intersectionality theory who wrote *I Am a Woman and a Human: A Marxist-Feminist Critique of Intersectionality Theory*. Cedric J. Robinson (1940–2016) was a social theorist who coined the notion of racial capitalism for analysing the relation of capitalism and racism. He is the author of *Black Marxism: The Making of the Black Radical Tradition*. David Roediger is a historian who studies the relationship between capitalism and racism. He is the author of the book *The Wages of Whiteness: Race and the Making of the American Working Class*. Marisol Sandoval is a critical theorist of culture and communication who has analysed cultural co-operatives, cultural labour in the cultural industries, the political economy of digital and alternative media, and the ideological character of corporate social responsibility initiatives. She is the author of the book *From Corporate to Social Media: Critical Perspectives on Corporate Social Responsibility in Media and Communication Industries*. Audrey Smedley is a historian with a particular interest analysis of the history of racism. She is the author of the book *Race in North America: Origin and Evolution of a Worldview*. Sylvia Walby is a sociologist and socialist feminist theorist. She is author of books such as *Theorizing Patriarchy; Patriarchy at Work: Patriarchal and Capitalist Relations in Employment*,

1800–1984; or *Theorizing Violence*. Carter A. Wilson is a political theorist whose work has a focus on the analysis of racism and who is the author of books such as *Racism: From Slavery to Advanced Capitalism*. Cornel West is a social theorist, public intellectual, and religious socialism. He is the author of works such as *The Ethical Dimensions of Marxist Thought*, *Race Matters*, and *Black Prophetic Fire*.

1.4 Alienation

Alienation is an important concept in Marx's works. He used throughout his life in his, including early works such as *Economic and Philosophic Manuscripts of 1844*, his middle period when he wrote manuscripts such as *Grundrisse*, and his later period when he worked on *Capital*. Alienation is one of Marxist humanism's key categories.

Marx develops and uses the term "alienation" in respect to political economy the first time in the essay *The Jewish Question* that he wrote in autumn 1843, and that was published in February 1844: "Money is the estranged essence of man's work and man's existence, and this alien essence dominates him, and he worships it" (Marx 1844b, 172). In his doctoral dissertation, Marx (1841, 64) spoke in the context of Epicurus' philosophy of the "alienation of the essence".

In 1843, in a reading of Hegel in the *Contribution to the Critique of Hegel's Philosophy of Law*, Marx argued that there is also political and ideological alienation: "It is indeed *estrangement* which matters in the so-called Christian state, but not *man*. The only man who counts, the *king*, is a being specifically different from other men, and is moreover a religious being, directly linked with heaven, with God. The relationships which prevail here are still relationships dependent on *faith*" (Marx 1843, 158). "Political emancipation is at the same time the *dissolution* of the old society on which the state alienated from the people, the sovereign power, is based." (Marx 1843, 165).

In the *Economic and Philosophic Manuscripts of 1844*, Marx specifies that capitalism results in the alienation of labour, which means a fourfold form of alienation (Marx 1844a, 276–277):

1) The alienation of humans from nature;
2) From their activities and species-being;
3) From their bodies and mind that form the human essence;
4) From the "product of his [the worker's] labour, from his life activity" (Marx 1844a, 276–277) and as a consequence from other humans and society.

In the *Grundrisse*, Marx presents economic alienation as the class relation between capital and labour:

> The emphasis comes to be placed not on the state of being objected, but on the state of being alienated, dispossessed, sold [Der Ton wird gelegt nicht auf das *Vergegenständlichtsein*, sondern das *Entfremdet-*, Entäußert-, Veräußertsein]; on the condition that the monstrous objective power which social labour itself erected opposite itself as one of its moments belongs not to the worker, but to the personified conditions of production, i.e. to capital. (Marx 1857/58, 831)

In *Capital Volume 1*, Marx argues that capital is an "alien power that dominates and exploits" workers and that in capitalism labour is "separated from its own means of objectification and realization" (Marx 1867, 716). In *Capital Volume 3*, Marx (1894) talks about alienation in chapters 5, 23, 27,36, and 48. He argues in chapter 23 that interest means the transfer of alienation from the realm of labour's exploitation into the realm of interest-bearing capital. In Chapter 48, he writes that alienation not just exists in the relationship between capital and labour, but that rent and interest are also expressions of economic alienation.

Taken together, we see that alienation for Marx, on the one hand, is the particular form of domination and exploitation that shapes the capitalist mode of production, in which labour creates commodities without owning the means of production and without controlling the conditions and the results of production. On the other hand, Marx sees alienation also as the universal form of domination, in which humans are not in control of the structures that affect their everyday lives. All class relations are economic forms of alienation. But alienation extends beyond the economy so that also the state and ideology alienate humans from the conditions of collective political decision-making and cultural meaning-making.

In his essay *Universal Alienation* in the present special issue, David Harvey (2018) defines alienation as universal in three respects:

1) Alienation in the economy not just entails capital's exploitation of labour, but also the realms of realisation, distribution and consumption, which means it extends to phenomena such as unemployment, consumerism, land seizure, deindustrialisation, debt peonage, financial scams, unaffordable housing, high food prices, etc.

2) Alienation entails processes beyond the economy, such as frustrations with politics, unaffordable public services, nationalist ideology, racism, police violence, militarism, warfare, alcoholism, suicide, depression, bureaucracy, pollution, gentrification, or climate change.
3) Alienation includes the geographic and social expansion of capital accumulation so that capital relations "dominate pretty much everywhere" (Harvey 2018, 427). "Alienation is everywhere. It exists at work in production, at home in consumption, and it dominates much of politics and daily life" (Harvey 2018, 429).

So, the universalisation of alienation means its extension beyond production, the economy and bounded spaces. Capital and capitalist society overcome and break down their own barriers in order to expand. In *Marx, Capital and the Madness of Economic Reason*, Harvey (2017, 47) argues that "a great deal of appropriation of value through predation occurs at the point of realization", which results in "[a]lienation upon realization" (Harvey 2017, 196).

In all forms of alienation, humans face asymmetric power relations and conditions that hinder their control over certain objects, structures or products (external nature, the means of production, the means of communication, the political system, the cultural system, etc.) so that aspects of their subjectivity are damaged (concerning human activities, well-being, consciousness, mind/psyche, body, worldviews, social relations). Alienation is neither purely objective nor purely subjective, but a negative relationship between social structures and humans in heteronomous societies.

In *Seventeen Contradictions and the End of Capitalism*, David Harvey (2014) devotes chapter 17 to the topic of "The Revolt of Human Nature: Universal Alienation". He argues that Marxists have often excluded alienation from consideration and have cancelled it off as "non-scientific concept" (Harvey 2014, 269). But the "scientific stance failed to capture the political imagination of viable alternatives" and "could not even confront the madness of the prevailing economic and political reason" (Harvey 2014, 269). Universal alienation is, therefore, a concept that in light of the danger that we may face "a less-than-human humanity" (Harvey 2014, 264) can provide prospects for alternatives. Alienation has always been a prominent concept in socialist/Marxist humanism (Fromm 1965, Alderson and Spencer 2017). Radical socialist humanism is the best way of opposing authoritarian capitalism's and neoliberalism's anti-humanism (Fuchs 2018).

Consequently, Harvey argues for both the use of the concept of universal alienation and for revolutionary humanism (Harvey 2014, 282–293 [Conclusion]). Humanism argues that "[w]e can through conscious thought and action change both the world we live in and ourselves for the better" and "that measures its achievements in terms of the liberation of human potentialities, capacities and powers" (Harvey 2014, 282–283). Harvey notes that humanism has been perverted and turned into a particularism that disguises itself as universalism but advances "imperialist and colonial cultural domination" (Harvey 2014, 285). He, therefore, argues for a "secular *revolutionary* humanism" that counters "alienation in its many forms and to radically change the world from its capitalist ways" (Harvey 2014, 287). Hardt and Negri (2017, 72–76) argue that there are parallels between autonomist and humanist Marxism: Both take subjectivity, social struggles and social change serious and oppose dogmatic Marxism and Stalinism.

Marx emphasises that the logic of accumulation characterises capitalism. This logic has its origin in the capitalist economy. But it also shapes modern politics and modern culture in capitalist societies. These systems are in capitalist society focused on the accumulation of political and cultural power. The accumulation of power takes the form of the accumulation of capital, the accumulation of decision-power, and the accumulation of definition-power. The consequences of accumulation are asymmetries of power, namely class structures, power structures and ideology (see Table 1.1).

Alienation means that humans are confronted with structures and conditions that cannot control and influence themselves. Under conditions of alienation, humans do not control the economic, political and cultural products that influence their lives and everyday life. Alienation means the "loss" of a product that does not belong to people. Use-values, collectively binding decisions and collective meanings are social products of human practices. In a capitalist society, however, they are controlled by only a few, which means that objectively alienating conditions exist.

TABLE 1.1 The antagonisms in three forms of alienation

Type of alienation	Dominating subjects	Dominated subjects
Economic alienation: exploitation	Ruling class, exploiters	Exploited class
Political alienation: domination	Dictator, dictatorial groups	Excluded individuals and groups
Cultural alienation: an ideology that results in disrespect	Ideologues	Disrespected individuals and groups

TABLE 1.2 The main actors in alienated and humanist society

	Alienated society	Humanist society
Economy	Exploiter	Socialist
Politics	Dictator	Democrat
Culture	Ideologue, demagogue	Friend

Table 1.2 illustrates the antagonism between alienated and humanistic society along the three societal dimensions of economy, politics, and culture. In alienated society, the main actors are the exploiter in the economy, the dictator in politics, and the ideologist/demagogue in culture. Humanism is the alternative to alienated society. In a humanist society, the main actors are the socialist in the economy, the democrat in politics, and the solidary friend in culture.

Literature

Adorno, Theodor W., et al. 1950. *The Authoritarian Personality.* New York: Harper & Brothers.
Alderson, David, and Robert Spencer. 2017. *For Humanism. Explorations in Theory and Politics.* London: Pluto.
Althusser, Louis. 1969. *For Marx.* London: Verso.
Althusser, Louis, and Étienne Balibar. 2009. *Reading Capital.* London: Verso.
Altvater, Elmar. 2016. "The Capitalocene, or, Geoengineering against Capitalism's Planetary Boundaries." In *Anthropocene or Capitalocene? Nature, History, and the Crisis of Capitalism,* edited byJason W. Moore, 138–152. Oakland, CA: PM Press.
Chibber, Vivek. 2013. *Postcolonial Theory and the Specter of Capital.* London: Verso.
Crutzen, Paul J. 2016. "Geology of Mankind." In *Paul J. Crutzen: A Pioneer on Atmospheric Chemistry and Climate Change in the Anthropocene,* edited by Paul J. Crutzen and Hans Günter Brauch, 211–215. Cham: Springer.
Foucault, Michel. 1969. "Qu'est-ce qu'un auteur?" In *Dits et écrits I 1954-1969,* 789-821. Paris: Gallimard.
Fromm, Erich. 1969. *Escape from Freedom.* New York: Avon.
———, ed. 1965. *Socialist Humanism. An International Symposium.* Garden City, NY: Doubleday.
Fuchs, Christian. 2020. *Communication and Capitalism: A Critical Theory.* London: University of Westminster Press. doi:https://doi.org/10.16997/book45.
Fuchs, Christian. 2018. *Digital Demagogue: Authoritarian Capitalism in the Age of Trump and Twitter.* Lon don: Pluto Press.

———. 2016. *Critical Theory of Communication: New Readings of Lukács, Adorno, Marcuse, Honneth and Habermas in the Age of the Internet.* London: University of Westminster. doi:https://doi.org/10.16997/book1.

———. 2011. *Foundations of Critical Media and Information Studies.* Abingdon: Routledge.

Hardt, Michael, and Antonio Negri. 2017. *Assembly.* Oxford: Oxford University Press.

Harvey, David. 2018. "Universal Alienation." *tripleC: Communication, Capitalism & Critique* 16 (2): 424–439. doi:https://doi.org/10.31269/triplec.v16i2.1026.

———. 2017. *Marx, Capital and the Madness of Economic Reason.* London: Profile.

———. 2014. *Seventeen Contradictions and the End of Capitalism.* London: Profile.

Horkheimer, Max. 1939/1989. "The Jews and Europe." In *Critical Theory and Society: A Reader*, edited by Stephen E. Bronner and Douglas Kellner, 77–94. New York: Routledge.

Lukács, Georg. 1971. *History and Class Consciousness.* London: Merlin.

Marx, Karl. 1894. *Capital Volume III.* London: Penguin.

———. 1867. *Capital Volume I.* London: Penguin.

———. 1857/58. *Grundrisse.* London: Penguin.

———. 1852. "The Eighteenth Brumaire of Louis Bonaparte." In *Marx & Engels Collected Works (MECW)*, 99–197. London: Lawrence & Wishart.

———. 1844a. "Economic and Philosophic Manuscripts of 1844." In *Marx & Engels Collected Works (MECW) Volume 3*, 229–346. London: Lawrence & Wishart.

———. 1844b. "On the Jewish Question." In *Marx & Engels Collected Works (MECW) Volume 3*, 146–174. London: Lawrence & Wishart.

———. 1843. "Contribution to the Critique of Hegel's Philosophy of Law." In *Marx & Engels Collected Works (MECW) Volume 3*, 3–129. London: Lawrence & Wishart.

———. 1841. "Difference Between the Democritean and Epicurean Philosophy of Nature." In *Marx & Engels Collected Works (MECW) Volume 1*, 25–107. London: Lawrence & Wishart.

Moore, Jason W. 2016. "The Rise of Cheap Nature." In *Anthropocene or Capitalocene? Nature, History, and the Crisis of Capitalism*, edited by Jason W. Moore, 78–115. Oakland, CA: PM Press.

———. 2015. *Capitalism in the Web of Life.* London: Verso.

O'Connor, James. 1998. *Natural Causes. Essays in Ecological Marxism.* New York/London. Guilford Press.

Warren, Rosie, ed. 2017. *The Debate on "Postcolonial Theory and the Specter of Capital".* London: Verso.

Žižek, Slavoj. 2007. *How to Read Lacan.* New York: W. W. Norton & Company.

Chapter Two
Erich Fromm and the critical theory of communication

2.1 Introduction
2.2 Communication
2.3 Ideology
2.4 Technology
2.5 Conclusion
Literature

2.1 Introduction

Erich Fromm (1900–1980) was a Marxist psychoanalyst, philosopher and socialist humanist[1] In the years from 1930 until 1939, he worked for the Institute for Social Research. Together with other Institute members such as MaxHorkheimer, he emigrated to the USA in 1934 after Hitler had come to power in Germany. He also worked at Bennington College, the New School for Social Research, the National Autonomous University of Mexico, Michigan State University, and NYU. Among his most well-known and most cited and read books are *Escape From Freedom*, *Sane Society*, *The Art of Loving*, *Man for Himself*, *To Have Or To Be?*, and *The Anatomy of Human Destructiveness*.

Fromm's work combined a humanist approach with the quest for socialism. Fromm's humanism stresses the need to realise all humans' potentials so that a good life for all is realised (Fromm 1965b, 207). Socialism is the realisation of humanism. "Marxism is humanism" (Fromm 1965b, 207). In contrast to other forms of humanism, socialist humanism does not believe that the Realisation of the potentials of humans and society cannot be achieved by education alone but requires the individuals' collective control and management of the economy, the political system and society (Fromm 1965a) so that "the full development of the individual" is "the condition for the full development of society, and vice versa" (Fromm 1965a, viii).

Given Fromm's socialist humanist approach, it is evident that the human being and social relations are key concerns of his works. Communication is the process through

---

[1] See Funk (2018) and Friedman & Schreiber (2013) for comprehensive introductions to Fromm's life and works.

which humans produce and reproduce sociality, social relations, social structures, groups, social systems, organisations, institutions, and society. Theories that focus on the human subject, such as the one by Fromm, are suited as starting points for a critical theory of communication. This chapter asks: How can Fromm's critical theory of communication be used and updated to provide a critical perspective in the age of digital and communicative capitalism?

In order to provide an answer, this chapter discusses elements from Fromm's work that allow us to understand the human communication process better. The focus is on communication (section 2), ideology (section 3), and technology (section 4). These three dimensions are connected: Communication is a general social process. Ideology is a particular form of communication that aims at creating reified consciousness. Technology is a means that humans use for achieving certain goals. In class societies, technology takes on an instrumental character and therefore acts as a means of domination and exploitation. Information and communication technologies (such as the computer) are particular types of technologies that organise the production, distribution and consumption of information. Fromm was particularly interested in the role of the computer in society (see section 4). The focus of this chapter on communication, ideology and technology is not accidental but is justified by the circumstance that these three categories are crucial for a critical theory of communication.

Each of the three main sections in this chapter consists of two sub-sections: The first sub-section presents Fromm's main arguments on the theme addressed in the section. The second sub-section updates Fromm's arguments and presents the present author's Frommian approach.

2.2 Communication

2.2.1 Erich Fromm on communication

One of the starting points of Fromm's works are the questions: What is the human being? What is the human being's essence? The human being is "*life aware of* itself" (Fromm 1964, 117). The human being is "a producing animal, capable of transforming the materials which he finds at hand, using his reason and imagination" (Fromm 1947/2003, 61). The human being "*must* produce in order to live" (61). Fromm (1947/2003, 28) argues that human beings differ from animals because they have self-awareness, reason and imagination (Fromm 1947/2003, 28; see also Fromm 1973/1997, chapter 10). These features enable them to reason morally, anticipate alternatives and consequences of action, and to dream. Dreams are "a common language of all humanity" (Fromm 1973/1997, 308; see also Fromm 1951). Reason and imagination among other things enable that they can "denote objects and acts by symbols" (Fromm 1947/2003, 28). The implication of the social use and production of symbols is that the human being is a language-using, communicating being. Fromm argues that the human being's productive orientation implies "*a mode of relatedness* in all realms of human experience. It covers mental, emotional, and sensory responses to others, to oneself, and to things. Productiveness is man's ability to use his powers and to realize the potentialities inherent in him" (Fromm 1947/2003, 61).

The relatedness of human existence implies that humans are co-operating beings:

> "One important element is the fact that men can not live without some sort of co-operation with others. [...] Each person experiences this need for the help of others very drastically as a child. On account of the factual inability of the human child to take care of itself with regard to all-important functions, communication with others is a matter of life and death for the child. The possibility of being left alone is necessarily the most serious threat to the child's whole existence"
>
> (Fromm 1941/1969, 35–36).

The human being is based on a dialectic of the body and the mind. The human has a need for "completeness in the process of living" (Fromm 1947/2003, 34) and strives to realise this need not just by envisioning something in thoughts, but "also in the process of living" (34). The dialectic of thinking and living is accompanied by the dialectic of "feelings and actions" (34).

Fromm (1965b) argues that the social character mediates between the economy and culture. The social character is "the matrix of the character structure *common to a group*" (Fromm 1965b, 210; see also Fromm 1956/2002, 76–81; Fromm 1941/1969, 304–327). The social character is the totality of the common psychological features of a particular social group. It is shaped by society's institutions such as political economy, the economic structure (the class structure in a class society), the education system, religion, literature, customs, and the ways parents raise their children, etc. (Fromm 1965b, 211; Fromm 1956/2002, 78–79).

Fromm argues that "*the social character is the intermediary between the socio-economic structure and the ideas and ideals prevalent in a society*" (Fromm 1965b, 212). He visualises this relationship as shown in Figure 2.1.

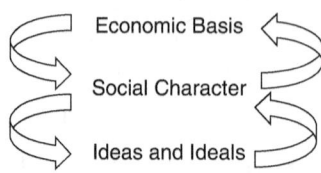

FIGURE 2.1 Erich Fromm's conceptualisation of the relationship between the economy and ideas (adapted from: Fromm 1965b, 212)

Fromm sees the relationship between "base" and "superstructure" as one where there is mutual interaction between levels. In 1970, Fromm wrote that the "ideological superstructure" is not a "reflex-like consequence of the socioeconomic structure" and that in "the concept of the social character, the connection between the economic basis and the superstructure is understood in their interaction. The practice of life, as it results from the socioeconomic structure, produces a certain social character which, in turn, produces the superstructure, which in turn reinforces the social character. The social character, in this view, is the intermediary between basic economic structure and superstructure" (Fromm and Maccoby 1970, 18 [footnote 24]).

In an essay first published in 1931, Fromm (1931/1989, 216) writes about "the dependence not only of social and political, but also of ideological, factors on economic conditions". He sees the task of psychoanalysis in the analysis of how "the economic condition [moves] through the mind and heart of a person to the ideological result" (216). Fromm in this essay refers positively to Engels' letter to Franz Mehring from 14 July 1893, where Engels (1893, 165) writes that there is an "interaction" and "a reciprocal influence" between the economy and ideology/consciousness. In a comparable letter to Joseph Bloch, Engels writes that there is "the interaction" (35) of "the economic moment" and "the various factors of the superstructure" (34).

For Fromm, humanism is the opposite of authoritarianism. As a consequence, he distinguishes between authoritarian and humanistic character, authoritarian and humanistic ethics, authoritarian and humanistic conscience (Fromm 1947/2003). This distinction can also be formulated as the one between "those who love death and those who love life, between the *necrophilous* and the *biophilous*" (Fromm 1964, 38). In contrast to Freud, who assumes that both the death instinct (Thanatos) and the life instinct (Eros) are part of human nature, Fromm (1964, 48–51) argues that only the life instinct is part of human nature, whereas necrophilia/the death instinct is psychopathological. Necrophilia is an intensification of sadism that takes on new qualities (Fromm 1973/1997, 463). In authoritarianism, "an authority states what is good for man and lays down the laws and norms of conduct", whereas in humanism the human being is "both the norm giver and the subject of the norms" (Fromm 1947/2003, 6). For Fromm (1973/1997), Hitler was an extreme example of the necrophilic character that loves "to destroy for the sake of destruction" and "to tear apart living structures" (441). Individuals, whom socialisation in capitalist society and authoritarian structures has turned into severely necrophilous persons, "become the executioners, terrorists, torturers; without them no terror system could be set up" (489).

Fromm differs in his interpretation of Freud's death instinct from other theorists in Marxist psychoanalysis. For Lacan (1991, 171, 326), the death instinct is part of the unconscious and the symbolic order. Herbert Marcuse (1956/1998, 83) argues that life "is the fusion of Eros and death instinct". In capitalism and class society, the death instinct gains "ascendency over the life instincts" and results in the externalisation of aggression in the form of violence (83). Whereas Lacan and Marcuse see the death instinct as a fundamental human drive, Fromm considers it as social psychopathology. Marcuse (1956/1998, 272) criticises Fromm, Karen Horney, and William Reich for the "revisionist rejection of the death instinct". Fromm (1955) answered to Marcuse that changes are needed to Freud's theory from a Marxist theory perspective in order to avoid "human nihilism" (349). The discussion shows that Marxist theories have interpreted Freud in different ways.

Fromm (1947/2003, 42–43) argues that socialisation (the way humans relate to others) and assimilation/acquisition (the way humans acquire things) are two fundamental aspects of human life. Assimilation is not a well-suited term because it sounds like humans do not actively and creatively change the world but merely adapt to it. The way humans acquire goods does not stand outside of social relations, which is why the separation of acquisition from socialisation is problematic. But one could say that socialisation is the one dimension of Fromm's analysis refers to the way humans organise their social relations, whereas the other dimension is about a particular type of social relation, namely the way that humans organise their economic relations. Fromm discerns two basic ways humans based on their social character structure organise the world: the non-productive (authoritarian) and the productive (humanistic) orientation. Fromm (1947/2003, 82, 84–86) argues that reception, exploitation, hoarding, marketing, masochism, sadism, destruction and indifference are characteristics of the authoritarian orientation and the authoritarian character structure that he also characterises as non-productive orientation.

In the realm of socialisation, the loving, reasoning social character type is opposed to the masochistic, sadistic, destructive and indifferent social character types. In the realm of economic socialisation, the working character type, who creates something, is opposed to the receiving, exploiting, hoarding and marketing character types (Fromm 1947/2003, 82).

Humanism is oriented on love to oneself, love to others, and love as a principle of society. The humanist organisation of communication(s) therefore implies the communication of love:

> "Love is possible only if two persons communicate with each other from the center of their existence, hence if each one of them experiences himself from the center of his existence. Only in this 'central experience' is human reality, only here is aliveness, only here is the basis for love. Love, experienced thus, is a constant challenge; it is not a resting place, but a moving, growing, working together; even whether there is harmony or conflict, joy or sadness, is secondary to the fundamental fact that two people experience themselves from the essence of their existence, that they are one with each other by being one with themselves, rather than by fleeing from themselves. There is only one proof for the presence of love: the depth of the relationship, and the aliveness and strength in each person concerned; this is the fruit by which love is recognized" (Fromm 1956, 103).

2.2.2 An update of Erich Fromm's concept of communication

What Fromm writes implies that social production is the essence of humans. Through production, humans create relations, relations to nature, relations to other humans, and relations to themselves. The implication is that the human being is a natural, social, co-operating and self-conscious being and that these characteristics are only possible through relations that humans produce in society. Also, communication is a process of social production, in which humans try to understand interpretations of the world by others and to share their understandings with others. The goal of communication is to understand how other humans understand the world. It is the understanding of understanding. Just like *communication is productive*, also *production is communicative*. In order to produce socially, that is in a co-operative manner, humans need to co-ordinate their work. For doing so, they use language in order to create, share and interpret symbols and meanings with the purpose of co-producing entities that satisfy certain human needs.

Fromm (1947/2003) speaks of a dialectic of feelings and actions. Also, the communication process is based on a dialectic of the body and the mind: In the communication process, thoughts produced in the human brain are externalised through speech created with the help by the combination of activities of the tongue, the lips, the teeth, the palate, the alveolar ridge, the uvula, and the glottis and bodily movements (the use of bodily gestures, our hands that write and type, the movement of our eyes that look at others in certain manners, etc.). The externalisation of thought through communication changes the social environment, which in turn acts as a system, in which other humans communicate so that individuals internalise signals that evoke further thoughts. Communication is a process of internalisation and externalisation of information in a social environment.

Fromm mentions that 20th-century capitalism advanced the social character of the "*homo consumens*" (Fromm 1965b, 214), who are socialised by capitalist culture and advertising to consume commodities. 21st-century culture is still a capitalist consumer culture. What has changed is that consumers are as prosumers (producing consumers) more actively asked and required to take part in the production of the commodities they consume. They self-assemble their furniture or create content, data and metadata on Facebook that is commodified to present targeted about to the users that want them to buy commodities. On commercial social media, human subjectivity creates a data commodity that enables that the same subjects are targeted with ads as consumers of commodities (Fuchs 2017b).

In a socialist society, consumption does not stop, but commodity consumption and commodity culture cease to exist. There is still individual consumption of goods in a socialist society, but there is also strong stress on social consumption of public goods and services and public events taking place, for example in "schools, libraries, theaters, parks, hospitals, public transportation, etc." (Fromm 1965b, 216).

Fromm does not reduce culture, ideology, and the psyche to the economy, but sees an interactive relationship between the economy and culture that is mediated by the social character. The social character is a mediating structure.

Raymond Williams (1977) acknowledges the dialectic character of such interactive approaches but argues that approaches that speak of mediation between the base and the superstructure are "not materialist enough" (97). They assume the existence of "separate and pre-existent areas or order of reality, between which the mediating process occurs" (99). In Williams' cultural materialism, the economy operates in culture, ideology, consciousness and politics, and the non-economic spheres also have emergent qualities that go beyond the economy. The economic and the non-economic are at the same time identical and different.

Williams' criticism applies to Fromm's model. The basic problem of how Fromm conceptualises the relationship of the economy and ideas (see Figure 2.1) is that he sees ideas and also the communication of ideas merely as a superstructure so that the economy and ideas are left separate although he connects them via mutual shaping processes. The phenomena of knowledge work that has become so prevalent in the 21st century and the role of the computer (an intellectual technology) as a key productive force show that ideas operate within the economy and are not a superstructure. Information and communication operate as part of the means of production both in the form of information technology and human knowledge. Furthermore, the relations of production are organised via human communication.

The economy is the realm where humans produce use-values that satisfy human needs. Culture is the realm, where humans make meaning of the world. That there is a dialectic of the economy and culture does not simply mean that these spheres interact, but rather that they are simultaneously identical and non-identical. Figure 2.2 shows the present author's model of how the economy and culture are related and the role of the social character.

Figure 2.2 visualises the present author's model of the dialectical relationship of the economy and culture and the role of communication and the social character in society. There is an economy inside and outside of culture and a culture inside and outside of the economy. The overlap of both is the cultural economy, the realm of society where mental workers create cultural products. These cultural products (e.g., a newspaper, a movie, a computer game, etc.) enter as inputs into non-economic social practices, including cultural practices. In cultural practices, humans co-create collective meanings of the world. Communication is the process through which social relations between humans are organised. Communication is, therefore, not the superstructural exchange of ideas. Rather, it takes place in all realms of society because all human activity is social and relational. Cultural products are an objectification of ideas. Collective meanings are the result of the communication of ideas about cultural products in the cultural system. Ideas operate in all realms of society, including the cultural economy and the cultural system. Collective meanings (such as an ideology, a worldview, a philosophy, a religion, etc.) influence other realms of society, including the economy and the cultural economy.

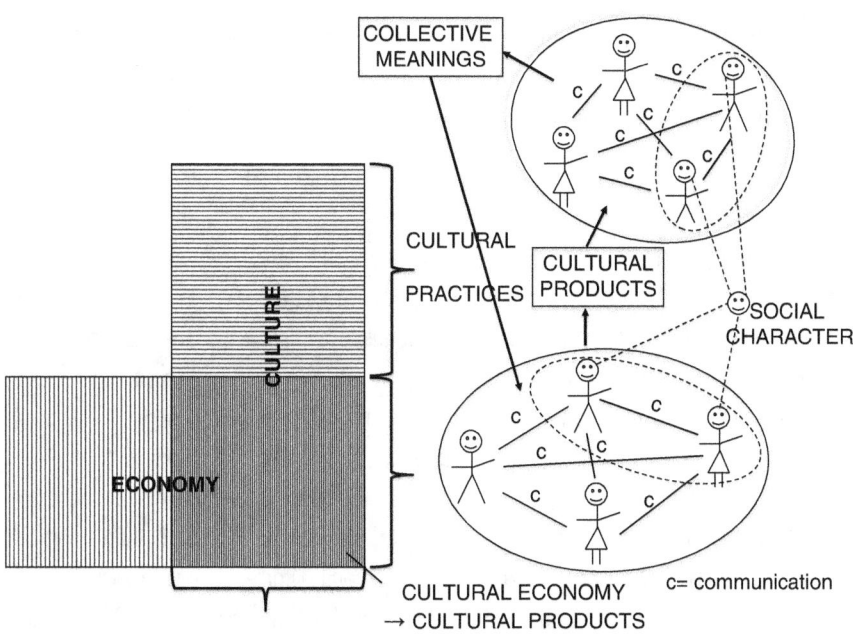

FIGURE 2.2 The relationship between the economy and culture

In each social system, certain social groups, who share certain social characteristics, operate. So, for example, in the capitalist economy workers form a social group, whose members share the social characteristic that they have to sell their labour-power in order to survive. What Fromm terms the social character is a group and psychological type whose members share certain psychological dispositions. The social character operates in several social systems at once. For Fromm, the authoritarian and the humanistic character are the two main types of the social character. Certain social groups have, by definition, a certain social character. But social groups and social characters are not the same. Different character types can be found in one and the same social group. So, for example, there are authoritarian workers and non-authoritarian workers. However, dominative groups are, to a certain degree, always authoritarian in character. For example, only individuals who have been socialised in capitalist society in such a manner that they have a desire to control and exploit others become managers or capitalists in a for-profit-corporation.

The social character mediates between the levels of the individual psyche and society. Humans, through communication in various social systems, form a particular social character, a character structure peculiar for a certain group in society. Through communication, the social character and social structures are formed and reproduced. The social character and social structures mediated through communication in the social relations that humans enter the condition, that is to enable and constrain individual thought and action.

Based on the distinction between the humanist affirmation of life and the authoritarian affirmation of death, Fromm (1973/1997) distinguishes between life-affirmative societies and destructive societies as two types of society (as well as non-destructive-aggressive societies as a third kind). The present author characterises these two societies, also as socialism and fascism. The human being is an individual being, but at the same time also a species-being. That the human is a species means that the human is a social and societal being. The individual can only live and realise their possibilities truly and to a full extent if all humans can live and realise their possibilities truly and fully. Therefore, humanism implies not just the good life of the individual, but the good life of all. Authoritarianism means that a particular individual, class or group coercively wants to enforce and enforces its will in society against others and considers its will as absolute and considers its will as absolute. The individual, particularistic will becomes the will of society. Conversely, a state of existence, where there are only unrelated individual wills results in an order of egoists, in which there is no sharing and no commonality. Such a state lacks relatedness. Both authoritarianism and individualism lack the dialectic of society and the individual that is at the heart of humanism.

Table 2.1 shows the present author's overview of different social characters that are based on the basic distinction between the authoritarian and the humanistic character.

The typology presented in Table 2.1 is based on the present author's distinction between the economic, the political and the cultural dimension of society (Fuchs 2008). All three realms are realms of production and teleological positing (Fuchs 2016): Production in the economy creates use-values that satisfy human needs. Production in the political system creates collectively binding decisions in society. Cultural production results in collective meanings of the world.

TABLE 2.1 The authoritarian and the humanistic character in the economy, politics and culture

	Authoritarian character	Humanistic character
Economy	The exploiter	The commoner
Politics	The dictator	The democrat
Culture	The ideologue/demagogue	The friend

Whereas the exploiter uses, instrumentalises and exploits others, the commoner advances the common good that benefits all and is controlled by all. Whereas the dictator coercively and with violence imposes his political will on others, the democrat deliberates with others in order to take collective political decisions. Whereas the ideologue tries to manipulate others, the friend helps others.

The capitalist economy is an authoritarian system of production, circulation and consumption, in which capital, the market, and the commodity form economic authorities. The mode of having is one of capitalism's guiding principles. In a political dictatorship, a political leader is an authority who shapes the political system. The mode of having also shaped dictatorships: Politics is all about having and accumulating political power. An authoritarian political system can accompany the authoritarian capitalist economy, but this does not necessarily have to be the case. The capitalist economy is compatible with dictatorship and liberal democracy. Generally speaking, authoritarianism means the undemocratic use of power and violence (the violence of the market, the state or ideology) to enforce the logic of having by turning humans into instruments that serve the interests of the powerful.

Generalising Fromm's analysis, we can say that the (ideal type) authoritarian character is destructive, exploitative and competitive in economic relations and aggressive and hateful in social relations in general, whereas the humanistic character is creative in economic relations and loving and co-operating in social relations in general. Based on Fromm, Table 2.2 presents the present author's distinction of social character types. Whereas productiveness means the capacity to realise human potentials and the potentials of humanity and society, authoritarianism and the mode of having are unproductive because they are based on the principle "I take what I need" from others (Fromm 1947/2003, 59). Exploitation is, therefore, the most fundamental aspect of the mode of having and authoritarianism. Those advancing the logic of exploitation do "not expect to receive things from others as gifts, but to take them away from others by force or cunning" (Fromm 1947/2003, 46). Exploitation's logic is a mode of economic appropriation that can permeate of realms of being, including economic production,

TABLE 2.2 The present author's variation of Fromm's general distinction of social character types (based on Fromm 1947/2003, 82)

	Authoritarian social character	Humanistic social character
Economic relations	Destructive, exploitative, competitive	Working, creating
Social relations in general	Aggressive, hateful	Loving, co-operating, helping others

TABLE 2.3 The present author's typology of authoritarian and humanistic forms of information and communication

	Authoritarian	Humanistic
Economic system	Knowledge and communication as commodities, exploitation of knowledge labour, means of communication as private property	Knowledge and communication as commons, co-ownership and co-production in self-managed knowledge-creating companies
Political system	Dictatorial control of knowledge and communication processes	Participatory knowledge and democratic communication
Cultural system	Ideological knowledge and communication	Socialist humanist knowledge and communication

love, affects, and also the world of knowledge, where exploiters "will tend not to produce ideas but to steal them" (Fromm 1947/2003, 47).

Based on these foundations, the present author draws a distinction between authoritarian and humanistic communication. In the realm of information, we can discern among authoritarian and humanistic knowledge and communication (see Table 2.3).

In the *authoritarian economic organisation of information*, communication and knowledge production operate within class relations. As a consequence, a dominant, property-owning class controls the means of communication as private property, exploits knowledge and communication workers who produce knowledge and organise forms of communication. In capitalism, this organisation of knowledge is a system, in which communication and knowledge are commodities that yield profit and are embedded in a system of capital accumulation. In the *humanistic economic organisation of information*, society's means of communication are owned collectively as a common good. Knowledge products are gifts and common goods and not commodities. The companies, in which public knowledge is produced, are self-managed co-operatives.

Fromm (1961/2008, 45) argues that in knowledge capitalism, alienation reaches deeply into the human mind because "symbol manipulators" have to sell "personality qualities" such as their smiles and opinions. All work requires the utilisation of the human being's dialectic of body and mind. However, there are types of work that are more based on the human being's exertion of physical energy than on the exertion of the brain and have a physical output. And there are types of work that are more based on the human being's exertion of the brain than of physical energy and produce information or social relations. Therefore, the distinction between physical and mental work makes sense.

The *authoritarian political organisation of knowledge and communication* implies that an individual or group acts as an authority that with the help of the state monopoly of the means of violence controls the means of public communication and the knowledge that is thereby produced and communicated. For example, in Nazi Germany broadcasting was politically controlled by the state. All regional radio companies were unified in one company, the state-controlled Reichs-Rundfunks-Gesellschaft (RRG, Reich Broadcasting Corporation). The Reichsrundfunkkammer (Reich Chamber of Broadcasting) registered all individuals working in the media industry and aligned the media system with Nazi ideology ("Gleichschaltung"). The RRG operated a total of twenty aligned radio stations and one television station (Deutscher Fernseh-Rundfunk). In authoritarian political communication, humans are unable to listen to themselves (Fromm 1947/2003, 120). "We listen to every voice and to everybody but not to ourselves. We are constantly exposed to the noise of opinions and ideas hammering at us from everywhere: motion pictures, newspapers, radio, idle chatter" (121). In authoritarian communication, humans have to listen or listen especially to a leader, which can be an individual, a group, a system or an ideology. Citizens are expected to follow the leader's orders. The problem of not listening to themselves is that humans do not trust and know themselves and cannot be alone with themselves (121).

The *humanistic political organisation of information* implies that the production of public knowledge and communication is democratically governed so that citizens and workers are represented in the decision-making structures of media organisations. A dictatorship does not centrally control voice. Rather, everyday citizens have a public voice and are represented in publicly disseminated information. "To be able to listen to oneself is a prerequisite for the ability to listen to others" (Fromm 1947/2003, 79). In a *humanist organisation of political communication*, humans listen to themselves and each other. They engage with each other.

> "While the having persons rely on what they have, the being persons rely on the fact that they are, that they are alive and that something new will be born if only they have the courage to let go and to respond. They come fully alive in the conversation, because they do not stifle themselves by anxious concern with what they have. Their own aliveness is infectious and often helps the other person to transcend his or her egocentricity. Thus the conversation ceases to be an exchange of commodities (information, knowledge, status) and becomes a dialogue in which it does not matter anymore who is right. The duelists begin to dance together, and they part not with triumph or sorrow-which are equally sterile-but with joy" (Fromm 1976/2008, 29)

An *authoritarian cultural system* publicly communicates ideological knowledge, that is the knowledge that justifies exploitation and domination and tries to convince the public from the belief that exploitation and domination are good, needed, unavoidable, or natural. In the communication of ideology, ideologues often use strategies such as dissimulation, lies, distortion, manipulation, scapegoating, personalisation, scandalisation, superficiality, brevity, acceleration, etc. Ideologues produce and communicate false knowledge and aim at producing and reproducing false consciousness. In contrast, a *humanist cultural system* is non-ideological. In it, humans produce and disseminate knowledge that supports the human capacities for and the human practices of critical, complex and creative thinking. "In the structure of having, the dead word rules; in the structure of being, the alive and inexpressible experience rules" (Fromm 1976/2008, 89).

In the authoritarian organisation of knowledge and communication, information and information producers are treated like things. The focus is on accumulating information or the accumulation of money, hegemony and power with the help of information. So, for example, in authoritarian, having-oriented learning knowledge is treated as a thing that is learned by heart, which is policed by authoritarian teachers in the form of exams and marks. "Students are supposed to learn so many things that they have hardly time and energy left to *think*" (Fromm 1947/2003, 56).

Based on these general foundations of theorising communication, we can next have a look at how Fromm's approach allows addressing ideology as a peculiar form of communication in class societies.

2.3 Ideology

2.3.1 Erich Fromm on ideology

Ideology is not an individual or collective idea, but a communication process through which classes and groups try to convince others to defend and favour certain structures of exploitation and domination.

Fromm (1965b, 217) argues that ideology is a kind of social unconscious that operates behind the back of individuals. Ideology prevents "thoughts from [...] becoming conscious", it represses "dangerous awareness" (218) that could threaten exploitation and domination. Ideology is a "social filter" (218) that covers up the true status of society. Ideology operates in "a) language, b) logic, and c) social taboos" (218). It is "socially produced and shared fiction" (218).

Fromm (1970/2010, 72) argues that insofar "as he is not an animal, man has an interest in being related to and conscious of reality, to touch the earth with his feet". "As long as he is only sheep [...] This reality is essentially nothing but the fiction built up by his society for more convenient manipulation of men and things" (72). The development of a sane society requires "that the social contradictions and irrationalities which throughout most of man's history have forced upon him a 'false consciousness' – in order to justify domination and submission respectively disappear or at least are reduced to such a degree that the apology for the existent social order does not paralyze man's capacity for critical thought" (73). Ideology is a communication process that aims at the creation of false consciousness that justifies domination and submission.

Fromm argues that since the 18th and 19th century when capitalism consolidated itself, "the concept of the self was narrowed down increasingly" (Fromm 1947/2003, 101). As a consequence, the ideology "I am what I have" (Fromm 1947/2003, 102; Fromm 1976/2008, 63, 91) became the dominant mindset and principle of society. It implies possessive individualism ("I am what I possess") and accumulation, "the wish to have much, to have more, to have most" (Fromm 1976/2008, 91). In 1961, Erich Fromm (1961/2008) edited an English translation of Marx's *Economic and Philosophic Manuscripts* that was accompanied by an introduction and analysis written by Fromm. Fromm (1961/2008, 30) argues that it was Marx who first stressed the "difference between the sense of *having* and the sense of *being*" as a fundamental aspect of capitalism. So, for example, Marx (1844, 309) argues that in capitalism, all "passions and all activity must [...] be submerged in *avarice*" (309) and that "the sense of having" (300) that is the "sense of *possessing*" (299) replaces "all physical and mental senses" (300). The mode of having is "a control-property-power orientation" (Fromm 1973/1997, 293).

Fromm (1976/2008) opposes the mode of having to the mode of being. Whereas the first is characteristic of capitalism and class society, the second is characteristic of socialist humanism.

> "In the having mode of existence my relationship to the world is one of possessing and owning, one in which I want to make everybody and everything, including myself, my property. [...] In the being mode of existence, we must identify two forms of being. One is in contrast to having [...] and means aliveness and authentic relatedness to the world. The other form of being is in contrast to appearing and refers to the true nature, the true reality, of a person or a thing in contrast to deceptive appearances as exemplified in the etymology of being" (Fromm 1976/2008, 21).

In the mode of being, humans define themselves not by what they possess, but by relating to each other through love: I am what I practice. I can only practice something in relation to others. I can only love myself if I love others. I can only love others if I love myself. I can only be myself fully if I do something that helps others. We can only fully be and only fully be ourselves if we create, sustain and live a society controlled by humans together – a society, in which humans own the means of production, work, decide, experience, laugh and cry together.

Fromm argues that the capitalist focus on having, that is its possessive individualism, instead of being has resulted,

> "in the growing use of nouns and the decreasing use of verbs in Western languages in the past few centuries. A noun is the proper denotation for a thing. I can say that I have things: for instance that I have a table, a house, a book, a car. The proper denotation for an activity, a process, is a verb: for instance I am, I love, I desire, I hate, etc. Yet ever more frequently an activity is expressed in terms of having; that is, a noun is used instead of a verb. But to express an activity by to have in connection with a noun is an erroneous use of language, because processes and activities cannot be possessed; they can only be experienced" (Fromm 1976/2008, 17).

The mode of having is not just an ideology that shapes the modern human's thought and behaviour. It also shapes language and communication that, as a consequence operates as ideological language and ideological communication:

> "Among the many forms of alienation, the most frequent one is alienation in language. If I express a feeling with a word, let us say, if I say 'I love you', the word is meant to be an indication of the reality which exists within myself, the power of my loving. The word 'love' is meant to be a symbol of the fact love, but as soon as it is spoken it tends to assume a life of its own, it becomes a reality. I am under the illusion that the saying of the word is the equivalent of the experience, and soon I say the word and feel nothing, except the *thought* of love which the word expresses. The alienation of language shows the whole complexity of alienation. Language is one of the most precious human achievements; to avoid alienation by not speaking would be foolish – yet one must be always aware of the danger of the spoken word, that it threatens to substitute itself for the living experience. The same holds true for all other achievements of man; ideas, art, any kind of man-made objects. They are man's

creations; they are valuable aids for life, yet each one of them is also a trap, a temptation to confuse life with things, experience with artifacts, feeling with surrender and submission" (Fromm 1961/2008, 38).

The ideology of having also dominates the realm of consumption and advertising. Advertising and consumption are propaganda for the purchase and use of ever more commodities: "Modern consumers may identify themselves by the formula: I am = what I have and what I consume" (Fromm 1976/2008, 23). According to the logic of advertising, humans are never satisfied, but always have an interest, a need and a desire for more and ever newer commodities. Advertising tries to make humans blind to potentially negative effects of certain commodities. It presents the commodity as an authoritative way of enhancing human life. Advertising,

"does not appeal to reason but to emotion; like any other kind of hypnoid suggestion, it tries to impress its objects emotionally and then make them submit intellectually. This type of advertising impresses the customer by all sorts of means: by repetition of the same formula again and again; by the influence of an authoritative image, like that of a society lady or of a famous boxer, who smokes a certain brand of cigarette; by attracting the customer and at the same time weakening his critical abilities by the sex appeal of a pretty girl; by terrorizing him with the threat of 'b.o.' or 'halitosis'; or yet again by stimulating daydreams about a sudden change in one's whole course of life brought about by buying a certain shirt or soap. All these methods are essentially irrational; they have nothing to do with the qualities of the merchandise, and they smother and kill the critical capacities of the customer like an opiate or out right hypnosis" (Fromm 1941/1969, 149).

Fromm argues that political propaganda just like advertising flatters "the individual by making him appear important, and by pretending that they appeal to his critical judgement, to his sense of discrimination" (Fromm 1941/1969, 151). Both work with appeals to fears and hopes, that is and appeals to feelings and promises of significance and importance to the individual in a world ruled by small, powerful groups.

2.3.2 An update of Erich Fromm's concept of ideology

Given Fromm's stress on false consciousness, there are clear parallels to Georg Lukács' approach. False consciousness is consciousness that "by-passes the essence of the evolution of society and fails to pinpoint it and express it adequately" (Lukács 1971, 50). False consciousness misses the "objective possibility" of consciousness, the "thoughts and feelings which men would have in a particular situation if they were *able* to assess both it and the interests arising from it in their impact on immediate action and on the whole structure of society" (Lukács 1971, 51). For Lukács, ideology aims at reifying consciousness, which means that it tries to turn humans' thoughts into things that can be controlled like things. Reified consciousness thinks in terms of "the abstract, quantitative mode of calculability" that in capitalism is the logic of capital accumulation and the commodity so that the reified individual "does not even attempt to transcend" class and domination (Lukács 1971, 93). Reified consciousness sees the qualities of society as "things-in-themselves in a mythologised" form (Lukács 1971, 192). Fromm (1970/2010, 96) implicitly also refers to Lukács' notion of reified consciousness when he writes that "reified man experiences little of life and instead follows principles which have been programmed for him by the machine". Fromm's appreciation of Lukács becomes evident when he writes that Lukács "was the first one to revive Marx's humanism" (Fromm 1961/2008, 59).

Like Lukács, Fromm shows that ideology is a communication process that aims at creating false consciousness. An example of how the mode of having as ideology shapes modern language and communication is the emergence of the English word "technology" in the 18th and 19th century. Although the word stems from the Greek *techne* that indicates an art or craft of doing system, the modern meaning of technology is "a system of [....] means and methods" (Williams 1983, 315), that is machines. The understanding of technology as machinery has emerged with the industrial revolution and the emergence of machines as capitalist means of production that are used in order to increase labour's productivity or what Marx (1867/1976, chapters 12 and 15) terms relative surplus-value production. Fromm argues that in a technological society, the logic of machines has also affected the way dominant groups treat dominated groups. Instrumental reason reduces humans to the status of machines and wants them to act like automatic machines:

> "Today we can meet a person who acts and feels like an automaton; we find that he never experiences anything which is really his; that he experiences himself entirely as the person he thinks he is supposed to be; that smiles have replaced laughter, meaningless chatter replaced communicative speech and dulled despair has taken the place of genuine sadness" (Fromm 1947/2003, 167).

Fromm (1941/1969) sees propaganda as a political form of advertising, manipulation and ideology. The present author defines advertising as propaganda for commodities, consumption and capitalism. Propaganda is not purely economic but has a political character as well because it advances the political interest of the capitalist class. And political propaganda is economical as well: It imitates and adopts the marketing techniques of advertising. Propaganda and advertising cannot be strictly separated. Advertising has the purpose of selling something to yield profit, whereas propaganda and public relations aim at convincing the members of the people of something, but often use the rhetorical and visual strategies of salespeople. For the present author, propaganda is a more general term that encompasses both economic propaganda (advertising) and political propaganda. Propaganda is the process of communicating and spreading ideological messages in the public that aim at convincing the members of the public to support dominative interests that want to advance instrumental reason, exploitation and domination. Whereas the notion of propaganda is more focused on the content of an ideological message, ideology is the corresponding, more general process that has both a social form and specific contents.

In other works, Fromm agrees with the present author that propaganda is not limited to politics and that advertising is product propaganda: "If a highly advertised brand of toothpaste is used by the majority of people because of some fantastic claims it makes in its propaganda, nobody with any sense would say that the people have "made a decision" in favor of the toothpaste." (Fromm 1956/2002, 180).

The discussion shows that Fromm advanced a critical notion of ideology that can inform a critical theory of communication. In the next section, we will have a look at Fromm's notion of technology.

2.4 Technology

2.4.1 Erich Fromm on technology

In the previous section, we already discussed the role of technology in capitalist society. The dominance of instrumental reason in capitalist society has brought about the reversal of means and ends: There is an "overemphasis on ends" (Fromm 1947/2003, 146). "We have the most wonderful instruments and means man has ever had, but we do not stop and ask *what they are for*" (Fromm 1947/2003, 146).

Technology is often uncritically accepted, affirmed and not questioned. It is treated as a fetish (technological fetishism). Fromm (1964, 59) argues that there is an "affinity between the necrophilous contempt for life and the admiration for speed and all that is mechanical". The admiration of machines, technology as means of domination and technological fetishism are based on the fascist principle "[l]ong live death" (Fromm 1973/1997, 33; see also 454–462). Technological fetishists love machines and commodities, that is dead labour, instead of having an interest in what is alive. "A new concept of the sacred and unquestionable is arising: that of calculability, probability, factuality" (Fromm 1970/2010, 61). The idea that social relations and human behaviour should be calculated aims at the control of the behaviour of workers, citizens and consumers in order to advance the accumulation of capital, political power and status.

Fromm (1970/2010) argues that the present technological society is grounded on the principles "that something *ought* to be done because it is technically *possible* to do it" (43) and the principle of "*maximal efficiency and output*" (43). The first principle is based on the naïve technological-optimistic and techno-deterministic assumption that technology must have positive impacts. The second principle advances the logic of accumulation, the "constant increase of quantity" (46) that disregards "the question of *quality*, or what all this increase in quantity is good for" (46).

Fromm (1970/2010, 53–64) is critical of the idea that computers that are like humans (including having feelings and thought) and act like humans. For Fromm, the idea that robots can be built that are like humans is the expression of a society ruled by instrumental reason, in which dominant forces want to make humans "act like robots" (54). Fromm argues that humans have a capacity for freedom, which means that they are "faced with alternatives" that entail a risk of failure" and "insecurity" (69). In order to exert control, dominant groups search for certainty in an uncertain, complex world, which has resulted in the "blind belief" (58) in the efficacy of the computer. The computer has become a technological fetish, "a substitute for God" (61). The belief that computers take value-free, unbiased decisions is erroneous because the construction and programming of computers "itself is based in built-in and often unconscious values" (63).

Fromm is not opposed to technology, but critical of its instrumental shaping and use. He argues for a humanised technology that "stimulates and furthers the growth and aliveness of man rather than cripples it" so that machines and computers become "*part in a life-oriented social system*" (Fromm 1970/2010, 103). Such a "new radical humanism" aims at "the growth of man with all his potentialities, the affirmation of life in all its forms against death and mechanization and alienation" (142).

Alternative use of computers – controlled by humans, quality instead of quantity:

Fromm argues for the use of alternative technology in the context of an alternative design of society, a participatory democracy that uses "participatory face-to-face groups" (Fromm 1970/2010, 121) that involve processes of "information exchange, debate, and decision-making" (112). In the economy, the system Fromm envisions takes on the form of self-managed companies. The "socialization of the means of production might be a *necessary*, but does not constitute a *sufficient* condition to achieve humanization" (156). Participatory democracy requires collective ownership of the means of production as one of its conditions, but must also be a political and cultural process of change. In the political system, Fromm has local grassroots town hall meetings in mind that are federated into a society-wide parliament. In the realm of culture, Fromm talks about the transition from spectator art to active art, an "active, participant culture" (119), which also includes critical pedagogy and the participation of students and learners in the administration of universities and other educational organisations and (120–121) and a stronger focus on public consumption of common goods instead of individual consumption of commodities. Fromm argues for the introduction of a basic income guarantee as the material foundation of participatory democracy (130–131).

Fromm (1960, 1970/2010) argues for computer-supported town meetings of citizens organised in workplaces and local communities, where key political matters are debated. These meetings are via computer technology organised as networks of "hundreds of thousands of small face-to-face-groups" who together form "a new type of Lower House" (Fromm 1960, 26). A precondition is that "the democratic process is transformed into one in which well-informed and responsible citizens express their will, not automatized mass-men" (Fromm 1960, 26). Consequently, also the town meetings can only work properly if the members are "well informed" (Fromm 1970/2010, 118). Fromm is well aware of the dangers of plebiscites and opinion polls and therefore argues that electronic democracy is "fundamentally different of a plebiscite or an opinion poll" because the meetings "would be based on information and debate their decisions" and their political influence would grow together with political education (Fromm 1970/2010, 118).

Fromm (1968, 20) speaks of the "problem of communication": Because of communication technologies, there are ever more potentials for communication, but true communication between humans has become more difficult. The causes of this development include the structure of the mass media, individualism, bourgeois culture, instrumentalism, dependency, the fear of war, etc. Fromm asks: "Do the words communion and community still make […] Social, psychological, and economic factors are many times combined to make communication in depth an impossible attempt" (Fromm 1968, 20).

2.4.2 An update of Erich Fromm's concept of technology

Fromm's analysis of the technological logic parallels Horkheimer and Adorno's notion of instrumental reason that they consider characteristic for the dialectic of the Enlightenment: "Bourgeois society […] makes dissimilar things comparable by reducing them to abstract quantities. For the Enlightenment, anything which cannot be resolved into numbers, and ultimately into one, is illusion" (Horkheimer and Adorno 2002, 4).

Capitalist society fetishises quantification: Its goal is the accumulation of capital and power, for which it needs to quantify and control the quantity of investments, labour-time, commodities, profits, political power, consumption, experience, consciousness the human being, and life.

A contemporary critique of big data and the capitalist Internet can build on Fromm's notion of technological fetishism. Big data is an example of how in contemporary capitalism, computer technology and its logic of calculation are fetishized. Big data is often defined as a massive increase of 3 Vs, namely the volume, variety and velocity of data (Kitchin 2014, 68). Big data studies is a fast-growing field of research (see Mayer-Schönberger and Cukier's 2013, Kitchin 2014, Mosco 2014). It deals with how big data transforms society, the environment, culture, the economy, and the political system. Whereas for uncritical accounts, big data is the consequence of Moore's Law that says that computing power doubles every 18 months (Mayer-Schönberger and Cukier's 2013, 8), more critical explanations stress that big data stands in the context of political and economic surveillance and targeted advertising-based capital accumulation models (Fuchs 2017a, 2017b, 2018c).

Big data has the logic of quantification and accumulation already in its name ("big"). The effect of data becoming so voluminous, variegated and fast that humans can no longer oversee it is that in big data applications and big data analytics, the human being is often pronounced as being dead. It is argued that computers and Artificial Intelligence are doing the job on their own independent of humans. If such scenarios become a reality, then the problem is that computers cannot have ethics because what is good and evil cannot be calculated and quantified. The effect is that moral irresponsibility or relativism might be built into digital machines. In the realm of big data analytics, the fetishism of quantification has resulted in a neglect of the study of how humans experience, assess and morally judge data (Fuchs 2017a).

Given the instrumental logic underlying big data, it is no wonder that conservative policy visions uncritically embrace, reify and fetishize big data. So, for example, a UK government policy paper outlining the UK's Industrial Strategy in the realm of Artificial Intelligence, argues: "In the same way that Gutenberg's press ushered in a new era of growth, data-driven technologies such as AI will underpin our future prosperity. [...] Creating an economy that harnesses artificial intelligence (AI) and big data is one of the great opportunities of our age" (HM Government 2018, 3, 8). Big data and AI are presented as revolutionary and as only having positive effects in society ("future prosperity", "great opportunities"). Potential negative effects of the use of big data in a capitalist society, such as the creation of a totalitarian surveillance society by data-based surveillance (dataveillance) or the increase of unemployment and precarious life by data-driven automation are not mentioned. New computing technologies are blindly trusted based on the logic that Fromm criticises, namely the assumption that what is technologically possible must be realised and must have positive effects in society.

Fromm anticipated discussions about digital democracy. Whereas digital democracy, in general means the practising of democracy with the help of computers (Hacker and van Dijk 2000, 1), one has to distinguish between different uses of computers in politics. The danger of digital plebiscites is real in a digital society. In a public sphere that is dominated by a culture of fake news, ideological scapegoating and high-speed, superficial, sensationalist tabloid news, point-and-click digital politics, in which citizen-users take society-wide decisions via their screens, can easily be used for passing laws that violate human rights and humanism. Furthermore, if authoritarian demagogues select the topics and define the questions asked in plebiscites, political decisions are prone to manipulation. For example, if a refugee is suspected of having committed a murder, an online plebiscite that builds on an anti-refugee campaign that ideologically exploits this case could result in a law that legislates the deportation or internment of all refugees.

What we need today is a combination of deliberative and participatory democracy (Fuchs 2018b). Deliberative democracy focuses on the direct political communication of citizens. In deliberative digital democracy, citizens only partly discuss politics online. They also come together for face-to-face debates that might be supported, but not substituted by online communication. Participatory digital democracy focuses on the extension of democracy beyond the realm of elections and the political system. It stresses the importance of economic democracy and cultural democracy, which means that questions of the collective control of resources, activity time and spaces and institutions play a role in enabling democracy. So, for example, the reduction of standard working hours without wage cuts or the introduction of a guaranteed basic income can give people more time for practising democracy. The collective ownership of digital communication platforms and their operation on a not-for-profit basis (public service Internet platforms, civil society Internet platforms) is a good foundation for creating citizen participation in democracy.

The rise of ever more digital communications (communication technologies such as the mobile phone and "social media") takes place in a political-economic context that results in less and less sustained communication. In the age of online fake news and Donald Trump, the political world is deeply polarised between right-wing authoritarians on the one side and humanists on the other side. We live in an age of authoritarian capitalism, where right-wing demagogues such as Donald Trump, Nigel Farage, Marine Le Pen, Viktor Orbán, Vladimir Putin, Marine Le Pen, Narendra Modi, H.C. Strache, Recep Erdoğan, Geert Wilders, etc. make use of social media for spreading nationalist and authoritarian ideology (see Fuchs 2018a, Fuchs 2019, Woolley and Howard 2019). The capitalist digital media's structures foster political communication and information that is brief, superficial, personalised, individualistic, anonymous, prone to harassment, tabloidized, and transmitted at high speed (Fuchs 2018a, chapter 7). Contemporary political online communication is dominated by authoritarian ideology, fake news, filter bubbles, algorithmic politics, and high speed online communication that does not leave space and time for real discussion (see Farkas and Schou 2019, Fuchs 2018a, 2019, McNair 2018, Pariser 2011). As a consequence, some authors have talked about the emergence of anti-social media in the age of authoritarian capitalism (Fuchs 2018d, Mair et al. 2018, Vaidhyanathan 2018). The Cambridge Analytica-scandal was characteristic of these developments.

Fromm argues for a different, democratic kind of communication that includes direct encounter ("true communication"):

> "While there will always be fanatics and more or less sick as well as stupid people who cannot participate in this kind of debate, an atmosphere can be created which, without any force, eliminates the effectiveness of such individuals within the group. It is essential for the possibility of a dialogue that each member of the group not only try to be less defensive and more open, but also that he try

to understand what the other person means to say rather than the actual formulation he gives to his thought" (Fromm 1970/2010, 115–116).

In the age of fake online news and authoritarian capitalism, societies have lost the capacity to foster engaged political debate between humans who have opposing opinions and interests. It is about time that political communication not just primarily takes place online between anonymous participants, but that we create hybrid forms, where humans first meet face-to-face in local communities and afterwards can decide to continue the discussion online. Club 2 was a legendary public service television debate format that featured open-ended, controversial, uncensored live debate. It had controversial debate topics, a living room atmosphere, and no studio audience. Austrian Broadcasting Corporation (ORF) broadcast Club 2 from 1975 until 1995. Club 2 was a democratic public sphere enabled by public broadcasting. In order to improve political communication and save democracy, every council flat needs its own Club 2 as social meeting places where political agreement and disagreement can take place. Political communication needs time, spaces and learning by doing. Such local debate clubs could also besides other realms become settings, where participants socially produce user-generated videos that are submitted to an electronic version of Club 2 ("Club 2.0").

Club 2.0 is the concept of Club 2 updated for the age of digital and social media (Fuchs 2017c). Club 2.0 operates based on a video platform that is not owned by corporations such as Google (YouTube), Amazon, or Netflix, but by a public service broadcaster such as the BBC. Club 2.0 is an example of a public service Internet platform (Fuchs 2018e). Club 2.0 includes forms of digital participation via online discussions, socially produced videos submitted by users, a selection of videos generated by user groups that feed into the television debate, non-anonymous online discussion. The online debate is decelerated by a limitation of the number of active users, the definition of a minimum length of discussion contributions that are submitted as text or video, and the limitation of the number of contributions a single user can make. Club 2.0 is an attempt to slow down and decommodify political communication in order to save democracy in the age of fake online news, filter bubbles and digital authoritarianism. Figure 2.3 visualises how Club 2.0 works.

2.5 Conclusion

A critical theory of communication can draw on several insights that we can gain from a reading and interpretation of Erich Fromm's works:

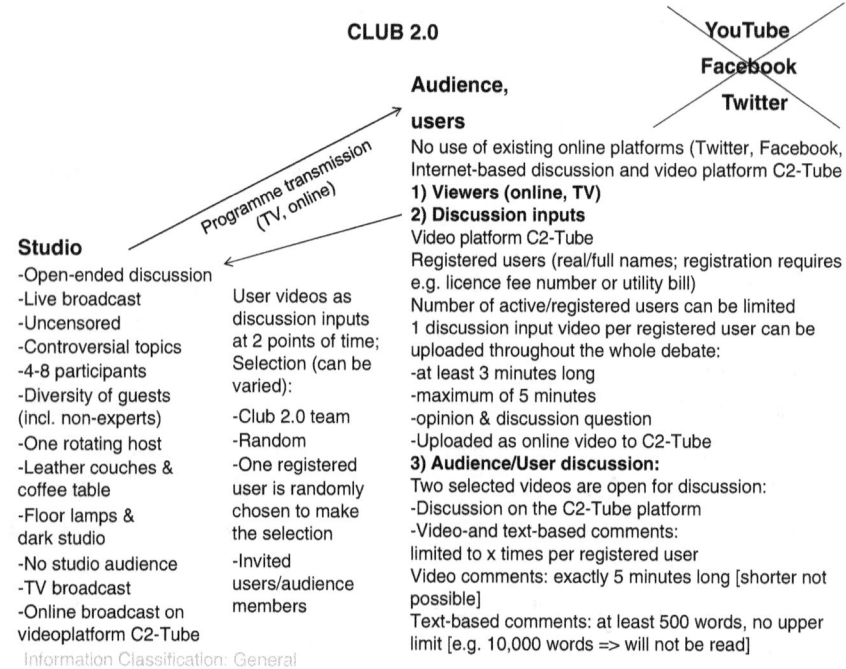

FIGURE 2.3 Club 2.0

- The human being:
  The human being is a natural, social, co-operating and self-conscious being. Social production is the essence of humans. Humans produce socially and communicate productively.
- The social character and communication:
  Fromm's notion of the social character is a concept that mediates between the levels of the individual psyche and society. Humans, through communication in various social systems, form a particular social character, a character structure peculiar for a certain group in society. Through communication, the social character and social structures are formed and reproduced. The social character and social structures mediated through communication in the social relations that humans enter condition, that is to enable and constrain individual thought and action.
- The authoritarian and the humanistic character:
  Fromm's basic distinction between the authoritarian and the humanistic character allows to analyse antagonisms in dominative societies: the contradiction between

the exploiter and the commoner in the class-structured economy, the antagonism between the dictator and the democrat in the political system, and the antagonism between the ideologue and the friend in the cultural system.

- Authoritarian and humanistic communication:

  Based on Fromm's approach one can draw a distinction between authoritarian and humanistic knowledge and communication. In the economy, this distinction expresses itself as knowledge commodities and private means of communication as private property on the one side and knowledge and communication commons on the other side. In the political system, we find dictatorial control of communication on the one side and participatory, democratic communications on the other side. And in the realm of culture, we can discern between ideological communication on the one side and socialist humanist communication on the other side.

- Ideology:

  For Fromm, ideology is a form of communication that operates as a social unconscious and filter that prevents certain knowledge about the world to become apparent. It covers up the true status of society. Fromm shares Lukács' critical notion of ideology as the attempt to create false, reified consciousness.

- The ideology of having:

  Fromm argues that a particular ideology, namely the ideology of having, dominates capitalist society. It is based on the logic of property and accumulation and the principle "I am what I have". In capitalist societies, the ideology of having expresses itself in the logic of the accumulation of capital, power and status. The ideology of having has negatively impacted on realms like language, communication, consumption, advertising, political propaganda.

- Capitalist technology:

  In capitalism, technology is fetishized, and the logic of quantification shapes social relations. Technological fetishism includes the uncritical acceptance of technology as it is, the assumption that everything that is technologically possible should be realised and will have positive effects on society.

- Alternative technology:

  Fromm is not opposed to technology, but critical of its instrumental shaping and use. He argues for the humanisation of technology, which includes participatory democracy and the mediation of participation by computer technology.

- Participatory computing:

Fromm's work on technology reminds us that the authoritarian and capitalist design and shaping of computing pose threats to democracy and human well-being. In contrast, the humanistic shaping and design of computer technology and society has the potential to advance participatory democracy.

Taken together, these results show that reading Erich Fromm today can inspire insights for the critical understanding of communication, ideology, technology, and computing. Fromm reminds us that we need to be aware of and should challenge authoritarian communication and authoritarian communication systems. Socialist humanism is the alternative to authoritarianism. The political quest is to create humanist technologies, humanist communication and a democratic-socialist society today.

Literature

Engels, Friedrich. 1893. "Letter to Franz Mehring, 14 July 1893." In *MECW Volume 50*, 163–167. London: Lawrence & Wishart.

———. 1890. "Letter to Joseph Bloch, 21/22 September 1890." In *MECW Volume 49*, 33–37. London: Lawrence & Wishart.

Farkas, Johan, and Jannick Schou. 2019. *Post-Truth, Fake News and Democracy*. New York: Routledge.

Friedman, Lawrence J., and Anke M. Schreiber. 2013. *The Lives of Erich Fromm: Love's Prophet*. New York: Columbia University Press.

Fromm, Erich. 1976/2008. *To Have or to Be?* London: Continuum.

———. 1973/1997. *The Anatomy of Human Destructiveness*. London: Pimlico.

———. 1970/2010. *The Revolution of Hope. Toward a Humanized Technology*. Riverdale, NY: American Mental Health Foundation Books.

———. 1968. "Introduction." In *The Nature of Man*, edited by Erich Fromm and Ramón Xirau, 3–24. New York: Macmillan.

———. 1965a. "Introduction." In *Socialist Humanism: An International Symposium*, edited by Erich Fromm, vii–xii. Garden City, NY: Doubleday.

———. 1965b. "The Application of Humanist Psychoanalysis to Marx's Theory." In *Socialist Humanism: An International Symposium*, edited by Erich Fromm, 207–222. Garden City, NY: Doubleday.

———. 1964. *The Heart of Man. Its Genius for Good and Evil*. New York: Harper & Row.

———. 1961/2008. *Marx's Concept of Man*. London: Continuum.

———. 1960. *Let Man Prevail. A Socialist Manifesto and Program*. New York: The Call Association.

———. 1956. *The Art of Loving*. New York: Harper & Row.

———. 1956/2002. *The Sane Society*. Abingdon: Routledge.

———. 1955. "The Human Implications of Instinctivist Radicalism." *Dissent* 2 (3): 342–349.

———. 1951. *The Forgotten Language: An Introduction to the Understanding of Dreams, Fairy Tales and Myths*. Oxford: Rinehart.

———. 1947/2003. *Man for Himself. An Inquiry into the Psychology of Ethics*. Abingdon: Routledge.

———. 1941/1969. *Escape from Freedom*. New York: Avon.

———. 1931/1989. "Politics and Psychoanalysis." In *Critical Theory and Society: A Reader*, edited by Stephen Eric Bronner and Douglas MacKay Kellner, 213–218. New York: Routledge.

Fromm, Erich, and Michael Maccoby. 1970. *Social Character in a Mexican Village*. Englewood Cliffs, NJ: Prentice-Hall.

Fuchs, Christian. 2019. *Nationalism on the Internet: Critical Theory and Ideology in the Age of Social Media and Fake News*. New York: Routledge.

———. 2018a. *Digital Demagogue: Authoritarian Capitalism in the Age of Trump and Twitter*. London: Pluto Press.

———. 2018b. "Digitale Demokratie und Öffentlich-Rechtliche Medien [Digital Democracy and Public Service Media]." In *ORF Public Value Studie 2017/2018: Der Auftrag: Demokratie [ORF Public Value Study 2017/2018: The Mission: Democracy]*, 94–138. Vienna: ORF (Austrian Broadcasting Corporation). https://zukunft.orf.at/rte/upload/texte/qualitaetssicherung/2018/orf_public_value_studie_demokratie_2018.pdf.

———. 2018c. "Karl Marx in the Age of Big Data Capitalism." In *Digital Objects, Digital Subjects: Interdisciplinary Perspectives on Capitalism, Labour and Politics in the Age of Big Data*, edited by David Chandler and Christian Fuchs, 53–71. London: University of Westminster Press. DOI: https://doi.org/10.16997/book29.d.

———. 2018d. "Socialising Anti-Social Social Media." In *Anti-Social Media: The Impact on Journalism and Society*, edited byJohn Mair, Tor Clark, Neil Fowler, Raymond Snoddy and Richard Tait, 58–63. Suffolk: Abramis.

———. 2018e. *The Online Advertising Tax as the Foundation of a Public Service Internet*. London: University of Westminster Press. DOI: https://doi.org/10.16997/book24.

———. 2017a. "From Digital Positivism and Administrative Big Data Analytics Towards Critical Digital and Social Media Research!" *European Journal of Communication* 32 (1): 37–49.

———. 2017b. *Social Media: A Critical Introduction*. London: Sage. Second edition.

———. 2017c. "Towards the Public Service Internet as Alternative to the Commercial Internet." In *ORF Texte No. 20 – Öffentlich-Rechtliche Qualität im Diskurs*, 43–50. Vienna: ORF. https://westminsterresearch.westminster.ac.uk/item/q3702/towards-the-public-service-internet-as-alternative-to-the-commercial-internet.

———. 2016. *Critical Theory of Communication. New Readings of Lukács, Adorno, Marcuse, Honneth and Habermas in the Age of the Internet*. London: University of Westminster Press. doi:https://doi.org/10.16997/book1.

———. 2008. *Internet and Society: Social Theory in the Information Age*. New York: Routledge.

Funk, Rainer. 2018. *Das Leben selbst ist eine Kunst. Einführung in Leben und Werk von Erich Fromm*. Freiburg: Herder.

Hacker, Kenneth L., and Jan van Dijk. 2000. "What is Digital Democracy?" In *Digital Democracy*, edited by Kenneth L. Hacker and Jan van Dijk, 1–9. London: Sage.

HM Government. 2018. *Industrial Strategy: Artificial Intelligence Sector Deal*. https://assets.publishing.service.gov.uk/government/uploads/system/uploads/attachment_data/file/702810/180425_BEIS_AI_Sector_Deal__4_.pdf.

Horkheimer, Max, and Theodor W. Adorno. 2002. *Dialectic of the Enlightenment*. Stanford, CA: Stanford University Press.

Kitchin, Rob. 2014. *The Data Revolution: Big Data, Open Data, Data Infrastructures & their Consequences*. London: Sage.

Lacan, Jacques. 1991. *The Seminar of Jacques Lacan. Book II: The Ego in Freud's Theory and in the Technique of Psychoanalysis 1954-1955*. New York: W.W. Norton & Company.

Lukács, Georg. 1971. *History and Class Consciousness*. London: Merlin.

Mair, John et al., eds. 2018. *Anti-Social Media: The Impact on Journalism and Society*. Suffolk: Abramis.

McNair, Brian. 2018. *Fake News: Falsehood, Fabrication and Fantasy in Journalism*. Abingdon: Routledge.

Marcuse, Herbert. 1956/1998. *Eros and Civilization: A Philosophical Inquiry into Freud*. London: Routledge.

Marx, Karl. 1867/1976. *Capital. A Critique of Political Economy. Volume One*. London: Penguin.

———. 1844. "Economic and Philosophic Manuscripts of 1844." In *Marx & Engels Collected Works (MECW) Volume 3*, 229–346. London: Lawrence & Wishart.

Mayer-Schönberger, Viktor, and Kenneth Cukier. 2013. *Big Data: A Revolution that will Transform How We Live, Work and Think*. London: Murray.

Mosco, Vincent. 2014. *To the Cloud: Big Data in a Turbulent World*. Boulder, CO: Paradigm.

Pariser, Eli. 2011. *The Filter Bubble*. London: Penguin.

Vaidhyanathan, Siva. 2018. *Anti-Social Media. How Facebook Disconnects Us and Undermines Democracy*. Oxford: Oxford University Press.

Woolley, Samuel C., and Philip N. Howard, eds. 2019. *Computational Propaganda. Political Parties, Politicians, and Political Manipulation on Social Media*. Oxford: Oxford University Press.

Williams, Raymond. 1983. *Keywords: A Vocabulary of Culture and Society*. New York: Oxford University Press. Revised edition.

———. 1977. *Marxism and Literature*. Oxford: Oxford University Press.

Chapter Three
Revisiting the Althusser/E. P. Thompson-controversy: Towards a Marxist theory of communication

3.1 Introduction

3.2 Background

3.3 Louis Althusser

3.4 Edward P. Thompson

3.5 Towards a critical theory of communication

3.6 Conclusion

Literature

3.1 Introduction

In contemporary society, there is much talk about the role of communication in society. One can hear and read a lot about social media, the information economy, the creative industry, the cultural industries, the digital economy, digital labour, the information society, the information economy, information work, etc. A critical theory of communication can guide our understanding of how communication shapes and is shaped by contemporary society's power structures. Jürgen Habermas' theory of communication takes a dualist approach that separates communication and power (see Fuchs 2016). Therefore, it is appropriate to explore how an alternative critical theory of communication can go beyond Habermas and for doing so, draw on various traditions of critical thought. This chapter contributes to this task by dealing with the question: How can Louis Althusser and Edward P. Thompson's controversy on base/superstructure and structure/agency inform a critical theory of communication?

The base/superstructure problem deals with the question of how the economic and the non-economic are ontologically related. The structure/agency problem is about the relationship of human subjects and their practices to society's structures. To find answers, we need theories of society. In one way or another, all social theories have to deal with these two problems. But Marxist theories have given particular attention to these questions because they are especially concerned with the role of the capitalist economy in society, capitalism's structural contradictions, and class struggles.

Althusser and Thompson have made two distinct contributions to this debate. The world of ideas and the communication of ideas have in Marxist theories especially been reflected in the categories of class-consciousness and ideology. The base-superstructure problem also poses questions about the relationship between the material and the ideational in society. One of its concerns is what role ideas have in relation to the economy and society. If we want to establish foundations of a critical theory of communication, it is, therefore, worthwhile to revisit discussions about the relationship of the economy and culture, the economic and the non-economic, and structure/agency.

Louis Althusser's works on Marxism are among the 20th century's most influential French contributions to critical theory. His most well-known works are *For Marx* (Althusser 2005 [1965]), *Reading Capital* (Althusser and Balibar 2009 [1968]), and the essay *Ideology and Ideological State Apparatuses* (Althusser 1971, 127–186). Althusser's approach of structuralist Marxism has influenced among others Alain Badiou, Antonio Negri, Ernesto Laclau, Étienne Balibar, Judith Butler, Jacques Derrida, Jacques Rancière, Manuel Castells, Michel Foucault, Nicos Poulantzas, Régis Debray, Stuart Hall, and Slavoj Žižek.

Edward P. Thompson is one of Britain's most well-known historians and Marxist scholars. Carl Winslow, editor of *E. P. Thompson and the Making of the New Left*, a collection of important essays of Thompson, characterises this influential Marxist scholar in the book's introduction as "one of the great figures of the post-Second World War left" (Thompson 2014, 9). His best-known works are *The Making of the English Working Class* (Thompson 1963) and a biography of *William Morris* (Thompson 2011 [1955]). Thompson was a humanist socialist who questioned structuralism's theoretical and political implications. Given Althusser's structuralism and Thompson's humanism, we can expect these authors to approach the base/superstructure problem and the structure/agency-question in quite different ways. And this difference gave rise to a controversy expressed in Thompson's (1978) book *The Poverty of Theory*. This work became one of the most well-known criticisms of Althusser. For example, it inspired Perry Anderson (1980) to write a 200 page long constructive engagement that discusses the commonalities of and differences between Thompson and Althusser.

This chapter proceeds by introducing the background (section 2), discussing Althusser's conception of base and superstructure (section 3), engaging with Thompson's critique of Althusser (section 4), and an outline of foundations of how a critical theory of communication can draw on and go beyond the Althusser and Thompson-debate (section 5).

Thompson is not just a historian but is also considered as a representative of cultural studies. There is a close relationship between cultural studies and communication studies. We, therefore, want to briefly discuss aspects of communication in cultural studies as background to the engagement with Thompson's works.

3.2 Background

Culture is a system of meaning-making, whereas communication is the process of (re)producing social relations, sharing and co-constructing meanings. Wherever there is culture, there is communication. Whenever we communicate, we create culture. Cultural studies and communication studies are, therefore, two closely related fields of study. Stuart Hall (1980) argues cultural studies is based on two paradigms: The "culturalism" of Raymond Williams, Richard Hoggart and E. P. Thompson on the one hand; and Althusserian structuralism on the other hand. Hall characterises Thompson's work as focusing on "classes as relations, popular struggle, and historical forms of consciousness, class cultures in their historical particularity" (Hall 1980, 61). Hall argues that for both Williams, Hoggart and Thompson culture is "interwoven with all social practices" and "sensuous human praxis" through which "men and women make history" (Hall 1980, 63). The "creative" and "historical agency" constitute "the two key elements in the *humanism*" (63) of what Hall terms *culturalism*. In contrast, structuralism foregrounds language, the whole, the mode of production and ideology as social structures and the human being as a bearer of structures. It stresses the "articulation of parts within a structure" (65) and "determinate conditions" (67).

Hall (1980, 72) argues that he wants to "think forwards from the best elements in the structuralist and culturalist enterprises". But in fact, his own work was more influenced by Althusser's and Laclau's structuralism than by so-called "culturalism". "Culturalism" is a derogatory term used by Hall. Marxist humanism is a more appropriate labelling for the approach of scholars such as Thompson and Raymond Williams. The structuralist character of his thought becomes evident in one of Hall's most read and cited works, the *Encoding/Decoding*-essay. In this paper, Hall applies Marx' dialectic of production, circulation and consumption to the means of communication. "Thus – to borrow Marx's terms – circulation and reception are, indeed, 'moments' of the production process in television" (Hall 1973, 3). Hall's paper visualises the communication process as a process of encoding and decoding that consists of structures of production, technological infrastructures, knowledge frameworks, meaning structures, discourses, and programmes (Hall 1973, 4). For Hall, communications are structures for the articulation, encoding and decoding of meanings and discourses. The human being and its work, creation and social production process are missing in this structuralist model.

Raymond Williams (1976) distinguishes between communication and communications: Whereas communication for Williams means "the passing of ideas, information, and attitudes from person to person" (9), a definition that foregrounds human beings and their relations, he sees as institutions, forms and systems, that is structures of communication. In Williams' terms, Hall focuses more on communications than communication.

Policing the Crisis is the work, where Hall's Althusserian structural Marxism comes to its height. Let us consider two brief, but typical, passages: The state "organises ideologically, through the cultural sphere and the education system – once again, progressively expanded and complexified as the productive needs it serves develop; through the means and media of communication and the orchestration of public opinion" (Hall et al. 1978, 205). "Events, as news, [...] articulate what the audience is assumed to think and know about the society." (56). Hall argues here that the ideological state apparatuses of the education system and the media system organise ideology and those news events articulate ideology. The point here is that cultural structures and not humans are said to act. Hall (1989, 48) says that in communication, meaning and ideology, "discourse is articulated to power" (Hall 1989, 48). Not humans are the subjects, but discourse is a subject that acts. Hall (1982) writes that humans are positioned and languaged (80), ideological discourses win their way (80), and discourse speaks itself through him/her (88). For Hall (1997, 5), "representational systems" such as language and music "communicate feelings and ideas".

The problem with all of these formulations is that they neglect the mentioning of active human beings who communicate with each other and so produce social relations. For Hall and structuralism, it is not humans who communicate ideology, ideas, discourse, feelings, etc. through language, music, news media and other representational systems. He assumes structures and systems language, speak, communicate, etc. Human communication is subsumed under communications, that is structures and systems of communication. Communication is reduced to the status of a structure. Such an approach misses that communication is a social process that connects humans and establishes and maintains relations between them. It is the social practice, in which humans produce and reproduce sociality and social relations by making sense of each other and the world. It is no surprise that the term "human" is not mentioned once in Hall's *Encoding/Decoding*-paper. Hall misses that discourses, communication, and ideology are the processes that relate humans and help to constitute particular power relations.

In the 1980s and 1990s, the major theoretical influence on Hall's approach was no longer exerted by Althusser's structural Marxism, but Foucault's post-structuralism and Laclau and Mouffe's post-Marxism. Hall's cultural studies thereby undertook a "shift away from its encounter with Marxism" (Sparks 1996, 95). What remained was the structuralist outlook, which becomes for example, evident in Hall's later works, such as the 1997 book *Representation*. While Althusser is not mentioned a single time, Hall conceives of representation based on Foucault's concepts of discourse, power, and knowledge, as well as Saussure's and Barthes' semiotics. Dealing with the question of the subject, Hall (1997, 54) argues that Saussure "tended to abolish the subject from the question of representation" and that for Foucault, it is "discourse, not the subject, which produces knowledge". Just like earlier in the 1970s, Hall also here takes a structuralist position and argues that it "is discourse, not the subjects who speak it, which produces knowledge", that the subject is merely "*produced within discourse*" and "*subjected to* discourse", and that the subject is "the bearer of the kind of knowledge which discourse produces" (Hall 1997, 55). In contrast to Hall, E. P. Thompson (2014) takes a socialist, humanist position. He explains in his essay *Socialist Humanism* that in this approach "real people" (73) and the "creative agency of human labour" (76) form the "centre of [...] aspiration" (73) and "man is human by virtue of his culture" (59). Whereas for Thompson, the human being's agency is at the core of attention, for Hall, it is structures and not humans that act as subjects. Thompson's approach is grounded in Marx's "new humanism" that struggles for society, in which every individual can fully and freely develop (Dunayevskaya 2000, 125) and where the "ultimate creation of freedom rests upon the shortening of the working day" (Dunayevskaya 2000, 89)

The analysis of structures is not unimportant, but it is insufficient to focus on how structures are articulated with each other and condition practices. There is a dialectic of structure and agency that any analysis of communication must take into account. The approach that I take is much closer to humanism, that is an approach that according to Marx starts from "the existence of living human individuals" (Marx and Engels 1845/46, 31) who produce in common. And to produce also means to communicate.

This approach constructs a critical theory of communication through the reading of humanist Marxist works from a communication perspective. This method also takes into account the dialectic of structure and practices but starts from human beings and their social relations of life and production. The approach I use on the one hand focuses on more well-known works, such as Raymond Williams works on communication, to argue for communicative materialism (Fuchs 2017). On the other hand, it also tries to reconstruct lesser-known works or elements in works from a communications perspective. E. P. Thompson is remembered as one of the primary historians of the English working class. He practised history as history from below, which means that he tells the history of the working class through the analysis of workers' everyday culture, customs, practices, experiences and struggles. By doing so, the question arises what the role is of communication in these processes. A reading of Thompson's work and its relation to Althusser is one of several entries into and starting points for a critical theory of communication. In his discussion of Williams' *Long Revolution*, Thompson warned of the assumption that "the central problem of society today is not one of power but of communication". This means that communication must in a critical analysis always be related to issues of power and class.

Whereas Thompson and Williams were life-long Marxists, Hall's relation to Marxian theory was ambivalent, "contingent and transitory" (Sparks 1996, 97). Furthermore, Thompson and Williams understood themselves explicitly as socialist humanists. These are two reasons why Thompson is one of the appropriate starting points for a critical theory that stands in the traditions of humanism and Marxism.

Given the outline of some background, we can next engage with the Althusser/Thompson-debate.

3.3 Louis Althusser

Althusser (2005) sees a social formation as consisting of various levels and instances (101) that together form an organic totality (102). He distinguishes between the economic mode of production and "the superstructures, instances which derive from it, but have their own consistency and effectivity" (100). The mode of production consists of the forces and relations of production (110) that form contradictions and are the social formation's "*conditions of existence*" (100, 110). The superstructure includes "the State, the dominant ideology, religion, politically organized movements, and so on" (106). The superstructure for Althusser consists of a political and an ideological level – "the State and all the legal, political and ideological forms" (111; see also Althusser 1971, 134). "So in every society we can posit, in forms which are sometimes very paradoxical, the existence of an economic activity as the base, a political organization and 'ideological' forms (religion, ethics, philosophy, etc.)" (Althusser 2005, 232). In the essay *Ideology and Ideological State Apparatuses*, Althusser (1971, 135–136) uses the metaphor of an edifice with different floors for describing the relationship of base and superstructure. It is "the base which in the last instance determines the whole edifice" (Althusser 1971, 136)

In Althusser's theory, we find a *"relative autonomy of the superstructures and their specific effectivity"*, but there is the *"determination in the last instance by the (economic) mode of production"* (Althusser 2005, 111). All levels are related and influence each other, but the economy is the overdetermining factor. Althusser says there is a "mutual conditioning" of levels and contradictions (205). "The superstructure is not the pure phenomenon of the structure, it is also its condition of existence" (205). Althusser takes from Mao (1937) the idea that there is always one overdetermining, principal, dominant, leading contradiction and structure (Althusser 2005, 101, 211). It would not in advance and eternally be determined what the "determinant-contradiction-in-the-last-instance" is, but the economy would in the last instance overdetermine other levels in the selection of the structure in dominance (213)[1]. For Althusser, one contradiction dominates other contradictions. One level dominates other levels. Althusser speaks of the structure in dominance (200). In capitalism, the contradiction between forces and relations of economic production is for him the "principal contradiction" (208).

The problem of the Althusserian approach is not just that it makes the economic the causally determining factor of society. It simultaneously under- and overestimates the role of the economic. The separation of society into economic, political and cultural levels underestimates the economy by ignoring that it operates in all social systems in the form of human production and work. Rules and ideologies do not simply exist. Humans produce and reproduce them. The political and the cultural are economic and non-economic at the same time (Fuchs 2015, chapters 2 and 3). Culture and politics are not just economic, the economic is also cultural and political. Althusser underestimates the operation of the non-economic in the economic realm. An example is that the ideologies of individual performance, developing the self, loving your work, etc. operate at the workplace. The cultural industries are a realm of the organisation of the economy, in which news, music, films, software, entertainment, art and other forms of

---

1 See also Althusser and Balibar (2009, 251).

knowledge are produced. These industries today form a significant part of the capitalist economy and are another example of culture operating inside of the economy. Althusser's separation of levels cannot adequately explain the dialectics of the economic and the non-economic.

That Althusser is a post-humanist philosopher becomes evident by the fact that in the language he uses (dominant structures, levels, instances, modes of production, contradictions, etc.), humans and their conscious agency are missing. Socialist humanism is a theoretical and political movement. During Soviet times, it formulated a critique of the Soviet-style regimes that aimed at the humanisation and democratisation of socialism. Its most important political moments were the 1956 Hungarian revolution and the 1968 Prague Spring. The Soviets crushed both uprisings militarily. In Marxist theory, humanism was a theory movement including the Yugoslav praxis group and writers such as C. L. R. James, Erich Fromm, Georg Lukács, Henri Lefebvre, Herbert Marcuse, Jean-Paul Sartre, Karel Kosík, Lucien Goldmann, or Raya Dunayevskaya. In Britain, E. P. Thompson was the main representative.

Althusser was critical of Marxist humanism in several respects: At the time when he wrote *For Marx* and *Reading Capital*, he saw humanist potentials in Chinese and Soviet socialism (Althusser 2005, 222, 236–239). Other than Marxist humanists, Althusser considered Marx's early philosophical writings as esoteric, ideological and unscientific. He propagated the existence of an epistemological break in the work of Marx that constitutes a division between an ideological Marx and a scientific Marx (Althusser 2005, 13). "In 1845, Marx broke radically with every theory that based history and politics on an essence of man" (Althusser 2005, 227). Marx would from then on have advanced a theoretical anti-humanism (229) and have focused on using "new concepts, the concepts of mode of production, forces of production, relations of production, superstructure, ideology, etc." (244).

Althusser overlooks the continuity of the notion of the human as a social being in Marx's works. In the *1844 Economic and Philosophic Manuscripts*, Marx speaks of the human species being a "social being" (Marx 1988, 105). Society is "the social fabric" of humans (ibid.). In class society, the exploitation of labour limits and cripples humanity, sociality, and society. Only a fully developed communism "equals humanism" (102). In 1845, Marx formulated the importance of human sociality in the sixth thesis on Feuerbach when he wrote that "the essence of man" is "the ensemble of social relations" and that the species "unites the many individuals" (Marx 1845, 570). The old Marx did not, as Althusser claims, abolish this insight, but applied it to the study of capitalism. *Capital* is a critique of political economy in that it shows the social and therefore historical character of commodities, labour, money, capital and class. Marx criticises capitalism's fetishist structure that makes capitalist society's structures appear as non-social and natural. *Capital* also criticises bourgeois thought that reifies capitalist categories in its theories. Marx elaborated a critical theory of capitalism that is a critical theory of fetishist society and thought. His analysis of capitalism in *Capital* is based on the insight that the majority of humans in capitalism produce goods and value that is not their property, but that the dominant class owns as capital and private property. In his early works, he for this phenomenon coined the term alienation.

The alienation of the social in capitalism is not just indirectly present in *Capital* in the form of the critique of fetishism, but also directly as the concept of alienation. Marx writes: "On the other hand, the worker always leaves the process in the same state as he entered it – a personal source of wealth, but deprived of any means of making that wealth a reality for himself. Since, before he enters the process, his own labour has already been alienated [entfremdet] from him, appropriated by the capitalist, and incorporated with capital, it now, in the course of the process, constantly objectifies itself so that it becomes a product alien to him [fremdem Produkt]" (Marx 1867a, 716). He also says in *Capital* that the production process is in capitalism a "pestiferous source of corruption and slavery", but will "under the appropriate conditions turn into a source of humane development ["Quelle humaner Entwicklung" in the German original]" (Marx 1867a, 621). Marx neither dropped the notion of alienation nor the concept of communism as humanism but developed both as part of a critical theory of capitalism. It is simply wrong that alienation and humanism are "ideological" concepts "used by Marx in his Early Works" (Althusser 2005, 249) and that they are only the "characteristic feature of the ideological problematic from which Marx emerged" (251).

Althusser is a relational thinker. He conceives a mode of production in relational terms as a specific set of "relations between men and relations between things" and as "relations between men and things" (Althusser and Balibar 2009, 193). He coins in this context the notion of the combinatory (194) for stressing the "*combination (Verbindung) of a certain number of elements*" (193). Also, society is for Althusser relational, it is an "articulation" of the "region of the economic [...] with other regions, legal-political and ideological superstructure" (198). Balibar argues that articulation means the "construction (Bau) or mechanism of 'correspondence' in which the social formation is presented as constituted out of different levels" – "an economic base, legal and political forms, and ideological forms" (228).

Étienne Balibar's section in *Reading Capital* is a more thorough engagement with Marx than Althusser's part. By and large, Balibar takes over Althusser's basic assumptions. He describes the mode of production as a connection of two connections (Althusser and Balibar 2009, 241): the relations of production (a property connection between humans, that is in capitalism between capital and labour) and the productive forces (a real/material appropriation connection between humans and nature).

The Althusserian concept of articulation is always either an articulation between structures or a determination of humans by structures. This becomes evident when Althusser writes that there is "a certain *attribution* of the means of production to the agents of production" (193). Relations of production determine "the *places* and *functions* occupied and adopted by the agents of production" (198) so that "they are the 'supports' (Träger) of these functions" (199). Humans are for Althusser not society's subjects. "*The true 'subjects' are these definers and distributors: the relations of production*" (199). Also, for Balibar, the combination of elements forms society's subject of history (280). Humans are for Balibar "supports for the connexions implied by the structure"; they "fulfil certain determinate functions in the structure" (283).

So, in Althusserianism, humans are always subordinated bearers of structures. This approach does not give attention to how structures need to be produced and constantly reproduced through human practices. Societal relations are not abstract but lived by humans in everyday social relations. Communication is humans' concrete production and reproduction of social relations. Human communication is the process, in which humans connect societal structures to their lived experiences and these lived experiences enter societal structures. Given that humans and their practices have a subordinated role in Althusser's approach, it is no surprise that communication is not a relevant concept. In *For Marx*, the term communication is not used a single time. In *Reading Capital*, the term communication appears twice. Once in a Marx quote that mentions means of communication (Althusser and Balibar 2009, 245) and another time in respect to the question of how to read Marx (355).

In the collection *Lenin and Philosophy and Other Essays*, Althusser uses the term communication for the presentation of a philosophical contribution (Althusser 1971, 23, 26–27) and in the context of ideological state apparatuses. The communications ideological state apparatus (ISA) is for Althusser one of eight ISAs (Althusser 1971, 143). It includes "press, radio and television, etc." (143). Althusser discerns communications from the cultural ISA that includes "Literature, the Arts, sports, etc." (143). Theatre, live music, sports entertainment certainly are also forms of communication just like the press, radio and television are forms of culture that communicate information that allows humans to reproduce their minds.

Overall, the notion of communication hardly plays a role in Althusser's works. In an anti-humanist approach that denies that humans are society's subject, it does not come as a surprise that there is no place for communicative practices. In the single instances where communication is mentioned in Althusser's works, it is reduced to ideological structures and is pluralised as communications (=communication systems).

In capitalism's economic mode of production, workers through communication co-operate in the production process, managers through authoritative communication command labour, money and exchange-value are the "language of commodities" (Marx 1867a, 143) that acts as means for communicating prices, etc. In the political system, parliamentary debates, election campaigns, demonstrations and programmes are specific forms of political communication. In the cultural system, an ideology communicates dominant ideas to the public in order to try to gain and secure hegemony. Production, control, exchange, politics, and ideology do not simply exist as structures, but are only possible through concrete communicative practices, in which humans relate to each other, make meaning of each other and the world, and produce and reproduce use-values and social structures. Althusser's theory remains too abstract and structuralist for making sense of communication.

3.4 Edward P. Thompson

The Poverty of Theory is Thompson's (1978) more than 200-page-long critique of Althusser and Althusserianism. Thompson argues that the notion of "men as träger", as bearers, supports and carriers of functions, was already during Marx's lifetime an ideology that "sought exactly to *impose* this structure upon the working class, and, at the same time, to convince them that they were powerless to resist these 'immutable' laws" (Thompson 1978, 147–148). "Althusser has simply taken over a reigning fashion of bourgeois ideology and named it 'Marxism'" (153). The problem is that structuralism sees humans as passive and not active beings. In this approach, humans "are *structured* by social relations" and "*thought* by ideologies" (153). Althusser overlooks the "*dialogue* between social being and social consciousness" that "goes in both directions" (9).

One should note that Marx does not exclusively use the term *Träger* (bearer) with respect to humans. He for example also writes that use-values are bearers of exchange-value (Marx 1867a, 126) and "bearers of value" (138). And he describes machinery as a "repository [Träger] of capital" (526). And Marx does indeed, as indicated by Thompson, not describe capital and labour as constituted by passive humans without subjectivity. An example is a passage, where Marx writes about the movement of capital:

> As the conscious bearer [Träger] of this movement, the possessor of money becomes a capitalist. His person, or rather his pocket, is the point from which the money starts, and to which it returns. The objective content of the circulation we have been discussing – the valorization of value – is his subjective purpose, and it is only in so far as the appropriation of ever more wealth in the abstract is the sole driving force behind his operations that he functions as a capitalist, i.e. as capital personified and endowed with consciousness and a will. Use-values must therefore never be treated as the immediate aim of the capitalist; nor must the profit on any single transaction. His aim is rather the unceasing movement of profit-making. This boundless drive for enrichment, this passionate chase after value, is common to the capitalist and the miser; but while the miser is merely a capitalist gone mad, the capitalist is a rational miser.
>
> (Marx 1867a, 254)

The capitalist (as well as the worker) is for Marx conscious, purposefully acting, wilful, passionate, and rational. Workers and capitalists are active subjects in the production and reproduction of capitalism. The labour contract between capitalist and worker is a structural form of violence that compels the worker to enter a relationship of exploitation. The point is that within capitalism, the worker has difficulty to escape the fact s/he must sell her labour-power because the market is an institutionalised form of economic violence or what Marx (1867a, 899) terms the "silent compulsion of economic relations".

Exchange-value and markets are principles that force the worker to actively seek to sell his/her labour-power on the market in order to be exploited. Class society's institutionalised violence conditions the possibilities and rights of classes and their members. The key aspect is the right to private ownership of the means of production that the bourgeois state defends. Capitalism's structural violence of markets and the state results in workers' actively seeking to sell their labour-power and capitalists' actively controlling the production process: The capitalist "proceeds to consume the commodity, the labour-power he has just bought, i.e. he causes the worker, the bearer of that labour-power, to consume the means of production by his labour. [...] First, the worker works under the control of the capitalist to whom his labour belongs;

[...] Secondly, the product is the property of the capitalist and not that of the worker, its immediate producer" (Marx 1867a, 291–292).

Thompson (1978) criticises two aspects of Althusser's and Althusserians' model of society:

a.) The dualistic separation of levels is undialectical.
b.) The causal reduction of levels to the economy is mechanistic, reductionist, and static.

Levels are "empty of all social and historical content" (95). Instances and levels "are in fact human activities, institutions, and ideas" that humans experience (97). For the British socialist thinker William Morris, culture would in contrast to Althusser not have derived from the economy. Rather, capitalist society is "founded upon forms of exploitation which are simultaneously economic, moral and cultural" (294). Thompson here forgot to mention the political. The reduction of the social to the economy is for Thompson not society's ontology, but a capitalist strategy. He, therefore, speaks of "capitalism's innate tendency to reduce all human relationships to economic definitions" (294). Althusser propagates a "total collapse of all human activities back into the elementary terms of a mode of production" (97) and constructs a "conceptual prison", in which "mode of production = social formation" (163).

Perry Anderson (1980) interposes to Thompson's critique that Balibar and Althusser see a plurality in the modes of production active in a social formation (67) and that Thompson's account of society is not so different from Althusser's: Thompson in *The Poverty of Theory* would just like Althusser break down society into the regions of the economy, polity, and culture (Anderson 1980, 70). The difference that Anderson overlooks is, however, that for Althusser these realms are much more separate from each other and determined by the economy, whereas Thompson argues that they dialectically operate in each other and that the economic mode of production is not determining society. Formulated differently, we can say that a societal formation is a totality, in which human agency produces, reproduces and is conditioned by dialectically interconnected and over-grasping economic, political, and cultural systems, institutions and structures. Thompson's approach comes much closer to a structure/agency-dialectic than the one of Althusser.

Thompson (1978) argues that "Althusserianism *is* Stalinism reduced to the paradigm of theory" (182) and "the attempt to reconstruct Stalinism at the level of theory" (131).

Althusser says that when he entered the Parti communiste français (PCF), philosophy was impossible. It would have been Stalin who "reduced the madness to a little more reason" (Althusser 2005, 22) and delivered "the first shock" (Althusser 2005, 27) so that Marxist philosophy became possible in the PCF. Thompson argues that Althusser here refers to Stalin's (1950/1972) *Marxism and the Problems of Linguistics*, a text for which Althusser "has always shown unusual respect" (Thompson 1978, 79).

Thompson was a member of the Communist Party of Great Britain (CPGB) from 1942 until 1956 (131), Althusser a member of the Parti communiste français (PCF) from 1948 onwards (131). The CPGB suspended John Saville and E. P. Thompson after they had founded the socialist humanist journal *The Reasoner*. Its subtitle was *A Quarterly Journal of Socialist Humanism*. Thompson and Saville commented: "The Executive Committee's statement makes it clear that a decisive factor in their action was our editorial condemning Soviet intervention in Hungary. The meaning of the Executive's decision is this: despite our own attempt to find some way for compromise, the leadership of the British Communist Party is determined not to permit discussion to develop in the party free from their control, since they fear that such discussion might lead on to the 'de-Stalinisation' of the British party – the ridding of the party of authoritarian methods and attitudes, and of political subservience to the Soviet leadership. [...] We do not intend to appeal against the Executive's decision, and we have both decided to resign from the party at once" (Saville 1994, 31).

Thompson (1978) asks: "*So where was Althusser in 1956?*" (132). In 1956, Althusser was a member of the PCF, whereas Thompson left the CPGB. "In 1956 it was, at length, officially 'revealed' that Stalinism had, for decades, been swatting down men like flies" (132). In 1946, the Soviet military also crushed the Hungarian uprising. PCF leader Maurice Thorez, who saw Stalin as "an eminent Marxist theoretician, a great organizer" (Thorez 1960b), argued that the Hungarian rebellion posed the threat of "fascist barbarism" (Thorez 1960a) and that Soviet military intervention was therefore needed. Thompson (1978) argues that Althusser's reaction to 1956 would have been a critique of socialist humanism (132). Socialist humanism was "the voice of a Communist opposition, of a total critique of Stalinist practice and theory" (132). Thompson argues that at the time when Althusser denounced socialist humanism, this was a typical move in defence of the Soviet regime (128–130). Althusser would have used a trick, in which "resurgent Stalinism presents itself as anti-Stalinism" (128). In contrast to Thompson, Althusser saw human potentials in Soviet socialism under Khrushchev and Brezhnev and in Chinese socialism under Mao.

Perry Anderson (1980) defends Althusser by arguing that he was not a Stalinist, but a Maoist (107–110), and that in the 1970s he spoke out against Stalinism and was in favour of the Workers' Defence Committee in Poland (111). Anderson misses that Thompson's main point is about the parallels between Stalin's and Althusser's theoretical approaches and their political implications.

Stalin was "a mixture of Marxist theorist, pragmatist, and hypocrite" (Thompson 1978, 141). For Stalin, history is a process without subject and human agency, humans are only "supports" or "vectors of ulterior structural determinations" (Thompson 1978, 79). Stalin (1939) describes the development of a society based on Engels' dialectics of nature in correspondence to natural laws. He sees history as a linear succession of modes of production determined by the economy. It is a "process of development from the lower to the higher" (Stalin 1939, 109). "This means that the history of development of society is above all the history of the development of production, the history of the modes of production which succeed each other in the course of centuries, the history of the development of productive forces and people's relations of production" (121). The economic mode of production would determine the superstructure: "Whatever is the mode of production of a society, such in the main is the society itself, its ideas and theories, its political views and institutions. Or, to put it more crudely, whatever is man's manner of life, such is his manner of thought" (121). Given the natural development of society, the October Revolution would have necessarily resulted in the establishment of a socialist society: "[T]he U.S.S.R. has already done away with capitalism and has set up a Socialist system" (Stalin 1939, 119).

The implication of these theoretical assumptions was for Stalin that anyone who was critical of him was a counter-revolutionary who opposed socialism and wanted to establish capitalism in Russia and therefore needed to be killed. This became, for example, evident when Stalin commented shorty after Nikolai Bukharin, one of the main Bolshevik theorists, had been arrested in 1937. Bukharin was put on trial together with others, was convicted to death for planning a conspiratorial coup, planning terrorism and for anti-Soviet espionage. He was executed in March 1938. Stalin said: "I think it is clear to everybody now that the present-day wreckers and diversionists, no matter what disguise they may adopt, either Trotskyite or Bukharinite, have long ceased to be a political trend in the labour movement, that they have become transformed into a gang of professional wreckers, diversionists, spies and assassins, without principles and without ideals. Of course, these gentlemen must be ruthlessly smashed and uprooted as the enemies of the working class, as betrayers of our country" (Stalin 1937, 277). Stalin's mechanistic interpretation of history and society justified the killing of his opponents. Mao (1937) was in his analysis of dialectical contradictions full of praise for Stalin's theory and politics: "Stalin's analysis provides us with a model for understanding the particularity and the universality of contradiction and their interconnection" (330). "The history of the Communist Party of the Soviet Union shows us that the contradictions between the correct thinking of Lenin and Stalin and the fallacious thinking of Trotsky, Bukharin and others did not at first manifest themselves in an antagonistic form, but that later they did develop into antagonism" (344).

Thompson was concerned about the parallels between mechanistic conceptions of society by the likes of Stalin and Mao and Althusserianism's concept of society that for example argues that "every mode of production necessarily *induces* the existence of the (superstructural) instances that specifically correspond to it" (Althusser 2003, 23) or that the "history of society can be reduced to a discontinuous succession of modes of production" (Althusser and Balibar 2009, 229). Thompson criticised both the theoretical homology and the political abuse that such theorising entails.

At this point, it will have become evident to the reader that my theoretical and political sympathies are with humanism and not structuralism. Thompson's approach has advantages and at the same time certain limits. His key category is class experience. Experience arises because humans are rational beings who "think about what is happening to themselves and their world" (Thompson 1978, 8). Changed experience "exerts pressures upon existent social consciousness" (8). Experience includes culture, ideas, instincts, feelings, norms, obligations, values, beliefs, affects, morals (Thompson 1978, 171), needs, interests, consciousness (164), myth, science, law, ideology (9), and thought (98). Experience in relation to class has to do with class-consciousness expressed in a class' culture, traditions, values, ideas and institutions (Thompson 1963, 10). Popular culture derives from common experience and customs in common (Thompson 1993).

It is evident that some of the terms that Thompson associates with experience relate to individual subjectivity, others to collective subjectivity, and some have to do with both. Experience is both social and individual. The theoretical problem that arises is when Thompson (1978, 98) argues that experience is a "middle term between social being and social consciousness" (Thompson 1978, 98) and that "as being is thought so thought is also lived – people may, within limits, *live* the social or sexual expectations which are imposed upon them by dominant conceptual categories" (Thompson 1978, 9).

The theoretical problem is to discern the individual's thoughts from everyday relations, in which humans live and act. Experience certainly includes both dimensions, but a term seems to be missing that allows us to distinguish human social experience from individual experience as well as collective from individual subjectivity. Whereas cognition and thinking are always ongoing in the individual's brain, they are only possible through and at the same time constitute the foundation of communication. Through communication, humans live, produce, and reproduce society's structures in everyday life and do so based on their individual subjectivity that in the communication process is symbolically externalised in mutual interaction with at last another human subject. Communication is a necessary condition for the formation of collective subjectivity (shared identities, norms and values, rules, common practices). Communication is the missing link in Thompson's work, the category that allows us to discern between individual subjectivity and collective subjectivity. Communication is the process, in which humans' individual subjectivities meet, share knowledge, and produce and reproduce a collective subjectivity.

Class is for Thompson (1963, 9) not a structure or category, but a historical and human relationship. Class happens "when some men, as a result of common experiences (inherited or shared), feel and articulate the identity of their interests as between themselves, and as against other men whose interests are different from (and usually opposed to) theirs" (Thompson 1963, 9). "Class is defined by men as they live their own history, and, in the end, this is its only definition" (Thompson 1963, 11). Classes "arise because men and women, in determinate productive relations, identify their antagonistic interests, and come to struggle, to think, and to value in class ways" (Thompson 1978, 106–107). Perry Anderson (1980, 42) importantly points out that it seems that for Thompson "class = class consciousness". Thompson's understanding of class faces the problem that classes "have frequently existed whose members did not "'identify their antagonistic interests' in any process of common clarification of struggle" (Anderson 1980, 40) and that it implies the possibility of class struggle without class and of class struggle operating only with the existence of a ruling class (42). That humans' position in the relations of production determines class status does not mean that class is an abstract structure. Rather class is lived in everyday economic relations in one's own class and between classes. And these social relations are established in and through communicative processes. Through communication, humans (re)produce social relations, including class relations. The decisive question is if the dominated class communicates politically and consciously about its class position and based on this conscious communication organises itself politically. Class is always objective (a class structure in society) and subjective (lived through communication) at the same time (class objectivity subjectified, class subjectivity objectified), but it is not always politically organised.

Ideology is certainly not a key category for Thompson, which means that an important form of subjectivity and consciousness is rather missing in his approach. He criticises that for Althusser ideology is in the form of ideological state apparatuses "imposed upon the innocent and utterly passive, recipient, man" (Thompson 1978, 174). Thompson argues that moral values are not mechanically imposed and "hailed", but "lived" (175). He does not reject the notion of ideology, he stresses that ideology not just works top-down but has a bottom-up hegemonic dimension: "This is not to say that values are independent of the colouration of ideology; [...] But to suppose from this that they are 'imposed' (by a State!) as 'ideology' is to mistake the whole social and cultural process. This imposition will always be attempted, with greater or lesser success, but it cannot succeed at all unless there is some congruence between the imposed rules and view-of-life and the necessary business of living a given mode of production" (175). Ideologies are situated in "the people's way of life" that is "culture's material abode" (176).

Thompson well points out the ideology's subject/object-dialectic. But the problem is that he assumes a certain determinism of resistance against ideology: "Moreover, values no less than material needs will always be a locus of *contradiction*, of struggle between alternative values and views-of-life" (175). "Conflicts of values, and choices of values, always take place" (175). Ideology is always a *communication process*, in which dominant groups try to justify and impose their moral values on others. If this attempt is (un)successful, partly (un)successful, or temporarily (un)successful depends on many factors, including the availability and distribution of power. If the dominant class can mobilise means of power (such as the mass media, public discourses, money, influence, reputation), then it can increase the likelihood to impose ideologies successfully. The ideological communication processes' outcomes are not arbitrary, but subject to power dynamics and asymmetries that confront dominated groups.

In the 832 pages of *The Making of the English Working Class*, Thompson (1963) uses the terms *communication(s)* and *to communicate* less than 30 times, always in theoretically rather unreflected manners (see pages 24, 134, 195; the words *communication, communications* and to *communicate* 14 times (on pages 110, 136, 174, 191, 221, 262, 266, 273, 336, 386, 391, 393). The analysis allows us to conclude that communication is a largely absent theoretical category in Thompson's works. His theoretical limit is that he ignores the role of communication in respect to experience, class and ideology.

Communication is the blind spot of both Althusser's and Thompson's approach and many other Marxist works and theories. A Marxist theory of communication is needed. What we can learn from the controversy between Althusser and Thompson is that thinking about the relationships between the economic and the non-economic and between structures and agency poses key theoretical questions for any social theory, including a Marxist theory of communication.

3.5 Towards a critical theory of communication

3.5.1 Communication in society: communication as the process of (re)producing social relations within societal relations

For Althusser and Balibar, articulation is an expression of society's relational character. But for them, articulation is a relation between structures, not between humans, who are for Althusserians just bearers of structures that are articulated with each other. For the two authors, the economy determines society "in the last instance". The economy in this approach determines in the last instance what a particular society's determining instance is. The problem here is not so much speaking of the last instance, but the notion of determination. Given that the social production of resources plays a role in all social systems, there can be no doubt that the economy is important everywhere in society. The notion of determination implies a too restrictive, one-sided and monocausal relationship. In the case of Althusser, articulation not just means relations, but economically (over-)determined relations. At the same time, Althusserian relations are abstract and detached from human practices. It is therefore no surprise that communication is a blind spot of Althusser's works. That structures mediate human agency means that they enable human communication through which social relations are produced and reproduced. At the aggregate level of society, communication produces and reproduces societal relations. Wherever there is a society, there are structure/agency-dialectics. And wherever there are structure/agency- dialectics, there is mediation by structures and communication. Society's structures mediate humans' communicative practices that (re)produce structures that are society's media.

We need to start the analysis of society with humans living in social relations. A social relation is a connection between humans that allows them to make meaning of each other. This is why Max Weber defines a social relationship as "the behavior of a plurality of actors insofar as, in its meaningful content, the action of each takes account of that of the others and is oriented in these terms" (Weber 1978, 26). A social relation can be ephemeral and transient. But it can also become a structure. A structure is a regularised social relation that has some stability (the behaviour is repeated or allows repeatability) in space-time. Structures provide a social system's reproducibility in space and time. They are the recursive result of humans' social practices: Humans produce and reproduce social structures in and through their actions and these structures condition, enable and constrain human behaviour and social action in society. There is a dialectic of structures and practices in society. Giddens, therefore, argues that "the structural properties of social systems are both medium and outcome of the practices they recursively organize" (Giddens 1984, 25; see Fuchs 2003 for a discussion).

One general sociological insight that plays a key role in Marx's works is that everything in society is a social relation. In *Capital*, Marx outlines a critical sociology of capitalism and shows that commodities, value, labour, money and capital are not things, but social relations. Capitalism is constituted through the class relationship between labour and capital.

Marx for example writes:

> [...] daß das Kapital nicht eine Sache ist, sondern ein durch Sachen vermitteltes Verhältnis zwischen Personen.
> (Marx 1867b, 793)

> Wert ist "etwas rein Gesellschaftliches".
> (Marx 1867b, 71)

> Die relative Wertform einer Ware" verbirgt "ein gesellschaftliches Verhältnis.
> (Marx 1867b, 71)

English translations of Marx are often not precise and translate *gesellschaftliches Verhältnis* as social relation and *gesellschaftlich* as social. In the Penguin-edition, the three passages above read:

> "capital is not a thing, but a social relation between persons which is mediated through things".
> (Marx 1867a, 932)

> Value is "something purely social"
> (Marx 1867a, 149)

> "The relative value-form [...] conceals a social relation"
> (Marx 1867a, 149)

Marx refers to the role of the social in society and therefore speaks of capital and value as societal relations and something purely societal. Humans in their everyday life constantly enter and leave social relations. Society is the totality of humans' social relationships. Given that social systems are interconnected through humans' multiple roles, relations and activities, they are interrelated. Social relations are always societal relations because society's realms of interaction shape and are shaped by everyday practices.

Georg Lukács (1971) expresses the societal and relational character of human existence with the help of the concept of mediation. Mediation is "a lever with which to overcome the mere immediacy of the empirical world" (162). "[O]bjects as they are given" (155) are not things-in-themselves. They are what they are only through relations and these relations are "*the real tendencies of the objects themselves*" (155). In Hegelian language, being-in-itself can only exist through being-for-another. A single individual is, as Marx says in the 6th thesis on Feuerbach "the ensemble of societal relations" (MEW 3, 6). Societal relations such as capital can continue to exist when one specific capitalist or worker dies because s/he can be replaced. This circumstance indicates the general character of societal relations. Social relations are in contrast concrete, they are the relations humans enter in their everyday life with each other; for example, the workplace, where Peter meets and co-operates with his colleagues Mary and Joe and where he has a quarrel with manager Sandra over working hours, overtime and payment. Sandra may leave the company, but this may not resolve the labour disputes as a similarly ruthless manager may replace her.

These everyday relations are organised day in and day out. They take place in particular spaces at specific times. Communication is an everyday process that establishes and maintains social relations. It is the production and reproduction of social relations. Peter and his colleagues only make known that they dislike working long hours and think that their pay is too low by telling Sandra about it, who is thereby forced to somehow respond on behalf of capital. Power relations are abstract societal relations that are instantiated, lived, enacted, reproduced and potentially challenged through processes of communication in everyday life.

Humans (re)produce social structures through communication in their everyday lives and thereby (re)produce societal structures that frame, condition, enable and constrain communicative production in everyday life. Society is the totality of societal relations. And each societal relation encapsulates manifold social relations. A societal relation (such as the class relation between capital and labour) is a totality of social relations. It is framed by and framing all other societal relations. The class relation is reproduced through multiple capitalist organisations, in which workers interact with each other and interact with capital. Society is the totality that is the result of and condition for human communication. The notion of the totality should not be understood as meaning that society in general or particular societies are totalitarian. Not just capitalism and class societies are totalities. Every society is a totality of over-grasping moments, that is systems that reach over into each other through human communication. Therefore, we are never isolated individuals, but all phenomena in society are truly concrete. The "truly concrete is not a particular, isolated phenomenon, but an aspect or 'moment' of a totality" (Lukács 1971, 344). Society is a "complex of complexes" (Lukács, 1986, 155; see also 181) that help reproducing society (182).

Neither the form nor the content of communication is immaterial. Communication is a material practice, which means that it is a social process, in which humans create concrete results. Society's materiality is that it is a realm of social production. Marx writes in this context that the "first premise of all human history is, of course, the existence of living human individuals" who "*produce* their means of subsistence" and thereby are "indirectly producing their material life" (Marx and Engels 1845/46, 31). Production is in society not conducted by isolated individuals but in social and societal relations. The human capacity to communicate is a fundamental human means of production that is needed for the (re)production of society and the social. "[C]ommunication and its material means are intrinsic to all distinctively human forms of labour and social organization" (Williams 1980, 50).

Communication and the production of physical and intangible products are not two separate processes. All economic production has a symbolic dimension of human interaction. Humans relate to each other in a symbolic way when they socially produce structures in order to make sense of each other and the world. Structures symbolise society's relations and thereby on behalf of humans something in society. Raymond Williams (1977) stresses in this context the "material character of the production of a social and political order" (93) and that culture and societies are realms of socio-material production (see Fuchs 2015, chapters 2 and 3). Communicative means are a "means of social production" (Williams 1980, 51) that has an "inherent role […] in every form of production" (53). Language, books, newspapers, the telegraph, the telephone and the Internet are examples of means of mass communication that disseminate information over space and make it persistent in time. Communication technologies allow the storage (making information durable) and transmission (transferring information from one social system and context to another) of information. In a more general sense, all social structures symbolise in complex ways the human activities that create them and communicate information about wealth, influence, and status. They are (general) means of communication.

For Lukács (1986), society is a complex of complexes, in which humans teleologically posit the world. By teleological positing, Lukács means the conscious, active production that is goal-oriented and realises subjective intentions in the objective world. It is a common feature of work and communication (see Fuchs 2016, chapter 2). Basic goals humans strive to achieve in society are the satisfaction of human needs (the economic positing), the management and organisation of complexity through collective decision-making (the political positing), and the recognition of subjectivity (the human body and the mind; the cultural positing). Communication is not another type of teleological positing that stands outside economic, political and cultural production, but is an immanent feature of all social production. Through communication, humans learn to understand each other and the world. Through cognition, they try to understand themselves and communication. Cognition is the foundation and a result of communication. The economic principle of production is universal in that all human activity produces results. The base/superstructure-model is not tenable because the production of the social operates in all realms of society and constitutes also politics' and culture's economy. Politics and culture are economic and non-economic at the same time and also work within the economy.

Communication has an economic dimension in the sense that it produces and reproduces sociality. At the same time the created meanings are not restricted to the economy, but matter in different social systems and realms of society. Communicative capacities and means of communication are social means for a means, a means that by producing an understanding of oneself, other humans and the world helps manage human needs, complexity and subjectivity in society.

3.5.2 Class and domination

In heteronomous societies, social and societal relations are organised based on power inequalities so that particular groups are privileged in the production of use-values, collective decisions, and reputation. They thereby are able to achieve more wealth, influence or reputation than others. Particularistic ownership, elitist politics and privileged status are economic, political and cultural principles of stratification that result in asymmetries and inequalities of ownership, influence and reputation. In the economy, power inequality and asymmetrical ownership are based on one class' exploitation of another class' labour. In politics and the economy, power inequalities take on the form of political and cultural domination. Domination means that a group has the means for achieving its will at the expense of others. Exploitation is an economic form of domination.

In modern society, the principle of the accumulation of money-capital has been generalised as a principle on which society is based. Modern society is a generalised form of accumulation, in which classes and social groups strive for the accumulation of economic power (money-capital), political power (influence on decision-making), and cultural power (reputation). Capitalism is not just an economic mode of production, but a societal mode of production, a societal formation that is based on the principle of accumulation. The capitalist economy's principle of accumulation is a model for the organisation of capitalist society, in which the subsystems have a relative autonomy and their specific forms and logics of accumulation. The logic of accumulation tends to result in power asymmetries and distributive injustices. In any heteronomous society, mediation takes on the form alienation: Specific groups control the products of teleological positings, whereas others do not exercise such control. This means that they can appropriate and own others' labour products, impose their political values on collective decisions, impose reputational hierarchies, or achieve combinations thereof. Different groups can control differing degrees of economic, political and cultural power. In general, money is however a privileged means that can easier be transformed into political influence and cultural reputation than the other way around.

In modern society, the fetishism of power structures imposes a structure on society, in which social structures appear natural, eternal, immutable, unchangeable, and thing-like. In economic fetishism, money and commodities appear natural. In political and cultural fetishism, offices and status-positions appear natural. Society appears to talk to us through things and elite-individuals. Money, commodities, political offices and status-positions symbolise and communicate power. Reified structures hide alienation's social and societal character and that it is therefore the result of power contradictions and struggles. Workers', citizens and subjects' economic, political and cultural struggles have the potential to strive for the abolishment of alienation and the establishment of a different order.

The structure of class and heteronomous societies is inherently contradictory. Contradictions tend to result in crises. It is, however, not determined whether contradictory power relations or an economic, political or cultural crisis resulting from such contradictions or a combination of crises results in social struggles on behalf of the dominated groups. Social struggles are always possible because history is conditioned, but within this conditionality are relatively open. The results are also not predetermined. But violent structures of domination can forestall social struggles. Violence threatens to destroy or severely impede human life. It can be physical, structural or ideological in character (Galtung 1990). It denies humans their need for survival, well-being, identity and freedom (Galtung 1990). Ideologies are a knowledge form implicated by fetishist structures that dominant groups communicate and spread in order to try to justify and naturalise domination and exploitation. Dominated groups react in specific manners to ideologies. The reactions range on a continuum from the subjective acceptance/reproduction of ideology on the one end and rejection and resistance to ideology on the other end.

3.5.3 Communication as societal commoning

Human reactions to violence, exploitation and domination are not determined. It can be that many people endure and do not resist because of conscious or unconscious fears of loss just like there can be the rapid or gradual emergence of resistance. Humans do not by nature subject themselves voluntarily and automatically to domination just like there is no automatism of social struggle. Their existential fears and needs for community, harmony, security and recognition can be channelled into the acceptance of domination, violence and ideologies. Dominated groups' social struggles mean risk-taking and acceptance of uncertainty. If a significant number of the dominated are willing to take risks and organise collectively, then collective action, protests, revolts, rebellions, or revolutions can emerge. A collective consciousness of the organisation emerges. Political organisation is a communication process, in which humans come together and interact in order to define their goals, their identity and their strategies, based on these they take actions that aim at transforming society. Political consciousness can be but is not necessarily and not automatically progressive in character. The individual and collective consciousness that questions domination is a possibility, but not a necessity. It can also be ideological (e.g., nationalist, racist, fascist) in character. Social struggles are not automatically politically progressive and there is no guarantee that their outcome is a better condition than before. A new social order can only emerge when objective contradictions are subjectively reflected in a collective manner so that political action aimed at societal transformation emerges.

The term communication in modern language is derived from the Latin verb *communicare* and the noun *communicatio*. *Communicare* means to share, inform, unite, participate, and literally to make something common. A heteronomous and class-divided society is a society based on particularistic control. Struggles for the commons in contrast aim at overcoming class and heteronomy and to make society a realm of common control. In a common economy, the means of production are owned collectively. In a common polity, everyone can directly shape and participate in collective decision-making. In a common culture, everyone is recognised. In such a participatory democracy, humans speak and communicate as a common voice. They own and decide together and give recognition to each other. A communicative society is not a society in which humans communicate because humans have to communicate in all societies in order to survive. A communicative society is also not an information society, in which knowledge and information/communication technologies have become structuring principles. A communicative society is a society, in which the original meaning of communication as making something common is the organising principle. Society and therefore also communication's existence then correspond to communication's essence. A communicative society is a society controlled in common so that communication is sublated and turned from the general process of the production of sociality into the very principle on which society is founded. A communicative society also realises the identity of *communicare* (communicating, making common) and *communis* (community). Society becomes a community of the commons. Such a society is a commonist society.

3.6 Conclusion

Althusser's structuralist theory is anti-humanist in character, which results in a theoretical subordination of humans under structures and the assumption that economic structures determine society. As a consequence, there is no space for communicative practices in this approach. Thompson's humanist Marxist approach foregrounds the notion of human experience. It takes the structure/agency- and base/superstructure-problems into dialectical directions, but fails to differentiate between individual and collective subjectivity, faces the dangers of a subjectivist notion of class, and overestimates resistance. Communication is the missing link in this approach.

A Marxist theory of communication needs to relate the notion of communication to the study of society, class, capitalism and the commons. Communication is the process, in which humans produce and reproduce social relations and thereby live, reproduce and potentially challenge societal relations (structures) in their everyday life by making meaning of each other and (re)producing the social and societal world. They do so based on their individual subjectivities that meet in the communication process. Communication does not stand outside of domination, but shapes and is shaped by structures of class, violence and resistance. It is the intermediate process that organises the dialectic of objective structures and human subjects in society as well as the dialectic of individual and collective subjectivity. The communicative production of sociality explodes the base/superstructure distinction and constitutes interwoven dialectics of the economic and the non-economic. A forgotten meaning of communication is that it is the very process of commoning. Communication shares knowledge but can as a principle of organising society also point towards a commonist society.

Literature

Althusser, Louis. 2005 [1965]. *For Marx*. London: Verso.

———. 2003. *The Humanist Controversy and other Writings (1966-67)*. London: Verso.

———. 1971. *Lenin and Philosophy and Other Essays*. New York: Monthly Review Press.

Althusser, Louis, and Étienne Balibar. 2009 [1968]. *Reading Capital*. London: Verso.

Anderson, Perry. 1980. *Arguments within English Marxism*. London: Verso.

Dunayevskaya, Raya. 2000. *Marxism & Freedom: From 1776 Until Today*. Amherst, NY: Humanity Books.

Fuchs, Christian. 2017. "Raymond Williams' Communicative Materialism." *European Journal of Cultural Studies 20* (6): 744–762. [= Chapter 4 in this book].

———. 2016. *Critical Theory of Communication: Lukács, Adorno, Marcuse, Honneth and Habermas in the Age of the Internet and Social Media*. London: University of Westminster Press. doi:https://doi.org/10.16997/book1.

———. 2015. *Culture and Economy in the Age of Social Media*. New York: Routledge.

———. 2003. "Structuration Theory and Self-Organization." *Systemic Practice and Action Research 16* (4): 133–167.

Galtung, Johan. 1990. "Cultural Violence." *Journal of Peace Research 27* (3): 291–305.

Giddens, Anthony. 1984. *The Constitution of Society. Outline of the Theory of Structuration*. Cambridge: Polity.

Hall, Stuart, ed. 1997. *Representation*. London: Sage.

———. 1989. "Ideology and Communication Theory." In *Rethinking Communication. Volume I: Paradigm Issues*, edited by Brenda Dervin, Lawrence Grossberg, Barbara J. O'Keefe and Ellen A. Wartella, 40–52. Newbury Park, CA: Sage.

———. 1982. "The Rediscovery of "Ideology": Return of the Repressed in Media Studies." In *Culture, Society and the Media*, edited by Michael Gurevitch, Tony Bennett, James Curran and Janet Woollacott, 56–90. London: Methuen.

———. 1980. "Cultural Studies: Two Paradigms." *Media, Culture & Society 2* (1): 57–72.

———. 1973. "Encoding and Decoding in the Television Discourse." Stencilled Occassional Papers #5, Birmingham Centre for Contemporary Cultural Studies.

Hall, Stuart et al. 1978. *Policing the Crisis*. London: Macmillan.

Lukács, Georg. 1986. *Zur Ontologie des gesellschaftlichen Seins. Zweiter Halbband Bände. Georg Lukács Werke, Band 14*. Darmstadt: Luchterhand.

———. 1971. *History and Class Consciousness. Studies in Marxist Dialectics*. Cambridge, MA: The MIT Press.

Mao, Tse-Tung. 1937. "On Contradiction." In *Selected Works Volume I*, 311–347. Peking: Foreign Language Press.

Marx, Karl. 1988. *Economic and Philosophic Manuscripts of 1844 and the Communist Manifesto*. Amherst, NY: Prometheus.

———. 1867a. *Capital. Volume 1*. London: Penguin.

———. 1867b. *Das Kapital. Band 1. MEW, Band 23*. Berlin: Dietz.

———. 1845. "Theses on Feuerbach." In *The German Ideology*, 569–574. Amherst, NY: Prometheus.

Marx, Karl, and Friedrich Engels. 1956–1990. *Werke (MEW)*. Berlin: Dietz.

———. 1845/46. "The German Ideology." In *MECW Volume 5*, 19–539. London: Lawrence & Wishart.

Saville, John. 1994. "Edward Thompson, the Communist Party and 1956." *Socialist Register 30*: 20–31.

Sparks, Colin. 1996. "Stuart Hall, Cultural Studies and Marxism." In *Stuart Hall: Critical Dialogues in Cultural Studies*, edited by David Morley and Kuan-Hsing Chen, 71–101. London: Routledge.

Stalin, Joseph V. 1950/1972. *Marxism and Problems of Linguistics*. Peking: Foreign Languages Press.

———. 1939. "Dialectical and Historical Materialism." In *History of the Communist Party of the Soviet Union*, 105–131. New York: International Publishers.

———. 1937. "Speech in Reply to Debate (April 1, 1937)." In *Stalin Works Volume 14 (1934–1940)*, 275–297. London: Red Star Press.

Thompson, Edward P. 2014. *E. P. Thompson and the Making of the New Left: Essays & polemics*, edited by Carl Winslow. New York: Monthly Review Press.

———. 2011 [1955]. *William Morris: Romantic to Revolutionary*. Pontypool: The Merlin Press. Reprinted with a New Foreword.
———. 1993. *Customs in Common*. London: Penguin.
———. 1978. *The Poverty of Theory & Other Essays*. London: Merlin.
———. 1963. *The Making of the English Working Class*. New York: Vintage Books.
———. 1961/2014. "The Long Revolution." In *E. P. Thompson and the Making of the New Left: Essays & Polemics*, edited by Cal Winslow, 187–214. New York: Monthly Review Press.
Thorez, Maurice. 1960a. *1956*. https://www.marxists.org/reference/archive/thorez/1960/1956.htm.
———. 1960b. Stalin. https://www.marxists.org/reference/archive/thorez/1960/stalin.htm.
Weber, Max. 1978. *Economy and Society. An Outline of Interpretative Sociology*. Berkeley, CA: University of California Press.
Williams, Raymond. 1980 [2005]. *Culture and Materialism*. London: Verso.
———. 1977. *Marxism and Literature*. Oxford: Oxford University Press.
———. 1976. *Communications*. Hamondsworth: Penguin.

Chapter Four
Raymond Williams's communicative materialism

4.1 Introduction
4.2 The materialist theory of communication
4.3 Communicative materialism and the "base"/ "superstructure"-problem
4.4 Ideology
4.5 Conclusion
Literature

4.1 Introduction

Raymond Williams (1921–1988) is today primarily remembered as a cultural and literary theorist and as a novelist. But to what extent was he also a communication theorist and to what extent can we use his approach for understanding digital communication? This chapter tries to answer these questions. Digital media analysis, in general, lacks theoretical foundations. Williams's approach can be used for mitigating this circumstance and for renewing cultural studies' engagement with Marxian theory.

Jim McGuigan (2014, xv) reminds us that "Williams's project was much broader than that of a literary scholar", and that Williams was an influential social theorist. In his often-overlooked book *Communications*, Williams (1976, 9) asks, "What do we mean by communication?". He then distinguishes between communications as systems and means of information communication and communication as human social process.[1] Given that Williams asks what we mean by communication, it is worthwhile asking if there are elements of a theory of communication in his works.

This chapter discusses the materiality of communication (Section 4.2), the base/superstructure problem (Section 4.3) and the notion of ideology (Section 4.4) in Williams's work. It shows that these dimensions are important for his materialist

---

1 Williams does not explain why he distinguishes communication from communications. Society is based on a dialectic of structures and agency. With the rising complexity of society, systems of communication have emerged (means of communication) that enable communication over spatio-temporal distances. There is a dialectic of communication and communications.

understanding of communication and that each of them helps us to understand digital media critically.

4.2 The materialist theory of communication

Culture and communication are closely connected. Williams (2005, 243) argues that his approach of cultural materialism stresses "the centrality of language and communication as formative social forces". It is well known that Raymond Williams understood culture as a whole way of life. Culture includes lived culture, recorded culture and traditional culture (Williams 2011, 70). All three require "characteristic forms through which members of the society communicate" (62). The creation of culture requires "communication and the making of institutions" (126). For Williams (1981a, 13), culture is a signifying system, consisting of practices through which "a social order is communicated, reproduced, experienced and explored" (Williams 1981a, 13). This means that wherever there is culture, there is communication. When we communicate, we constitute culture. We need a theory of communication in order to have some idea of how communication relates to community, how it relates to society, what kind of communication systems we now have, what they tell us about our society, and what we can see as reasonable directors for the future. And we can only do this by theory (Williams 1989b, 20)

Rejecting both purely subjectivist and objectivist approaches, Williams (1976) distinguishes between communication and communications. Communication is the "passing of ideas, information, and attitudes from person to person", and communications are "the institutions and forms in which ideas, information, and attitudes are transmitted and received" (Williams 1976, 9). Whereas communication is a human social process and a practice (Williams 2014, 175), communications are systems, institutions and forms. There is a dialectic of communication and communications: Humans communicate by means of communication, whereas communications are created and re-created by human co-production and communication.

Williams (1976, 130–137) in his book *Communications* distinguishes between authoritarian, paternal, commercial and democratic organisational forms of the media (see Sparks 1993). The first three communications systems are political, cultural and commercial expressions of instrumental reason. Authoritarian communications involve state control, manipulation and censorship of the media. The "purpose of communication is to protect, maintain, or advance a social order based on minority power" (Williams 1976, 131). Paternal communications are authoritarian communications "with a conscience: that is to say, with values and purposes beyond the maintenance of its own power" (131). In such communication systems, there is ideological control that aims to impose certain moral values on audiences. The controllers of paternal communication systems assume that specific morals are good for citizens and that the latter are too silly to understand the world. In commercial communications, there is commercial control: "Anything can be said, provided that you can afford to say it and that you can say it profitably" (133). All three forms have an instrumental character: Authoritarian, paternal and commercial communications instrumentalise communication and turn it into a tool for control and domination.

In contrast, democratic communications are for Williams based on cooperative rationality. Such media systems are based on the freedom to speak and the free choice of what to receive. Such communications are "means of participation and of common discussion" (Williams 1976, 134). Williams (1976, 1983b) argues for a "cultural democracy" that combines public-service media, cultural co-operatives and local media (see also p65–72). Such a democracy establishes "new kinds of communal, cooperative and collective institutions" (Williams 1983b, 123). The core of Williams's proposal is that public ownership of the basic means of production [the means of communication and cultural production] should be combined with leasing their use to self-managing groups, to secure a maximum variety of style and political opinion and to ensure against any bureaucratic control (Williams 1979, 370). The idea of public service must be detached from the idea of public monopoly, yet remain public service in the true sense (Williams 1976, 134).

Instrumental and co-operative media are contradictory forces. Practically speaking, one can assess the instrumental and co-operative character of a medium by asking to which degree it is based on collective control and advances critique and reflection. Only cultural forms of class struggle can drive back the capitalist colonisation of communications. Democratic communications are the dominant form of communication in a socialist society, in which "the basic cultural skills are made widely available, and the channels of communication widened and cleared, as much as possible" (Williams 1958, 283).

Williams was a thorough reader and interpreter of Marx. He found particular interest in Marx's quest for an alternative to capitalism. Marx is a constant point of reference throughout Williams's oeuvre. Frequently being asked, "You're a Marxist, Aren't You?" (Williams 1989b, 65–76), Williams rejected the derogatory implications the question often had and criticised the lack of engagement that it brought along. He writes about how orthodox Marxists often declared that a specific position "has nothing in common with Marxism" and how every socialist theorist was flatly "referred to as a Communist whether or not one actually carried the party card of membership in the Communist Party" (Williams 1989b, 65). Williams rejected both Stalinist orthodoxy and anti-Marxism but made clear that for him, Marx "was the greatest thinker in the socialist tradition" (66). He argued that his approach of Marxism was one that stressed: "the connections between a political and economic formation, a cultural and educational formation, and, […] the formations of feeling and relationship which are our immediate resources in any struggle" (76). Contemporary Marxism that focuses on "the real meanings of totality", the questioning of capitalism and domination as totalities, would be "a movement to which I find myself belonging and to which I am glad to belong" (76). Given that such an understanding guided Williams's works, it is no surprise that he, as we will see next, also related the concept of communication to Marx's theory.

Williams (2005) argues that the political transformation of society has to include communications and that socialism entails, as Marx says, "'the production of the very form of communication', in which, with the ending of the division of labour within the mode of production itself, individuals would speak '*as* individuals', as integral human beings" (57). Williams, here, refers to Marx's Feuerbach chapter in the *German Ideology*, where Marx writes in a note that conditions of human self-activity mean "Production der Verkehrsform selbst" (Marx and Engels 1845a, 72) – "Production of the form of intercourse itself" (Marx and Engels 1845b, 91). In the *German Ideology*, Marx uses the term *Verkehrsform* for what he later termed the relations of production (*Produktionsverhältnisse*). He later spoke of Verkehr as "Kommunikations- und Transportmittel" (Marx1867b, 405) ["means of communication and transport", Marx 1867a, 506] and continued to use the term "Produktions- und Verkehrsverhältnisse" (Marx 1867b, 12) ["relations of production and forms of intercourse", Marx 1867a, 90). So Marx used the term "forms of intercourse" and not, as Williams translates the term, the "very form of communication".

Marx situates the notion of *Transportmittel* at the level of the productive forces and the concept of *Verkehrsverhältnisse* at the level of the relations of production. *Transport* means the shifting of an object in space from position A to position B. *Verkehr* is more general and has three meanings: (a) transport, (b) contact/relation and (c) sexual intercourse. Marx speaks of the means of communication as part of the productive forces but uses the term *Verkehr* in a general sense as social relations in the sense of (b). When Williams says that, for Marx, socialism means that humans produce and control the form of communication, the imprecise translation also contains two truths:

1) Socialism is a fundamental change of the productive forces, which includes changes in the means of communication.
2) Socialism changes the relations of production, that is, the social relations that are established and maintained in and through communication.

Williams's quest for an alternative society and alternative communications remains of key importance in the age of digital media: In the digital media world, what Williams in *Communications* terms commercial communications is dominant. This becomes evident when one, for example, thinks of monopoly capitalist firms such as Google (search engines), Facebook (social networks), Microsoft (operating systems) and Amazon (online shopping). Also, authoritarian communications are present on the Internet, which becomes evident when we think of Edward Snowden's revelations about online surveillance, the Chinese Internet and the way right-wing authoritarians such as Donald Trump use social media (Fuchs 2017b, 2017a). The alternative type of communications that Williams described as having democratic potential exists on the Internet but is relatively marginal. Two well-known examples are Wikipedia and non-profit, radical open access journals and books.

The instrumental logic of society and the Internet that manifests itself as the exploitation of digital labour, domination online, and ideologies of and on the Internet is never perfect, but always prone to attack by social struggles. Such struggles are not an automatic reaction to domination but are always a possibility. Raymond Williams's stress on alternative communications reminds us that the dominant, instrumental Internet is not an inevitable endpoint: that a commons-based Internet and a public-service Internet are feasible alternatives that are possible but are at the moment marginal. Williams also understood that political action is needed. He, for example, argued for "selective and variable levels of taxation" (Williams 1976, 164) and for taxing advertising. Today, online giants such as Google make use of tax avoidance strategies to maximise their profits and defend their monopolies. An online advertising tax could be a strategy aimed at forcing the online giants to pay taxes. Taxing large corporations' profits could fund a participatory media fee: In this model, the state collects corporate taxes and re-distributes a part of it to citizens via participatory budgeting to citizens, who receive annual media cheques that they are obliged to donate to non-profit Internet and media projects. Public-service media could create and operate an alternative, advertising-free YouTube that makes their programme archives available for remixing and re-use.

Williams (1977) advanced the approach of cultural materialism, especially in the book *Marxism and Literature* (Williams 1977). Cultural materialism has an "emphasis on production" (Williams 1981b, 12) and is the "analysis of all forms of signification [...] within the actual means and conditions of their production" (Williams 1983a, 210). Williams (1983b) argues that communication is not secondary to the forces and relations of production because "relations between people in the society are often seen most easily by looking at the institutions of communication" (22) and because "it is through communication systems that the reality of ourselves, the reality of our society, forms and is interpreted" (23). Seeing communication as the material allows us to stress that the production of social relations through communication is a key feature of society.

Williams rejects the orthodox Marxist assumption that language is a reflection of material reality that lies outside of it and was created after human labour came into existence. In *Marxism and Literature*, Williams (1977) stresses that it is important to see that language is an activity (20). It is material because, in it, the "physical body" produces "agitated layers of air, sounds" (29). It is a social relationship (30). "Language is in fact a special kind of material practice: that of human sociality" (165). For Williams, spoken words are material because they make use of immediate human resources, whereas written words would be material because they make use of non-human resources (169). Language and communication are part of that material reality, not external to it. He stresses the important influence of Valentin Vološinov's (1929/1986) *Marxism and the Philosophy of Language* on the development of a materialist theory of language. Vološinov against reflection theory recovered "the full emphasis on language as activity, as practical consciousness" (35). "Signification, the social creation of meanings through the use of formal signs, is then a practical material activity; it is indeed, literally, a means of production" (38).

Given that all communication offers meanings of the world to others, we can also say that all social relations inherently involve communication. Communication is the process in which humans produce meaning and thereby constitute culture. Whereas communication is the social production of meanings, culture is the system in which communication takes place. Culture is the totality of social meanings and meaning-making practices that shapes, conditions, enables and constrains our everyday communication that reproduces the cultural system and its structures. Economic, political and other social systems all have their "own signifying system – for they are always relations between conscious and communicating human beings" (Williams 1981a, 207). And they are "necessarily elements of a wider and more general signifying system" (207). This means that culture is "a system in itself" (208). It operates intrinsically to all social systems. Culture and social systems are "mutually constitutive" (217).

In his 1978 essay *Means of Communication as Means of Production*, Williams (2005, 50–63) stresses that culture and communication are not simply ideas but also material because they require means of communication:

> [M]eans of communication, from the simplest physical forms of language to the most advanced forms of communications technology, are themselves always socially and materially produced, and of course reproduced. Yet they are not only forms but means of production, since communication and its material means are intrinsic to all distinctively human forms of labour and social organization, thus constituting indispensable elements both of the productive forces and the social relations of production.
> (Williams 2005, 50)

The means of communication are "intrinsic, related and determined parts of the whole historical social and material process" (52). Orthodox Marxist approaches exclude communications from the means of production. They associate the means of production with "mechanical formulations of base and superstructure", in which communication is seen as "a second-order or second-stage process, entered into only *after* the decisive productive and social-material relationships have been established" (53). One of the reasons why such a position is untenable is that communications have become important industries and play an important general role in the economy (53). Means of communication have a history that is part of, but not reducible to, the history of the general means of production, to which it stands in a variable relation (Table 4.1).

Williams established a typology of the means of communication (see Figure 4.1).

Digital media result in a convergence of these types of means of communication: The Internet is convergent information, communication and co-operation technology, on which the various types of means of communication that Williams identifies converge. In the online realm, we can find verbal communication in the form of written text (e.g., chat rooms) or spoken text (e.g., Skype), non-verbal communication (images, memes, digital music, etc.), the amplification of reception (e.g., BBC iPlayer and file sharing), storage (e.g., Dropbox and iCloud) and alternative (non-profit and non-instrumental) communications (e.g., Wikipedia and Democracy Now!).

Williams argues that historically amplificatory and durative communications have come under the dominant class' control. In capitalism, this has resulted in concentrated and monopolised communications industries that in new ways, make voice, visibility and access selective and a realm of asymmetric power. The basic problem is the expropriation and commodification of the means of communication (Williams 1989b, 26; Williams 2005, 62).

The discussion shows that Williams takes a materialist approach for understanding communication and that there is an implicit theory of communication in Williams's works that can be re-constructed. Given that Williams foregrounds the material character of communication, we can characterise his approach not just as cultural materialism but also as communicative materialism. Speaking of communicative materialism implies that one has to re-visit the problem of base and superstructure.

4.3 Communicative materialism and the "base"/ "superstructure"-problem

In Marxist theory, culture, ideas, communication, information, knowledge, morals and ideologies are often described as belonging to an immaterial superstructure that is spatially built on a material, economic base and came temporally into existence after that base. The base/superstructure problem asks the question of how the economic and the non-economic are related to each other. The strength of the Marxist theory is

TABLE 4.1 Williams's typology of the means of communication (based on Williams, 2005, 53–63; 1981a, Chapter 4)

Communication based on immediate human physical resources	Verbal communication	Spoken language, written language: poetry, songs,
	Non-verbal communication	Body language: dance, postures, gestures, facial expressions,
Communications based on non-human materials socially produced by human labour	Amplificatory communications	Megaphone, television, radio, cable and satellite television
	Durative communications (storage)	Seals, coins, medals, paintings, sculptures, carvings, woodcuts, written texts, printed texts, sound recordings, film, video, cassettes, discs
	Alternative communications	Alternative speaking, listening, seeing, recording featuring democratic communal use, self-management, autonomy, collective cultural production, e.g., community radio

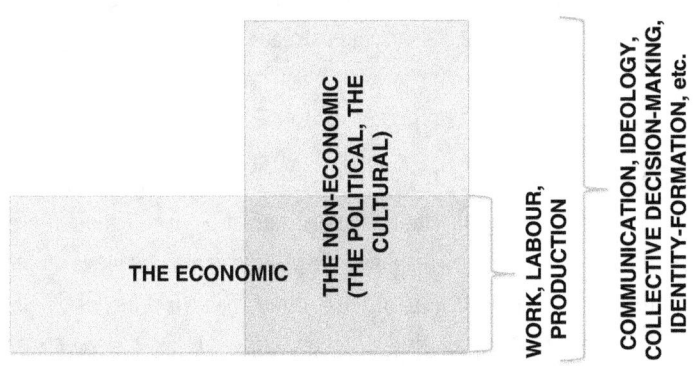

FIGURE 4.1 The relation of the economic and the non-economic in society

that it has the potential to make us aware of the fact that when we talk about politics and culture, we need to also think of the economy and the other way around.

In *Marxism and Literature*, Williams (1977) reviews solutions to the base/superstructure problem in Marxist theory. He argues that the term superstructure tends to be associated with institutions, forms of consciousness, political and cultural practices (77). He challenges seeing culture as "dependent, secondary, 'superstructural': a realm of 'mere' ideas, beliefs, arts, customs, determined by the basic material history" (19). It is idealist to separate "'culture' from material social life" (19). In such a separation, "intellectual and cultural production [...] appear to be 'immaterial'" (Williams 1989c, 205). According to Williams (1977), many Marxist approaches separate base (the mode of production) and superstructure either temporally ("first material production, then consciousness, then politics and culture") or spatially (various levels and layers all built on the layer of the economic base; 78). Such approaches forget that Marx in *the German Ideology* argues "against the separation of 'areas' of thought and activity (as in the separation of consciousness from material production)" (78).

One has to see the "direct material production of 'politics'" and "the material character of the production of a cultural order" (93) in order to critically understand society today as much as in Williams's days:

> The social and political order which maintains a capitalist market, like the social and political struggles which created it, is necessarily a material production. From castles and palaces and churches to prisons and workhouses and schools; from weapons of war to a controlled press: any ruling

> class, in variable ways though always materially, produces a social and political order. These are never superstructural activities. They are the necessary material production within which an apparently self-subsistent mode of production can alone be carried on. (93)

The categories used in Marxist theory for describing the relationship of base and superstructure include determination, reflection, mediation, typification (representation and illustration), homology and correspondence. All these notions leave culture and the economy separate and are not "materialist enough" (Williams 1977, 92, 97). So Williams's criticism is that Marxist theory has too often assumed a dualism of culture and the economy, as, for example, in Habermas's theory of communication (Fuchs 2016a). Through Williams's criticism, we can re-consider Marx and establish a materialist and truly dialectical theory of communication.

In *Marxism and Literature*, it also becomes evident that Williams in 1977 had changed his position on how to think of the base/superstructure problem in comparison to the 1973 *Base and Superstructure* article (Williams 2005, 31–49) and *Culture & Society* (Williams 1958). In the two earlier works, he ascertained the differentiation between base and superstructure and basically took a position of interactive dualist mediation, in which the two realms interact, condition and exert pressure on each other, and set each other limits. In *Marxism & Literature*, he rejects the notion of mediation and the strong and soft forms of determination as dualist and idealist. He instead argues that cultural materialism holds the position that culture and communication are material and that they are part and not part of the economy at the same time. Figure 4.1 visualises the relationship between the economic and the non-economic.

The non-economic includes the political (processes of collective decision-making) and the cultural (processes of collective meaning-making). Passing laws in a parliament is a form of production. It involves human work of not just politicians but also consultants, researchers, party secretaries and officials, administrators, archivists, public relations officials, security personnel and so on. A newspaper is a cultural artefact. Its production involves journalists, editors, designers, advertising experts, web editors, social media experts, printers and so on. Both the law as a political artefact and the newspaper as a cultural artefact do not just have this economic dimension of production but have an effect all over society. They are produced and used, economic and non-economic phenomena. We can learn from Williams that the materialist concept of social production explodes the base/superstructure model that separates the economic and the non-economic and interprets the political and the cultural as "immaterial".

What is the role of communication in the model shown in Figure 4.1? Communication is the social process of symbolic interaction that brings together and relates different actors in the production and use of objects (artefacts and specific social structures). In the economic production of use values (including political and cultural use values), humans communicate in order to coordinate the production process. In the use and application of these use values in society, they also communicate and use means of communicative production in order to make meaning of society, which means making meaning of other humans and one's relation to them.

An example: When one eats a meal prepared in a restaurant, then the process of eating is a bodily activity aimed at nourishment. If eating is organised as dinner, then it is also an opportunity for socialising through communication, for example, with friends. And what food we choose, where we eat and go out, how we dress and so on have also a symbolic dimension that communicates something about our status, habitus, cultural distinction, reputation and so on. Food is an object that is co-produced by nature and humans. Its use produces and reproduces not just the human body but also sociality, status, reputation and power. It is thereby simultaneously economic, biological, social, cultural and political. Communication is the activity that sets food in the example and other entities, in general, as an object into the relationship between humans. Given that communication is the social production of meaning in culture and culture as the system is in its process-dimension communication, cultural production operates through communication in any social system. There is a dialectic of communication and culture.

For Williams (1977), Gramsci's concept of hegemony is important for cultural materialism. Hegemony "is a whole body of practices and expectations, over the whole of living: our senses and assignments of energy, our shaping perceptions of ourselves and our world. It is a lived system of meanings and values – constitutive and constituting – which as they are experienced as practices appear as reciprocally confirming" (110). Hegemony is culture as "lived dominance and subordination of particular classes" (110). Art, ideas, aesthetics and ideology are "real practices, elements of whole material social process" (94). Cultural production is "social and material" (138; see also Williams 1989b, 1989c, 206):

> Cultural work and activity are not [...] a superstructure: not only because of the depth and thoroughness at which any cultural hegemony is lived, but because cultural tradition and practice are seen as much more than superstructural expressions – reflections, mediations, or typifications – of a

> formed social and economic structure. On the contrary, they are among the basic processes of the formation itself.
>
> (Williams 1977, 111)

Ideas are "elements of a hegemony", the "whole area of lived experience" (111). Although Williams argues that hegemony is "continually resisted" (112), for Gramsci the concept predominantly has to do with the reproduction of domination in everyday life. Gramsci (1971) argues that there are "two major superstructural 'levels'" (12): civil society and the state. Civil society is the realm of hegemony that "the dominant group exercises throughout society", and that is the "'spontaneous' consent given by the great masses of the population to the general direction imposed on social life by the dominant fundamental group; this consent is 'historically' caused by the prestige (and consequent confidence) which the dominant group enjoys because of its position and function in the world of production" (12).

Hegemony for Gramsci only covers what Williams (1977, 121–127) terms dominant culture and part of what he terms residual culture and selective tradition, but not what Williams terms emergent culture, by which he understands "new meanings and values, new practices, new relationships and kinds of relationships" that are ' "substantially alternative or oppositional" (Williams 1977, 123; see also Williams 2005, 37–42; Williams 1981a, 204–205).

Another concept Williams (1977) uses is "structures of feeling", by which he refers to "meanings and values as they are actively lived and felt", "structures of experience", "affective elements of consciousness and relationship", and "thought as felt and feeling as thought" (132). In *Culture & Society*, Williams (1958) uses the term structure (in the singular) of feeling multiple times without defining it. In *The Long Revolution*, he defines the structures of feeling as "the meanings and values which are lived in works and relationships" (Williams 2011, 337). Hegemony and structures of feeling are terms that Williams employs for mediations of and between society and the individual, and also between social structures and individual agency. However, just like hegemony, a structure (of feeling) cannot describe the *process* that connects individuals and society. A specific category is missing, namely the one of communication.

Whereas cognition is always ongoing in the human brain, they are only possible through and at the same time constitute the foundation of communication. We experience the world both individually and socially. Social experience conditions individual experience and vice versa. Communication is the process that organises the relationship of individual and social experience and relates the individual to other individuals and thereby to groups, organisations, social systems, institutions, social spaces and society. Communication connects the individual to society.

Information society theories tend to advance the ideology of the immaterial. This ideology fetishises the new that it presents as a radical rupture from the old. Concepts such as the post-industrial society, network society, knowledge-based society and information society therefore often imply the end of capitalism. Along with these concepts, it is regularly assumed that with the rise of the Internet, labour and production have become weightless and immaterial. Notions such as immaterial labour, cloud computing and weightless economy imply that we live in an immaterial world of communication(s).

Raymond Williams's cultural materialism is a reminder that we need to look at the conditions of production of the Internet and digital media. In 2015, the Internet consumed 8 per cent of the world's global electricity production (De Decker 2015). Given that green energy forms only account for a small share of worldwide energy generation, operating the Internet is environmentally unsustainable.

According to estimations, around 50 million tonnes of e-waste are generated per year and predictions are that within 4 years, there will be a further growth by 33 per cent (Vidal 2013; see also Maxwell and Miller 2012). This amount of e-waste is around 7 kg per person in the world. Up to 45 per cent of the total e-waste is treated informally and illegally (Rucevska et al. 2015, 4, 7). Large volumes of e-waste end up in developing countries such as Ghana, Nigeria, Cote D'Ivoire, the Republic of the Congo, China, Hong Kong, Pakistan, India, Bangladesh and Vietnam, where they pollute the soil and poison e-waste workers who dismantle the technologies.

Communicative materialism means critically questioning the social production of communication(s). Digital media are produced and used based on an international division of digital labour (IDDL; Fuchs 2014, 2015). In it, we, for example, find slave workers who extract minerals under the threat of being killed and low-paid component assemblers working under harsh conditions at Foxconn in China. There are also highly paid and highly stressed software engineers at Google and other tech companies who suffer from leisure time poverty. Furthermore, we in the IDDL find low-paid Indian programmers and users who as digital workers produce value when using targeted-advertising-based platforms such as Facebook, YouTube, Weibo and Twitter. There are also precarious freelancers working in the digital media industries, online crowd workers and so on.

The IDDL involves both manual and mental labour. Williams (1983a) argues that definitions of the working class as either blue-collar wage earners or broader definitions that include also white-collar wage workers exclude "the whole diverse body of people who are not, in such terms [of earning a wage], 'economically active'" (159). Feminist Marxism stresses, in this context, the importance of houseworkers in the reproduction of capitalism. Today, an entire shadow economy of "housewifised" workers, who are unpaid or precarious, has emerged. The use of targeted-advertising-based social media platforms is just one of the numerous examples of shadow labour (Lambert, 2015) and digital labour (Fuchs, 2014, 2015, 2017b)

Donald Trump's success in becoming the 45th US President displays the materiality of communication that Raymond Williams writes about. Trump shows the interwovenness of communication, politics, the economy and ideology. Trump cannot simply be explained as an economic, political or ideological phenomenon. His economy, politics and ideology are staged and communicated as a public spectacle that gives his supporters psychological opportunities for identification, which is an expression of anger and anxiety (Fuchs 2017a). Trump shows that communication is indeed, as Raymond Williams argued, a basic foundational and material aspect of contemporary society. Trump is also a communicative phenomenon, a phenomenon of capitalist, authoritarian, ideological, neoliberal and nationalist communication. He is "a one-man megabrand" (Klein 2017, 10), an economic and entertainment spectacle that has turned into a political spectacle.

For a critical theory of communication, ideology is an important category. The next section draws attention to the notion of ideology in Williams's works.

4.4 Ideology

Williams (2005, 245, 242) is sceptical of general theories of ideology because they ignore lived experience in class society. He criticises structuralism and structuralist theories of language and ideology for downplaying "the practical encounters of people in society" (Williams 1989a, 157) and saw Althusser's concepts of ideology and ideological state apparatuses as theoretical decline and abstractions (174).

Williams did, however, dedicate *Marxism and Literature*'s fourth chapter to the concept of ideology (Williams 1977, 55–71). He argues that there are three understandings of ideology in Marxist theory: (a) meanings and ideas; (b) a specific class or group's system of beliefs; and (c) a system of false, illusory beliefs and false consciousness (55).

He shows that Marx and Engels gave a polemical meaning to the term, using it for thought that neglects or ignores "the material social process of which 'consciousness' was always a part" (58). The danger would be to think of ideologies as separate from and reflexes of material reality (59). Marx would have stressed that ideas are themselves material products (60). Thinking and imagining will always be social processes associated with physical ways "in voices, in sounds made by instruments, in penned or printed writing, in arranged pigments on canvas or plaster, in worked marble or stone" (62). Labour and social relations necessarily require imagination and language (61–62).

The concept of ideology as false consciousness aims as in Lukács' *History and Class Consciousness* at identifying "truth with the idea of the proletariat" (Williams 1977, 68). Williams does not go into any details but says he finds Lukács' approach unconvincing (68). If "ideology were merely some abstract, imposed set of notions, if our social and political and cultural ideas and assumptions and habits were merely the result of specific manipulation, of a kind of overt training which might be simply ended or withdrawn, then society would be very much easier to move and to change than it in practice has ever been or is" (Williams 2005, 37)

Ideology is lived in educational institutions, the family and so on, where the dominant culture is learned and incorporated, but there is always the potential it can also be challenged by alternative and oppositional forms that constitute an emergent culture (Williams 2005, 39–42).

Williams (1977) points out the different uses of the term ideology in Marxism but does not give his own definition. Marxist understandings of ideology hover "between 'a system of beliefs characteristic of a certain class' and 'a system of illusory beliefs – false ideas or false consciousness' – which can be contrasted with true or scientific knowledge" (66). Williams (2005) is critical of two positions that characterise two opposite poles of Marxist concepts of ideology. He, on one hand, questioned left populism that considers ways of how "the people see it" (241) as automatically good, progressive and authentic. On the other hand, he disagrees with positions that show "contempt of people" (241) which assumes that "the people" are "simply being betrayed or manipulated", which ignores "the changes that were being lived into the fibres" (242).

Williams did not, however, completely reject the notion of manipulation and ideology as false consciousness. Let us next look at a series of examples of how he applies the ideology concept in different contexts. He describes strategies of the *Sun, Mail* and *Express* as powerful "manipulative methods" (Williams 2003b, 217) supported by press concentration. We can also find other instances, where he is closer to the positions of Lukács and the Frankfurt School than he admitted.

For example, Williams (1983c, 239–256) gave a lecture about Robert Tressell's (2012) 1914 novel *The Ragged-Trousered Philanthropists*. Tressell's book is about the difficulties the worker Frank Owen encounters when trying to convince his fellow workers of socialism. They believe in the ideology of their masters. Williams comments that Owen thinks "the real enemy [...] are the people who soak in the daily evidence of their condition and yet remain content; who displace their dissatisfaction onto other people" (Williams 1983c, 252). They are "inside the condition of the class, outside its consciousness" (252), "vulnerable not only to propaganda and the self-justifications of others who have an interest in perpetuating ignorance, but an ignorance that gets built in, inside people themselves; an ignorance that becomes their common sense" (256). The strength of Tressell's book, however, is in the attitude it communicates: "You are a prisoner, and you'll only get out of this prison if you'll admit it's a prison. And if you won't call it a prison, I will, and I'll go on calling it a prison, come what may" (256). Williams's characterisation of internalised anti-socialism as "soaking in", "displacement", "outside of working class consciousness", "propaganda", "ignorance" and "prison" is not so far from the assumption that the workers in *The Ragged-Trousered Philanthropists* have and live an ideological, false consciousness.

Williams also sees advertising as an ideology in the negative sense of the term. There are many examples in his work, all still relevant. In his essay *Advertising: the Magic System*, Williams (2005) defines advertising as "a major form of modern social communication" (185) that is "an institutionalized system of commercial information and persuasion" (170). Advertising is a magical system, "a highly organized and professional system of magical inducements and satisfactions, functionally very similar to magical systems in simpler societies, but rather strangely coexistent with a highly developed scientific technology" (185). The alternative between capitalism and socialism includes a fundamental choice between "man as consumer and man as user'. Advertising is 'a functional obscuring of this choice" (186) and obscures "the real sources of general satisfaction" (189). It is "organized fantasy" that presents corporations' decisions as "your choice" (193), a "world of suggestion and magic" (Williams 1983b, 71). Advertising "permeates the whole communications system, [...] its methods have been [...] widely extended into public relations and politics" (Williams 1976, 163–164). Advertising is a "huge area of cultural production as commercial persuasion" (Williams 1981b, 13). Advertising is selling "both consumer goods and 'a way of life'" (Williams 2003a, 36). "It is a way organizing and directing a consuming public, which is given real but only limited and marginal choices" (Williams 1968, 44). Williams (2003a, chapter 4) shows in an empirical analysis that advertising-based television tends to privilege commercial content over public-service programming and that the news on such stations tends to take on the style, form and language of advertisements.

For Williams, advertising tries to "persuade", to "induce", to "obscure" and to create fantasies by appearing to operate like magic. Williams (1989b) uses the language of ideology critique, but in *Advertising: The Magic System*, he does not speak of advertising as commodity and consumption ideology. In another essay, he says advertising is part of "the false ideology of communications" (29).

Although Williams in other places criticises ideology critique such as Lukács and the Frankfurt School, he uses the same vocabulary. He is certainly right that we cannot assume that ideology works automatically and is always accepted and reproduced. But, at the same time, ideology is not automatically resisted either. Where ideology works, it is not just communicated but also lived and experienced, and thereby internalised by consumers and citizens. There are many attempts to make ideologies work, but we only know in hindsight which ones do. In the case of advertising, commercial ideology works when consumers consciously or unconsciously have positive feelings and associations with specific ads that increase the likelihood that in particular situations they purchase and consume the advertised commodities. So critical studies of advertising must look at the whole cycle of the production, content, distribution and consumption of ads and commodities, including the ideological content, as well as the meanings and desires the consumers and advertisers associate with them. Scholars have acknowledged that Williams has anticipated the importance of the symbolic and lifestyle aspects of branding and advertising (Wharton 2013). Williams (2005) argues that given that capitalism's structure of feeling, meanings and values gives no answer to "problems of death, loneliness, frustration, the need for identity and respect" (190), magical systems create meanings and work as an ersatz culture. Other approaches have used the term ideology instead of magical systems: Williams's approach is certainly compatible with thinking in the line of thought of the Frankfurt School.

Williams saw mainstream communication studies as ideological, instrumental, administrative and uncritical. The focus on Lasswell's formula "Who says what how to whom with what effect?" leaves out the question "with what purpose?" and excludes intention (Williams 2005, 181). This general criticism of mainstream communication theory was a foundation for Williams's critique of technological determinism: In *Television*, Williams (2003a) criticises the technological determinism of McLuhan and others as an ideology – "an ideological representation of technology as a cause" (131) that is "a self-acting force which creates new ways of life" (6). He opposes this view by a dialectic of intentions and the social order, on one hand, and technology, on the other (132–138). Williams (1983b, 128–152) challenges technological optimism as much as technological pessimism as a form of technological determinism that defends established institutions against change.

When Williams (1983b) criticises Thatcherism and neoliberalism as ideologies in the early 1980s, he argues that "a new politics of strategic advantage" (244) that he termed "Plan X" is a code for "a neoliberal hegemony" (McGuigan 2015, 27) and the "neoliberal structure of feeling" (McGuigan 2016, 23). The defining factor of Plan X is to protect capital and the political elite's advantage, it does not care about broader effects on society, and therefore is "a willed and deliberate unknown" (Williams 1983b, 245).

Although Williams does not define ideology, we can from his examples of tabloid news, anti-socialism, advertising, technological determinism and Thatcherism deduce a definition. Ideology is a particular form of instrumental communication. It is a communicative strategy that the ruling class uses in order to try to achieve strategic advantage and convince and persuade others of specific dominant interest by manipulation, displacement, ignorance, inducement, mystification, inducement, obscuration, the organisation of fantasies and desires.

Williams's discussions of ideology show that he was struggling with finding a definitive understanding of the term. He was critical of general concepts of ideology that make ideology synonymous with culture and of understanding ideology as manipulation and false consciousness. The solution to the problem of how to understand ideology is to assume that ideology is a communicative strategy that aims at legitimating dominative interests by specific communication strategies. Williams stresses that we in hindsight can understand which ideologies are successful because they have become actively lived by human subjects and associated experiences, feelings, desires, sentiments and subjectivities in everyday life.

In the world of the Internet today, we find *ideologies of the Internet* and *ideologies on the Internet*. Ideologies of the Internet are a form of public communication that fetishises instrumental control of online communication. It is instrumental communication about instrumental communications, a meta-form of communication that justifies and defends the application of instrumental reason to the Internet. Neoliberal ideologies of the Internet, for example, present the online world as a frontier for investments that will create a better world. They leave out questions of inequality, digital labour, class and exploitation. Google describing itself in its ten core principles as showing that "democracy on the web works" because "Google search works because it relies on the millions of individuals posting links".

Democracy is reduced to user-generated content production online and the notion of participatory online culture. Questions relating to the secrecy of Google's search algorithm, its monopoly power in the search market, users and employees' lack of control of its means and so on are not asked. Ideologies of the Internet in the context of the state justify state surveillance, censorship and control of the Internet and leave out questions of privacy and freedom of speech. Ideologies on the Internet are the expressions of fascism, racism, right-wing extremism, nationalism, classism, sexism, anti-Semitism and so on online. Right-wing ideology flourishing in many societies is also highly present online and on social media. Ideology on the Internet tends to make use of audio-visual means generated by users (such as memes, videos, images, animations and music) and tabloidisation (simplification, few words, emotionalisation, scandalisation, polarisation, banalisation, manipulation, fabrication, etc.). User-generated ideology is the phenomenon that ideology production is no longer confined to professional ideologues but is produced and reproduced by users' everyday online life (Fuchs 2016b, 2016c).

4.5 Conclusion

Raymond Williams's work contains key foundations for and elements of a materialist theory of communication. His approach can together with other social theories be used as a foundation for a critical theory of communication (Fuchs 2016a). Williams's communicative materialism allows us to theorise communication and aspects of the communication process, such as its role in society, its various types, the dialectic of communication and communications, ideology as a peculiar form of communication, the role of communication(s) in capitalism and alternative, democratic communication(s).

Stuart Hall, in his last interview, said that contemporary cultural studies often do not expand "a Marxist tradition of critical thinking – [...] and that is a real weakness" (Jhally 2016, 338). He argues for a "return to what cultural studies should have been about and was during the early stages" (338). Williams's materialist concept of culture is one way that can allow media and cultural studies to renew its engagement with Marx and Marxist theory. Williams engaged closely with Marx's works and established his own humanist version of a Marxist theory of society and culture that gives attention to the production and reproduction of communication as one of the foundations of the social order. Williams argues that, for Marx, materialism means that humans produce and reproduce the social and thereby society. "By producing their means of subsistence men are indirectly producing their material life: (Marx and Engels 1845b, 37). Williams argues that communications are such means of human subsistence. The mode of production "must not be considered simply as being the reproduction of the physical existence of the individuals. Rather it is a definite form of activity of these individuals, a definite form of expressing their life, a definite *mode of life* on their part" (Marx and Engels 1845b, 37).

Williams stresses that communication is the mode of production of the social and society, and the mode of social and societal life.

Stuart Hall grounded his notion of communications in Marx's theory. At the time when Hall wrote his famous *Encoding/Decoding* article in 1973, he also worked on a new reading of Marx's (1857/1858)*Introduction to the Grundrisse*. This interpretation of Marx was published as the first essay in the Centre for Contemporary Cultural Studies' *Stencilled Occassional Papers-Series* (Hall 1973a). Hall stressed the importance of Marx's dialectic of production, circulation and consumption. The *Encoding/Decoding* essay is an application of this dialectic to communications: "Thus – to borrow Marx's terms – circulation and reception are, indeed, 'moments' of the production process in television" (Hall 1973b, 119). In Hall's famous visualisation of the encoding/decoding process and its description, we cannot find human beings but rather technical infrastructures, structures of production, knowledge frameworks, meaning structures, discourses and programmes. Communications are for Hall (1973b) structures for the articulation, encoding and decoding of meanings and discourses. The encoding/decoding model later influenced the cultural circuit model (Johnson 1986/1987, Du Gay et al. 1997), in which communication does not feature prominently as a concept.

Whereas Hall provides a more structuralist model of communications grounded in Marx's *Introduction*, Williams – based on Marx's *German Ideology* – sees communication as a human social agency, humans' production of social relations, sociality and society. For Hall (1980), Williams represents cultural studies' "culturalist" tradition. To be more precise, one should say that Williams advanced a humanist, cultural-materialist and communicative-materialist version of Marxism, in which the communication concept played an important role. In his most detailed discussion of Williams's works, Hall (2016, 25–53) argues that "human practice" as "the material activity of human beings" forms the core of Williams's approach (39). Williams's humanist position sees language and communication as practices, whereas in structuralism, language and communications are discursive structures (72). Today, in the age of digital capitalism, it is worth re-engaging with the Marxist foundations of cultural studies, including Williams's writings, Hall's explicitly Marxist works, Marx's writings and the long and diverse traditions of Marxist theory.

In communicative materialism, communication is a process of social production, through which humans produce and reproduce meanings, culture, social relations, sociality, social structures, social systems and society. Communication is the process of the constitution of social relations. It requires a means of communication as a means of production. Cultural and communicative materialism allows a dialectical and materialist understanding of digital media phenomena such as digital labour, ideologies on and of the Internet, the digital commons and so on. For Williams (1958, 319–338), working-class culture is not a particular form or a type of content but a common and collective idea of culture. This involves access to education and culture for all. "The human fund is regarded in all respects common, and freedom of access to it as a right constituted by one's humanity; yet such access, in whatever kind, is common or it is nothing" (Williams 1958, 326). Only a resource that is owned and used in common can benefit all. Williams's approach speaks against digital capitalism and for the digital commons.

The "sharing society" has to "begin by really sharing what it has, or all its talk of sharing is false or at best marginal" (Williams 1983b, 101). Uber, Airbnb, crowdsourcing and crowdfunding are ideological forms of sharing that are not about sharing the means of communication as a means of production and the benefits these means produce among all citizens and users. An alternative sharing society has to be non-capitalist in character.

Literature

De Decker, Kris. 2015. "*Why We Need a Speed Limit for the Internet.*" Low-Tech Magazine, October 19.

Du Gay, Paul, Stuart Hall, Linda Janes, Anders Koed Madsen, Hugh Mackay, and Keith Negus. 1997. *Doing Cultural Studies: The Story of the Sony Walkman.* London: Sage.

Fuchs, Christian. 2017a. "Donald Trump: A Critical Theory-Perspective on Authoritarian Capitalism." *tripleC: Communication, Capitalism & Critique 15* (1): 1–72.

———. 2017b. *Social Media: A Critical Introduction*. 2nd ed. London: Sage.
———. 2016a. *Critical Theory of Communication: New Readings of Lukács, Adorno, Marcuse, Honneth and Habermas in the Age of the Internet*. London: University of Westminster Press. doi: https://doi.org/10.16997/book1.
———. 2016b. "Racism, Nationalism and Right-Wing Extremism Online: The Austrian Presidential Election 2016 on Facebook." *Momentum Quarterly – Zeitschrift für sozialen Fortschritt* 5(3): 172–196. doi:https://www.momentum-quarterly.org/ojs2/index.php/momentum/article/view/1772/1427.
———. 2016c. "Red Scare 2.0: User-Generated Ideology in the Age of Jeremy Corbyn and Social Media." *Journal of Language and Politics* 15(4): 369–398.
———. 2015. *Culture and Economy in the Age of Social Media*. New York: Routledge.
———. 2014. *Digital Labour and Karl Marx*. New York: Routledge.
Gramsci, Antonio. 1971. *Selections from the Prison Notebooks*. New York: International Publishers.
Hall, Stuart. 2016. *Cultural Studies 1983*. Durham, NC: Duke University Press.
———. 1980. "Cultural Studies: Two Paradigms." *Media, Culture & Society* 2 (1): 57–72.
———. 1973a. *A 'Reading' of Marx's 1857 Introduction to the Grundrisse*. Birmingham: Centre for Contemporary Cultural Studies.
———. 1973b. "Encoding/Decoding." In *Culture, Media, Language*, edited by Stuart Hall, Doothy Hobson, Andrew Lowe, and Paul Willis, 117–127. London: Routledge.
Jhally, Sut. 2016. "Stuart Hall: The Last Interview." *Cultural Studies* 30 (2): 332–345.
Johnson, Richard. 1986/1987. "What is Cultural Studies Anyway?" *Social Text 16*: 38–80.
Klein, Naomi. 2017. *No Is Not Enough: Defeating the New Shock Politics*. London: Allen Lane.
Lambert, Craig. 2015. *Shadow Work: The Unpaid, Unseen Jobs That Fill your Day*. Berkeley, CA: Counterpoint.
McGuigan, Jim. 2016. *Neoliberal Culture*. Basingstoke: Palgrave Macmillan.
———. 2015. "A Short Counter-Revolution." In *Raymond Williams: A Short Counter Revolution: Towards 2000*, Revisited, edited by Jim McGuigan, 19–46. London: Sage.
———. 2014. "Introduction." In *Raymond Williams on Culture & Society: Essential Writings*, edited by Jim McGuigan, xv–xxvi. London: Sage.
Marx, Karl. 1867a. *Capital Volume I*. London: Penguin Books.
———. 1867b. *Das Kapital Band 1. Marx Engels Werke (MEW) Band 23*. Berlin: Dietz.
———. 1857/1858. "Introduction." In *Grundrisse*, edited by Karl Marx, 81–114. London: Penguin.
Marx, Karl, and Friedrich Engels. 1845a. *Die Deutsche Ideologie. Marx Engels Werke (MEW) Band 3*. Berlin: Dietz.
———. 1845b. *The German Ideology*. New York: Prometheus.
Maxwell, Richard, and Toby Miller. 2012. *Greening the Media*. Oxford: Oxford University Press.
Rucevska Ieva, et al. 2015.*Waste Crime – Waste Risks: Gaps in Meeting the Global Waste*

Challenge. A UNEP Rapid Response Assessment. Arendal: United Nations Environment Programme and GRID.

Sparks, Colin. 1993. "Raymond Williams and the Theory of Democratic Communication." In *Communication and Democracy*, edited by Slavko Splichal and Janet Wasko, 69-86. Norwood, NJ: Ablex.

Tressell, Robert. 2012. *The Ragged Trousered Philanthropists.* Ware: Wordsworth.

Vidal, John. 2013. *"Toxic "E-Waste" Dumped in Poor Nations, says United Nations."* The *Guardian*, December 14.

Vološinov, Valentin N. 1986/1929. *Marxism and the Philosophy of Language.* Cambridge, MA: Harvard University Press.

Wharton, Chris. 2013. *Advertising as Culture.* Bristol: Intellect.

Williams, Raymond. 2014. *On Culture & Society*, edited by Jim McGuigan. London: Sage.

———. 2011 [1961]. *The Long Revolution.* Cardigan: Parthian.

———. 2005 [1980]. *Culture and Materialism.* London: Verso.

———. 2003a [1974]. *Television.* London: Routledge.

———. 2003b. *Who Speaks for Wales? Nation, culture, identity*, edited by Daniel Williams. Cardiff: University of Wales Press.

———. 1989a. *Politics of Modernism.* London: Verso.

———. 1989b. *Resources of Hope.* London: Verso.

———. 1989c. *What I Came to Say.* London: Hutchinson Radius.

———. 1983a. *Keywords: A Vocabulary of Culture and Society*, rev. ed. New York: Oxford University Press.

———. 1983b. *Towards 2000.* London: Chatto & Windus.

———. 1983c. *Writing in Society.* London: Verso.

———. 1981a. *Culture.*Glasgow: Fontana/Collins.

———. 1981b. "Introduction." In *Contact: Human Communication and Its History*, edited by Raymond Williams, 7–20. London: Thames and Hudson.

———. 1979. *Politics and Letters: Interviews with New Left Review.* London: Verso.

———. 1977. *Marxism and Literature.* Oxford: Oxford University Press.

———. 1976. *Communications.* Harmondsworth: Penguin.

———, ed. 1968. *May Day Manifesto 1968.* Harmondsworth: Penguin.

———. 1958. *Culture & Society: 1780-1950.* New York: Columbia University Press.

Chapter Five
Henri Lefebvre's theory of the production of space and the critical theory of communication

5.1 Introduction

5.2 The history and contemporary status of Marxist communication theory

5.3 Henri Lefebvre's theory

5.4 Lefebvre and communication theory

5.5 Conclusion

Literature

5.1 Introduction

This chapter asks: How can Henri Lefebvre's humanist Marxism contribute to the foundations of a critical theory of communication?

Henri Lefebvre (1901–1991) was a French Marxist theorist. He published 72 books (Elden 2004, 4) on topics such as social space, Karl Marx, dialectical materialism, modernity, metaphilosophy, everyday life, structuralism, existentialism, urban politics, state theory, globalisation, and social struggles. He held professorships at the Universities of Strasbourg (1961–1965) and Paris X-Nanterre (1965–1973), among other positions. Some see him as a philosopher, while others regard him as an urban theorist, geographer, sociologist, political scientist, or historian. But there "is only one category he would have accepted – Marxist – and all that this implies; that is, being a philosopher, sociologist, historian and foremost, politically *engagé*" (Elden and Lebas 2003, xii).

The *Production of Space* is Lefebvre's best known and most widely read work. It was first published in French in 1974. He was both a critic of structuralism (especially Louis Althusser's version) and existentialism (especially Jean-Paul Sartre's approach). He joined the Parti communiste français (PCF) in 1928. Because of his critique of Stalinism, the PCF excluded him in 1958. Lefebvre can be considered the most important French representative of Marxist humanism. Stuart Elden (2004 19) characterises Lefebvre together with Althusser and Sartre as the 20th century's central French Marxist and as a "polymath in the range of topics he discussed" (4).

The majority of his works remains untranslated into English (Brenner and Elden 2009, 2), which has certainly limited their reception. The critical theorist Stanley Aronowitz (2015, 133) argues that because of Lefebvre's radical transdisciplinarity and the large influence of Althusserian structuralism that opposes Hegelian Marxism and Marxist humanism, for "decades Marxists, sociologists and others in the social sciences and philosophy ignored him." Also, Lefebvre's works on globalisation and the state have largely been ignored (Brenner and Elden 2009, 2). Lefebvre was much more than a critical theorist of space. This excess of Lefebvre always relates to space, while simultaneously transcending it. This chapter contributes to the discovery of an alternative Lefebvre by asking how his works can contribute to the foundations of a critical theory of communication. It does so by reflecting on the role of communication in *The Production of Space* and *Critique of Everyday Life*. I do not claim that Lefebvre was a communication scholar. But given that he as humanist Marxist gave attention to human's social and productive role on society, his theory may be one of the traditions within Marxism that we can take as an interesting starting point for thinking about a Marxist theory of communication.

The chapter first gives a brief overview of some aspects of Marxist communication theory and its status today (Section 5.2). It then presents an overview of Lefebvre's work (Section 5.3) in order to introduce those interested in communication theory to his main body of works. Third, a Lefebvre's work is discussed and situated in the context of critical communication theory (Section 5.4).

5.2 The history and contemporary status of Marxist communication theory

Critical communication studies' history goes back to the works of Marx and Engels. Their notion of ideology and Marx's concept of fetishism have played a role in the foundations of ideology critique of mediated communication. Marx, for example, stressed the material character of communication, analysed the role of technology – including communication technologies that he referred to as the "means of communication" – in capitalism in a dialectical manner, and anticipated the emergence of informational and digital capitalism with his analysis of the general intellect (see Fuchs 2016b for a detailed analysis). Although Marx dialectically combined a structural analysis of capitalism with an analysis of the role of praxis, agency, and social struggles, in the history of Marxian-inspired social theory approaches emerged that are either structuralist in character (structural Marxism) or agency-based (workerism, class-struggle oriented Marxism). A third type tries to integrate structure and agency approaches dialectically.

Based on Marx, Georg Lukács (1923/1971) tried to combine the two approaches in his major work *History and Class Consciousness*. He stressed both aspects of class struggle and ideology as reification and reified consciousness. Recently it has been stressed that Lukács also made direct contributions to the study of language, semiotics and communication, especially in his last books (Fuchs 2016a, 2018b). Antonio Gramsci's (1971) philosophy of praxis was established at the time of Lukács's early works. His concepts of culture, organic intellectuals and hegemony have in communication theory had a major influence on scholars such as Raymond Williams and Stuart Hall.

Lukács's notion of reification had a direct influence on the development of the Frankfurt School's notion of instrumental reason (Horkheimer 2004). In respect to culture and communication, the concept of instrumental reason has been applied to Horkheimer and Adorno's (2002) critique of the culture industry and Marcuse's (1964) analysis of the one-dimensional man that includes a critique of one-dimensional language and one-dimensional media. Horkheimer and Adorno took a more structuralist approach that was grounded in Marx's notion of exchange-value and focused on the analysis of the negative impacts of the universalisation of exchange-value on society and culture. Marcuse shared this approach but tried to dialectically mediate it with an analysis of the role of social struggles in establishing potential alternatives to capitalism and the logic of exchange-value and the structural limits that activism faces in capitalist society.

Jürgen Habermas took the Frankfurt School's work into a new direction. He applied the notion of instrumental reason and its Lukácsian foundations to the analysis of economic and political systems that colonise the lifeworld and argued that communication was a missing element in the works of Horkheimer, Adorno, and Marcuse. Habermas certainly is the most influential critical communication theorist today. However, the Marxian origins of his works, as present in *The Structural Transformation of the Public Sphere* (Habermas 1991), were later lost and turned into a dualist critique that separates communication and domination (Fuchs 2016a). Habermas conceives of communication as dominationless and thereby separates it in a dualist manner from structures of domination and exploitation, whereby Marx's original stress on the dialectical character of communication and technology as ambivalent forces in capitalism have been lost. Most communication scholars will today agree that Habermas is a critical communication theorist, but only a very small number will characterise him as a Marxist theorist.

Marxian analysis has also had an influence on cultural studies. Stuart Hall (1980) has distinguished between the culturalist and the structuralist paradigm of cultural studies. The first is represented by the humanist Marxist works of Raymond Williams and Edward Thompson. The second came about by the influences that Louis Althusser's structural Marxism and the post-Marxist approach of Ernesto Laclau and Chantalle Mouffe had on the study of culture. Stuart Hall is himself a representative of the structuralist paradigm. He focused his analyses on structures of encoding, decoding, articulation and representation.

The approaches of E. P. Thompson (1963) and Raymond Williams (1977) can be characterised as humanist because they start from human experiences and human consciousness that are situated in class relations. But these are not purely agency-based approaches that fetishize the individual and social struggles. Rather, Williams and Thompson base their analysis of society and culture on a dialectic of structure and agency, as evidenced for example by Williams' concept of the structure of feelings and Thompson's notion of class experience that both operate at the two mediated levels of individual consciousness and collective consciousness as represented by organisations and institutions.

Marxist theory has a 175-year long history and has advanced a complex multitude of approaches, categories and focuses.[1] In light of the prominence of the New Left and social movements in the aftermath of the 1968 rebellions, Marx and Marxian-inspired theory played a major role in the social sciences and humanities and universities around the world. The rise of neoliberalism, postmodernism, and the collapse of the Soviet Union weakened the influence of Marx in the social sciences and humanities since the 1990s. But at the same time, class inequalities and the economy's crisis-proneness increased progressively, which exploded into the 2008 world economic crisis and political crises. Ever since, there has been a large growth of the academic and political interest in Marx, culminating in "Marx-year 2018" on the occasion of Marx's bi-centenary. Since 2008, there has also been a significant increase in interest in and engagement with Marx and Marxian approaches in media and communication studies. The new interest in Marx and Marxian-inspired communication research has resulted

---

1 1843 can be taken as a decisive year that marks the beginning of Marxian theory because in this year Marx wrote and published the first works that are today still widely read and cited, including the *Critique of Hegel's Philosophy of Law* that includes the famous introduction, where Marx characterises religion and ideology in general as "*opium* of the people" (Marx 1843, 175).

in a significant number of books, articles, special issues, reading groups, workshops, and conferences.

Since the start of the new millennium, autonomist Marxism, especially Michael Hardt and Antonio Negri's books *Empire* (2000), *Multitude* (2004), *Commonwealth* (2009), and *Assembly* (2017), formed the Marxist approach that has most influenced discussions of communication. Hardt and Negri have stressed the emergence of cognitive capitalism that has recomposed the working class so that dominance of immaterial/knowledge labour has emerged as well as new forms of the expropriation of the commons (including the cultural and digital commons) together with new potentials for the appropriation of digital machines for progressive purposes.

In the context of the increased interest in Marxist communication research and theory, Henri Lefebvre's approach offers a distinct opportunity for communication theory. His approach allows us to (a) re-think the relationship of humanism and structuralism as well as of agency and structure, (b) think about the relationship of space and communication, and (c) reflect on the role of information and communication technologies in capitalism.

Lefebvre's approach shares the Marxist humanist perspective and the criticism of structuralism, functionalism and Althusserianism with the approaches of E. P. Thompson, Raymond Williams, Georg Lukács, and other humanist Marxists. Engaging with Lefebvre is, therefore, part of a larger project that combines humanism and Marxism for theorising communication (Fuchs 2019, 2018b, 2017a, 2016a) and aims at renewing humanist Marxism in order to challenge authoritarian capitalism (Alderson and Spencer 2017; Fuchs 2018a).

5.3 Henri Lefebvre's theory

The task of this section is to introduce the readers to aspects of Lefebvre's works that matter for communication theory. There are three aspects in Lefebvre's work that are relevant for a critical theory of communication. They will be discussed subsequently in the following three sub-sections:

a) Humanism and structuralism;

b) The social production of space;

c) Information and communication technologies in capitalism.

5.3.1 Humanism and structuralism

Lefebvre argues in his book *Dialectical Materialism* (first published in 1940) that like Marx's *Economic and Philosophic Manuscripts*, the dialectical- materialist analysis of society must start with *humans producing in society*. He takes a humanist Marxist perspective that focuses on creativity, activity, praxis, Hegelian dialectics, human essence, alienation, and the total human. In another place, he adds the importance of human needs to these concepts (Lefebvre 1982, 39–42). Lefebvre stresses that the "problem of man [...] is central for dialectical materialism" (Lefebvre 2009, 94). He argues that Marx's later economic analyses were "integrated with humanism" (89) At that time, Stalinism showed a "deep mistrust" of "Marx's early writings" (1) because they could be read as an anti-Stalinist Marxism. Lefebvre's 1940 book can be read as a Marxist critique of Stalin.

Lefebvre (1982, 18–19) opposes the orthodox Marxist interpretation that Marx applied universal dialectical laws to the development of society and capitalism. He argues that Marx is not a sociologist, economist, historian, anthropologist, philosopher, etc., but all of that and more. And he ascertains that "*Marx is not a sociologist, but there is a sociology in Marx*" (Lefebvre 1982, 22). Generalising this thought, we can say: Marx is not a sociologist, economist, philosopher, political scientist, historian, anthropologist, etc., but there is sociology, economics, philosophy, politics, history, anthropology, etc. in Marx.

As a Marxist humanist, Lefebvre has been very critical of structuralist theories. Structuralism is a functional reductionism that "gives a privileged status to one concept" (Lefebvre 1991, 106), namely to structures over agency. Lefebvre was particularly opposed to Louis Althusser's structural Marxism. He argued that Althusser's approach is a "withdrawal into scientism" (Lefebvre 2003, 38), reducing Marxism to an epistemology that "sideline[s] practice and its problems," is a "fetishistic philosophy of 'pure' knowledge," and results in the "elimination of the dialectic" (40).

The Production of Space contains numerous references to language's role in space. This is especially because Lefebvre was a critic of structuralist linguistics, a tradition founded by Ferdinand de Saussure and followed by authors such as Roland Barthes, Jacques Derrida and Julia Kristeva. Lefebvre (1991, 5) criticises that in structural linguistics, "the philosophico-epistemological notion of space is fetishized and the mental realm comes to envelop the social and physical ones". Authors in this field would presuppose "an identity between mental space (the space of the philosophers and epistemologists) and real space" (6).

Lefebvre criticises reductionist approaches:

> In its most extreme form, reductionism entails the reduction of time to space, the reduction of use value to exchange value, the reduction of objects to signs, and the reduction of 'reality' to the semiosphere; it also means that the movement of the dialectic is reduced to a logic, and social space to a purely formal mental space.
>
> (Lefebvre 1991, 296)

He also criticises in this context structural linguistics' reducationism: "Man does not live by words alone" (35); "The systematic study of language, and/or the study of language as a system, have eliminated the 'subject' in every sense of the term" (61). Lefebvre warns that one should not overestimate the social and political roles of language: "The Word has never saved the world and it never will" (134).

In Lefebvre's view, structural linguistics subsume space, society and everything under language. He, on the other hand, argues that space subsumes language. Space is material and humans in its production also produce a code and language of space. Lefebvre criticises viewing "the spoken and written word" as "(social) practice" (Lefebvre 1991, 28). For him, language does not precede space, but the production of space follows the production of a language and code (16–18). Lefebvre argues that a theory of space should be a unitary theory that sees a unity between the fields of the physical, the mental and the social (11). This unity would be constituted by the fact that all spaces are produced.

Lefebvre (1991) sees space as a means of production and therefore as part of society's base. Space "is at once a precondition and a result of social superstructures" (85). He distinguishes between mode of production on the bottom and "the state and the superstructures of society" (85) at the top.

Space is located as a means of production in the economy and interacts with the "superstructures." For Lefebvre, there are various levels of society: "The forces of production and their component elements (nature, labour, technology, knowledge); structures (property relations); superstructures (institutions and the state itself)" (85). Social space "underpins the reproduction of production relations and property relations" and

> is equivalent, practically speaking, to a set of institutional and ideological superstructures that are not presented for what they are (and in this

capacity social space comes complete with symbolisms and systems of meaning – sometimes an overload of meaning) (349)

The spatial code "is a superstructure, which is not true of the town itself, its space" (47).

5.3.2 The social production of space

Lefebvre (1991, 299, 346) argues that a new political economy should be a critique of the political economy of space and its production. He wants to advance a Marxist approach that does not stress products (structural Marxism), but production (26). Like Marx, he starts the analysis of society from humans who "as social beings are said to produce their own life, their own consciousness, their own world" (68). In production, humans would mobilize spatial elements, including resources (materials) and tools (matériel) in a rational manner so that they organise "a sequence of actions with a certain 'objective' (i.e. the object to be produced) in view" (71). Lefebvre's key idea in *The Production of Space* is that humans not only produce social relations and use-values but in doing so also produce social space. In more general terms, extending beyond social space to all physical spaces, one can say that "each living body *is* space and *has* its space: it produces itself in space and it also produces that space" (170). In society, humans produce social spaces. There is a dialectic of social relations and space: "Social relations, which are concrete abstractions, have no real existence save in and through space. *Their underpinning is spatial*" (404).

Social space contains the social relations of reproduction (personal and sexual relations, family, reproduction of labour-power) and the relations of production (Lefebvre 1991, 32). Space is not a thing (73) and not a container (94). It is a product and a means of production (85). Human beings "*have* a space and […] *are* in this space" (294). Space "is neither subject nor object" (92). It is a "social reality," and "a set of relations and forms" (116). It subsumes products and their interrelations (73). There is a dialectic of social space and human action: "Itself the outcome of past actions, social space is what permits fresh actions to occur, while suggesting others and prohibiting yet others" (73). Space is part of a dialectic of production: "Space is at once result and cause, product and producer" (142). Social space is "always, and simultaneously, both a *field of action* […] and a *basis of action*" (191). Social space interrelates "everything that is produced either by nature or by society" – "living beings, things, objects, works, signs and symbols" (101).

Let us briefly focus on Lefebvre's concept of the boundary of social space. Because of its form, a space is circumscribed (Lefebvre 1991, 181). A social space has physical borders and conceptual boundaries that are socially produced, but always interpenetrates and superimposes other spaces (86). Humans "demarcate, beacon or sign [...] space, leaving traces that are both symbolic and practical" (192). How are boundaries communicated? Space can be marked physically or by discourse and signs so that it becomes a symbol (141). On the one hand, it can be nature that "communicates" the physical boundary of a space to us. A habitable valley bounded by mountains into all directions has natural borders. The valley cannot easily be extended physically because the mountains border it. Only if something such as an earthquake or rockfall changes the mountain and the valley's geography can such natural boundaries change. Humans in society can intentionally produce signs to make objects symbolise and take on specific meanings that are culturally created, stored, disseminated, and communicated. The border of a nation-state is physically marked by blockages of the national territory controlled by organs of the state, with the monopoly of violence. It is discursively marked by a distinction between citizens and non-citizens, communicated in the form of passports that grant access to, and provide certain rights within, a national territory.

The passport is a socially produced sign, a symbol of political power that constitutes an inside and an outside of the nation-state. The physical borders of the nation-state are the historical results of wars and political struggles. The nation state's physical borders are politically and socially defined and produced. Political conventions bound a particular natural territory.

The nation's physical boundaries are signified and communicated by border crossings, territorial maps, world maps, etc. Both the natural and informational boundaries of the nation-state are political conventions defined by those in power. Both the physical border and the passport are symbols that communicate closure of the national territory.

Lefebvre distinguishes three levels of social space that are shown in Table 5.1. I have gathered characterisations of these spaces scattered across *The Production of Space*. These are collected in the table. Lefebvre distinguishes between perceived social practices, conceived representations of space, and lived spaces of representation. He argues that a "dialectical relationship [...] exists within the triad of the perceived, the conceived, and the lived" (Lefebvre 1991, 39). Everyday life forms representational spaces (116).

TABLE 5.1 Lefebvre's three levels of social space (based on information from: Lefebvre 1991, 32–33, 38–43, 362, 50, 116, 233, 288)

	Spatial practice	Representations of space	Representational space
Subjects	Members of society, family, working class	Experts, scientists, planners, architects, technocrats, social engineers	Inhabitants and users who passively experience space
Objects	Outside world, Locations, spatial sets, urban transport routes and networks, places that relate the local and the global, trivialised spaces of everyday life, desirable and undesirable spaces	Knowledge, signs, codes, images, theory, ideology, plans, power, maps, transportation and communications systems, abstract space (commodities, private property, commercial centers, money, banks, markets, spaces of labour),	Social life, art, culture, images, symbols, systems of non-verbal symbols and signs, images, memories
Activities	Perceiving, daily routines, reproduction of social relations, production	Conceiving, calculation, representation, construction	Living, everyday life and activities

Lefebvre (1991) distinguishes between dominated and appropriated space (164–167). A dominated space is "a master's project" (165). In capitalism, the nation-state (a bounded territory controlled by the monopoly of violence and enabling national markets and a power balance between classes and class fractions, see Lefebvre 1991, 111–112, 280–281) forms political space. The unity of the workplace (the space of work and production), the city (urban space), markets and centres of commerce and consumption (spaces of consumption, leisure and entertainment) forms economic space. The nation-state and capitalist space are the capitalist forms of dominated space, spaces dominated by state power and the power of capital. The nation-state and capitalist spaces are instrumental spaces (281, 306).

Lefebvre argues that capitalism is based on an antagonism between conceived, planned space that is organised as abstract space, and the lived spaces of everyday life. He writes that this as a result of this antagonism, "lived experience is crushed" (Lefebvre 1991, 51). Abstract space is the organisation of abstract labour (49) and exchange (57). It is "the space of the bourgeoisie and of capitalism" (57) and "the location and source of abstractions" (348) – the abstractions created by abstract labour, money, commodities and capital (348). The nation-state institutes abstract space (285). It is a relation between things that renders objects' social nature invisible (49). It is a space of calculation and quantification (49). Time in capitalism serves "to measure space" – "the time appropriate to the production of exchangeable goods, to their transport, delivery and sale, to payment and to the placing of capital" (278). Lefebvre introduces the notion of dominant spaces: "The dominant form of space, that of the centres of wealth and power, endeavours to mould the spaces it dominates (i.e. peripheral spaces)" (49). And he ascertains that human beings make spaces by living in them: "The user's space is lived – not represented (or conceived). When compared with the abstract space of the experts (architects, urbanists, planners), the space of the everyday activities of users is a concrete one, which is to say, subjective" (362). It is a "space of 'subjects' rather than of calculations" (362). Abstract space is based on a logic that fragments and cuts up space (89). It results in the creation of sectors, subsystems, and partial logics (311). In capitalism, social space is the milieu of accumulation (129). Abstract space is a "medium of *exchange*" (307). The commodity is organised in abstract spaces: "The commodity is a *thing*: it is *in space*, and occupies a location" (341).

Commodities are produced, exchanged, and consumed, which results in special spaces for their production, exchange and consumption. The notion of abstract space clarifies why Lefebvre distinguishes between lived and conceived space. He wants to point out that conceived space entails the possibility of a dominant group organising and instrumentalising social space in its interest to achieve advantages at the expense of other groups.

Alfred Sohn-Rethel (1978) points out that abstract thought is the equivalent to the exchange abstraction in the world of knowledge. Class societies divide mental and physical labour in a division of labour. The consequence is mechanistic, quantifying, mathematical logic. For Sohn-Rethel, the "unity of mental and manual work" (181) is a precondition of socialism. Lefebvre applies the critique of abstract thought to the critique of space and argues that abstraction in class societies not just produces abstract thought, but also abstract space along with it. Conceptual space is a particular form of social space, in which human experts produce planning information that guides the organisation of space. They also live this conception in everyday work practices and relations. So, conceived space is a subdomain of lived space. Conceived space does not necessarily take on dominant and dominated forms. In a socialist society, conceived space is appropriated by a human interest in such a way that the information that plans space benefits not dominant class, but all those living in a space. There is also the possibility of participatory design and planning so that citizens are integrated into the planning of the spaces they live in.

Marx (1867, 165) understands commodity fetishism as the form of appearance, in which "the definite social relation between men themselves" is presented as "a relation between things". The commodity appears as natural, unsocial and out of history. Commodity fetishism makes it difficult to imagine alternatives to capitalism. Marx's project was the "unmasking of things in order to reveal (social) relationships" (Lefebvre 1991, 81). He writes: "Fetishism is both a mode of existence of the social reality, an actual mode of consciousness and human life, and an appearance or illusion of human activity" (Lefebvre 2009, 81). Lefebvre is interested in a critique of the spatial dimension of fetishism. Abstract space hides what it contains with the help of "fantasy images, symbols which appear to arise from 'something else'" (Lefebvre 1991, 311). In capitalism, through what Guy Debord describes as the society of the spectacle, "the visual gains the upper hand over the other senses" (286).

Abstract space is a contradictory space (Lefebvre 1991, 306). Lefebvre identifies contradictions between dominant space vs dominated space; instrumental space vs differential, appropriated space; abstract, conceived space vs lived space; and centre vs periphery. For Lefebvre, the principal contradiction that subsumes the one between centre and periphery is the one between globalising space and fragmented space:

> Where then is the principal contradiction to be found? Between the capacity to conceive of and treat space on a global (or worldwide) scale on the one hand, and its fragmentation by a multiplicity of procedures or processes, all fragmentary themselves, on the other. Taking the broadest possible view, we find mathematics, logic and strategy, which make it possible to represent instrumental space, with its homogeneous – or better, homogenizing – character. This fetishized space, elevated to the rank of mental space by epistemology, implies and embodies an ideology – that of the primacy of abstract unity. Not that this makes fragmentation any less 'operational'. It is reinforced not only by administrative subdivision, not only by scientific and technical specialization, but also – indeed most of all – by the retail selling of space (in lots).
>
> (Lefebvre 1991, 355)

Capitalism has a tendency to globalise the economy to make use of strategic spatial advantages (resources, price of labour-power, political climate, etc.) for accumulation. At the same time, it creates ever more specialised instrumental spaces. Capitalism fragments space and interconnects the fragments at the regional, national, international, and global levels. This contradiction would be the spatial expression of what Marx (1867) terms the contradiction between productive forces and relations of production (Lefebvre 1991, 357): The development of the means of production allows the production of spaces. In capitalism, dominant interests shape social spaces and instrumentalise them as means of control, power and capital accumulation. Social spaces are via the logic of capitalism turned into abstract, dominated, instrumental spaces.

Lefebvre analyses a capitalist spatial contradiction between the centre and the periphery. He also sees abstract space as imperialist in character, as the logic of the commodity is expansive and tries to "occupy all space" (Lefebvre 1991, 219). The result is imperialist centre-periphery geography:

> In the so-called underdeveloped countries, plundered, exploited, 'protected' in a multitude of ways (economic, social, political, cultural, scientific), the obstacles in the way of growth and development become increasingly daunting. Meanwhile, the advanced countries use the more backward as a source of labour and as a resource for use values (energies, raw materials, qualitatively superior spaces for leisure activities).
> (Lefebvre 1991, 346–347)

The "centre continues effectively to concentrate wealth, means of action, knowledge, information and 'culture'. In short, everything" (Lefebvre 1991, 332–333).

5.3.3 Information and communication technologies in capitalism

In the third part of the *Critique of Everyday Life* that was published in French in 1981, Lefebvre dedicates one remarkable section to "Information Technology and Daily Life" (Lefebvre 2014, 808–825). He warns that we, via the rise of the computer, are facing the danger that capitalism's abstract logic of commodification is extended to the realms of information and communication.

Information would always have played a role in capitalist markets and exchange, but "for many centuries, information as such did not appear on the market" (Lefebvre 2014, 817). Lefebvre characterises informational capitalism: "What is novel about the contemporary world is that there is a world market in information, which positively 'drives' the other markets, through advertising, propaganda, the transmission of positive knowledge, and so on." (817). Information technology faces the "danger of being administratively and institutionally controlled either by the national state, or by transnational forces" (819).

In *The Production of Space*, Lefebvre stresses the importance of land for a Marxist theory of space. Marxism would have advanced a binary model of class oppositions between capital and labour (Lefebvre 1991, 323–325) and forgotten the importance of land in capitalism. In contemporary capitalism, the land would play a crucial role through the commodification of "underground and above-ground resources – of the space of the entire planet" (324). He distinguishes between markets in land and works: "There are two markets whose conquest represents the ultimate triumph of the commodity and money: the market in *land* (a precapitalist form of property) and the market in *works* (which, as 'non-products', log remained extra- capitalist)" (342). Here Lefebvre points out that the commodification of land and culture/information signifies commodification becoming ultimate.

In *Information Technology and Daily Life*, there is a comparable passage about the commodification of information: "Is not information, the supreme commodity, also the ultimate commodity? Does it not complete the great cycle of the commodity, its extraordinary expansion – in short, the realization of the world of commodities in that of the mode of production, in the global?" (Lefebvre 2014, 817). Information technology "perfects and completes the world of commodities" (818).

5.4 Lefebvre and communication theory

Based on the overview of some of Lefebvre's works in section 3, we can next discuss its relevance for theorising communication. In doing so, we will follow the same structure and sequence of topics as used in section 3

5.4.1 Humanism and structuralism

Lefebvre reminds us that society is neither pure structure nor pure practice, but a dialectic of social structures and human practices. In respect to communication this means that communication is neither linguistic structures nor individual speech acts, but a dynamic, complex production process the creates and re-creates semiotic and social structures as well as individual consciousness and actions.

Today, Manuel Castells is considered as one of the major figures in communication studies. He did however not start as a communication theorist, but as an urban theorist who was heavily influenced by Althusser's structural Marxism. Castells (1977) elaborated a structuralist approach of space and the urban that is explicitly directed against Lefebvre. Castells argues that "Lefebvrian humanism" assumes that "society creates space" and that space and society are "the ever-original work of that freedom of creation that is the attribute of Man, and the spontaneous expression of his desire" (92). He claims that Lefebvre assumes the "spontaneism of social action and the dependence of space upon it" (92). Castells argues that to start with the human being means a voluntarist theory that ignores any influence and structural conditioning of action. He overlooks that to start social theory with the human *who produces society* implies that the human is the social being. With the human, the social – and therefore also social relations and social structures – is immediately posited. Lefebvre shows that one cannot think about the human without the dialectic of structures and agency.

Castells takes an Althusserian approach, in which the "relation between society and space" is "a function of the specific organisation of modes of production that coexist historically (with a predominance of one over the others) in a concrete social formation, and of the internal structure of each of these modes of production" (Castells 1977, 64). In contrast to Lefebvre, Castells reduces the structure/agency-dialectic to structures and sees "space as an expression of the social structure" (126).

Although Lefebvre elaborates a fairly dialectical theory, *The Production of Space* is not free from functionalist formulations, in which not humans, but structures or things, act. Lefebvre writes for example: "[E]very society [...] produces a space, its own space" (Lefebvre 1991, 31); the "ancient city had its own spatial practice" (31); "Representational space is alive: it speaks" (42); "Peasant houses and villages speak" (165). Space is not a subject that acts. Rather humans are the subjects who speak to each other within, conditioned by and through producing social space. To be fair, one must say that such problematic formulations are the exception from the rule in Lefebvre's works that overall strives to conceive of social space and society as a dialectic of structure and agency.

Marx's understanding of the materialist character of society is that humans are "living human individuals" who "*produce* their means of subsistence" and thereby "their material life" and "a definite mode of life" (Marx and Engels 1845/1846, 37). Humans in their social production of life produce and reproduce sociality itself, which includes language as a means of communicative production and social relations. In communication, humans create and maintain social relations by making use of language. Communication takes place in, and creates, social space.

Lefebvre's approach poses the question of what kind of space consciousness is. If one assumes that consciousness is not simply individual, but necessarily social, then this implies that language is not simply a mental space. Any language that is not concretely lived is non-existent. Language is a communicative means of production that humans use in the communication process for creating and reproducing social relations. Communication is the concrete process that connects social space and mental space, society and the individual. Raymond Williams (2005, 50–63) in this context points towards the material character of communication by stressing that means of communication are means of production. Languages are "forms of social production" that make use of the human body's resources, whereas other means of communication use "non-human material" (Williams 2005, 55; see also Williams 1981, 87–90). Because of his scepticism of structural linguistics, Lefebvre somewhat underestimates the material character of language and communication.

Classical Marxist approaches have separated base and superstructure, the economy and culture, work and discourse, labour and ideology. This separation does not hold because of two arguments:

1) The material unity of society is, as Lefebvre also stresses, that humans produce and reproduce their sociality. Just like cars, roads, houses, shops, factories, railways, and cities are products of human activities, words, texts, songs, culture and ideologies are also human products. The difference is that culture can be simultaneously consumed by an endless number of humans, whereas a train can only carry a limited number of people.
2) In the 21st century, culture and communication have become an important industry that employs a significant number of people and produces cultural commodities. It can therefore not stand outside the economy. As an example, 8.8% of UK jobs in 2014 were located in the cultural economy (advertising, marketing, architecture, crafts, design, IT, film and broadcasting, museums, libraries, music, arts, publishing) (DCMS 2015). In London, the share was even larger at 16.4%.Department for Culture, Media & Sports (DCMS) 2015

In this context, Williams argues that "[c]ultural work and activity are not […] a superstructure […] because cultural tradition and practice are […] among the basic processes of the [societal] formation itself" (Williams 1977, 111). He uses the term "cultural materialism" to signify a position that foregrounds the materiality of culture: "Cultural materialism is the analysis of all forms of signification, including quite centrally writing, within the actual means and conditions of their production" (Williams 1983, 201). Cultural materialism argues that consciousness and its products are "parts of the human material social process" (Williams 1977, 59). Ideas are created in the human brain and always require some physical medium that they are associated with. Matter is a process-substance of the world. Natural matter is the object of the natural production process, through which nature produces and organises itself as *causa sui*. Social matter is the object of human subjects in society and the process of its production. There are qualitative differences between natural and social matter. In society, both interact in a dialectical manner when humans appropriate and transform nature.

For Lefebvre, the dialectic of society is one between subjects and objects that are mediated by activities of social production. This dialectic produces and is conditioned by social space in the form of spatial practices, representations of space, and spaces of representation (see Table 5.1).

5.4.2 The social production of space

We can learn from Lefebvre that humans produce and reproduce social relations whenever they relate to each other mutually and so make meaning of each other and the social world. A social system is a social relation between a specific number of humans that is regularised in space and time. It does not exist ephemerally but has some continuity. All social systems have an economy, a political structure of governance and culture. However, for every specific system, one of these dimensions is dominant. So, for example, a workplace is an economic social system, but also has certain political rules of behaviour and specific work culture. All social systems are dialectics of practices and specific structures (use-values, rules, and collective meanings). Structures are the properties that make social systems durable, enable and constrain the continuity of practices within social systems, and are produced and reproduced by these practices. Institutions are large-scale social systems that play a key role in society. Both social systems and institutions are more enduring features of a society, but institutions have key relevance in society and can contain many social systems within them. Examples include the parliamentary system, the legal system, the market system, the education system, the health care system, etc. A social space is a bounded combination of social relations, structures, practices, social systems, and institutions. Every social system has its space and is an element of larger spaces. When Lefebvre says that by producing social relations, humans produce social space, it is important to add to that insight that there are various levels of social organisation that humans re-create in everyday life, including structures, social systems and institutions. We could say that space is a bounded collection of many subjects, objects, and their relations.

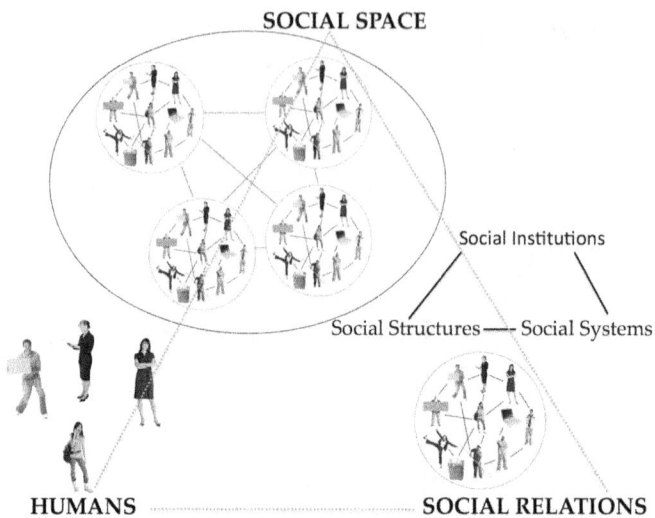

FIGURE 5.1 The dialectic of humans – social relations – social space

Figure 5.1 visualises the dialectic of humans – social relations – social space.

Humans produce social relations that are bounded, related and organised in social spaces. In the production of social relations, they produce and reproduce social structures that enable and constrain the practices in social systems. Specific social systems form society's key institutions. Humans produce and reproduce social relations, social structures, social systems, institutions, and social spaces that in a dialectical manner condition (enable and constrain) human practices and are the medium and outcome of such practices.

The dialectic of humans and social space, as visualised in Figure 5.1, is immanent in Lefebvre's approach. He does not fully elaborate what the role of communication is in social production, which requires that we extend and amend Lefebvre's approach: Social systems, institutions, and social space have a more continuous and enduring existence in society. This means that they do not necessarily break down if one or more particular individuals is no longer a member and so ceases to act in a particular social role. Another individual may substitute the one who left. So if in a software engineering company a Java programmer leaves, another may be employed who possesses the same skills. Social systems, institutions, and spaces are real abstractions from individual existence. But given their more abstract character, how can they exist? They require being lived by a specific number of individuals, who socially relate to each other in everyday life. *Communication* is the process in which structures, social systems, institutions and social spaces are lived and thereby reproduced by humans in a concrete manner in everyday life. They do so by making use of particular communicative means of production (verbal and non-verbal codes/languages, information, and communication technologies) that enable the production and reproduction of the social: Humans produce social relations by making meaning of each other and thereby reproduce the structures, systems, institutions, and spaces that enable and constrain their communication. Communication is the way in which humans live and produce social relations that, in turn, constitute structures, systems, institutions, and spaces.

Lefebvre speaks of a dialectic of perceiving, conceiving, and living. How exactly are these processes related? All social life is a unity of mentally perceiving the physical and social world; mentally conceiving this world in particular cognitive ways as thoughts; and living the world in social relations in which humans communicatively produce themselves, use-values, collective decisions, rules, morals, norms, collective meanings, etc. Perceiving and conceiving are mental and informational activities. They are social and material practices that are part of living and producing a society. Perceiving is the mental conception of the lived physical and social world, the cognitive production of nature and society. Conceiving is a particular form of perceiving; a creative way of living the world by producing information about it. And living the world means perceiving, conceiving and producing society.

Given that there is no easy way to separate these processes, Lefebvre's model results in the description of thoughts (the perceived) and information (the conceived) as non-social. Perceiving, conceiving and living are all social practices, which makes it difficult to call one level of social space "spatial practices". This implies that the other two levels are not forms of practice. The three levels are ordered, nested and overlapping. Spatial practice is conceptually the most unclear and least utilised level: "[S]patial practices mediate between the conceived and the lived, [...] spatial practices keep representations of space and representational space together, yet apart" (Merrifield 2000, 175).

All objects in society take on certain appearances. Their form and content represent meanings that are given to them by discourses in society and ideologies in heteronomous societies. Via objects, those who control them communicate meanings indirectly to those who consume, use or encounter these objects. Lefebvre (1991) says in this context that there is a "language of things and products" (80). So language is not just a code that enables the direct symbolic encounter between humans – also the form and content of structures and things can function as symbols and convey meanings to us; meanings that specific humans or groups encode into them via symbolic production.

In this context, Marx (1867, 143) characterises value as the "language of commodities." The price you pay for a commodity (the money-form of value) is a symbol that not solely communicates how cheap or expensive it is, but also tells you something about the amount of labour that has gone into the product. Furthermore, it allows you to distinguish and compare commodities in an abstract way. The structural language of objects is not necessarily dominative, but can take on a dominative form:

> The "language of things is as useful for lying as it is for telling the truth. Things lie, and when, having become commodities, they lie in order to conceal their origin, namely social labour, they tend to set themselves up as absolutes".
>
> (Lefebvre 1991, 81)

There are also political and ideological forms of fetishism in which specific institutions or ideas (e.g., the nation, war, racism) are presented as natural properties of society, although they only represent particular power relations and interests. Fetishism is a particular form of communication in class societies in which the social becomes reified and reduced to the status of a thing. This reification is communicated as a natural property of society. When things symbolise something, it appears to us as though they communicate. But actually, they only exist and are able to function as symbols because human social labour produces them within social relations and is contained in them. Through commodities and markets, the owners, who are the sellers of these goods, speak to us and attempt to persuade us to buy. Via the thing-character of commodities, they conceal the origin of the goods: the exploitation of labour and class relations. Commodity fetishism empties commodities of meanings, which creates a void that can then be filled by advertising. It propagates and communicates commodity ideologies to convince us that we should consume and that commodities create magic betterments of our lives. Commodity fetishism makes it impossible for us to see and communicate with the immediate producers and obscures the fact that producers who organise in the division of labour speak with each other. Indeed, it takes a political organisation for them to come together, formulate and communicate political demands.

Lefebvre's analysis shows clear parallels to world systems theory. The first part of Immanuel Wallerstein's (1974) multi-volume book *Modern World System* was just like Lefebvre's book *The Production of Space* published in 1974. Wallerstein (1974) characterises the "capitalist world-economy" as "built on a worldwide division of labour in which various zones of this economy (that which we have termed the core, the semiperiphery, and the periphery)" are assigned "specific economic roles" (162).

In the global space of the capitalist world system, the international division of labour takes on a fetishistic form so that workers who produce different parts of a commodity in different places are not aware of each other, cannot communicate with each other, and cannot politically organise. In digital capitalism, we find an international division of digital labour at the heart of the production of digital media, in which African slaves, Chinese assemblers, highly stressed and highly paid software engineers, precarious online freelancers, unpaid digital user workers, etc. constitute the collective digital worker (Fuchs 2014, 2015, 2016c).

5.4.3 Information and communication technologies in capitalism

Lefebvre's section on "Information Technology and Daily Life" in *Critique of Everyday Life* bears strong parallels to Raymond Williams' cultural materialism as Lefebvre argues that the production of information renders the distinction between base and superstructure superfluous:

> Information is produced. It is consumed. Information technology confirms the outmoded character of the classical Marxist contrast base and superstructure. Information is not – or not merely – a superstructure, since it is an – exchangeable – product of certain relations of production. What was regarded as superstructural, like space and time, forms part of production, because it is a product that is bought and sold.
> (Lefebvre 2014, 816)

Such cultural materialism, as can both be found in Williams and Lefebvre, matter today. For example, Edward Snowden's revelations of the existence of a surveillance-industrial complex, in which secret services such as the NSA co-operate with private security companies and communications corporations such as Google, Facebook, Microsoft, Yahoo!, Skype, Apple, etc., shows that today the two dangers Lefebvre identified have joined forces and resulted in the combined corporate and state control of personal data.

The commodification of information is another important theme in "Information Technology and Daily Life". Nature and communication are both common goods that all humans require in order to survive. Every human needs a place to live and to communicate to survive. You can survive without a car because it is likely that you can use other means of transport for travelling from point A to B. But you cannot survive without access to land, food and water – basic natural resources – and without the communicative interaction with other humans. The difference between land and information is that the fruits of the land are used up in consumption, and only a limited number of people can live on the land. Information, on the other hand, does not deplete. An unlimited number of people can use information at the same time. By arguing that land and information as commodities signify a new stage in the development of commodification, Lefebvre anticipated discussions about the commodification of the commons, as discussed in general theories of the commons as well as in Marxist theories of the commons (see: Hardt and Negri 2009; Hess and Ostrom 2007). So one here can certainly find parallels between Lefebvre and autonomist Marxism.

Information faces a contradiction between commodification and commonification. The movement of information becoming a commons undercuts the commodification of information. Examples are creative commons, file-sharing platforms, open access publishing, open wireless communities, free software, Wikipedia, etc. In this context, Yochai Benkler (2006) speaks of commons-based peer production in the digital media age. But open and gratis access knowledge communities do not necessarily undermine commodification. A range of capital accumulation models providing gratis access to knowledge, networking, software and online services has emerged, but they commodify user data and user activities. Google and Facebook are the best examples (Fuchs 2017b). Communication and digital communication are contested realms in which we find complex dialectics of the commodity and the commons.

5.5 Conclusion

Lefebvre stresses that the production of space also produces a code and language and sees communication and culture as secondary superstructures. Means of communication are (just like social space) means of production through which humans produce social relations and therefore also social space. The aspect of Lefebvre's theory that can be most fruitfully integrated into a critical theory of communication is his Marxist humanist stress on the role of human production in society. Humans produce social relations and thereby a dialectic of human action and the production of social space. Communication is the concrete dialectical mediation of the individual and society. It is the process in which humans produce social relations, structures, systems, institutions, and social spaces that enable and constrain human action. Lefebvre's concept of abstract space is a spatial dimension of abstract labour and commodity fetishism. Fetishism and the logic of abstract space create the impression that things communicate and act, ultimately hiding the social character of capitalism and domination. *Information Technology and Daily Life* bears striking parallels to Raymond Williams' cultural materialism and contains an anticipation of the discussions of the commodification of the communicative commons.

Humanist Marxism is not just dialectical in character; it is also a class struggle-Marxism that aims at thinking and realising alternatives to capitalism and domination. Lefebvre, therefore, stresses that only class struggle can challenge the capitalist domination of space. It can generate differences and re-appropriate spaces. In this context, Lefebvre (1991) speaks of differential space and counter-space as being alternative. These are communal and shared spaces based on "the collective management of space" (103).

Differential space foregrounds quality of life over quantity (381) and use-value over exchange-value (410).

Given the commodification of information and information technology, dialectical Marxism seeks to identify potential alternatives in the realm of information technology. Lefebvre asks in this context: "Is not technologizing the social and political, as opposed to socializing and politicizing technology, a choice and a decision?" (Lefebvre 2014, 821). And he continues:

> The relations of self-managed units, enterprises or territories, are already in conflict with the market and the state. These conflictual relations interfere with the relations of these units to information technology. Will self-management be realized and actualized by acquiring a content and meaning in information technology? Or will technological and political pressures reduce self-management to a sham? That is the question.
>
> (Lefebvre 2014, 824)

In the age of digital media, Lefebvre's work reminds us that digital capitalism creates spaces of alienation and that a humane digital society requires a self-managed and socialised Internet and digital media landscape.

In times when humanity is under strong threat by anti-humane forces such as far-right movements, nationalism, authoritarianism and potential new fascisms, engaging with the tradition of humanist Marxism that Lefebvre belongs to enables reflections on the causes and consequences of society's problems and how social struggles for alternatives can intervene. Communication is a foundational aspect of such practices.

Literature

Alderson, David, and Robert Spencer, eds. 2017. *For Humanism. Explorations in Theory and Politics*. London: Pluto Press.

Aronowitz, Stanley. 2015. *Against Orthodoxy: Social Theory and its Discontents*. Basingstoke: Palgrave Macmillan.

Benkler, Yochai. 2006. *The Wealth of Networks*. New Haven, CT: Yale University Press.

Brenner, Neil, and Stuart Elden. 2009. "Introduction: State, Space, World." In *State, Space, World: Selected Essays by Henri Lefebvre*, 1–48. Minneapolis, MN: University of Minnesota Press.

Castells, Manuel. 1977. *The Urban Question. A Marxist Approach*. London: Edward Arnold.

Department for Culture, Media & Sports (DCMS). 2015. *Creative Industries: Focus on Employment*. https://www.gov.uk/government/uploads/system/uploads/attachment_data/file/439714/Annex_C_-_Creative_Industries_Focus_on_Employment_2015.pdf.

Elden, Stuart. 2004. *Understanding Henri Lefebvre*. London: Continuum.

Elden, Stuart, and Elizabeth Lebas. 2003. "Introduction: Coming to Terms with Lefebvre." In *Henri Lefebvre: Key Writings*, edited by Stuart Elden, Elizabeth Lebas and Eleonore Kofman, xi–xix. London: Continuum.

Fuchs, Christian. 2019. "Revisiting the Althusser/E.P. Thompson-Controversy: Towards a Marxist Theory of Communication." *Communication and the Public* 4 (1): 3–20. https://doi.org/10.1177/2057047319829586 [= chapter 3 in this book].

———. 2018a. *Digital Demagogue: Authoritarian Capitalism in the Age of Trump and Twitter*. London: Pluto Press.

———. 2018b. "Towards a Critical Theory of Communication with Georg Lukács and Lucien Goldmann." *Javnost – The Public* 25 (3): 265–281. doi:https://doi.org/10.1080/13183222.2018.1463032 [= chapter 6 in this book].

———. 2017a. "Raymond Williams' Communicative Materialism." *European Journal of Cultural Studies* 20 (6): 744–762. doi:http://dx.doi.org/10.1177/1367549417732998 [= chapter 4 in this book].

———. 2017b. *Social Media: A Critical Introduction*, 2nd ed. London: Sage.

———. 2016a. *Critical Theory of Communication. New Readings of Lukács, Adorno, Marcuse and Habermas in the Age of the Internet*. London, UK: University of Westminster Press. doi:https://doi.org/10.16997/book1.

———. 2016b. "Digital Labor and Imperialism." *Monthly Review* 67 (8): 14–24. doi: http://dx.doi.org/10.14452/MR-067-08-2016-01_2.

———. 2016c. *Reading Marx in the Information Age. A Media and Communication Studies Perspective on "Capital Volume I"*. New York, NY: Routledge.

———. 2015. *Culture and Economy in the Age of Social Media*. New York, NY: Routledge.

———. 2014. *Digital Labour and Karl Marx*. New York: Routledge.

Gramsci, Antonio. 1971. *Selections from the Prison Notebooks*. New York: International Publishers.

Habermas, Jürgen. 1991. *The Structural Transformation of the Public Sphere. An Inquiry into a Category of Bourgeois Society*. Cambridge, MA: MIT Press.

Hall, Stuart. 1980. "Cultural Studies: Two Paradigms." *Media, Culture & Society 2* (1): 57–72.

Hardt, Michael, and Antonio Negri. 2017. *Assembly*. Oxford, UK: Oxford University Press.

———. 2009. *Commonwealth*. Cambridge, MA: Harvard University Press.

———. 2004. *Multitude, War and Democracy in the Age of Empire*. London: Penguin.

———. 2000. *Empire*. Cambridge, MA: Harvard University Press.

Hess, Charlotte, and Elinor Ostrom, eds. 2007. *Understanding Knowledge as a Commons*. Cambridge, MA: The MIT Press.

Horkheimer, Max. 2004. *Eclipse of Reason*. London, UK: Continuum.

Horkheimer, Max, and Theodor W. Adorno. 2002. *Dialectic of Enlightenment*. Stanford, CA: Stanford University Press.

Lefebvre, Henri. 2014. *Critique of Everyday Life. The One-Volume Edition*. London, UK: Verso.

———. 2009. *Dialectical Materialism*. Minneapolis, MN: University of Minnesota Press.

———. 2003. *Key Writings*. London, UK: Continuum.

———. 1991. *The Production of Space*. Malden, MA: Blackwell.

———. 1982. *Sociology of Marx*. New York: Columbia University Press.

Lukács, Georg. 1923/1971. *History and Class Consciousness. Studies in Marxist Dialectics*. Cambridge, MA: The MIT Press.

Marcuse, Herbert. 1964. *One-Dimensional Man. Studies in the Ideology of Advanced Industrial Society*. Boston, MA: Beacon Press.

Marx, Karl. 1867. *Capital. Volume 1*. London: Penguin.

———. 1843. "Contribution to the Critique of Hegel's Philosophy of Law & Introduction." In *Marx & Engels Collected Works (MECW) Volume 3*, 3–129, 175–187. London: Lawrence & Wishart.

Marx, Karl, and Friedrich Engels. 1845/1846. *The German Ideology*. Amherst, NY: Prometheus.

Merrifield, Andy. 2000. "Henri Lefebvre: A Socialist in Space." In *Thinking Space*, edited by Mike Crang and Nigel Thrift, 167–182. London: Routledge.

Sohn-Rethel, Alfred. 1978. *Intellectual and Manual Labour: A Critique of Epistemology*. London: Macmillan.

Thompson, Edward P. 1963. *The Making of the English Working Class.* New York: Vintage Books.
Wallerstein, Immanuel. 1974. *The Modern World-System I.* New York, NY: Academic Press.
Williams, Raymond. 2005. *Culture and Materialism.* London: Verso.
———. 1983. *Writing in Society.* London: Verso.
———. 1981. *Culture.* Glasgow: Fontana.
———. 1977. *Marxism and Literature.* Oxford, UK: Oxford University Press.

Chapter Six
Towards a critical theory of communication with Georg Lukács and Lucien Goldmann

6.1 Introduction

6.2 Aspects of communication in Georg Lukács's *Eigenart des Ästhetischen*

6.3 Aspects of communication in Lucien Goldmann's works

6.4 Conclusion

Literature

6.1 Introduction

This chapter asks: What elements for a critical theory of communication can we find in Lukács's major aesthetic work *Die Eigenart des Ästhetischen* (*The Specificity of the Aesthetic*) and Lucien Goldmann's works? It aims to show that socialist humanism unites the approaches of Lukács and Goldmann and can ground a critical, Marxian theory of communication.

When we hear someone talking about the critical theory of communication, most of us think immediately of Jürgen Habermas' (1984, 1987) theory of communicative action. But critical theory is to a significant degree associated with the works of Karl Marx, their influence, and the Marxian tradition at large. Rolf Wiggershaus (1995, 5) stresses in this context that the Frankfurt School used the term critical theory as "a camouflage label for 'Marxist theory'". Habermas has over time become very critical of Marx. This also led to the discarding of dialectical thought. Habermas' theory of communicative action is dualist (Fuchs 2016a, Chapter 6): It separates communication and the lifeworld from labour and the economy as well as from power and politics.

Habermas (1987, 281) characterises his approach as a "media dualism" that identifies "two contrary" types of media – communicative action that enables social integration and the steering media of money and power that enable system integration. This assumption results in a sharp contrast between the lifeworld, language and communicative action on the one side and the economic and political system, money and power on the other side. Habermas (1987, 183) criticises the "transfer of action co-ordination from language over to steering media". Steering media "may not be understood as a functional specification of language; rather, they are a substitute for special functions of language" (Habermas 1987, 263). The consequence of such a theorisation of communication is that it is conceived as inherently democratic and free of the logic of capitalism and domination. Lucien Goldmann (1977b, 43) characterises dualism as a mode of thought, where the object is "represented as a purely external objectivity, independent of or opposed to the subject". For Habermas, the human subject is part of the lifeworld, whereas reified objectivity forms systems outside of communication.

The problem of Habermas' approach is that (a) communication is not inherently democratic, but is in corporate contexts also an instrumental strategy, which is why one also speaks of strategic communication or corporate communication; (b) manipulative communication (e.g. "fake news") aims at instrumentally distorting political communication; (c) not all economic action is instrumental in the sense of aiming at profit-maximisation, but can in the case of non-profit self-managed organisations also be oriented on co-operation (Fuchs 2016a, 188). Marx (1867, 143) argues that a commodity's value and price form "the language of commodities". So other than Habermas, Marx suggests that language also operates within capital and power, not outside of it.

Habermas' theory of communication is dualist because he situates communication on the progressive side of the contradiction between domination and democracy. An alternative approach sees communication as in itself contradictory so that in a capitalist society it is both a means of domination and democracy (Fuchs 2016a). The question that arises then is how to advance democratic communication. A critical theory of communication needs to transcend the Habermasian approach and consider communication in a critical and contradictory manner. We need an alternative, Marxist theory of communication (Fuchs 2016a).

Maeve Cooke (1997, 15) stresses that for Habermas, the lifeworld is "a background to everyday processes of communication", forms a resource for communication that it enables and that the lifeworld, "as an enabling condition of communicative action, is itself reproduced by the integrative mechanisms of communicative action". Cooke argues that there is a dialectical relationship between the lifeworld and communicative action. One can certainly agree with this view. But Habermas falls short of developing a truly dialectical theory. The distinction between lifeworld and communication alone does not make a critical theory because aspects of the political economy need to be taken into account. For doing so, thinking about the relationship between economy/culture, work/communication, and production/language is necessary. Habermas externalises the category of work from culture, the lifeworld and communication and so does not apply the dialectic to this relation.

In the history of Marxist theory, we find authors who have engaged with elements of a theory of communication. Their contributions are today largely forgotten. Georg Lukács (1885–1971) and Lucien Goldmann (1913–1970) are two of these authors. Lukács's (1923/1971) book *History of Class Consciousness* has been one of the most influential Marxist books of the 20th century and has become an indispensable work for understanding ideology. Goldmann's works are today by and large forgotten. He is best remembered for work on the sociology of the novel (Goldmann 1975). This chapter asks: What elements for a critical theory of communication can we find in Georg Lukács's aesthetic works and Lucien Goldmann's works? It aims to show that both authors made important contributions to the foundations of such a theory.

Lukács's book *Die Eigenart des Ästhetischen* (*The Specificity of the Aesthetic*) and Goldmann's cultural writings contain insights into how to theorise communication. Therefore both authors matter for the development of a critical theory of communication. But their relevance has thus far been overlooked. In September 2017, 6,445 bibliographic references to Lukács's *History and Class Consciousness* had been made, but only 215 to his major aesthetic book *Die Eigenart des Ästhetischen* (*The Specificity of the Aesthetic*)[1] (Lukács 1963a, 1963b). The latter is a voluminous work consisting of two volumes with a total of 1,737 pages (volume 1: 851 pages; volume 2: 886 pages). One reason why the book has not received much attention is that just like Lukács's (1986a, 1986b) *Ontologie des gesellschaftlichen Seins* (*Ontology of Social Being*), also his book on aesthetics has thus far not been translated into and published in English. At the same time, the reception of Lukács has focused on *History and Class Consciousness* so much that his other works have been forgotten (see Fuchs 2016a, chapter 2). I have in a previous work shown that Lukács's *Ontology* is a key work in his oeuvre and that it is an important contribution to the foundations of a critical theory of communication (Fuchs 2016a, chapter 2). Section 2 of this chapter asks what elements we find in Lukács's *Die Eigenart des Ästhetischen* that contribute to the clarification of elements of a critical theory of communication. János Kelemen (2014, chapter 2) argues that Lukács's in the *Ontology of Social Being* and *The Specificity of the Aesthetic* theorised language as part of an ontological and aesthetic theory.

---

1 Data source: Google Scholar, accessed on September 17, 2017.

Whereas Lukács's reception is reductionist, the reception of Goldmann does today almost not exist at all. He is a forgotten Marxist theorist. Goldmann considered Lukács a main influence. He was a Lukácsian Marxian scholar, which is why it is feasible to discuss certain aspects of Lukács's and Goldmann's contributions to a critical theory of communication together.

The two books by Goldmann most relevant for the foundations of a critical theory of communication are Essays on Method in the Sociology of Literature (Goldmann 1980) and CulturalCreation in ModernSociety (Goldmann 1977a). UntilSeptember2017, these two books had received 134 and 131 citations respectively.[2] This relatively small number indicates how undiscovered Goldmann's approach is. By engaging with undiscovered, forgotten, repressed and hidden Marxist theories today, we can try to put the richness and importance of the Marxian theory tradition on the agenda of the contemporary social sciences and humanities and critical communication theory (see also Fuchs 2017a, 2017b, 2017c, 2017d).

Section 6.2 of this chapter asks what elements of communication we can find in Lukács *Eigenart des Ästhetischen*. Section 6.3 engages with elements in Goldmann's work that contribute to the foundations of a critical theory of communication. The conclusion (Section 6.4) summarises the main and points out the relevance of the two thinkers' humanist Marxism.

6.2 Aspects of communication in Georg Lukács's *Eigenart des Ästhetischen*

For Lukács (1963a, 13), everyday life is the "starting and end point of all human activity".[3] Everyday life has to do with the "practice and habit of work, traditions and manners of humans living and producing together and fixing these experiences in language".[4] Language is the "indispensable medium of communication" that enables "working together and living together in the everyday life of societal being"[5] (1986a, 187).

---

2 Data source: Google Scholar, accessed on September 17, 2017.
3 "Das Alltagsverhalten des Menschen ist zugleich Anfang und Endpunkt einer jeden menschlichen Tätigkeit".
4 "Übung und Gewohnheit in der Arbeit, Tradition und Sitte im Zusammenleben und Zusammenwirken der Menschen, Fixieren dieser Erfahrungen in der Sprache".
5 "Die Sprache, als unentbehrliches Medium der nur gesellschaftlich möglichen Kommunikation, des Zusammenwirkens und Zusammenlebens schon im Alltag des gesellschaftlichen Seins, ist gerade in dieser letztthinnigen Einheitlichkeit ein Zeichen der gleichfalls letztthinnigen Einheitlichkeit des neuen, nicht mehr stummen Gattungsprozesses selbst".

> This means that if we imagine everyday life as a large river, then science and art branch out as higher forms of reality's reception and reproduction that differentiate themselves, develop according to their specific aims, reach their pure form in the peculiarity that emerges from societal life's needs in order to then, because of their effects on human life, flow again into the river of everyday life. So the latter constantly enriches itself with the human mind's highest results that it assimilates to its everyday, practical needs, whereof then again new branches of higher organisational forms emerge as questions and demands.[6]
>
> (Lukács 1963a, 13)

For Lukács, the world is a dynamic flow of everyday life, the life of production, from which alternative streams flow out and back and enrich production. He uses the river as a metaphor for describing how human production and the organisations and institutions that are realms of mental production relate to each other. The traditional Marxist metaphor has been a building in which the economic basement is the foundation of and carries the upper political and cultural floors. The building metaphor is, however, too static and cannot take the constant processes of human production into account. The building is only a spatial metaphor, whereas the river is a spatio-temporal metaphor.

In dialectical philosophy, the world is contradictory, and contradictions are productive in that they are the potential for and source of change. Lukács uses the metaphor of the river for dialectics in order to stress this dynamic character of everyday life. At the same time, he also stresses that rivers can branch out to create a new stream, which stresses the productive and contradictory nature of dialectics. An alternative metaphor for dialectics that Heraclitus used is a fire that extinguishes and kindles itself (Fuchs 2014).

In his final work Zur Ontologie des gesellschaftlichen Seins (On the Ontology of Societal Being), which like Die Eigenart des Ästhetischen is a neglected book, Lukács systematically works out an ontology of society that is based on the concept of teleological

---

6 "D. h. wenn man sich den Alltag als einen großen Strom vorstellt, so zweigen in höheren Aufnahme- und Reproduktionsformen der Wirklichkeit Wissenschaft und Kunst aus diesem ab, differenzieren sich und bilden sich ihren spezifischen Zielsetzungen entsprechend aus, erreichen ihre reine Form in dieser – aus den Bedürfnissen des gesellschaftlichen Lebens entspringenden – Eigenart, um dann infolge ihre Wirkungen, ihrer Einwirkungen auf das Leben der Menschen wieder im Strom des Alltagslebens zu münden. Dieser bereichert sich also andauernd mit den höchsten Ergebnissen des menschlichen Geistes, assimiliert diese seinen täglichen, praktischen Bedürfnissen, woraus dann wieder, als Fragen und Forderungen, neue Abzweigungen der höheren Objektivationsformen entstehen".

positing (see chapter 2 in Fuchs 2016a for a detailed discussion of the importance of Lukács's Ontology for a critical theory of communication): Human activity is teleological because humans in it consciously create with a purpose, orientation and goal (Lukács 1986a, 5) so that intentions take on an objective form as products of human activity. Lukács's notion of teleological positing stresses that human production is a key aspect of all social systems. So, one can say that all systems have a common economic foundation. Lukács argues that work's teleological positing structurally changed the subject-object-relationship so that the relations of the individual and the totality brought about transformations such as the emergence of language (Lukács 1986a, 52).

In *Die Eigenart des Ästhetischen*, Lukács describes the commonality of all societies and all social systems metaphorically as the river of everyday life, the flows, networks and processes of everyday production. Communication is the production of sociality and social relations. Humans do not produce alone but in relation to and together with (and in class societies also *against*) others. Everyday life is always production, which requires communication, the production of communication as well as communicative production. Communication and work, the social and the economic, are identical and non-identical at the same time. There is a dialectic of work and communication – the dialectic of the production of communication and communication in production – that is grounded in humans' teleological positing. The social production of communication is the creation and reproduction of social relations that enable different forms of production. These different forms branch out of the river of everyday life as dialectical spirals, in which humans produce new qualities of society that flow back into the stream of everyday life and take effect there. Lukács (1963a, 38, 86) argues that work and language are inseparable: That humans have to say something to each other develops in and through the complexity of work. Work and language are the "basic forms of the specifically human mode of life"[7] (39). Both are based on the "teleological principle"[8] (40), namely that humans can imagine the result of production before they produce something.

Lukács described how during human evolution society became increasingly disembedded from nature, which means that the level of immediate interaction with nature in production decreased. The natural barriers of human behaviour decreased, although humans always remain connected to nature in metabolisms as social beings who are also natural

---

7 "Grundformen der spezifisch menschlichen Lebensweise".
8 "telelogischen Prinzips".

beings (Lukács 1963a, 470). Relatively autonomous spheres of society emerge from human production that are dialectically part of, related to, and different from everyday life. These spheres flow out of and into society (Lukács 1963a, 207, 362). In Die Eigenart des Ästhetischen, Lukács analyses science and the arts as two such institutions, in Zur Ontologie des gesellschaftlichen Seins the economy and ideology. In capitalism, the expansion of the productive forces and with it of science does not have natural limits (Lukács 1963a, 165), but only socio-economic ones (the crisis). Science strongly shapes everyday life. But in a negative dialectic, scientific and technological progress under conditions of capitalist profitability turns into inhumanity and anti-humanism (Lukács 1963a, 197). Lukács argues that the role of art in capitalism's fetishized world of commodities is the tendency that it has de-fetishising character.

Lukács (1963a) argues that communication does not just communicate content, but also aims at appealing to and evoking feelings: "Every societal communication goes from the total human to the total human and therefore cannot content itself with the simple transmission of conceptually clarified content, but rather also appeals to the partner's emotional life"[9] (Lukács 1963a, 377). Communication has an evocative character, it tries to evoke "some kind of action, behaviour, etc."[10] in the communication partner (Lukács 1963a, 378). Language is "the decisive medium and […] main regulator of the intercourse of humans" (1963b, 39)[11]. It creates a distance between humans and the world of objects (1963b, 48, 66).

Communication is a process of symbolic interaction that is based on information from the external world that acts as a signal for cognition and communication. One of the aspects of Lukács's aesthetic writings that matters for a theory of communication is his concept of signal systems. Lukács (1963b) deals with human information processes in detail in the chapter Das Signal system 1' (The Signal System 1') of Die Eigenart des Ästhetischen (Lukács 1963b, 11–192). He argues that humans have three signal systems. Based on Ivan Pavlov's work, he distinguishes between the reflex system that reacts to natural input signals (signal system 1) and language that reacts to the social world (signal system 2). The second signal system that uses spoken and visual words would be specifically human. Lukács (1963b, 21) criticises that Pavlov does not see a generic

---

9 "daß jede gesellschaftliche Kommunikation vom ganzen Menschen zum ganzen Menschen geht und darum sich nicht mit dem einfachen Weitergeben von begrifflich geklärten Inhalten begnügen kann, sondern auch an das Gefühlsleben des Partners appelliert".
10 "sie zu irgendeinem Handeln, Verhalten etc. veranlassen".
11 "So wird die Sprache zum entscheidenden Medium und zum Hauptregulator des Verkehrs der Menschen miteinander".

connection between work and language. Lukács introduces the signal system 1' that just like signal system 2 is a system dealing with signals of signals (1963b, 73). It generalises and makes conscious signals of signals (1963b, 27). It identifies typical aspects of relations (1963b, 58). Lukács discusses examples of phenomena created by signal system 1': Phantasy, thoughts, creativity, knowledge of human nature, love, comprehension, spontaneous decision-making, tactics, the aesthetic reception of art and culture. When Lukács says that "signal system 1' especially serves human cognition"[12] (1963b, 68) and determines psychological life (108), it becomes evident that by signal system 1' he means the system of human cognition and psyche that is located in and organised by the brain.

Signal system 1' creates novelty based on existing foundations (Lukács 1963b, 33), a dialectic of continuity and discontinuity (35). There is "complex, contradictory co-operation of signal systems 1' and 2"[13] (1963b, 64). Signal system 1' transforms the signals (forms and contents) obtained via signal system 2 (1963b, 91). There is a dialectic of human cognition and communication: Humans act in and perceive the natural and social world. The perceived signals are transformed by and processed in the human brain. The human brain coordinates the interaction with other humans and the social and natural environment. In the communication process, humans externalise parts of their thoughts and internalise parts of the thoughts of others. Humans in the cognition process through signal system 1' produce knowledge of the world. In the communication process, humans engage with each other and produce and reproduce social relations and their own sociality, that is their existence as social and societal beings.

Both cognition and communication are according to Lukács grounded in human work, which means that they are purposeful production processes creating novelty. Lukács (1986a, 1986b) speaks in this context of teleological positing. In the metabolism with nature and communication with other humans, humans re-produce themselves naturally and socially and thereby society. In the work process, humans create through bodily and cognitive activity and communication physical and non-physical use-values that satisfy human needs. Work requires communication, communication is the work of human sociality, and cognition is the work of the human brain. Figure 6.1 visualises these processes. The three signal systems that Lukács identifies allow humans to automatically react to influences according to their instincts (signal system 1), to reflect on the world (signal system 1'), and to communicate with each other (signal system 2).

12 "Signalsystem 1' vor allem der Erkenntnis des Menschen dient".
13 "So sehen wir überall auf relativ entwickelter Gesellschaftsstufe, eine komplizierte, widerspruchsvolle Zusammenarbeit der Signalsysteme 1' und 2 ".

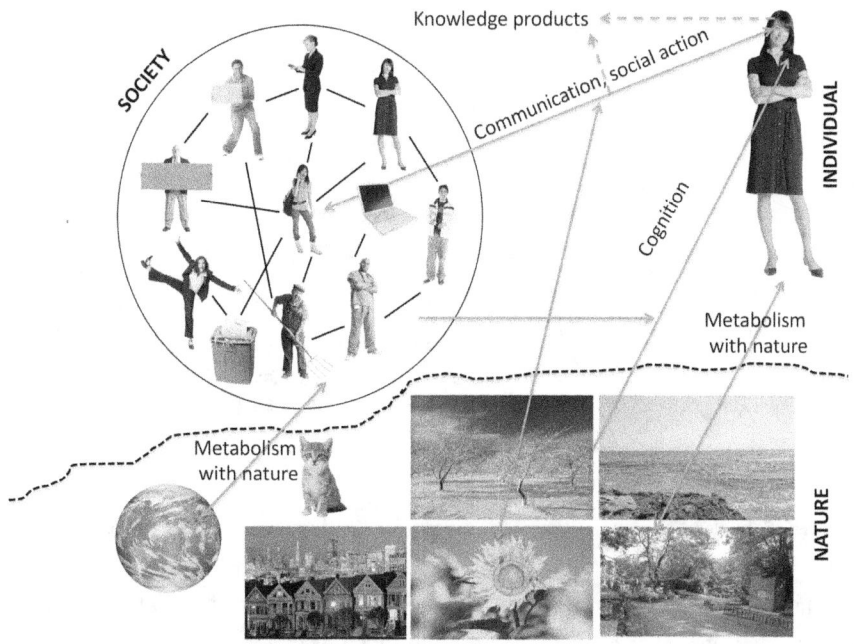

FIGURE 6.1 Human interactions in society and with nature

For explaining the relationship of signal systems 1′ and 2, Lukács (1963b, 31–32) refers to the third part of Hegel's Encyclopaedia, the Phenomenology of Mind. Imagination is for Hegel, as part of the subjective mind, an important aspect of representation (Vorstellung). Representation is the dialectic of recollection, imagination and memory (Hegel 1830/2007, §451). Imagination for Hegel is the dialectic of reproductive imagination, associative imagination, and sign-making imagination (§§455–459, see also Figure 6.2): Humans have the capacity to produce and reproduce mental images in their engagement with the world. They can mentally relate different mental images to each other. Hegel mentions the following example: "For example, I have before me the image of an object; this image is connected quite externally to the image of persons with whom I have spoken about this object, or who possess it, etc." (Hegel 1830/2007, §455 [Zusatz]). Based on images and relations of images, humans create signs, new representations of the world: "The sign is some immediate intuition, which represents a wholly different content from that it has for itself" (§458). The production of signs is the dialectic of sound, speech, and language (§459). "Sound articulating itself further for determinate representations, speech, and its system, language, give to sensations,

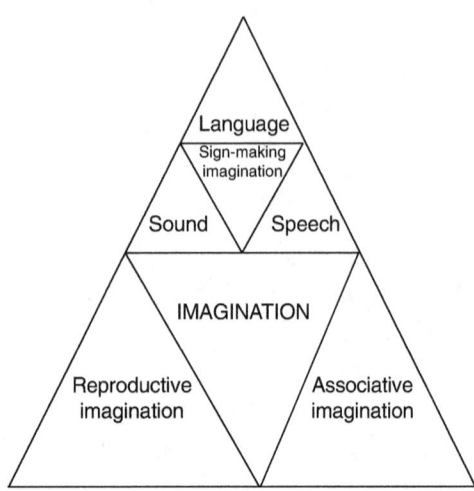

FIGURE 6.2 Hegel's dialectic of imagination (visualisation based on Hegel 1830/2007, §§455–459)

intuitions, representations a second, higher reality than their immediate one, in general, an existence that carries weight in the realm of representation" (§459).

For Hegel, human imagination is where what Lukács terms signal systems 1' and 2 are connected. For Hegel, both thought and communication are part of the subjective and theoretical mind. In his idealist manner, Hegel sets the human mind as an absolute substance of the world, something that exists and does not need to be grounded and explained. Cognition and communication are therefore reduced to the mind.

Whereas cognition and communication are for Hegel aspects of the subjective mind, he sees work as a dimension of the objective mind. He locates work as part of ethical life, civil society, and the system of needs (Hegel 1830/2007, §524). So Hegel separates work and communication as two very different dimensions of the human mind. He cannot answer the question of what communication and work have in common. Lukács (1963b, 33) in contrast stresses that the human being is "a product of his own work"[14]. Humans mentally conceive reality in the form of concepts and communicate with each other because "of the necessity to form concepts for work in the work process"[15] (1963b, 81).

---

14 "Produkt seiner eigenen Arbeit".
15 "Wir glauben – gerade von den Darlegungen Engels überzeugt -, daß die Ausbildung der artikulierten Sprache bei den Menschen mit der Notwendigkeit, in der Arbeit, für die Arbeit Begriffe auszubilden, zusammenhängt, und daß dieses imperative Bedürfnis der menschgewordenen Existenz die Artikulation allmählich durchgesetzt hat".

Teleological positing means that a human production is a form that is based on human work and shapes human activities, including cognition and communication that produce thoughts and sociality.

In *Das System der spekulativen Philosophie* (*System of Speculative Philosophy*), one of his philosophical systems developed in Jena, Hegel (1803/1804, 185–232) argues that spirit is expressed as language and work. Spirit results for Hegel on the one hand in language (226) and on the other hand in work and property (227). Language and work have for Hegel in common that they relate individuals (227, 229).

In the article *Arbeit und Interaktion* (*Work and Interaction*), Habermas (1968) builds on Hegel's Jena philosophy and introduces a differentiation between work as strategic action and communication as non-strategic action aimed at achieving understanding. His later differentiation between system and lifeworld goes back to this earlier work and Hegel's differentiation of work and interaction in the Jena system of philosophy.

Hegel in his Jena philosophy and based on him Habermas fall back behind Hegel's later dialectical *Logic*, in which a contradiction does not simply mean two separate entities, but two entities that are separate and identical at the same time and therefore "overgrasp" into each other (for a detailed discussion, see Fuchs 2015, chapter 3; Fuchs 2016b, 36–38). Hegel uses in this context in his *Logic* the term "übergreifen" that has been translated as "overgrasping". "Hegel uses übergreifen to express the positive aspect of the process of Aufhebung. The concept that results from speculative 'comprehension' (begreifen) reaches back and 'overgrasps' the opposition of the moments produced by thought in its dialectical stage" (Translators' Introduction, in: Hegel 1830/1991, xxvi). Hegel (1830/1991, §20) for example says that "thought is itself and its other, that it overgrasps its other and that nothing escapes it".

Applied to the relationship of work and communication, this means that work and communication overgrasp into each other: Communication is a form of work, work only acquires a social character through communication. Work has a communicative character just like communication has work character. Habermas cannot adequately analyse this dialectic.

Marx (1867, 284) describes human production as "purposeful activity". He argues that "what distinguishes the worst architect from the best of bees is that the architect builds the cell in his mind before he constructs it in wax. At the end of every labour-process, a result emerges which had already been conceived by the worker at the beginning, hence already existed ideally. Man not only effects a change of form in the materials of nature; he also realizes [verwirklicht] his own purpose in those materials"

(Marx 1867, 284). Human self-consciousness and complex reflection enable us to anticipate the potential result of our action and production. From this feature of purposeful, reflective action follows that humans have the capacity for ethical reflection, forming moral values about what is good and evil, organising a political system, struggling for what they consider as injustices, and potentially establishing a just society without domination, classes and exploitation.

Ideologies are attempts to reduce humans to the status of machines that think, communicate and act reflex-like and in an automated manner. An ideology is a particular form of communication that aims at manipulating humans in such a way that they think and act in the particular interest of a dominant class or group. As a consequence, not all, but only that particular class of humans benefits. And it does so at the expense of others. Ideology is what the Frankfurt School called instrumental reason and technological rationality (Horkheimer 2004; Marcuse 1941). Ideology tries to instrumentalise humans and to turn their consciousness and behaviour into automatic machines. It is of course not self-evident that this always works, but what is decisive is that in class and dominative societies, there is constant production and dissemination of ideologies which attempts to stabilise and reproduce the system.

Exploitation, ideology and domination are specific types of purposeful action, namely instrumental actions that instrumentalise humans for the benefit of the few. Socialism in contrast is based on a different sort of purposeful action that overcomes instrumentalisation and creates benefits for all/the many. Such action can be termed co-operative action or commons-based action.

The notions of ideology and instrumental reason and technological rationality build on Lukács's (1923/1971) idea of reified consciousness that he bases on Marx's notion of fetishism. Ideologies try to create reified consciousness by presenting society in a thing-like, immutable, unchangeable and naturalised way. It is the attempt to turn consciousness into a thing. Lukács's distinction between signal systems 1, 1′ and 2 allows us to understand ideology as a reduction: Ideology tries to reduce human communication and cognition to signal system 1 so that humans think and act in a pre-determined and instrumental manner just like machines and Pavlov's dog does. Society is created in social relations. Because social relations are variable, humans can change social situations and society. Ideology tries to present social relations as thing-like and unchangeable.

Ideologies for example advance the idea that immigrants are by nature lazy "parasites" and that their lifestyle is by nature incompatible with the national one. The behaviour of "foreigners" is presented as being determined by their nationality, not by the totality of social relations. If one assumes the latter, then it is clear that no individual has by nature certain features and that human beings in a society can therefore manage and find ways to live together, learn from each other and become friends. Racist ideology reifies humans and reduces them to a specific nature with the aim of fostering division, hatred, exclusion, discrimination, conflict, war and in the last instance, annihilation.

Signal system 2 organises communication and therefore the production of social relations. Signal system 1' organises reflection. Ideology aims at humans "switching off" or reducing the activity of signal systems 1' and 2. In the example, racism aims at human beings encountering others through ideologically formed prejudices, not through reflection on society's complexity and communication with immigrants that encounters them as fellow human beings and potential friends. Ideology tries to reduce human thought and action to automatic reflexes of signal system 1 that lack reflection and communicative encounter. All ideology in the last instance, through the reduction of the complexity of humans and society to signal system 1, tries to dehumanise society and humans. Dehumanisation means that ideology denies certain groups and individuals being human. It denies its victims humanity and wants to see them suffer and being excluded or even exterminated. It tries to deny those whom it tries to convince to act against the scapegoat full human complexity by aiming at reducing the complexity of cognition and communication to a one-dimensional pattern. Ideology is a non-dialectical form of consciousness, communication and practice that reduces the dialectical complexity of thought, communication, action and society to naturalised prejudices, stereotypes and other irrationalities.

6.3 Aspects of communication in Lucien Goldmann's works

Lucien Goldmann tried to combine Hegel, Kant, Marx, Lukács, Piaget, and Heidegger. Goldmann adopted "Piaget's vocabulary to reformulate Lukács' holism" (Jay 1984, 320). After Goldmann's death, Raymond Williams (2005, 11–30) wrote a contribution that commemorated the French thinker. Williams (2005) argues that Goldmann's interpretation of Lukács was a "critical sociology" (17) that acted as "a critical weapon against this precise deformation" that advances the reification of "life and consciousness" and as a critical weapon "against capitalism itself" (21).

The books of Goldmann most relevant for a critical theory of communication are the two collections Essays on Method in the Sociology of Literature (Goldmann 1980) and Cultural Creation in Modern Society (Goldmann 1977a).

Goldmann opposes both structuralism and individualism. What he terms genetic structuralism is a form of social theory that foregrounds the dialectics of "structure-process, fact-value, subjectivity-objectivity, comprehension-explanation and determinism-freedom" (Goldmann 1980, 36). There is "continuity in discontinuity, freedom in determinism, the presence of values in the establishing of facts, and so on" (Goldmann 1980, 37). Structuring and production constitute a dynamic process in society (93). Structuralism denies humans' "creative role and transfers the creativity factor to structures alone" (149).

Goldmann opposes linguistic structuralism that proclaims the death of the subject and sees language and communication as pure discourse structures. One "cannot simply imagine that [linguistic] structures effect transformations, through a mere internal process of change. There are subjects and it is they who make history, i.e. transform structures" (Goldmann 1980, 39). This includes that humans make "the history of ideas and thought" (Goldmann 1980, 43). Goldmann is opposed to structuralist French theory in the tradition of Althusser and Foucault and structural linguistics in the tradition of Saussure and Roland Barthes. We can here see a clear parallel between Goldmann and Lukács's stress that communication and thought are forms of teleological positing and human production. For Goldmann (1980, 45), there is a dialectic of the subject and object of knowledge: "The subject is also part of the object of thought and, conversely, the object (capitalist society) is part of the mental structure of the subject". Goldmann's key argument against structural linguistics is that linguistic structures do not act and that rather humans act and communicated mediated by language. "Language does not love or hate, it is neither pessimistic nor optimistic because its function is to permit love or hate, hope or despair" (Goldmann 1980, 51).

> Contrary to linguistically based structuralism, genetic structuralism asserts that in no instance could structures replace man as historical subject, even if they do characterize human thought, behaviour and emotions. [...] I do not believe that language produces, interprets, governs or creates. It is men who do so, through language and by using it as a privileged instrument (Goldmann 1980, 149)

Groups are transindividual subjects (Goldmann 1980, 97) that produce worldviews, that is collective consciousness (60). "By 'world view' we mean a coherent and unitary perspective concerning man's relationships with his fellow men and with the universe" (111). Goldmann terms the actual consciousness of a group real or effective consciousness. In contrast, he speaks of possible consciousness as a consciousness that conforms to reality (65). Possible consciousness is "an adequate and coherent consciousness" (87). Goldmann applies Hegel's notions of essence and existence to the collective consciousness and argues that today real and possible consciousness rarely match (66). "The possible is based on the real, but the possible only becomes real insofar as it is an overcoming and a modification of the real as it exists" (118). Goldmann criticises positivism as only focusing on real consciousness and ignoring potential consciousness (68). Reification involves in general the "replacement of the qualitative and human by the quantitative" (99).

Goldmann (1980, 118) sees the major problem of contemporary Western societies in the "danger of reduction or even elimination of man's possibilities". He stresses that he shares this insight with the Frankfurt School. What Goldmann formulates in abstract terms means that exploitation destroys the possibility for workers' wealth and equality, political domination destroys the possibility for participation and democracy, war destroys the possibility for life. Ideology destroys the possibility for a public sphere, in which humans on equal grounds together interpret and make meaning of the world.

For Goldmann (1977a), the creation of actual and potential consciousness is a communication process. He argues that there can be certain forms of manipulation of communication and speaks in this context of "distortion" and "obstruction": Certain messages are "developed and transmitted", others are "distorted, [...] the elaboration and transmission of whole series of messages" are "obstructed" (37). Although Goldmann speaks of obstruction and distortion, in these cases he does not term the communication process "ideology". He does not work out a clear critical understanding of ideology.

Lukács (1923/1971) based on Marx's notion of fetishism characterises ideology as reified and false consciousness that "obscures the historical, transitory character of capitalist society" by making its determinants appear as "timeless, eternal" and "valid for all social formations". Ideology ignores dialectic totalities and sees a whole just as a "'sum' of the parts" so that "isolated parts" appear as "a timeless law valid for every human society" (Lukács 1923/1971). Ideology exists for Lukács only in class societies: "Ideology presupposes 'societal structures, in which different groups and conflicting interests act and strive to impose their interest onto the totality of society as its general interest. To put it shortly: The emergence and diffusion of ideologies appears as the general characteristic of class societies'[16] (Lukács 1986b, 405).

---

16 Translation from German: "Die Hauptfrage ist demnach, daß das Entstehen solcher Ideologien Gesellschaftsstrukturen voraussetzt, in denen verschiedene Gruppen und entgegengesetzte Interessen wirken und bestrebt sind, diese der Gesamtgesellschaft als deren allgemeines Interesse aufzudrängen. Kurz gefaßt: Entstehen und Verbreitung von Ideologien erscheint als das allgemeine Kennzeichen der Klassengesellschaften".

Goldmann shared Lukács's concept of ideology, but applied it without developing his own theory of ideology. He conducted applied sociological Lukácsian work without engaging in theorising the underlying categories of ideology and reification that he took for granted from Lukács's works. That he shares Lukács's concept of ideology as reified and false consciousness and society become evident from the way Goldmann uses the term. Let us look at some examples.

In his book *Lukács and* Heidegger, Goldmann explains that for Lukács reification means "the separation between subject and object, between judgment f fact and value judgment", so that the world and psychic structures "appear as the property of things" and "practical human relations no longer exist except through the price, on the market, between buyer and seller, between individuals apparently free, isolated, and equal" (Goldmann 1977b, 33). Reification creates "a world of spectacle where [...] social relations are hidden as such and appear as the property of things outside of them" (43).

Goldmann does not provide his own or Lukács's definition of ideology. But he makes clear that for Lukács, there is a difference between the "falseness or truth of consciousness, its ideological or non-ideological character" (Goldmann 1977b, 55), which is an understanding of ideology as a process that tries to distort, misrepresent, one-dimensionally present or dissimulate reality in order to legitimate or hide the interests of a ruling class or group (Fuchs 2015, chapter 3). Such a critical concept of ideology differs from general theories of ideology that equate ideology with consciousness or worldviews.

Goldmann (1973, 62) characterises individualism as "the ideology of a rising class". In his book on Kant, Goldmann (1971, 199) speaks of the Enlightenment as an "ideology", in which "progress had become a natural law" that suppressed "qualitative difference between present and future, and the need for action". Jansenism was a Catholic movement that believed in predestination, the original sin and divine grace. It had influence during the 17th and 18th centuries, especially in France. In *The Hidden God*, Goldmann (1964/2013) analyses Jansenism and how Pascal and Racine related to it. He analyses Jansenism as "the only ideology that was peculiar to [...] [the] nobility" in France (104) and argues that the works of Pascal and Racine were the "most important philosophical and literary expression of this ideology" (142).

The positive aspect of the mass media is for Goldmann (1977a, 41) that there has been "an increase in the number of people actually having access to culture". But one has to go beyond quantity and must also look at the qualities of communication (42). Based on

Lukács, Goldmann defines the reification of consciousness as the disappearance of "transcendence and totality", "the entire social structure, the global character of interhuman relations […] from the consciousness of individuals. […] an individualistic, atomized vision of men's relations with other men and with the universe is created. Community, positive values, the hope of transcendence [dépassement] and all qualitative structures tend to disappear from men's consciousness, yielding to the faculty of understanding [l'entendement] and the quantitative. Reality loses all transparency and becomes opaque; man becomes limited and disoriented" (43).

Monopoly capitalism has destroyed independent spheres of human activity that "permitted the organization of a public opinion functioning as significantly in political and social life as in cultural life" (Goldmann 1977a, 44–45). Monopoly capitalism negatively impacts the public sphere. Reification also takes place through the media system. The "mass of information" bombarding us "can be disorienting" (47). Consumer culture tries to focus human activities on commodities (85). In politics, an elite of technocrats dominates decision-making (45, 88). Goldmann distinguishes between active and passive reception (47) and argues that media use is contradictory and dialectical (49). The political task is according to Goldmann overcome one-dimensional media and follow a "strategy which would permit efficacious action by those trying to use mass media toward effectively creative, cultural ends" (49). Humans face two tendencies, namely "the tendency to adapt to the real, and the tendency to overcome the real toward the possible – toward a beyond which men must create by their behaviour" (57). Social struggles determine which tendency asserts itself over the other in a particular event or situation. The alternative that Goldmann envisions is "economic democracy and self-management" (47). In the realm of the media, this means democratic, self-managed media that replace capitalist media. At the level of communication and consciousness, the struggle for alternatives involves dialectical thought that aims at understanding the totality and is a "radical critique of all positivism" (112).

It is noticeable that Goldmann in the same way as Lukács uses Hegelian dialectical language for ascertaining that capitalism constitutes a gap between actuality and possibility and between existence and essence. But Goldmann, other than Lukács, avoids speaking of ideology as a form of communication that aims at creating false consciousness. Ideology is a term that Goldmann hardly uses. He completely avoids speaking of false consciousness. So Lukács's categories could in a way be said to be more critical than the categories of actual and potential consciousness that do not immediately imply a critique of domination, although Goldmann, of course, gives them a critical content. Goldmann goes a step further than Lukács in that he advances a critique of capitalist media based on Lukács.

6.4 Conclusion

We can summarise some of the main findings of this chapter, whose task has been to find out what elements there are in Lukács's Eigenart des Ästhetischen and Lucien Goldmann's works that contribute to the foundations of a critical theory of communication.

Lukács describes everyday life metaphorically as a river that produces new qualities. Production is for him a flow, from which emergent qualities and novelty arise. The metaphor of society as a river is much more dynamic than the one of a building. In a building, there is a basement and there are floors that sit on top of the basement. The river in contrast is a productive flow that constantly produces something new through which the flow and the river as a system reproduce themselves. Based on Lukács, we can see the importance of the production of communication and communicative production in society: Communication is one of the processes of production in society's everyday flows. It produces social relations, social systems, sociality and society. Lukács grounds communication as a phenomenon of flows and production that helps us to overcome static and mechanistic base/superstructure conceptions of society.

Lukács in Die Eigenart des Ästhetischen also theorises the communication process itself. He in this context distinguishes between the signal systems 1, 1' and 2. He conceives of these systems not in a mechanistic manner, as Pavlov did, but in a dialectical way. For Lukács, communication is based on a dialectic of thought and language and a dialectic of nature and society. The three signal systems (instincts, cognitive capacity/the brain, language) are media that help to organise these dialectics. What Lukács describes as teleological positing, by which he means human production, is the common feature of instinctual behaviour, cognition and communication. The unconscious is the process that produces instinctual behaviour. Cognition is the process in the brain that produces thoughts. Communication is the human social process that produces social relations and sociality.

Lukács's Eigenart des Ästhetischen also allows us to better understand how ideology works. Ideology tries to reify consciousness by reducing human activities to the automatism of signal system 1 and by reducing the activities of signal systems 1' and 2 to signal system 1 so that social relations are presented as thing-like. Based on ideology, complex reflection about society and the causes of its problems are reduced to one-dimensional patters. Ideological judgements are based on irrational prejudices and naturalisations and not on communicative encounters. Ideology is a practice, discourse and form of consciousness that tries to reduce society and humans to a thing- and machine-like automatism and instrumentalism. Ideology denies humans their humanity. It is the attempt to create inhumanity by communicating to humans that other humans are not like them but are lower forms of humans and that society is not a complex, dialectical whole, but a form of unchangeable and thing-like nature.

Goldmann opposes structuralism and structural linguistics for their neglect of the human subject. He argues for a dialectic of subject and object and stresses that language does not act, but that rather humans act mediated by language.

Goldmann took up Lukács notion of the reification of consciousness and formulated it as a contradiction between real consciousness and potential consciousness. Reified structures would limit human potentials and potential consciousness so that which exists appears as the only possible reality.

Goldmann in a manner comparable to Marcuse, Horkheimer, and Adorno applies Lukács notion of reification to capitalism's media system. He argues that capitalist media in manifold ways limit potential consciousness. Goldmann tends in contrast to Lukács to avoid the terms "ideology" and "false consciousness". He criticises capitalist media as aiming at the reification of consciousness and argues for an alternative, self-managed democratic media and dialectical communication in order to strengthen the public sphere. The quest for socialist humanism is a political task that unites Lukács, Goldmann, and the Frankfurt School.

Taken together, Lukács, and Goldmann provide perspectives on some of the most important foundational questions of a critical theory of communication, such as the dialectical relationship of subject and object, communication as production, the dialectic of communicative production and the production of communication, communication as a dialectic of thought and language and the dialectic of nature and society mediated by three sign systems, ideology as the reduction of humans and society to the first sign system, ideology as a contradiction of actual and potential consciousness, capitalist media as creators of reified consciousness, and the struggle for alternative communications (see also Fuchs 2016a).

There are profound parallels and complementarities between Lukács's and Goldmann's works. This is no surprise because Goldmann understood himself as a Lukácsian. Both approaches contribute to the foundations of a critical humanist theory of communication.

Literature

Cooke, Maeve. 1997. *Language and Reason: A Study of Habermas's Pragmatics*. Cambridge, MA: The MIT Press.

Fuchs, Christian. 2017a. "Günther Anders' Undiscovered Critical Theory of Technology in the Age of Big Data Capitalism." *tripleC: Communication, Capitalism & Critique 15* (2): 584–613. doi: https://doi.org/10.31269/triplec.v15i2.898.

———. 2017b. "Preface: Horst Holzer's Marxist Theory of Communication [Preface to Christian Fuchs' translation of Horst Holzer's article "The Forgotten Marxist Theory of Communication & Society"]." *tripleC: Communication, Capitalism & Critique 15* (2): 686–706. doi: https://doi.org/10.31269/triplec.v15i2.908.

———. 2017c. "Raymond Williams' Communicative Materialism." *European Journal of Cultural Studies 20* (6): 744–762. [= Chapter 4 in this book]

———. 2017d. "The Relevance of Franz L. Neumann's Critical Theory in 2017: "Anxiety and Politics" in the New Age of Authoritarian Capitalism." *tripleC: Communication, Capitalism & Critique 15* (2): 637–650. doi: https://doi.org/10.31269/triplec.v15i2.903.

———. 2016a. *Critical Theory of Communication: New Readings of Lukács, Adorno, Marcuse, Honneth and Habermas in the Age of the Internet*. London: University of Westminster Press. doi: https://doi.org/10.16997/book1.

———. 2016b. *Reading Marx in the Information Age. A Media and Communication Studies Perspective on "Capital Volume I"*. New York: Routledge.

———. 2015. *Culture and Economy in the Age of Social Media*. New York: Routledge.

———. 2014. "The Dialectic: Not Just the Absolute Recoil, but the World's Living Fire that Extinguishes and Kindles Itself. Reflections on Slavoj Žižek's Version of Dialectical Philosophy in "Absolute Recoil: Towards a New Foundation of Dialectical Materialism"." *tripleC: Communication, Capitalism & Critique 12* (2): 848–875. doi: https://doi.org/10.31269/triplec.v12i2.640.

Goldmann, Lucien. 1980. *Essays on Method in the Sociology of Literature*. St. Louis, MO: Telos Press.

———. 1977a. *Cultural Creation in Modern Society*. Oxford: Basil Blackwell.

———. 1977b. *Lukács and Heidegger: Towards a New Philosophy*. London: Routledge & Kegan Paul.

———. 1975. *Towards a Sociology of the Novel*. New York: Tavistock.

———. 1973. *The Philosophy of the Enlightenment. The Christian Burgess and the Enlightenment*. London: Routledge & Kegan Paul.

———. 1971. *Immanuel Kant*. London: NLB.

———. 1964/2013. *The Hidden God. A Study of Tragic Vision in the Pensées of Pascal and the Tragedies of Racine*. London: Routledge.

Habermas, Jürgen. 1987. *The Theory of Communicative Action. Volume 2*. Boston, MA: Beacon Press.

———. 1984. *The Theory of Communicative Action. Volume 1.* Boston, MA: Beacon Press.

———. 1968. "Arbeit und Interaktion. Bemerkungen zu Hegels Jensener "Philosophie des Geisters"." In *Technik und Wissenschaft als "Ideologie"*, 9–47. Frankfurt am Main: Suhrkamp.

Hegel, Georg Wilhelm Friedrich. 1830/2007. *Phenomenology of Mind.* Oxford: Oxford University Press.

———. 1830/1991. *Encyclopaedia of the Philosophical Sciences, Part 1: The Encyclopaedia Logic.* Indianapolis, IN: Hackett.

———. 1803/1804. *Jenaer Systementwürfe I: Das System der spekulativen Philosophie* Hamburg: Felix Meiner Verlag.

Horkheimer, Max. 2004. *Eclipse of Reason.* London: Continuum.

Jay, Martin. 1984. *Marxism and Totality: The Adventures of a Concept from Lukács to Habermas.* Berkeley, CA: University of California Press.

Kelemen, János. 2014. *The Rationalism of Georg Lukács.* New York: Palgrave Macmillan.

Lukács, Georg. 1986a.*Zur Ontologie des gesellschaftlichen Seins. 1. Halbband Georg Lukács Werke, Band 13.* Darmstadt: Luchterhand.

———. 1986b. *Zur Ontologie des gesellschaftlichen Seins. 1. Halbband Georg Lukács Werke, Band 14.* Darmstadt: Luchterhand.

———. 1963a. *Die Eigenart des Ästhetischen. 1. Halbband. Georg Lukács Werke, Band 11.* Darmstadt: Luchterhand.

———. 1963b. *Die Eigenart des Ästhetischen. 2. Halbband. Georg Lukács Werke, Band 12.* Darmstadt: Luchterhand.

———. 1923/1971. *History and Class Consciousness. Studies in Marxist Dialectics.* Cambridge, MA: The MIT Press.

Marcuse, Herbert. 1941. "Some social Implications of Modern Technology." In *Technology, War and Fascism: Collected Papers of Herbert Marcuse, Volume 1*, edited byDouglas Kellner, 39–65. London: Routledge.

Marx, Karl. 1867. *Capital Volume One.* London: Penguin.

Wiggershaus, Rolf. 1995. *The Frankfurt School. Its History, Theories, and Political Significance.* Cambridge, MA: The MIT Press.

Williams, Raymond. 2005. *Culture and Materialism.* London: Verso.

Chapter Seven
Günther Anders's critical theory of technology

7.1 Introduction
7.2 The Promethean gap
7.3 Günther Anders's analysis of television and radio
7.4 Conclusion
Literature

7.1 Introduction

Günther Anders (1902–1992) was an Austrian philosopher, critical theorist, political activist, and a writer of poems, short stories, novels, letters, diaries, and short stories. He studied art, history and philosophy in Hamburg, Freiburg and Marburg. His teachers included Edmund Husserl, Martin Heidegger, and Ernst Cassirer. He defended his dissertation in 1923 at the University of Freiburg. Husserl was his PhD supervisor. Just like Herbert Marcuse, Anders turned against his former teacher Martin Heidegger because of the latter's role in the Nazi regime (for a comparison of Anders's and Marcuse's works, see Fuchs 2002). Anders published texts against Heidegger, arguing that his former teacher's philosophy was pseudo-concrete. Anders was married to Hannah Arendt from 1929 until 1937.

As a son of Jewish parents, Anders, like his second cousin Walter Benjamin, had to flee from Germany after Hitler had come to power in 1933. He went first to Paris and then to the USA. The rise of Hitler, Auschwitz, and the dropping of atom bombs on Hiroshima and Nagasaki were politically formative events for Anders that he reflected in his writings. In 1950, Anders and his then-wife Elisabeth Freundlich returned to Europe. They married and settled in Vienna where he lived until his death in 1992.

In distinction to the Frankfurt School critical theorists, Anders explicitly called himself a critical theorist of technology. In his principal work *Die Antiquiertheit des Menschen*, he studied the transformations of the soul in the age of the second industrial revolution. The German version of the two-volume work consists of 818 pages. The book has until this day not been published in English. The title can be translated as *The*

Antiquatedness of the Human Being, *The Outdatedness of the Human Being*, or *The Obsolescence of the Human Being*.

Anders (1980a, 9) characterises his approach explicitly as "philosophy of technology". Other critical theorists, such as Herbert Marcuse, also wrote about technology, but did not devote entire books to such analysis and did not define their approaches as a critical theory of technology. So, Anders's approach is special in that he devoted a lot of attention to the critical analysis of technology's role in society. Anders argued that there are contradictions in society that shape technology and its use (126). He opposed the blind belief in technological progress as well as scepticism towards all technology. A dialectical philosophy of technology has "to discover and determine the dialectical point at which our 'yes' to technology has been transformed into scepticism or into a straightforward 'no'"[1] (Anders 1980b).

Günther Anders's "genuine interest in different aspects of what he analyses as a global issue of power abuse and repression [...] established him as a transnational intellectual" (Molden 2014, 69). Konrad Paul Liessmann characterises Anders as philosophy's outsider: Anders was a truly interdisciplinary thinker, who wrote: "poems, novels, fables and tales as well as philosophical essays and treatises" (Liessmann 2014, 73). Transcendence was a key feature of Anders's works, as he "did not want to commit himself: neither to a provenance, nor to a future; neither to a style, nor to a genre; neither to a philosophical school, nor to an ideology; neither to an institution, nor to an identity; neither to a discipline, nor to a category" (Liessmann 2014, 73).

Anders (1956, 8) characterises his philosophy as occasional philosophy: It takes political and other events as occasions for philosophical intervention. Exaggeration is one of his philosophical methods (1956, 15). Anders (1980a, 411–414) says that his writings do not form a system and that Hegel worked out the last systematic philosophy. Because of a lack of translation of his works into English, Günther Anders remains one of the undiscovered critical theorists of society and technology. This essay is an introduction to Anders's main works. It asks: How did Günther Anders analyse modern technology? In which respects does his thought remain relevant in digital capitalism?

This chapter proceeds by discussing the relevance of Anders's concept of the Promethean gap (Section 7.2) and his analysis of broadcasting (Section 7.3). Section 7.4 draws conclusions.

---

1 "den dialektischen Punkt ausfindig zu machen und zu bestimmen, wo sich unser Ja der Technik gegenüber in Skepsis oder in ein unverblümtes Nein zu verwandeln hat" (Anders 1980a, 127).

7.2 The Promethean gap

Günther Anders argues that contemporary society is a system of machines: "The machine system is our '*world*'"[2] (Anders 1956, 2). In this world, we encounter what he (16) terms the Promethean gap, an asynchronicity of humans and products. The Promethean gap entails gaps between the relations of production and ideology, production and imagination, doing and feeling, knowledge and conscience, the machine and the body (18), production and needs (19). We are unable to imagine the vast negative consequences that contemporary technologies' uses can bring about. In the case of catastrophes induced by technologies, we are unable to show grief and remorse because the number of deaths and the extent and intensity of devastation are so excessive.

7.2.1 Prometheus

The Greek myth of Prometheus appears in *Theogony* (Hesiod 2006), which is a poem by Hesiod, who lived around the time of the 8th and 7th century BC. Prometheus challenges Zeus' power by tricking him into choosing an inferior gift that looks like a superior one. He furthermore steals fire from Mount Olympus and gives it to the humans. Zeus, the king of the gods, unleashes his anger against Prometheus by eternal punishment. Prometheus is chained to a rock and every day an eagle eats up his liver. The liver is restored overnight so that the whole procedure repeats itself daily. Finally, Heracles frees Prometheus. In this myth, Prometheus gives fire to the humans as a means of production because he thinks it emancipates them. But Zeus' wrath is more powerful than Prometheus, whose deed is eternally punished. The attempt of emancipation ends up in suffering, failure and domination. Anders applied the myth of Prometheus as an allegory of modern technology that was first created for emancipating humanity from scarcity and hardship but has unleashed new destructive powers. We can think of the fire in the Prometheus myth as a symbol of technological progress, while Prometheus' eternal punishment is equivalent to technology and society's negative dialectic that turns against progress and has negative impacts.

The Promethean gap means a "*confusion of creator and creation*"[3] (Anders 2016, 31 [German: Anders 1956, 25]). When "feeling 'Promethean shame' humans also prefer

---

2 Translation from German: "Das Gerätesystem ist unsere ‚*Welt*'".
3 Translation from German: "*Vertauschung von Macher und Gemachtem*".

what was made over the maker"[4] (Anders 2016, 31 [G: Anders 1956, 25]). Taking up Marx's notion of alienation and Lukács's concept of reification, Anders argues that there are three stages of reification:

1.) The loss of human control of the means of production;
2.) "Thing-shame", the human feeling of *"shame at not being a thing"*[5] (Anders 2016, 35; [G: 1956, 30]);
3.) Humans' feelings of inferiority to the machine, the "self-degradation in front of fabricated things"[6] (Anders 2016, 35 [G: 1956, 30]).

When Anders says that humans desert to the camp of the machines (2016, 36 [G: 1956, 31]), he means that ideology *"inverts the relation between freedom and unfreedom"*[7] (2016, 38 [G: 1956, 33]). Humans who adhere to this ideology think that things *"are free and human beings are unfree*[8]*"* (2016, 38 [G: 1956, 33]).

7.2.2 Technological fetishism

As an example of technological fetishism, Anders (2016, 58–62 [G: 1956, 59–64]) tells the story of Douglas MacArthur who was UN commander in the Korean War. MacArthur fed data into a computer in order to calculate whether the US should intervene in Korea or not. As all computers used for instrumental reasons, the machine was exclusively fed "with the type of data that did not offer any resistance to quantification"[9] (2016, 59 [G: 1956, 61]). Data and computing cannot make moral judgements because only humans have moral capacities. Questions about "the annihilation of human lives or the devastation of countries" were reduced to "figures of profit or loss"[10] (2016, 60; [G: 1956, 61]) – moral qualities were reduced to calculable quantities. A key decision about life and death was left to a machine.

In *Capital Volume 1* (1867), Marx describes in the chapter *Machinery and Large Scale*

---

4 In the German original: "auch in seiner ‚promethischen Scham' zieht der Mensch ja das Gemachte dem Macher vor".
5 In the German original: *"Scham, kein Ding zu sein"*.
6 In the German original: "Selbsterniedrigung vor Selbstgemachtem".
7 In the German original: *"die Subjekte von Freiheit und Unfreiheit sind ausgetauscht"*.
8 In the German original: *"Frei sind die Dinge: unfrei ist der Mensch"*.
9 In the German original: "mit solchen Daten, die einer Quantifizierung keinen Widerstand entgegensetzten".
10 In the German original: "was natürlich automatisch zur Folge hatte, daß (zum Beispiel) die Vernichtung von Menschenleben oder die Verwüstung von Ländern, aus methodischen Sauberkeits- und Eindeutigkeitsgründen nur als Profit- oder Verlustgrößen eingesetzt und bewertet werden konnten".

Industry (see Fuchs 2016, chapter 15) how capitalist technology's rise was associated with an inversion of means and ends so that humans became a means exploited with the help of machinery for the end of capital accumulation. The "automaton itself is the subject, and the workers are merely conscious organs, co-ordinated with the unconscious organs of the automaton, and together with the latter subordinated to the central moving force" (Marx, 1867, 544–545). Anders describes a state of the world in which alienation not just takes place in the factory and the office, but also at a global scale so that the human world is turned into a machine that instrumentalises (almost) all human activity.

In chapter 1.4 of *Capital*, Marx (1867, 163–177) introduces the notion of commodity fetishism. In capitalism, social relations are not immediately visible to humans but are veiled and naturalised by the commodity form. We perceive the world as being made up of commodities and do not see how labour produces these commodities. Anders argues that advanced reification results in a worldwide form of reification and reified consciousness so that human alienation is not just a matter of non-control, blindness, and disregard, but also one of love: humans love things that are used to control, dominate and exploit them.

Apocalyptic technologies such as the atom bomb explode the means-ends relationship (Anders 1956, 247–351). They are not means (to ends such as production, exploitation, or victory over an enemy), but destroy all ends by having the potential to annihilate humanity. But if there can be no ends, then there is no means to an end. The nuclear bomb is rather the ultimate meanness that has the potential to terminate humanity. In contemporary capitalism, humans are turned into resources, which is why Anders (1980a, 21) speaks of the *homo materia* and says that today "being is being-raw-material"[11] (1980a, 33).

The optimistic version of technological determinism (technological optimism) is an ideology that corresponds to the love and worship of the machine that Anders criticises. Technological determinism considers machines as autonomous actors that determine the development of society. In technological optimism, it is argued that machines result in positive developments in society. In technological pessimism, it is argued that they bring about or strengthen the negative features of society. In digital determinism, digital technologies such as the computer, the Internet, web platforms,

---

11 Translation: "*Sein ist Rohstoffsein*".

data, the mobile phone, etc. are treated as fetish objects that are said to determine society's development. For Anders, technology and society stand in a dialectical relationship so that society shapes and is objectified in technology and technology shapes society. Technology is, for Anders, not a neutral thing that can have different effects depending on its contexts of use. He rather stresses that the social production of technology results in ingrained objective qualities that can unfold complex dynamics and contradictions in society when technologies are used and institutionalised. In a contradictory society, we will likely find contradictory technologies that have contradictory effects on society that cannot be fully predicted.

7.2.3 Big data fetishism

Today, ideologues argue that big data is a new technological revolution that changes everything. An example: The "world of big data is poised to shake up everything from businesses and the sciences to healthcare, government, education, economics, the humanities, and every other aspect of society" (Mayer-Schönberger and Cukier 2013, 11). "The benefits to society will be myriad, as bid data becomes part of the solution to pressing global problems like addressing climate change, eradicating disease, and fostering good governance and economic development" (Mayer-Schönberger and Cukier 2013, 17).

Wired Magazine is one of the publications at the forefront of spreading the ideology of optimistic digital determinism. *Wired* and similar neoliberal magazines like *The Economist* celebrate the "big data revolution":

- *Wired* for example reported that big data could cure cancer: "In fields like genetics, neuroscience, and cancer biology, we've built tools that have enabled us to acquire mountains of data. […] associate professor of systems biology at the University of Cambridge, and senior researcher at Cambridge's Microsoft Research Lab, Fisher is mastering machine power to solve one of our biggest chronic health threats: cancer. Her research relies on the vast amounts of available data on cell biology, generated over the last several decades and plugged into computers to produce models that mimic how cancer cells behave. […] The more data that's factored in, the higher-resolution the models become, allowing better and quicker predictions about cell behaviour" (Bryce 2017).
- *The Economist* in an issue with the front-page headline "The world's most valuable resource: Data and the new rules of competition" sees data as "the oil

of the digital era" (*The Economist*, May 6, 2016, p. 9). "Data are to this century what oil was to the last one: a driver of growth and change" (p. 17).

- *Wired* claimed that big data will boost productivity in general and agricultural productivity in particular: "The UK should invest much more in agricultural R&D if it is to guarantee its food security. Productivity in UK agriculture has been relatively static for the last ten years. [...] Now, just as the green revolution was based on a change in plant genetics, a new data-led revolution is needed to ensure that productivity continues to grow in a sustainable and resilient way" (Tiffin 2015).
- Another *Wired* claim was that big data in smart cities would result in overcoming urban problems: "Known as Bristol is Open, the project will effectively turn Bristol into a giant laboratory and look at how big data can be used to solve problems such as air pollution, traffic congestion and assisted living for the elderly. [...] Sensors and other internet of things devices will be hooked up to the network to collect huge amounts of data from the city" (Temperton 2015).
- Quantifying the human self with big data devices would personalise health care as well as prevent and cure illnesses: "we've [...] seen an explosion of various wearables, apps and digital health devices [...] Smartwatches regularly capture heart rate, and soon may add cuffless continuous blood pressure monitoring and glucose measures. [...] Integrated home diagnostic 'medical Tricorder' platforms and connected pill bottles are coming to market. These will be paired with Amazon Echo and Your.MD and similar healthcare chatbots as interfaces. Mental health can be discerned from analysing our speech and the 'digital exhaust' from our smartphones. Breath can be analysed for more than alcohol, to track hydration status and molecules that can indicate a metabolic or malignant disease. Sensors in our beds can readily track the quantity and quality of sleep. Connected onesies or sensor-fitted pacifiers can track the vitals and activity of our newborns. [...] Increasingly, software will check and parse the data from these streams to help identify trends and alert the patient and their care teams much earlier. Startups such as Sentrian (founded by Harley Street physician Jack Kreindler) are making sense of remote patient data to decrease preventable hospital admissions by making predictions, alerting patients and caregivers to act early in the course of changes or deterioration. [...] The quantification of health will have true uses, can be crowdsourced and shared, and will improve outcomes (and perhaps even lower costs) across healthcare" (Kraft 2017).

- Big data would prevent social unrest and terrorism: Big data can "pick up where the next bout of social unrest will appear in the Middle East, or reveal a new history of the US Civil War [...] news mining can track changes in the public discourse that might foreshadow social unrest" (Steadman 2013).
- Big data algorithms would make perfect choices among job applicants and would make selection panels a thing of the past: "Talent management startup Clustree uses big data to help human-resource departments find the right internal candidate for job vacancies. It does this by analysing millions of CVs to discern career paths and improve job recommendations. In October 2015, the startup, launched in 2013 by Bénédicte de Raphélis Soissan, raised $2.9 million from Alven Capital" (Medeiros 2016).

All of these examples share the same logic: It is claimed that collecting and analysing more data results in the better prevention of and the capacity to overcome problems society faces. As a result, big data would make humans healthier, wealthier and more educated and society safer, cleaner and more democratic. To increase the quantity of the computational analysis of society and the data it generates would give rise to better qualities.

Big data logic disregards that society's problems are grounded in power structures. Physical and mental health have to do with environmental influences such as pollution, radiation, human stress, working conditions, human happiness, the amount of available free time, the education system, etc. Productivity depends on human capacities and the development of human skills. Air pollution is predominantly the outcome of fossil fuel-based capitalism. Social unrest, crime and terrorism are grounded in social inequalities and the asymmetric distribution of power. Finding the best candidate for a job is not simply a matter of formal qualification, but also of informal, communicative and social skills. Big data's logic of digital positivism only stresses potential positive impacts datafication could have. It disregards potential negative impacts.

In the time of neoliberal health care, where public investments are scarce, big data can be used for identifying who should be treated (e.g. who are wealthy enough) and who should go without treatment. Big data in urban and political settings can be used for trying to predict who may become a criminal or a terrorist. But such predictive algorithms can result in false positives, undermine democracy and contribute to the creation of a fascist police state. Collecting big data about applicants and employees can foster economic surveillance that violates privacy and installs totalitarian management controls. Datafication requires server farms and ever more digital devices, which increases energy consumption. Energy sources are today predominantly based on fossil fuels or nuclear energy and only to a smaller degree on renewable and clean energy sources (Fuchs 2017b). Increasing big data can therefore have negative rebound effects on the environment.

The big data fetishism of *Wired* and *The Economist* is a good example of digital fetishism. The authors, entrepreneurs, consultants and stories featured in such magazines express constant astonishment about what computers can do. "My god – it's incredible what *it* – the machine – can do!"[12] (Anders 2016, 34 [G: Anders 1956, 28]). Big data fetishism disregards the societal context, contradictions and power structures, into which computer technologies are embedded. It argues for the replacement of human decisions and actions by algorithmic logic.

In the age of big data and the Internet of things, human activity continues to be automated. Automation is not just limited to the economy but extends into all realms of everyday life. Drone-bombs, self-driving cars and trains, Twitter bots, automated phone calls with computer-generated voices, algorithmic auctions and trading, the automated regulation of water, energy and heating in smart homes, and smart retail and shopping are only some of the examples. A study estimates that in the third 2016-US presidential election debate, political bots accounted for 36.1% of the pro-Trump tweets (Kollanyi, Howard, and Woolley 2016). Politics has become semi-automated. It has become difficult to discern what has been written, posted, liked, and re-posted by a human being or machine. Algorithms today strongly influence politics. The problem is that machines cannot make political judgements. They do not have morals or the ability to reflect. They cannot make judgements that are based on morals or politics. Fake attention and fake news can, to a certain degree, influence and thereby manipulate political decisions. Automated politics undermines democracy.

Anders (1962/2014, 193) argued that in the age of the antiquation of the human being, reification takes on a form where products and technologies "transform themselves into pseudo-persons". This insight has obtained an important truth today, where it is problematic that, in semi-automated politics and action in the age of big data, it can be difficult to discern whether humans or machines create information, visibility and attention. Secret algorithms determine your Facebook newsfeed and Google results. Social media bots are algorithms that try to intervene in these algorithms and to create

---

12 In the German original: "'Mein Gott, was *die* kann!' (nämlich die Maschine)".

artificial attention. Attention and visibility thereby not just become semi-automatic, but also communication power-asymmetries can be enforced. Post-truth politics on social media does not democratise politics. It does not shift away from power from experts towards citizens, but rather enforces giving attention power to an elite.

7.2.4 Post-humanist ideology

Humans' Promethean shame and desire to become identical with machines is most evident in post-humanist ideology. Originating in structuralism's announcement of the death of the human subject, post-humanism aims at overcoming human existence and turning humans into machines. The computer scientist Ray Kurzweil argues that the miniaturization of computers will result in nanobots that can enter and repair the human body. Human life could thereby be prolonged to the stage where it would become possible to download the human brain onto computers, making humans immortal:

> The power (price-performance, speed, capacity, and bandwidth) of information technologies is growing exponentially at an even faster pace, now doubling about every year.[...] Human brain scanning is one of these exponentially improving technologies. [...] Nonbiological intelligence will be able to download skills and knowledge from other machines, eventually also from humans. [...] We will be able to reengineer all of the organs and systems in our biological bodies and brains to be vastly more capable. [...] Nanobots will have myriad roles within the human body, including reversing human aging (to the extent that this task will not already have been completed through biotechnology, such as genetic engineering).
> (Kurzweil 2005, 25, 26, 27, 28)

Kurzweil sees the computer as God, an omnipotent force that can radically transform nature. In Kurzweil's ideology, the human being's inferiority complex and admiration of the computer is taken to an extreme level so that the extinction of the human species is planned in order for humans to become parts of machines. Post-humanism is the ideological dream of the human "to become equal to his deities, the machines"[13] (Anders 2016, 40 [G: 1956, 36]). Kurzweil and other post-humanists solve the mind-

---

13 In the German original: "Sein Traum wäre es natürlich, seinen Göttern: den Apparaten, gleich zu werden, richtiger: ihnen ganz und gar, gewissermaßen ko-substanziell zuzugehören".

body problem in a dualistic manner by assuming that the human mind can exist independently from the body in a computer. In reality, there is a dialectic of the mind and the body. When one of the two dies, the other dies too. If becoming immortal by becoming a cyborg were technically possible, then in a capitalist society it would be likely that this capacity would be used for perfecting and immortalising the ruling class and fostering the annihilation of all those who do not fit into the capitalist models of productivity and entrepreneurship and of those who are ideologically scapegoated as harming capitalist growth. To "leave the human condition behind and stop being human" implies "the *climax of all possible dehumanisation*"[14] (Anders 2016, 44 [G: 1956, 41–42]). Given that capitalism always has fascist potentials, and we live in times of crises that can produce fascism, fostering post-humanism can also easily foster fascism. The combination of cyborgism and capitalism is likely to result in cyber-fascism, post-human fascism.

7.3 Günther Anders's analysis of television and radio

The second part of the first volume of *Die Antiquiertheit des Menschen* is dedicated to the analysis of broadcasting (Anders 1956, 97–211). It holds the title *Die Welt als Phantom und Matrize* (*The World as Phantom and Matrix*). Anders criticises that commercial broadcasting addresses the audience as consumers of commodities in order to increase sales. "*The world* has now *become an 'exposition'*; and certainly an advertising exposition that is impossible not to visit, because we always already find ourselves in the middle of it"[15] (Anders 1980a, 161).

Anders focuses on three aspects in his critique of commercial broadcasting: labour, ideology, and alternatives.

7.3.1 Audience and consumer labour

As the *first aspect* of his critique, Anders stresses the role of *labour* in commercial media. He argues that consuming commercial broadcasts is a form of labour: "Everyone is in a way employed and occupied as a *homeworker*. [...] The process

---

14 In the German original: "das Mensch-Sein hinter sich bringen'. [...] ist [...] der Klimax möglicher Dehumanisierung".
15 Translation from German: "*Die Welt ist* nun *zur 'Ausstellung' geworden,* und zwar zu einer Werbeausstellung, die nicht zu besuchen unmöglich ist, weil wir uns immer schon ohnehin in ihr befinden".

becomes completely paradoxical insofar as the homeworker has to pay for his labour instead of being paid for his cooperation; he namely has to pay for the means of production (the device and, in many countries, even for the broadcasts) [...] So he pays for selling himself"[16] (Anders 1956, 103). Consumption of a TV commercial programme is "camouflaged labour"[17] (Anders 1980b).

The first volume of Anders's principal work *Die Antiquiertheit des Menschen* was published in 1956. Around the same time, the Canadian Marxist Dallas Smythe formulated foundations of a critique of the political economy of commercial media that has striking parallels with Anders's approach (see Smythe 1951, for a detailed discussion, see Fuchs 2012). Smythe later developed this approach into the theory of the audience commodity and audience labour. He argues that the content of advertising-funded media is not a commodity, but a "free lunch" (Smythe 1977, 5). The audience's attention would be the commodity of advertising-funded media. Audiences would by watching commercial television, listening to commercial radio, or reading commercial publications, produce an audience commodity that is sold by corporate media to advertising clients. Smythe, therefore, speaks of audience labour as a productive form of labour that produces the audience commodity. Audiences "work to market [...] things to them- selves" (Smythe 1981, 4). "Because audience power is produced, sold, purchased and consumed, it commands a price and is a commodity. [...] Your audience members contribute your unpaid work time and in exchange, you receive the program material and the explicit advertisements" (Smythe 1981, 26, 233).

Smythe and Anders share the insight that in advertising-based consumer capitalism, consumers become productive workers whose selves are sold. Anders in this context uses the notion of the homeworker, Smythe the concept of audience labour. It is unlikely that the Austrian philosopher and the Canadian political economist were aware of each other's works when they were developing these ideas in the early 1950s. They independently developed a critical theory update of the concept of labour for the age of consumer capitalism.

In big data capitalism, the homeworker, audience labour and the audience commodity have been transformed (Fuchs 2017a). Social media are based on user-generated

---

16 Translation from German: "Jedermann ist gewissermaßen als *Heimarbeiter* angestellt und beschäftigt. [...] Vollends paradox wird der Vorgang dadurch, daß der Heimarbeiter, statt für diese seine Mitarbeit entlohnt zu werden, selbst für sie zu zahlen hat; nämlich für die Produktionsmittel (das Gerät und, jedenfalls in vielen Ländern, auch für die Sendungen) [...] Er zahlt also dafür, daß er sich selbst verkauft".

17 "getarnte Arbeit" (Anders 1980a, 182).

content, data and metadata. To a certain degree, Internet users behave like classical audiences who consume, watch, listen and read. But to a particular extent, they are also producers of content, data and social relations. All audiences produce meanings in consumption. But in producing such meanings, users of commercial social media also produce data and metadata that make their interests, relations and behaviour traceable. Big data emerged from the surveillance interests of online corporations and state agencies that want to control users' behaviours to accumulate profits and intelligence. Via big-data-based surveillance, online ads are being targeted and personalised. Predictive algorithms are used to try to predict online behaviour. The price of the big data commodity is set in algorithmic auctions. By turning into the big data commodity and digital labour, the audience commodity and audience labour have become data- and surveillance-based, targeted, and algorithmic. Anders's homeworker has today become a digital homeworker and Smythe's audience worker a user-worker.

Anders (1980a, 210–246) argues that one of the consequences of the capitalist world machine is that privacy becomes antiquated. The result of the application of surveillance technologies is according to Anders that "[n]ot only is it true that 'The world is delivered to your home', but also: 'Your home is delivered to the world'"[18] (Anders 1980b). Surveillance means *"the delivery of man to the world"*[19] (Anders 1980b). "*As surveillance devices are used routinely, the main premise of totalitarianism is already created and, with it, totalitarianism itself*"[20] (Anders 1980b).

In the age of the Internet and surveillance capitalism, the world is constantly and in real-time delivered to us. We – and our activities, our interests, our communication, our contacts – are constantly delivered not to the world, but our contacts and at the same time to online corporations and state security authorities. Edward Snowden's revelations have shown that big data capitalism is driven by data corporations' interest in amassing data about as many of our online activities as possible and state authorities' interest in monitoring data flows because they pretend to assume or seem to assume that they can thereby prevent terrorism. The problem of this approach is that it creates a huge political-economic surveillance machine in which humans are reduced to the status of consumers and are at the same time treated as if all of them are

---

18 "*Nicht nur gilt: „Die Welt wird ins Haus geliefert' sondern auch: „Das Haus wird der Welt ausgeliefert"* (Anders 1980a, 210).
19 "*Auslieferung des Menschen an die Welt*" (Anders 1980a, 210).
20 "Wo *Abhörapparate mit Selbstverständlichkeit verwendet werden, da ist die Hauptvoraussetzung des Totalitarismus geschaffen; und damit dieser selbst*" (Anders 1980a, 221).

terrorists. Categorical exploitation and categorical suspicion fuse, the combination of big data capital and the big data state create a totalitarian surveillance machine that undermines privacy and civil rights.

7.3.2 Ideology and the media

Ideology is the *second aspect* of Anders's critique of commercial media. In the tradition of Georg Lukács and the Frankfurt School, Anders understands ideology as the production of false consciousness. But he argues that false consciousness is just an immediate goal that ideologues want to achieve. They would also aim at creating a false will and ultimately false action: Ideology's "immediate goal consists in producing '*false consciousness*'", but it is an "apparatus for the production of *false action*"[21] (Anders 1980b). "*The truth of ideology* (that is: true compliance with the interest that lies at the basis of its production) *is false praxis*"[22] (Anders 1980b).

Anders argues that the commercial broadcast is a phantom world that is half present and half absent (Anders 1956, 111). The flood of images by "showing the world, veils the world"[23] (Anders 1956, 4). The difference between appearance and being would disappear (111), the event would be shaped by the "matrix of its reproduction"[24] (111). "*Reality is transformed into the reproduction of its images*"[25] (179).

Anders argues that broadcasting results in *banalisation* (*Verbiederung*) and that it neutralises politics and critique. The cause of these forces would not be technological but political-economic in nature: "The fundamental neutraliser is [...] the commodity character of all phenomena"[26] (121). Commercial media manufacture reality: "There are really numerous events that happen as they happen in order to be useable as broadcasts"[27] (191). According to Anders, the commodity requires banalisation to be bought and sold. "Since the broadcast is a commodity, it too must be served in status that is pleasant to our eyes and ears, optimally ready for consumption, alienated,

---

21 "Mag auch ihr Nächstziel darin bestehen, ‚falsches Bewußtsein' herzustellen", so ist Ideologie "das Gerät zur Produktion *falschen Handelns*" (Anders 1980a, 190).
22 "*Die Wahrheit der Ideologie* (das heißt: die wahre Erfüllung des ihrer Herstellung zugrundeliegenden Interesses) *ist die falsche Praxis*" (Anders 1980a, 191).
23 "die Welt zeigend, die Welt verhüllten".
24 Translation from German: "Matrize ihrer Reproduktion".
25 Translation from German: "*daß das Wirkliche zum Abbild seiner Bilder wird*".
26 Translation from German: "Der fundamentale Neutralisator [...] ist der Warencharakter aller Erscheinungen".
27 Translation from German: "Wirklich gibt es zahllose Geschehnisse, die nur deshalb so geschehen, wie sie geschehen, damit sie als Sendungen brauchbar seien".

removed from its core, and assimilated; that is, in a manner that it addresses us as our *simile*, custom-designed, as if it were *part of us*"[28] (Anders 1956, 122). Anders's notion of banalisation has parallels to Herbert Macuse's (1964) notion of one-dimensional man. Marcuse analyses how the commercialisation of culture creates "one-dimensional thought and behavior in which ideas, aspirations, and objectives that, by their content, transcend the established universe of discourse and action are either repelled or reduced to terms of this universe" (Marcuse 1964, 14).

Unilateralism is another aspect of ideological media. "*The relation human-world becomes unilateral*"[29] (Anders 1956, 129). By the unilateralism of communication, Anders means a one-sided information flow: "Since the devices speak on our behalf, they also deprive us of language; they deprive us of our capacity to speak, our opportunities to speak, and of our pleasure to speak"[30] (Anders 1956, 107). "*Without the radio the massive successes of Hitler would have been unthinkable. Fascism and radio went hand in hand*"[31] (Anders 1980b).

The one-dimensional human is for Anders at the same time dualistic, a phantom. It is present and absent and lives at the same time in different realities (the real and the imagined world, reality and fiction, reality and simulation). It is occupied with many activities at the same time and can therefore not be focused. It is not an individual, but a di-vidual (*Divisum*). The divided individual is "divided into a multiplicity of functions"[32] (Anders 1956, 141)

Anders argues that commercial media present the micro-world as the macro-world and the macro-world as the micro-world (Anders 1956, 152–153). There is both *sensationalism* and *anti-sensationalism* (153). The unimportant is presented as sensation and spectacle, whereas truly important and dangerous developments are minimised. Whereas sensationalism makes mountains out of molehills, anti-sensationalism makes molehills out of mountains (153).

---

28 Translation from German: "Da nun auch die Sendung eine Ware ist, muß auch sie in augen- und ohrengerechtem, in einem optimal genußbereiten, entfremdeten, entkernten, assimilierbaren Zustande serviert werden; also so, daß sie uns als unser *Simile*, nach unserem Maße Zugeschnittenes, als *unsereins* anspricht".
29 Translation from German: "*Die Beziehung Mensch-Welt wird unilateral*".
30 Translation from German: "*Da uns die Geräte das Sprechen abnehmen, nehmen sie uns auch die Sprache fort; berauben sie uns unserer Ausdrucksfähigkeit, unserer Sprachgelegenheit, ja unserer Sprachlust*".
31 In the German original: "*Ohne dieses [das Radio] sind die Massenerfolge Hitlers nicht denkbar. Faschismus und Rundfunk sind Korrelate*" (Anders 1980a, 88).
32 Translation from German: "in eine Mehrzahl von Funktionen zerlegt".

So, for Anders, commercial media's manufacturing of reality entails *banalisation, unilateralism, di-vidualism, sensationalism, and anti-sensationalism*. One can say that these are ideological strategies. But for Anders, capitalism is today "post-ideological" and ideology has become antiquated. It is not that ideologies no longer exist. Anders rather says they are no longer needed because false statements and lies about the world have become the world (Anders 1956, 193; see also Anders 1980a, 188–192). Ideology produces post-ideology. Anders (1980a, 261) argues that ideologies are theoretical systems that interpret the whole (although in a false manner):

"*The images coming from all over the world* that are ceaselessly transmitted to us have nothing to do with what were still called, only fifty years ago, *images of the world*. Now they are always only single trees, not the forest"[33] (Anders 1980b).

The ideological strategies of *banalisation, unilateralism, di-vidualism, sensationalism, and anti-sensationalism* remain relevant and have taken on new qualities in big data capitalism.

Contemporary networked digital media platforms operate at extremely high speed and publish an immense amount of content. In the world of big and ultra-accelerated content and data, attention is a scarce good. In order to attract attention online, content today tends to be compressed, short, superficial, and ephemeral. The feudalisation of the public sphere, the world of engagement, publishing and debate, has in the age of Twitter and reality TV taken on the form of highly accelerated *banalisation* and tabloidisation that appears to democratise the public sphere (user-generated content as "participatory culture"), but is, in essence, the antiquation of engaging political information, political communication and political debate.

Also, *unilateralism* has taken on new forms in the world of social media and user-generated content. The broadcast media's monopoly of voice has been broken. Now (almost) everyone can speak, broadcast, post, comment, etc. online. A computer is a universal machine, a tool for the production, dissemination and consumption of information. The technological convergence of what in traditional broadcasting are different technologies and institutions has enabled the emergence of prosumption (productive consumption, consumers who are producers of information). But the

---

33 In the German original: "Die '*Bilder aus aller Welt*', die man uns pausenlos zuleitet, haben mit dem, was man noch vor fünfzig Jahren '*Weltbilder*' nannte, überhaupt nichts mehr zu tun. Immer sind es einzelne Bäume statt des Waldes" (Anders 1980a, 261–262).

capitalist world of prosumption is far from democratic. It is driven by the logic of accumulating profits and attention. Online attention is time. Time is scarce. Time is money. Online attention turns into money. Given the capitalist stratification of the online world, we also find a stratification of attention: Celebrities, corporations and some others dominate online visibility. They together form the online elite that achieves high attention and visibility. In contrast, proletarian users can speak and post but are hardly heard. The result is a class conflict between online celebs that accumulate and are rich in attention and online proletarians that are the capitalist online attention economy's poor.

In the age of social media, the *di-vidual* has already become antiquated and has turned into a *multi-vidual*. We are constantly confronted with a vast amount of content, opinions, choices, new releases, updates, requests for inputs, messages, etc. The problem is that the multiverse of information is to a large degree one and the same type of superficial information that distracts attention from information and communication that really matters and can make a difference to the world. Critical, dialectical information often remains buried and unrecognised in the vast flow of big data. One-dimensionality disguises itself as a plurality. Information that stands out from big data and achieves mass attention as *sensation and spectacle* is often banal and trivial. Meanwhile, critiques and thoughtful ideas that could make a real difference, which are based on complex arguments and require space and time for development, are mostly overlooked, ignored and repressed *anti-sensations*.

Although there is also classical censorship in the online world, the main form of repression online is equal to what Herbert Marcuse (1969) terms repressive tolerance:

> All points of view can be heard: [...] in endlessly dragging debates over the media, the stupid opinion is treated with the same respect as the intelligent one, the misinformed may talk as long as the informed, and propaganda rides along with education, truth with falsehood. This pure toleration of sense and nonsense is justified by the democratic argument that [...] all contesting opinions must be submitted to 'the people' for its deliberation and choice. [...] Other words can be spoken and heard, other ideas can be expressed, but, at the massive scale of the conservative majority (outside such enclaves as the intelligentsia), they are immediately 'evaluated' (i.e. automatically understood) in terms of the public language--a language which determines 'a priori' the direction in which the thought process moves.
>
> (Marcuse 1969, 94, 96)

On social media, all opinions can be posted and all content can be assessed and commented on in real-time. But given the asymmetries of visibility and attention in the flood of information (e.g., due to sponsored/branded content, targeted advertising, reputational hierarchies, etc.), non-trivial, complex and critical voices have a harder time to be recognised and to make a difference.

In the age of social media and prosumption, we forget that we are working and when we are working. Anders's notion that there is a Promethean gap between doing and feeling has reached a new level, as we in real-time can access lots of information about the world and communicate with many parts of the world, but at the same time labour no longer feels like, and hardly is perceived as, exploitation and a class relation.

In classical commodity fetishism, the "definite social relation between men themselves" assumes "the fantastic form of a relation between things" (Marx 1867, 165). In the world of capitalist social media, commodity fetishism has become antiquated and has turned into inverse commodity fetishism. When using Facebook or Google, we cannot see and experience the commodity, but rather experience sociality as if it were unmediated by the commodity form. We do not pay money for accessing social media because it provides access as a "free lunch". In reality, this lunch is not for free but is a means for exploiting our digital labour so that personal data is turned into a commodity behind our backs, not visible to and not directly experienceable for us. In inverse commodity fetishism, the social hides the commodity form. Alienation appears as social and non-alienated fun and pleasure. Günther Anders anticipated this development: "Despite the fact that we really live in an alienated world, the world is presented to us as if it is a world for us, as if it were our own and like ourselves"[34] (1956, 116).

"As consumers we contemporaries are today consistently '*secret agents*'" [35] (Anders 1980a, 171) because it is kept secret "*that, for what and for whom he performs his activity when he sits in front of his goggle-box*"[36] (170). The goggle-box has today turned into the Google-universe. In the case of the goggle-box that broadcasts advertising-funded programmes, audience labour is kept ideologically secret through

---

34 Translation from German: "*Obwohl wir in Wahrheit in einer entfremdeten Welt leben, wird uns die Welt so dargeboten, als ob sie für uns da wäre, als ob sie unsere wäre und unseresgleichen*".
35 Translation from German: "Als Konsumenten sind wir Heutigen durchweg ‚*Geheimagenten*'".
36 Translation from German: "*weil vor ihm selbst geheimgehalten wird, daß er, wofür er und für wen er, wenn er vor seiner Schüssel sitzt, seine Tätigkeit ausübt*".

the consumers' enjoyment and relaxation. In the Google universe of social media, inverse commodity fetishism creates the immediate experience of sociality so that communication and sociality act as the forces that keep the status of users as workers secret.

7.3.3 Alternatives

When reading Anders, one must always bear in mind that he uses exaggeration as a means of criticism. What drove Anders's radical critique was a deep-seated humanism and concerns about the human being's situation in capitalist societies. He was not opposed to alternative forms and organisations of communication. He argues that the key task is the formation of moral phantasy that aims at overcoming the Promethean gap (Anders 1956, 273). Anders favoured means that allow humans to develop such phantasy.

In the preface to the 5th edition of the first volume of *Die Antiquiertheit des Menschen*, Anders argues that the Vietnam war, where television and the media showed images of killed civilians, which would have had an enlightening effect:

> It has, in fact, been shown that, in certain situations, television images can deliver the reality, in which we would otherwise not participate in at all, into the home and can shake us up and motivate us to take historically important steps. Perceived images are worse than perceived reality, but they are better than nothing. The images of the Vietnam War that were channelled into American homes day by day, really 'opened' the screen-gazing eyes of millions of citizens eyes who were staring at the screen, triggering a protest that greatly contributed to the end of the genocide that took place at that time.[37] (1956, VIII)

The question is how alternative media and digital media that strengthen human

---

37 Translation from German: "Unterdessen hat es sich nämlich herausgestellt, daß Fernsehbilder doch in gewissen Situationen die Wirklichkeit, deren wir sonst überhaupt nicht teilhaftig würden, ins Haus liefern und uns erschüttern und zu geschichtlich wichtigen Schritten motivieren können. Wahrgenommene Bilder sind zwar schlechter als wahrgenommene Realität, aber sie sind doch besser als nichts. Die täglich in die amerikanischen Heime kanalisierten Bilder vom vietnamesischen Kriegsschauplatz haben Millionen von Bürgern die auf die Mattscheibe starrenden Augen erst wirklich ‚geöffnet' und einen Protest ausgelöst, der sehr erheblich beigetragen hat zum Abbruch des damaligen Genozids" (Anders 1956, VIII).

imagination could look like today. Certainly, they have to be non-commercial and pursue a non-profit agenda.

Club 2 in Austria and *After Dark* in Britain were prototypes of slow broadcast media. The *Club 2* debate format originated in the 1970s in the context of the Austrian Broadcasting Corporation (ORF), Austria's public service broadcaster. *Club 2* was an open-ended, live, uncensored, controversial debate with diverse participants. *Club 2* was a true public sphere.

We need slow media. Offline and online. Slow media. And slow media 2.0. Is a new version of *Club 2* possible today? What could *Club 2.0* look like? Speaking of a second version can on the one hand mean that the *Club 2* concept could be revived to help to strengthen the public sphere in times of authoritarian capitalism. On the other hand, one has to consider that society does not standstill. Rather, it develops dynamically and has created new realities such as the Internet that has become a key part of public communication. *Club 2.0* therefore also means a somewhat updated concept of *Club 2* that sticks to its ground rules but also extends the concept. If *Club 2.0* can go from a possibility to reality is not simply a technical question. It is a question of political economy. It is a political question because it requires the decision to break with the logic of commercial, entertainment-oriented TV dominated by reality TV and comparable formats. *Club 2.0* requires a political choice in favour of public service media and public interest media. *Club 2.0* is also an economic question because realising it requires breaking with the principles that shape the media today, such as high speed, superficiality, brevity, the algorithmisation and automation of human communication, post-truth, the spectacle, etc. *Club 2.0* is a question of resources and changing the media system's power relations.

Figure 7.1 visualises a possible concept of *Club 2.0*. This model is a basic idea that certainly can be varied in many ways and is merely one of many possible versions. The key aspects are the following:

- *Club 2/After Dark's ground rules*: Club 2.0 uses and extends the traditional principles of *Club 2/After Dark*. The live television part requires all of the traditional principles of *Club 2/After Dark*. These ground rules are key for the format's success. *Club 2.0*'s broadcasts need to be open-ended, live, and uncensored.
- *Cross-medium:* Club 2.0 is a cross-medium that brings together live television and the Internet.

- *Online video*: Club 2.0 live broadcasts are available online via a video platform.
- *Autonomous social media, no traditional social media*: Existing commercial social media platforms (YouTube, Twitter, Facebook, etc.) are not suited because they are not based on the principles of slow media and public interest. Broadcasting *Club 2.0* over YouTube would for example result in frequent advertising breaks that would disrupt and disable discussion.
- *Autonomous video platform C2Tube*: *Club 2.0* requires its own video platform that we can provisionally call C2Tube. C2Tube poses the possibility for viewers to watch the debate online and via a diversity of technical devices.
- *Interactivity*: C2Tube also allows interactive features that can be used to a certain degree.
- *User-generated discussion inputs*: There is the possibility for discussion inputs generated by users. Such a feature requires that users are non-anonymous and register on the platform. Anonymity encourages Godwin's law that says that "as an anonymous online discussion grows longer, the probability of a comparison involving Hitler approaches 1". Setting an upper limit of registrations or activating only a certain number of users during a specific debate allows limiting the number of registered and active users. The selection of active users can for example be made randomly. Or all users can be allowed to participate. User-generated discussion inputs should ideally be in video format. The number of user-generated discussion inputs that can be generated should best be limited (ideally to just one per active user). User-generated discussion inputs can be uploaded to the C2 platform.
- *Interfacing the studio debate with user-generated videos*: At certain points of time during the live broadcast, user-generated video input is chosen and broadcast and informs the studio debate. Users in such videos formulate their own views and can also provide a question for discussion. Ideally, during a two to three-hour-long debate, about two user-generated videos could be broadcast. Inevitably a selection mechanism is needed for deciding which user-generated videos are broadcast. There are several principles such as random selection, selection by the *Club 2.0* production team, random choice of a registered user who is enabled to choose the video, special guests who make the selection, etc.
- *User discussion*: *Club 2.0* also enables discussion between users. A discussion could take place simultaneously to the live broadcast and/or after it. The two selected user-generated C2 videos can be opened up for discussion on the C2 platform. Ideally, video- and text-based comments should be possible. There

should be a minimum length for text-based comments and maybe a maximum length for video comments. In order to stick with the principle of slow media and avoid the Twitter effect of accelerated standstill, the number of video and text comments a single user can post per debate should be limited.

- *Forgetting data:* Videos are fairly large and storage-intensive. Therefore, the question is what should happen to all those videos that are uploaded, but not broadcast and not opened for discussion. Given that they have no practical use, they could be deleted. This means that the users must be aware of the fact that uploading a video means loss of data. Contemporary social media store all data and meta-data forever. Forgetting data can therefore be used as a counter-principle. The online debates that feature text and video comments could either be preserved or deleted after a certain period of time.
- *Privacy-friendliness:* Contemporary social media use data and user surveillance for economic and political purposes, that is for making monetary profits by selling targeted advertisements and implementing a political surveillance society that promises more security but undermines privacy and installs a regime of categorical suspicion. *Club 2.0*'s way of dealing with data should be privacy-friendly, only store the minimum amount of data necessary for operating the platform, not sell user data, and in general use good practices of data and privacy protection. This principle is also called privacy-by-design, which means that privacy is designed into the platform and the format. This does however not mean that users who debate publicly are anonymous. Privacy rather relates to the way user data is stored and handled.
- *Social production:* Contemporary social media are highly individualistic. The production of user-generated *Club 2.0* input videos could, in contrast, take on the form of social production that transcends individualism and creates truly social media content by integrating *Club 2.0* into educational institutions (schools, universities, adult education, etc.) where individuals together learn by co-creating video content as input for discussions. For doing so, the topic of a specific *Club 2.0* evening needs to be known in advance, which can be achieved by publishing a description. Groups of individuals can get together and prepare videos that they can on the evening of the broadcast upload to C2Tube once the uploading possibility is enabled.

Club 2.0 alone would not achieve a better world. In times of authoritarian, high-speed capitalism, complexity and critique are largely missing from the news and political information and communication. *Club 2.0* could contribute to strengthening the public

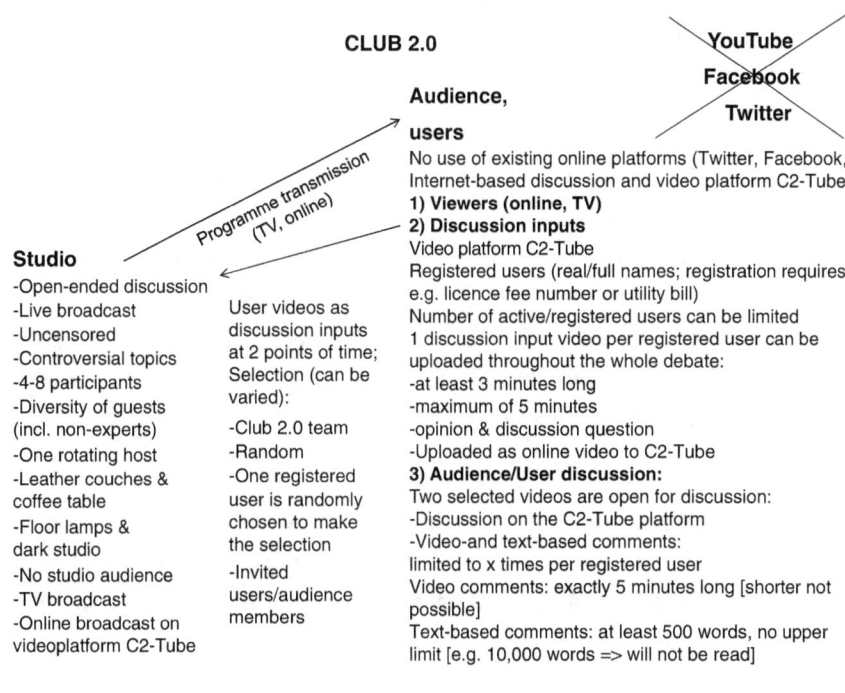

FIGURE 7.1 Concept of Club 2.0

sphere. Public sphere communication is part of society's critical capacities. With the rise of authoritarian capitalism, we have witnessed intensifying attacks on critical capacities. Imagine Donald Trump sitting on the *Club 2.0* leather couch together with some of his hardest critics: In this situation, there is no Twitter that allows him to reduce interaction to throwing short sound bites into the anonymous virtual space from a distance. There is only face-to-face live discussion without escape, where claims and counterclaims are explored, ideologies are questioned, opposite opinions are given time to meet and clash, etc. *Club 2.0* would bring back a bit of dialectics into a one-dimensional world, in which the public sphere is under attack by authoritarian capitalism.

7.4 Conclusion

The philosophy of technology is very frequently associated with Martin Heidegger. Anders has in contrast and opposition to Heidegger elaborated a critical theory of technology. For Anders, technology is not simply a world of tools. Capitalism and imperialism are themselves world machines for the accumulation of capital and power that shape and are shaped by machines reciprocally. Anders allows us to critically analyse how the technological fetishism associated with the Promethean gap takes on new forms today, such as that of digital positivism, big data fetishism, or post-humanist ideology.

In his analysis of commercial television and radio, Anders stresses aspects of labour, ideology and their alternatives. Today, the users of social media are what Anders termed homeworkers. Their use of platforms such as Google, YouTube and Facebook are digital labour that produces a big data commodity that is sold for enabling targeted advertising. The world of the Internet appears to have democratised communications, but it is today shaped by new power asymmetries in the online attention economy that features new forms of banalisation, unilateralism, di-vidualism, sensationalism, and anti-sensationalism.

Anders stresses that the interaction between technology, capitalism and imperialism generates annihilatory potentials. Given that capitalism and imperialism continue to exist and today tend to take on authoritarian forms, what Anders termed annihilism (annihilatory nihilism) remains a constant threat.

At the international level, Günther Anders's work has thus far remained rather un-discovered, which has to do with the fact that his principal work *Die Antiquiertheit des Menschen* is yet to be published in English. Anders's works remind us that confronting the negative dialectics of contemporary society requires critical intellectuals and political praxis.

Literature

Anders, Günther. 2016. "On Promethean Shame." In *Prometheanism: Technology, Digital Culture and Human Obsolescence*, edited by Christopher John Müller, 29–95. London: Rowman & Littlefield International.

——— 1980———. 1980a. *Die Antiquiertheit des Menschen 2. Über die Zerstörung des Lebens im Zeitalter der dritten industriellen Revolution*. Munich: C. H. Beck.

——— Pérez 1980———. 1980b. *The Obsolescence of Man, Volume II: On the Destruction of Life in the Epoch of the Third Industrial Revolution*. Translated by Josep Monter Pérez. https://libcom.org/files/ObsolescenceofManVol%20IIGunther%20Anders.pdf.

——— Bischof 1962———. 1962/2014. "Theses for the Atomic Age." In *The Life and Work of Günther Anders: Émigré, Iconoclast, Philosopher, Man of Letters*, edited by Günter Bischof, Jason Dawsey and Bernhard Fetz, 187–194. Innsbruck: Studienverlag.

——— 1956———. 1956. *Die Antiquiertheit des Menschen 1: Über die Seele im Zeitalter der zweiten industriellen Revolution*. Munich: C. H. Beck.

Bryce, Emma. 2017. "Cancer Vs. The Machine: How to Personalise Treatment Using Computing Power. Jasmine Fisher Is Reverse Engineering Cancer." *Wired Online*, March 9.

Fromm, Erich. 1942/2001. *The Fear of Freedom*. Abingdon: Routledge.

Fuchs, Christian. 2017a. *Social Media: A Critical Introduction*, 2nd ed. London: Sage.

——— 2017———. 2017b. "Sustainability and Community Networks." *Telematics and Informatics 34* (2): 628–639.

——— 2016———. 2016. *Reading Marx in the Information Age: A Media and Communication Studies Perspective on Capital Volume I*. New York: Routledge.

——— 2012———. 2012. "Dallas Smythe Today – The Audience Commodity, the Digital Labour Debate, Marxist Political Economy and Critical Theory. Prolegomena to a Digital Labour Theory of Value." *tripleC: Communication, Capitalism & Critique 10* (2): 692–740. doi:https://doi.org/10.31269/triplec.v10i2.443.

——— Röpcke 2002———. 2002. "Zu einigen Parallelen und Differenzen im Denken von Günther Anders und Herbert Macuse." In *Geheimagent der Masseneremiten – Günther Anders*, edited by Dirk Röpcke and Raimund Bahr, 113–127. St. Wolfgang: Edition Art & Science.

Hesiod. 2006. *Theogony. Works and Days. Testimonia*. Cambridge, MA: Harvard University Press.

Kollanyi, Bence, Philip N. Howard and Samuel C. Woolley. 2016. *Bots and Automation over Twitter during the Third U.S. Presidential Debate*. Accessed August 14, 2020. http://blogs.oii.ox.ac.uk/politicalbots/wp-content/uploads/sites/89/2016/10/Data-Memo-Third-Presidential-Debate.pdf.

Kraft, Daniel. 2017. "*Quantified Self to Quantified Health: How Tech Helps Doctors Fill Gaps in Patient Records*." *Wired Online*, March 9.

Kurzweil, Raymond. 2005. *The Singularity Is Near*. London: Viking Penguin.

Liessmann, Konrad Paul. 2014. "Between the Chairs: Günther Anders – Philosophy's Outsider." In *The Life and Work of Günther Anders: Émigré, Iconoclast, Philosopher, Man of Letters*, edited by Günter Bischof, Jason Dawsey and Bernhard Fetz, 73–82. Innsbruck: Studienverlag.

Marcuse, Herbert. 1969. "Repressive Tolerance." In *A Critique of Pure Tolerance*, 81–123. Boston: Beacon Press.

——— 1964 ———. 1964. *One-Dimensional Man*. London: Routledge.

Molden, Berthold. 2014. "Günther Anders as a Transnational Intellectual in the 1960s." In *The Life and Work of Günther Anders: Émigré, Iconoclast, Philosopher, Man of Letters*, edited by Günter Bischof, Jason Dawsey and Bernhard Fetz, 59–69. Innsbruck: Studienverlag.

Marx, Karl. 1867. *Capital Volume I*. London: Penguin.

Norris, Robert S., and Hans M. Kristensen. 2010. "Global Nuclear Weapons Inventories, 1945–2010." *Bulletin of the Atomic Scientists 66* (4): 77–83

Mayer-Schönberger, Viktor, and Kenneth Cukier. 2013. *Big Data. A Revolution That Will Transform How We Live, Work and Think*. London: Murray.

Medeiros, João. 2016. "*Europe's Hottest Startups 2016: Paris*." *Wired Online*, September 12.

Smythe, Dallas W. 1981. *Dependency Road: Communications, Capitalism, Consciousness, and Canada*. Norwood, NJ: Ablex.

——— 1977———. 1977. "Communications: Blindspot of Western Marxism." *Canadian Journal of Political and Social Theory 1* (3): 1–27.

——— 1951———. 1951. "The Consumer's Stake in Radio and Television." *The Quarterly of Film, Radio and Television 6* (2): 109–128.

Steadman, Ian. 2013. "*Big Data and the Death of the Theorist*." *Wired Online*, January 25.

Stockholm International Peace Research Institute (SIPRI). 2016. *Global Nuclear Weapons: Downsizing but Modernizing*. Accessed on August14, 2020. https://www.sipri.org/media/press-release/2016/global-nuclear-weapons-downsizing-modernizing.

Temperton, James. 2015. *Bristol Is Making a Smart City for Actual Humans*. *Wired Online*, March 17.

Tiffin, Richard. 2015. "*Boost Agriculture with Big Data*." *Wired Online*, March 2.

Chapter Eight
Jean-Paul Sartre as social theorist of communication. A theoretical engagement with "Critique of Dialectical Reason"

8.1 Introduction

8.2 Language and communication in society

8.3 Communication in capitalism

8.4 Ideology and reification

8.5 Conclusion

Literature

8.1 Introduction

Jean-Paul Sartre was a public intellectual who made use of modern media for public and political interventions. As a writer, the theatre and the newspaper were beside the book the media of his preferred use. He also appeared on radio and television but was much more sceptical of these media types (Scriven 1993). Sartre did not just make use of the media to communicate publicly but also contributed to theorising communication. This chapter focuses on his *Critique of Dialectical Reason* (*CDR*). It asks: How can Sartre's *Critique of Dialectical Reason* inform a critical theory of communication?

CDR is a two-volume book that in its English edition has a total of 1,304 pages. The French original of volume 1 was published in 1960, volume 2 posthumously in 1985 after Sartre's death in 1980. *In Search for a Method* (*SM*) is an accompanying text published as a separate book. This total of around 1,500 pages shows Sartre at the height of his dialectical, Marxist phase of development.

In her Sartre-biography, Annie Cohen-Solal (2005) argues that the work of Sartre on his major philosophical books always reflected political experiences. Between 1950 and 1956, Sartre was particularly close to the French Communist Party (PCF). This period started at the beginning of the Korean War. After the Soviet military clampdown of the Hungarian revolution, Sartre strongly criticised the PCF and argued that communism needed to be de-Stalinised (see Cohen-Solal 2005, 329; Sartre 1968). For Sartre, a period "of general reassessment" followed after 1956 and he embarked on "the production of a theoretical work" (Cohen-Solal 2005, 375), the *Critique of Dialectical Reason*.

In his foreword to the 2004 English edition of *CDR*'s first volume (*CDR1*), Frederic Jameson remarks that *Critique of Dialectical Reason* has not achieved the attention it deserves. James argues that this circumstance has to do with the popularity of (post-)structuralism, the unfinished character of the book, and especially its "notorious stylistic difficulty" (xiii) and "occasional unreadability" (xiv). *CDR* is "difficult to penetrate even by Sartre's standards of complexity" (Cox 2008, 52). When mentioning Sartre, poststructuralists such as Foucault, Derrida, Lyotard, and Deleuze focused on stressing "they were *not* like Sartre" (Churchill and Reynolds 2014, 218). Poststructuralism has not just degraded Hegel and Marx, but also Sartre.

There is the relatively widespread assumption that Sartre wrote *CDA* under the influence of drugs and that it is, therefore, a weird book. Often, this claim keeps individuals from reading *CDA*. In reality, it might just be an excuse of having to avoid the difficulty and intellectual dialectic of torture and pleasure experienced when reading *CDA*. It is an intelligent strategy and an excuse for not having to take serious *CDA*. It is true that Sartre was taking large amounts of the amphetamines Corydrane and Orthédrine while writing *CDA*. This stimulant was unlike opiates and cannabis. It helped Sartre to think and write fast and focus lots of time to his work. Sartre said that it helped him to adapt the speed of and time committed to writing to his speed of thinking (De Beauvoir 1984, 174, 318–319, 328). But the pills did not alter or manipulate his state of mind, which is why the assumption that *CDA* is a silly, unserious, drug-infused book is a prejudice used by people as an excuse for not reading, engaging with, discussing, and writing about the book.

Although Sartre in the *Critique* makes an important contribution to theorising communication, this work has been by and large ignored in communication theory. Sartre is hardly mentioned both in the *Encyclopedia of Communication Theory* (Littlejohn and Foss 2009) and *The International Encyclopedia of Communication Theory and Philosophy* (Jensen and Craig 2016). Discussions of Sartre in the context of communication theory tend to focus on *Being and Nothingness* or Sartre's relation to Merelau-Ponty. *CDR* as Sartre's opus magnum has thus far remained rather undiscovered in communication theory. There are interesting exceptions, such as Peck (2002, 2006), who argues that Sartre can help media and cultural theory to avoid separations of culture and the economy and to overcome the gap between Political Economy of Communication and Cultural Studies. The lack of attention given to *CDR* certainly has to do with the difficulty of the book's style and language, which has resulted in the circumstance that hardly anyone has read it in the field of media and communication studies. On the one hand, it looks like scholars are intellectually too lazy to invest the time and patience needed to read Sartre's *Critique*. On the other hand, many seem to see Sartre's dialectic as irrelevant and too complicated. This lack of engagement with Sartre in communication theory is, however, a weakness because Sartre's book can be an important inspiration for a critical, dialectical theory of communication. This chapter is a contribution to the illumination of the role of communication in Sartre's Marxist theory works.

Also, within Sartre scholarship, only a little attention has been given to communication. In the English *Sartre Dictionary* (Cox 2008), there are no entries for language and communication. In the French *Dictionnaire Sartre* (Noudelmann and Philippe 2004), there is no entry for "communication" and a three-page entry for "langue" (Tamassia 2004). The latter dictionary item's main message is that "Sartre never wrote a systematic linguistic theory nor did he develop a true philosophy of language" and that Sartre's interest in culture was primarily "focused on literary language" (Tamassia 2004, 274, translation from French). The few published works on Sartre and language have indeed largely focused on Sartre and literature and in his early philosophical works (see e.g., Anderson 1996; Busch 1999, chapter 4; Berendzen 2006; Busch 2010; Clarke 1999; Hung 2015; Leak 2008; Rae 2009). Although there are important exceptions that acknowledge the importance of language in *CDR* (e.g., Anderson 2002), the widely dominating view is that Sartre, including the Sartre of CDR, "has no explicit philosophy of language" and communication (Flynn 1997, 228).

It is evident that there has thus far not been much interest in Sartre as a contributor to a critical, dialectic theory of communication. In Sartre's works on dialectical Marxist theory, there are widely overlooked elements that can inform such a theory. The goal of this chapter is to analyse Sartre's understanding of communication and language in *CDR* and to discuss the book's relevance to the critical analysis of media, communication and society.

Whereas Sartre's earlier works such as *Being and Nothingness* were by Marxist critics seen as "idealistic mystification" (Marcuse 1948, 330) and as reducing "human phenomena to one level", the level of individual consciousness (Lukács 1949, 261), *Critique of Dialectical Reason* marked a profound change, namely Sartre's turn towards humanist Marxism (Spencer 2017, 127). Sartre shifted "his focus from consciousness to *praxis* (roughly, purposive human activity in its socioeconomic field)" (Flynn 2014, 331).

From "the first page of volume one to the last page of volume two, the *Critique* is self-consciously bound up with the fate of Marxism" (Aronson 2010, 274). Earlier critics such as Lukács (1984, 395, translation from German) therefore expressed "greatest respect" for "Sartre's turn to Marxism"[1]. *Critique of Dialectical Reason* promises to be one of the theoretical works that contain widely disregarded elements that can inform the establishment of a critical, dialectical, Marxist-humanist theory of communication.

Critique of Dialectical Reason is a work of social ontology (Flynn 2014, 335) and therefore has, as will be repeatedly pointed out in this chapter, parallels to Lukács' forgotten opus magnum *Ontologie des gesellschaftlichen Seins* (*Ontology of Societal Being*) (see Fuchs 2016, chapter 2). Bernard-Henri Lévy (2003, 436) remarks that Sartre's Critique "is reminiscent of the Marxism of Lukács" because both Lukács and the late Sartre were Hegelian Marxists.

Section 2 discusses Sartre's analysis of language and communication in society. Section 3 focuses on how Sartre can inform our understanding of communication in capitalism. Section 4 gives attention to Sartre's analysis of ideology. Some conclusions are presented in Section 5

8.2 Language and communication in society

The Sartre of *Search for a Method* (*SM*) and *Critique of Dialectical Reason* (*CDR*) wanted to combine Marxism and existentialism in order to provide an analysis of the mediation of society and the individual (Flynn 2014, 326). The task was to "reconquer man within Marxism" (*SM*, 83). The fusion of existentialism and Marxism that Sartre has in mind in these books seek the human "*where he is*, at his work, in his home, in the street" (*SM*, 28).

Critique of Dialectical Reason is a dialectical, humanist, critical theory of society and capitalism. Sartre starts by working out the foundations of a practice-oriented social theory. "We repeat with Marxism: there are only men and real relations between men" (*SM*, 76). For Sartre, the group mediates between the individual and society. Group relations form "a screen between the individual and the general interests of his class"

---

1 Although there are strong parallels between Sartre's *CDA* and Lukács' *Ontology of Societal Being* and *History and Class Consciousness*, Sartre seems to have never forgiven Lukács for the latter's initial critique. In the talk "Marxism and Existentialism" that he gave in 1961, one year after the publication of *CDA1*, Sartre (2016, 5–10) criticises Lukács as idealist objectivist who reduces human subjects to "'carriers' of economic relations" and "obliterates all subjectivity" (5).

(*SM*, 67). For Sartre, it is important to analyse how "collective objects" are grounded in "the concrete activity of individuals" (*SM*, 77).

Praxis

Praxis is one of the key concepts of Sartre's dialectic. He writes that "the dialectic is the rationality of *praxis*" (*CDR1*, 39). There is a "complex play of *praxis* and totalisation" (*CDR1*, 39). Praxis exists because humans want and need and desire to satisfy their needs that arise from the lack of something (*CDR1*, 79–88). Praxis "makes the environment into a totality" (*CDR1*, 85). Praxis is "directly revealed *by its end*", which means that there are efforts "in accordance with present givens in light of the future objective" (*CDR1*, 549). Praxis is the "dialectical organisation of means with a view to satisfying need" (*CDR1*, 736). For Sartre, transcendence as the process of going beyond current conditions towards the future, synthetic unity, totalisation, and dialectical reason are important features of praxis (*CDR2*, 385). Praxis "as a transcendence (and preservation) of *hexis*, creates totalization – as an ever open, never finished, spirality of temporalization" (*CDR2*, 347). Praxis goes beyond an inert, stable condition (hexis) and transforms it dialectically by at the same time going beyond and preserving the old condition in a new condition. This process is open. Therefore, any praxis as change is a change of society taking place in time (and space) as dialectical spirals. In Hegel's language, we can say that any social condition has contradictions, which means there is a negative condition. Change in society means praxis brings about the negation of the negation, which involves determinate negation that posits a new sublated (*aufgehoben*) condition that preserves and eliminates the old condition and lifts it up to a new level where we can find emergent qualities.

Marx, Gramsci, and the Yugoslav Praxis School use the notion of praxis different from Sartre. What Sartre terms "praxis" is for them "practice". They see praxis as a practice that reproduces or aims at creating a commons-based society. For Gramsci, praxis aims at "absolute humanism" (Gramsci 1971, 417). Marx's (1845a, 1845b) first, second, third, and eight theses on Feuerbach stress the revolutionary character of praxis. Marx defines praxis as "revolutionary" and "practical-critical" activity (Marx, 1845b, 3). Praxis is a political practice that aims at creating a *"free community of free personalities"* (Petrović 1967, 133). These terminological differences do not imply fundamental disagreements on the level of the content of theory between Sartre and other philosophers of praxis.

The dialectic of structures and practices

Louis Althusser characterises Sartre's Marxist approach as "historicist humanism" that "takes the form of an exaltation of human freedom" (Althusser and Balibar 1970/2009, 158). Althusser overlooks the dialectic of structures/system/social field (the practico-inert) and practices (praxis) in Sartre's *Critique*, which allows him to attack Sartre incorrectly as a humanist idealist. Like Marx, Sartre bases his theory on a dialectic of structuration and practices. In society, there is a dialectic of practices and structures/systems, products and production. "A product of his product, fashioned by his work and by the social conditions of production, man *at the same time* exists in the milieu of his products and furnishes the substance of the 'collectives' which consume him" (*SM*, 79). The human being is "*at once the product of his own product and a historical agent*" (*SM*, 87). Sartre refers in this context to the well-known passage about the dialectic of humans making history and circumstances that shape and condition them from Marx's *Eighteenth Brumaire* (*CDR1*, 35) and Engels' letter to Borgius from 25 January 1894 (*SM*, 31). For Sartre, there is a dialectic of structures and practices in society. He sees the dialectic as constituting and constituted by humans: "man must be controlled by the dialectic in so far as he *creates* it, and *create* it in so far as he is controlled by it" (*CDR1*, 36). The human being is "at once both the product of his own product and a historical agent" (*SM*, 87).

In the context of the analysis of the dialectic in society, Sartre speaks of the "dialectic of the subjective and the objective" as "the joint necessity of 'the internalization of the external' and 'the externalization of the internal'" (*SM*, 97; an almost similar formulation can be found in *CDR1*, 71). Praxis is for Sartre the internalisation of the practico-inert structures and the creation and reproduction of these structures in work processes that externalise and objectify human energy and thoughts in products and structures. The group is the level where the dialectic of subjectivity and objectivity, the individual and society, is organised through practices. Sartre does here not mention the role of communication. Elsewhere he argues that the human is "externalizing himself in the materiality of language" (*SM*, 113). Social production is the practice that externalises human ideas and energy which result in products. In his earlier works from the late 1940s, Sartre already conceived of communication as practice: "Communication does not exist – it must be brought about" (Sartre 1992, 9).

Work and communication

Humans are characterised by praxis as the capacity of and the project to go "beyond a situation" that defines them (*SM*, 91) and the capacity of "transcending the given toward the field of possibles" (93) so that the negative conditioning by structures opens up the possibility for creating that "what *has not yet* been" (92). Humans transcend the situation they find themselves in "by means of work and action" (*SM*, 99). "What makes this undertaking 'existentialist' is its emphasis on the project of the labourer" (Flynn 2014, 331). Work is for Sartre the key form of praxis. He stresses: "The essential discovery of Marxism is that labour, as a historical reality and as the utilisation of particular tools in an already determined social and material situation, is the real foundation of the organisation of social relations" (*CDR1*, 152, footnote 35).

Work is, as both Sartre and Lukács (1984 1986) stress, the model of social production. There are strong parallels between Sartre's (*CDR1*, 90) formulation that work is "the original *praxis*" and Lukács' (1978, 46) argument that work is the "model for all social practice". Both Lukács (1984 1986) and Sartre (*CDR1*) see work as purposeful action where humans achieve goals with defined means. Lukács speaks in this context of teleological positing, Sartre of a means/end-relation (*CDR1*, 90).

Humans produce products in social relations and also produce and reproduce the social relations they are part of. Communication is the process of the production of human sociality and social relations (Fuchs 2020). It is the process that guides social production. There is a dialectic of work and communication (Fuchs 2020): Humans communicate in production. Work has a communicative character. And communication is productive in that it creates and reproduces social relations and produces an understanding of the world. Communication is a work process. At the level of practices (or what Sartre calls "praxis"), there is a dialectic of communication and work that organises social production (Fuchs 2020).

Mediation and communication

Sartre argues that human relations are not just dyadic relations but always ternary relations where a "human mediator" acting as "third party" links "two individuals who are ignorant of each other" and actualise "the reciprocity of their relation" (*CDR1*, 106). The "unity of a dyad can be *realised* only within a totalisation performed from outside by a third party" (*CDR1*, 115). A group is for Sartre not a "binary relation" but a "ternary relation" (*CDR1*, 374).

If we think of a party where two people who do not know each other meet and become lifelong friends, it becomes evident how humans mediate other human beings' communication. Human mediation is less evident in situations such as when two friends communicate on Facebook or face-to-face at home. The private home, the family, etc. are social systems and collective human actors that influence and shape everyday human communication and are shaped by social systems and structures. Facebook is not simply an Internet platform or communication technology, but a for-profit company that is founded on class relations between owners and digital workers (Fuchs, 2021). Media and communication technologies are techno-social systems grounded in social relations and human action. Sartre stresses the importance of concrete human beings who shape social systems, techno-social systems, subsystems of society, and society as a totality. All of these social realms shape besides single individuals (who act as communicators and human mediators) the communication process.

The communication process can potentially result in emergent sociality, which means that humans who communicate create a new social form (such as a friendship, a community, an organisation, etc.) that plays a role in society and thereby feeds back on society and creates impacts in society. Figure 8.1 visualises these aspects of the communication process based on Sartre. The model indicates that humans, social systems, techno-social systems (such as communication technologies), subsystems of society (such as the economy, the political system, culture), and society as a totality are forms of sociality that act as mediators of communication.

The filled arrows indicate a necessary relationship, while the striped arrows symbolise a potential relationship. Any human needs to communicate in order to live in society. And any communication needs a form of social mediation. These are aspects of society's necessities and human needs. But not any communication results in emergent sociality and impacts on society. Emergent sociality is a potential but not a necessary feature of communication.

Sartre argues that the human relationship involves one side "being an object" for other humans and the one side's "subjectivity getting its objective reality through them as the interiorisation of my human objectivity" (*CDR1*, 105). In any social relation, humans sensually perceive each other mutually by processes such as hearing, seeing, speaking, bodily movements, touching, feeling, smelling, and tasting. One side becomes an object of perception of the other side and actively perceives the other side. And on the side of the other actor, the same process takes place in a mutual and reciprocate manner so that each involved individual is subject and object of perception and communication. The mutual symbolic interaction between humans in the social process is the communication process. In *CDR*, Sartre does not term this process communication but rather speaks of praxis as "the dialectic as the development of living

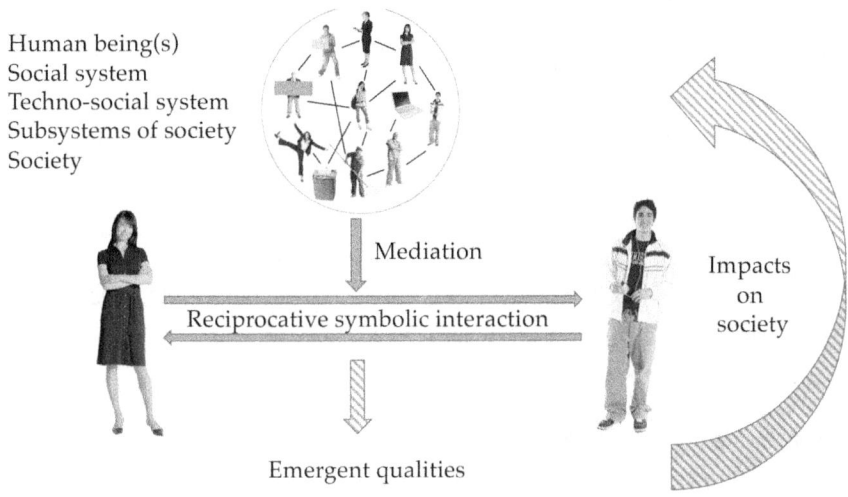

FIGURE 8.1 A model of the communication process based on Sartre's critical theory of dialectical reason

action" that is not an "*a priori* communication engineered by a kind of Great Telephone Operator" (*CDR1*, 106). But Sartre's terminology is here somehow ambivalent because he also speaks of the "practical mediation" that enables "them to communicate" (*CDR1*, 104), which affirms the category of communication. Sartre wants to foreground the role of humans in social relations and is careful not to overstress the role of communication technologies. He stresses the human and social character of technologies. Communication technologies are not simply tools, media, or machines. They are techno-social systems. Communication is a human and social process, so by using the term communication one does not automatically create a technological determinist concept of the social.

The practico-inert and language

The practico-inert is an important category in Sartre's theory. "In his *Critique*, as just mentioned, Sartre reserves an ontological place for structure and structuralist studies in the domain of the 'practico-inert' and the analytic reasoning that it supports" (Flynn 2006, 116). Structures and systems are an objectification of past practices. That's why Sartre calls them the practico-inert. He also speaks of worked matter in order to signify that social structures are the results of human work. They are inertia emerging from social practices. By the practico-inert, Sartre means "the sedimented prior praxes that both limit and facilitate present praxes the way natural language limits and facilitates speech acts" (Flynn 2006, 112).

Sartre situates language in the realm of the practico-inert. "Ontologically, language belongs to the category of 'being-for-others' in *Being and Nothingness* and to the domain of the 'practico-inert' in his *Critique of Dialectical Reason*. [...] Language, on this account, is a basic technique for appropriating the world rather than the means of constituting it, as poststructuralists would insist" (Flynn 2006, 111). Language is a structure that enables, conditions, and constrains communicative practices. We can say that there is a dialectic of language and communication, the structural and the practice aspect of information in society.

Language and communication make their first important appearance in *Critique of Dialectical Reason* in section 2.1 of book I in Volume 1. Book I's second chapter, to which the section in question belongs to, discusses human relations as mediation. Sartre stresses the role of words and language in communication. Words "carry the projects of the Other into me and they carry my own projects into the Other" (*CDR1*, 98). "Language might well be studied on the same lines as money: as a circulating, inert materiality, which unifies dispersal; in fact this is partly what philology does. Words live off the death of men, they come together through men; whenever I form a sentence its meaning escapes from me, is stolen from me; meanings are changed for everyone by each speaker and each day; the meanings of the very words in my mouth are changed by others." (*CDR1*, 98). "'Human relations' are in fact inter-individual structures whose common bond is language and which actually exist at every moment of History" (*CDR1*, 99).

For Sartre, language is a system and totality where we find a dialectic of words as moments and the language system as a totality: "every word is the whole language" (*SM*, 172; see also Sartre 1974/2008, 51–52). "There can be no doubt that language is in one sense an inert totality. But this materiality is also a constantly developing organic totalisation. Nor can there be any doubt that speech separates as much as it unifies; or that it reflects the cleavages, the stratifications and the inertias of the group; or that dialogues are partly dialogues of the deaf" (*CDR1*, 98). Language as a structure is a medium that acts as a tool: "language is a *tool* as soon as I speak or listen to someone else" (Sartre 1963/2012, 276). The "totality of language as a set of internal relations between objective senses is given, for and to everyone; words are simply specifications expressed against the background of language; the sentence is an actual totalisation where every word defines itself in relation to the others, to the context and to the entire language, as an integral part of a whole" (*CDR1*, 99).

Language is a totality that lives through practice: "language contains every word and every word is to be understood in terms of language as a whole; it contains the whole of language and reaffirms it. But this fundamental totality can only be praxis itself in so far as it is directly expressed to others; language as the practical relation of one man to another is praxis, and praxis is always language (whether truthful or deceptive) because it cannot take place without signifying itself" (*CDR1*, 99). Using "a word is praxis, since it tends to create a group. For the word tends simultaneously to mediate and create reciprocities. [...] communication is effected not through the word, but by reference to the word: at once as an institution, as a direct relation to the context, and as a serialized third party" (*CDR2*, 426).

The word is an "institution, an inertia", a "tool", by which "I make myself inert and act upon the inert" (*CDR2*, 426). "I make myself inert by speaking, but in order to awaken inertia the other" (*CDR2*, 426). The word is "utilized *in a praxis* [...]; it awakens the inert in the other, inasmuch as this inert may be the beginning of a praxis: *order*" (*CDR2*, 426). When Sartre says that language is praxis and praxis is language, what he means is that the communication process is a productive practice that produces and reproduces a group, that is sociality. Sartre does not explicitly say so, but the implication of this conceptualisation is that communication is a form of work.

For Sartre, language and communication are not immaterial, but part of human materiality. "Of course, language is materiality, action is effort" (*CDR1*, 429). "But language cannot have come to man, since it presupposes itself: for an individual to discover his isolation, his alienation, for him to suffer from silence or, for that matter, to become integrated into some collective undertaking, his relation to others, as manifested in and by the materiality of language, must constitute him in his own reality" (*CDR1*, 99). The same understanding can be found in Raymond Williams' cultural materialism and Lukács' ontology. Williams (1989, 206) conceives of "cultural practice as from the beginning social and material". Lukács (1986, 169, translation from German) argues that language is an organ, medium, and complex that enables the reproduction of society, the "preservation of the species within a constant change of all subjective and objective moments of reproduction".

Sartre worked out a dialectical social theory that allows us to not only conceive of the social and society as a dialectic of subject and object as well as praxis and the practico-inert but also to ground a dialectical understanding of communication and language. There is a dialectic of communication and language as part of the dialectic of subject and object, praxis and the practico-inert.

Language not just mediates social relations, but the ensemble of social relations that humans are part of also shapes their language and the use of language and words. For example, members of a certain socio-economic class develop in a certain region develop a particular accent and give particular emphasis to certain words in their language-use. Sartre argues that language is shaped by human beings' "*insertion in the world*" (Sartre 1974/2008, 274) and "*being-in-the-world*" (Sartre 1974/2008, 275). Language is a "materiality which mediates between men to the extent that men are mediator between its different aspects (a materiality that I have elsewhere called practico-inert)" (Sartre 1974/2008, 271). Sartre here refers back to *CDA* and argues that language can only act as a medium of social relations because social relations and structures, the practico-inert, is a medium that shapes language and language-use. There is an interaction, a dialectic, of language and society.

A critical theory does not stop at the level of society in general. It also has to analyse capitalism as a concrete social formation. The next section, therefore, discusses the relevance of Sartre's approach for the analysis of language and communication in capitalism.

8.3 Communication in capitalism

Direct and indirect communication

The development of "particular systems of ideas" stands in the context of the development of the productive forces and the relations of production (*SM*, 112). In class society, culture, language and communication therefore often have an antagonistic character. "Thus the general categories of the culture, the particular systems, and the language which expresses them are already the objectification of a class, the reflection of conflicts, latent or declared, and the particular manifestation of alienation" (*SM*, 113).

For Sartre (*CDR1*), there are two major forms of mediation. The first one is the series. It is characterised by instrumentality, impersonality, domination, imitation, separation, isolation, massification, and interchangeability (*CDR1*, 256–269). Reciprocity, freedom, co-operation, fraternity, community, synthesis, and union characterise the second form of mediation – the fused group (*CDR1*, 345–404). In the case of a series, the practico-inert dominates and mediates praxis, whereas it is the other way around in the case of a fused group. In a fused group, individuals become "common individuals" because of fraternity, which is the obligation "to help one another in general" or in the context of a task or action (*CDR1*, 437).

Sartre distinguishes between direct social relations that are based on presence "permitting the immediate establishment of relations of reciprocity between two individuals, given the society's techniques and tools" (*CDR1*, 270) and indirect gatherings defined by absence so that humans cannot talk to each other (*CDR1*, 270–276). Sartre here draws a distinction between reciprocal communication on the one hand that can take place face-to-face or in a mediated manner (e.g. telephone, Internet) and one-way mass communication on the other hand. Interpreting Sartre, we can distinguish between direct and indirect social relations. Both can take on the form of a series and a reciprocating form (see Table 8.1).

Sartre discusses the radio audience as an example for a series with indirect communication and absence: "the mere fact of *listening to the radio*, that is to say, of listening to a particular broadcast at a particular time, establishes a serial relation of *absence* between the different listeners. In this way, the practico-inert object not only produces a unity of individuals outside themselves in inorganic matter, but also determines them in separation and, in so far as they are separate, ensures *their communication through alterity* (and the same applies to all 'mass media')" (*CDR1*, 271). The "radio listeners [...] constitute a *series* in that they are listening to the common voice which constitutes each of them in his identity as an *Other*" (*CDR1*, 276).

Communication and power

Sartre points out that communication stands in the context of power. When "I listen to a broadcast, the relation between the broadcaster and myself is not a human one: in effect, I am passive in relation to what is being said, to the political commentary on the news, etc. This passivity, in an activity which develops on every level and over many years, can to some extent be resisted: I can write, protest, approve, congratulate,

TABLE 8.1 Examples of two Sartrean forms of direct and indirect social relations

	Direct social relation	Indirect social relation
Series	Individuals waiting at a bus stop	Audience listening to a radio broadcast
Reciprocative group	Friends meeting and chatting in a bar	Friends chatting via e-mail, individuals discussing via an e-mail list

threaten, etc. But it must be noted at once that these activities will carry weight only if a majority (or a considerable minority) of listeners who do not know me do likewise. So that, in this case, reciprocity is a gathering with one voice" (*CDR1*, 271).

Sartre characterises an indirect serial relation that is based on absence, such as a radio broadcast, as "a reifying relation in which the voice is given as *praxis* and constitutes the listener as the object of *praxis*" (*CDR1*, 272). One can switch off an "ideological broadcast", but this is merely an individual negation that does not negate the speaker's voice (*CDR1*, 272). It is impossible that one directly responds. One cannot convince, "*one by one*, the listeners all of whom it [the radio broadcast] exhorts in the common isolation which I create for all of them as their inert bond" (*CDR1*, 273).

Sartre does not like techno-determinists such as Marshal McLuhan, Martin Heidegger, or Friedrich Kittler assume that the technological features of the means of communication determine these technologies' use and effects in society. But he points out that one-way communication technologies such as the radio, the television, and the newspaper can be appropriated and centralised by capitalists and/or governments and/or cultural hegemony in order to centralise communication power. "Moreover, radio stations represent the point of view of the government or the special interests of a group of capitalists; so the listeners' activities (about programmes or about the opinions that are expressed) are unlikely to have any effect" (*CDR1*, 271).

Sartre argues that centralised communication is a form of alienation: the "negation of direct reciprocity is centralisation, as the necessity that two given sub-groups whose practices are complementary should go through 'the departments' or 'the Council' in order to adapt their actions reciprocally. The alienation of indirect reciprocity is that mediation is itself a modifying action on this reciprocity" (*CDR1*, 614).

For Sartre, public speaking is different from broadcasting and mediated communication: "Thus the public speaker really does address us, in that both individual reciprocity (*I* shout out my approval or my criticism) and collective reciprocity (we applaud him or shout our disapproval at him) are perfectly conceivable. All listeners to the public speaker are "in a position to contradict or even insult him" (*CDR1*, 272).

Democratic and capitalist communication

Sartre distinguishes between democratic and capitalist forms of television:

1.) Democratic television/communications means "total distribution and popular culture" where "production is intensified for culture. An interior practico-inert" (*CDR2*, 440).
2.) Television "in a capitalist society" is "an organ of restricted distribution of non-vulgarized bourgeois culture" (*CDR2*, 440). "But mass production creates the mass media. So class and government propaganda cannot ignore these. Production thus creates a practico-inert: TV as a talking machine, and this talking machine demands its own *voice* in the present situation of capital. And its voice is governmental, and a class ideology. It demands its own voice, and its institutionalization. It is the machine that demands its own unity. On this basis: either the State directly, or interchangeable private sets (competition barely differentiates them). There are accidents, of course: most of the directors harassed by McCarthyism worked in TV" (*CDR2*, 440). "On this basis, there is TV thought, TV behaviour, etc., which belong to the practico-inert. It is simultaneously other-direction and senseless discourse" (*CDR2*, 441).

It is, of course, possible to organise a communication system such as a radio or television station in a non-capitalist manner. The profit imperative can be dropped. Workers and audience members can co-own and co-govern the station. There can be formats that allow stronger audience participation. Also, public service media are an example of non-capitalist organisation forms of radio and televisions.

Sartre focuses much more on the analysis of the capitalist and alienated character of communication than on democratic and appropriated forms of communication. But his critique points towards what Williams (1976) calls democratic communications, means of communication that are for-public-benefit instead of for-private-profit, "means of participation and of common discussion" (134), and foundations of a cultural democracy" that combines public-service media, cultural co-operatives, and local media.

German critical theorists such as Max Horkheimer, Theodor W. Adorno, Herbert Marcuse, Walter Benjamin, Bert Brecht, and Hans Magnus Enzensberger are just like Sartre concerned about questions of the mass media's communication power. Brecht (1932/2000, 42) argued that the radio could be "the finest possible communication apparatus [...] if it understood how to receive as well as to transmit, how to let the listener speak as well as hear, how to bring him into a network instead of isolating him". Building on Brecht, Hans Magnus Enzensberger (1982, 62) distinguishes between emancipatory and repressive media use. Sartre, Brecht, and Enzensberger share the critique of centralised programme-production and distribution where there is "[o]ne transmitter, many receivers" (Enzensberger 1982, 62).

YouTube is not participatory culture, but serial communication

The question that arises from all of these approaches, including Sartre's, is if we automatically see the emancipation and democratisation of communication when it becomes possible that each receiver/consumer of information can transmit and produce information. The Internet and social media platforms pose such potentials for information prosumption (productive consumption). Thinkers such as Henry Jenkins (2008) therefore argue that the Internet advances participatory culture. But did capitalist Internet platforms such as YouTube, Facebook, Instagram, Twitter, really bring about a democratisation of culture and communication? Table 8.2 shows a list of the ten most-watched YouTube videos of all time.

YouTube's attention economy shows that making everyone a potential speaker does within a capitalist society not automatically bring about a democratic culture. Giving users the opportunity to comment, like, and repost content is a capitalist strategy of social media corporations that try to fix users' attention for long times on the platform in order to present targeted ads to them. "Participatory culture" has a capitalist purpose, namely the sale of targeted ads and the sale of commodities in general. Entertainment provided by for-profit media companies dominates YouTube. Eight of the ten most-watched videos on YouTube are music songs whose copyright is owned by one of the big-three music corporations Sony, Universal, and Warner. Attention power is asymmetrically distributed on YouTube and other social media platforms. Everyone can speak and produce, but not everyone is heard and seen. The everyday user is mostly invisible and unheard. Corporations, celebrities, and politicians are in contrast much more seen and heard than ordinary users on social media. YouTube uses targeted ads in order to yield profit. Corporate social media are first and foremost advertising platforms and capitalist ventures. A major use of social media is that capitalist corporations use social media for promoting their commodities via advertisements and publishing content.

Capitalist social media allow users to produce content and to talk to each other. But they remain forms of communication and information shape by what Sartre terms a series because the instrumental reason of capital and commodification shapes these

TABLE 8.2 The most viewed YouTube videos of all times (source: https://en.wikipedia.org/wiki/List_of_most-viewed_YouTube_videos, accessed on 16 February 2020)

Rank	Title	Type	Owner	Views
1	Luis Fonsi – Despacito	Music	Universal Music (Vivendi)	6.6 billion
2	Ed Sheeran – Shape of You	Music	Warner Music	4.6 billion
3	Pinkfong Kids' Songs & Stories – Baby Shark Dance	Children's music	SmartStudy (Samsung Publishing)	4.6 billion
4	Wiz Khalifa – See You Again	Music	Warner Music	4.4 billion
5	Masha and the Bear – Recipe for Disaster	Children's entertainment	Animaccord Animation Studio	4.2 billion
6	Mark Ronson – Uptown Funk	Music	Sony Music	3.8 billion
7	Psy – Gangnam Style	Music	YG Entertainment (distributed by Universal)	3.5 billion
8	Justin Bieber – Sorry	Music	Universal Music (Vivendi)	3.3 billion
9	Maroon 5 – Sugar	Music	Universal Music (Vivendi)	3.1 billion
10	Katy Perry – Roar	Music	Universal Music (Vivendi)	3.0 billion

platforms' logic. In addition, the individualism that aims at fostering capitalist consumerism (the purchase of commodities) is built into these platforms' technological structures. YouTube, Facebook, Twitter, Instagram, etc. afford that users have individual profiles, where they accumulate followers and likes. On the capitalist Internet, capitalism's economic logic translates at the cultural level into the accumulation of online reputation. Corporate social media are part of the cultural logic of digital capitalism. Facebook and Google control the majority of digital advertising revenue, which shows that there are duopolistic structures in this industry.

Enzensberger argues that for the creation of democratic communications "the elimination of capitalistic property relationships is a necessary but by no means sufficient condition" (Enzensberger 1982, 54–55). If users owned YouTube/Google, a democratic attention economy wouldn't be the automatic result. The capitalist logic of accumulation needs to be abolished in society at large and be replaced by the logic of the commons and the community in order to advance a democratic culture and economy. Platform co-operatives and public service Internet platforms are examples of non-capitalist organisation forms of digital media (Fuchs 2021). Platform co-operatives are Internet platforms that are owned and governed by a community of users and workers. Public service Internet platforms are platforms operated by public service media organisations for advancing public values such as democracy, education, political and cultural participation, and the public sphere. An alternative Internet is possible.

Sartre's distinction between the series and the group allows us to distinguish between different forms of the media. Instrumental reason rules capitalism. Capitalism instrumentalizes human labour and also our forms of communication in order to accumulate capital, political power, and cultural hegemony. Capitalism is not just a political and an economic system, but also an ideological formation that aims at instrumentalising human consciousness in the interest of the ruling capitalist class interest. The next section focuses on Sartre's concept of ideology.

8.4 Ideology and reification

Alienation and reification

Sartre argues that in capitalism, alienation is the result of the conflict between productive forces and relations of production (*SM*, 13–14) and "irreducible to an idea" (*SM*, 14). He writes that oppression, including racism, colonialism, slavery and any tyranny, consists "in treating the Other as an *animal*" (*CDR1*, 110) or "*like a dog*" (*CDR1*, 111). In alienation, the human being "subordinates the human to what is Other than" the human, which results in "the hatred" of the human being (*CDR1*, 181). For Sartre, reification is not "[a] metamorphosis of the individual into a thing" (*CDR1*, 176), but has to do with mechanical rigidity, alien laws, atomisation of the group so that it becomes a mechanical system (ibid.). Sartre argues that bourgeois humanism is an ideology that "identifies the bourgeois with man in opposition to the *other-species*, to the anti-human, the worker" (*CDR1*, 752). Also, racism is a bourgeois (anti-)humanism that defines the racialised group as the anti-human opposite of the human (752).

In respect to the working class, alienation means for Sartre that the worker is "a product of capitalism" and "works for wages and produces goods which are taken from him and uses industrial machinery which belongs to individuals or to private groups" in order to "produce [...] an expansion of capital" (*CDR1*, 309). An exploited class is "a totalised series of series" (*CDR1*, 309). The working class is characterised by the non-ownership of the conditions of production, including machines and other means of production (*CDR1*, 679). Workers are exchangeable. If they do not politically organise themselves, they are atoms and cogs in a socio-economic machine. They are non-owners. The property they produce is separate from them. For capitalism to work, there is a series of workers in every capitalist company. And the totality of all series is the working class. Class struggle means that the series is negated into a "*wholly active class, all of whose members are integrated into a single praxis*" (*CDR1*, 317). In socialism, "man will be his own product instead of the 'product of his product'" (*CDR1*, 320). For Sartre, the existence of classes has to do with scarcity (*CDR2*, 14), including the scarcity of time, means, knowledge (9).

Ideology

Sartre's approach to ideology is comparable to the one that Georg Lukács' (1971) takes in his famous book *History and Class Consciousness*. Lukács speaks of reification in general and the reification of consciousness. Also, Sartre sees reification operating at the level of human practices (exploitation, oppression) and consciousness (ideology).

In *Critique of Dialectical Reason*, Sartre does not give an explicit definition of ideology. But he argues that ideology is "imposed on the exploited class by the exploiting class by means of propaganda" (*CDR1*, 673). Sartre argues that the dominant class strives to use the media system for "diffusing its own ideology (i.e. the practical justification of its praxis)" (*CDR2*, 439). There is a parallel of Sartre here to Lukács' concept of ideology. Lukács stresses that "the emergence and diffusion of ideologies appears as the general characteristic of class societies" (Lukács 1984, 405, translation from German). For Sartre, alienation in class society also takes on the form of alienated language: "Many words, detached from objects, are adrift", humans "have a feeling that language does not quite belong to them" (Sartre 1963/2012, 276). Alternative speaking and an alternative language mean "a community which has forged a language of its own against the bourgeois tongue" (Sartre 1963/2012, 285).

Sartre (1974/2008) argues that ideology affirms (234) and is a weapon of the ruling class (235), masks and hides (251), and that emancipatory movements along with class society want to "abolish all ideology" (266). In *CDR2*, Sartre speaks of ideology as "false consciousness, that is as praxis that does not recognize itself" (*CDR2*, 294). There are parallels to Lukács' (1971) notions of reified consciousness and false consciousness, by which he, in general, refers to consciousness that "by-passes the essence of the evolution of society and fails to pinpoint it and express it adequately" (50) and in capitalism to consciousness that veils "the nature of bourgeois society" and is a form a deception aimed at ensuring the subordinated classes' consciousness remains "amorphous" (66).

Sartre's critique of ideology operates along multiple dimensions. We will discuss some example dimensions: analytical reason, advertising and consumer capitalism, racism, and Stalinism.

Analytical reason

Sartre opposes dialectical reason to *analytical reason*. The latter naturalises society and reduces "human relations to the functional relations of quantitative variables" (*CDR1*, 712). It is also atomistic (*CDR1*, 65), positivist (802), and guided by the logic of the natural sciences (827). This results in the claim that *"[t]his is how things are"* and that they cannot be changed, which is an "empirical irrationality" (712). Sartre sees in the assumption of a dialectic of nature a form of analytical reason. Sartre's critique of analytical reason as an ideology is parallel to Horkheimer and Adorno's critique of instrumental reason and Lukács' critique of reified consciousness.

In the Dialectic of Enlightenment, Horkheimer and Adorno (2002) argue that in capitalism, instrumental reason means that there are "instruments of power – language, weapons, and finally machines" (29). In capitalism, such instruments of power are, for example, the capitalist economy, positivism, the capitalist machinery, ideology, and the culture industry. "Reason serves as a universal tool for the fabrication of all other tools […] Reason's old ambition to be purely an instrument of purposes has finally been fulfilled" (Horkheimer and Adorno 2002, 23). Lukács (1971) criticises the logic of quantification as an aspect of capitalism's fetishist structure. It is part of the "nature of capitalism to" reduce "the phenomena to their purely quantitative essence, to their expression in numbers and numerical relations" (Lukács 1971, 6). Already Marx stressed the connection of capitalism and instrumental reason: "Time is everything, man is nothing; he is, at the most, time's carcase. Quality no longer matters. Quantity alone decides everything; hour for hour, day for day" (Marx, 1847, 127). There are parallels of Sartre's critique of analytical reasons to Marx, Lukács, and Horkheimer/Adorno. All of them oppose instrumental reason to dialectical reason.

Computational social science and big data analytics as analytical reason

In digital capitalism, computational social science and big data analytics have developed as new approaches that transform academia and science. The focus is on the collection and quantitative analysis of very large datasets from various sources such as the Internet or digitisation projects. "[B]ig data analytics strives to provide insight to enable business decisions from vast amounts of data which are often ambiguous, incomplete, conditional and inconclusive" (Ghavami 2020, 14). Paraphrasing Sartre, we can say that big data analytics reduces "human relations to the functional relations of quantitative variables" (*CDR1*, 712). Big data analytics cannot understand the qualitative features of social life, such as experience, ethics, motivations, fears, desires, morals, norms, etc. Big data analytics is a new form of positivism, digital positivism that constitutes, as Sartre says, an "empirical irrationality" (*CDR1*, 712).

Advertising and consumer capitalism

Sartre argues that propaganda "is the manipulation of series and of the masses as such" (*CDR1*, 642). He discusses *advertising* as an example of manipulated seriality. It is a form of mediation that creates an illusion (644). A group of experts becomes "a *definite power*" (645) that tries to create "alienated evaluations" (646), to turn individuals into "the instruments of well-organised collectives", which creates "total alienation" (649) and "a false totality" (650). These are general features of all ideology. It is specific for advertising that it tries to control consumption and distribution of commodities and to make consumers "adapt their budgets" to capitalist interests (651). Advertising is one of the "techniques of other-direction" (651).

Advertising tries to direct the interests of humans to commodities and thereby into the direction of corporations. Capitalist logic comes to define human action. Advertising on the Internet is targeted and personalised. It is based on and enabled by big data collection and algorithm-driven big data analytics. In digital advertising, big data's digital positivism is a new technique of other-direction that directs a user's attention towards personalised ads and thereby towards corporations that sell commodities in order to accumulate capital. In digital capitalism, advertising's other-directedness turns from mass-direction of ads towards personalised targeting. What remains the same is that consumers' and workers' interests are by (targeted) ads directed towards another, foreign interest, namely capitalist interest.

Advertising is a general feature of consumer capitalism. Sartre writes that the emergence of the culture industry, including entertainment and sports, stands in the context of the second industrial revolution (*CDR2*, 42). He argues that competitive sports, such as boxing, in class society has an ideological role. Sports produces and reproduces competition "in all its nakedness as the concrete event that a popular audience approves and supports" (*CDR2*, 47).

Racism

Sartre argues that the colonial system requires *racism* as "Other-Thought" in order to advance "super-exploitation" (*CDR1*, 714). In his preface to Frantz Fanon's book *The Wretched of the Earth*, Sartre (1963a) argues that colonisers use all means necessary to subdue the humans who live in the colonies. The colonisers dehumanise the colonised in order to be able to destroy, dominate, and exploit them. Physical violence is one method they use, cultural control another one:

> Our soldiers overseas, rejecting the universalism of the mother country, apply the 'numerus clausus' to the human race: since none may enslave, rob, or kill his fellow man without committing a crime, they lay down the principle that the native is not one of our fellow men. [...] the order is given to reduce the inhabitants of the annexed country to the level of superior monkeys in order to justify the settler's treatment of them as beasts of burden. Violence in the colonies does not only have for its aim the keeping of these enslaved men at arm's length; it seeks to dehumanize them. Everything will be done to wipe out their traditions, to substitute our language for theirs and to destroy their culture without giving them ours.
>
> (Sartre 1963a, 15)

Stalinism

Sartre saw *Stalinism* as "absolute idealism" (*SM*, 23) that was based on a "separation of theory and practice" (*SM*, 22). It was "blind to events" (*SM*, 126). The action was guided by ideology made in party offices and not an experience of reality. The Communist Party leaders "feared that the free process of truth, with all the discussions and all the conflicts which it involves, would break the unity of combat; they reserved for themselves the right to define the line and to interpret the event" (*SM*, 22). They disregarded that "[c]oncrete thought must be born from *praxis* and must turn back upon it in order to clarify it" (*SM*, 22). The result was the "terrorist practice" of liquidating particularity and the "physical liquidation" of "particular people" (*SM*, 28).

Stalin was an "iron-fisted opportunist" (*CDR2*, 101) who advanced the ideology of "socialism in one country", whereby communist universalism and internationalism was destroyed (*CDR2*, 95–117). Stalin privileged "the singular over the universal and the national over the international" and presented him as the incarnation of the singular

(*CDR2*, 213). Stalin defined the Soviet system and thereby himself as the essence of socialism. As a consequence, he saw it as the primary task of non-Soviet communism to defend the Society system and thereby Stalin as the essence of socialism. Stalin turned socialism into an ideology and into particularism. Socialism was defined as one country and one person in that country. The ideological consequence was that any "opposition would be defined as treason" (*CDR2*, 103). When Soviet shoulders shot at the rebelling Hungarian workers in 1956, pro-Soviet communists justified the killing and wounding of thousands based on the faith that the Soviet Union was socialist and that any critique of it was pro-capitalist and therefore in their view needed to be stopped by violence (Sartre 1968, 18). Sartre saw the 1956 Hungarian Revolution as an aspect of de-Stalinisation (Sartre 1968, 93) and the Soviet intervention as the triumph of neo-Stalinism (111).

Sartre stresses that the problem of low productivity reinforced Stalin's dictatorship and terror in agriculture and the problem of trying to transform an agricultural into an industrial society and the contradictions industrialisation and urbanisation created (*CDR2*, 118–183). The economic situation did not leave time for the transformation process, so the collectivisation of agriculture was conducted by force. Sartre argues that collectivisation and development could have been achieved without violence and that the decisive factor was Stalin's ideology to "subordinate man to the construction of machines (i.e. subordinate men to worked materiality)" (*CDR2*, 206). Stalin dehumanised humans and thought of them as things and cogs in a machine that can be smashed and replaced.

The analytical reason, advertising/consumer culture, racism, and Stalinism have in common that they are ideologies that try to manipulate the consciousness of everyday people in the interest of dominant economic and political groups. These example ideologies share with all ideologies their class nature and that they try to manipulate the public and the ideas of the public's members in such manners that the members of the public accept, adopt, practice, and support the logic of quantification (analytical reason), capitalist consumerism (advertising, entertainment), and terror (racism/fascism, Stalinism, nationalism). Sartre stresses that ideology denies certain humans their humanity in order to justify their domination. Ideology can only start ceasing to exist in "a socialism of abundance" (Sartre 1993, 171).

8.5 Conclusion

Sartre has been overlooked as a contributor to communication theory. His *Critique of Dialectical Reason* (*CDR*) shows Sartre at the height of his Marxist phase. A critical theory of communication can draw on ideas from *CDR*. Communication is the human process of the production of sociality. *CDR* is a Marxist-humanist theoretical approach. Sartre's dialectical, Marxian humanism can inform the development of a critical, dialectical, humanist theory of communication.

We can summarise the main insights of this chapter:

- For Sartre, society and the social are based on a dialectic of practices (praxis) and structures (the practico-inert). Unlike Marx, Gramsci and the Praxis School, Sartre does not use the term praxis for emancipatory political action, but he shares with these thinkers the stress on human action in society.
- At the level of information, the dialectic of the practico-inert and praxis is for Sartre a dialectic of language and communication.
- Just like for Lukács, work is also for Sartre the model of human action. Based on Sartre and Lukács, we can argue that there is a dialectic of work and communication. Communication is based on work because it is productive. It is the process of the production of sociality. And work is communicative because it has a social character.
- Sartre stresses that social relations and therefore also the communication process are not binary but ternary relations where a third party mediates the relation between humans. We can add that this third party can be a human being, a group, a social system, a techno-social system, a subsystem of society, or society as a whole.
- Sartre distinguishes between the series and the group as two major forms of social relation. The first is characterised by instrumentality and separation, the second one by co-operation and community.
- In the realm of communication, Sartre gives examples for serial forms of communication and relates this form to capitalist power relations and authoritarian political power. Although he gives much more attention to capitalist than to democratic communication, the political implication of Sartre's approach is the demand to turn capitalist means of communication into what Raymond Williams terms democratic communications.
- Internet platforms enable consumers of information to become producers of information. But the emergence of social media and user-generated content platforms has not democratised the Internet and culture but created new monopolies (Facebook, Google, etc.), structures of asymmetric online attention,

voice, and visibility, as well as online individualism. Capitalist Internet platforms are not democratic communications but what Sartre characterises as series.
- Just like Lukács, Sartre sees reification and alienation operating at the level of human practices (exploitation, oppression) and consciousness (ideology).
- Although there is no explicit definition and theory of ideology in *Critique of Dialectical Reason*, Sartre provides foundations of a critical concept of ideology. He stresses that ideology aims at a society that dehumanises humans. Example ideologies that he discusses include analytical reason, advertising, racism, and Stalinism. Struggles for socialism are for Sartre also struggles against an ideology and for a dialectical reason.

We live in times where we experience the extension and intensification of anti-humanism. There are new forms of nationalism, right-wing authoritarianism, and fascism that deny certain groups their humanity. Posthumanism, poststructuralism, theories of the Anthropocene, "New Materialism", Actor Network Theory, Deep Ecology, computational social science, big data analytics, etc. are intellectual and ideological projects that decentre the importance of human practice and praxis and of the human being in society. A revival of Marxist and socialist humanism is needed today in order to show that such attacks serve a political and economic purpose in the restructuring of capitalist society. The works of Marxist-humanist thinkers such as the Sartre of *Critique of Dialectical Reason*, Theodor W. Adorno, Günther Anders, Kevin Anderson, Simone de Beauvoir, Ernst Bloch, Angela Davis, Raya Dunayevskaya, Zillah Eisenstein, Barbara Epstein, Frantz Fanon, Erich Fromm, Lucien Goldmann, André Gorz, David Harvey, Max Horkheimer, C. L .R. James, Karl Korsch, Karel Kosík, Henri Lefebvre, Georg Lukács, Herbert Marcuse, Maurice Merleau-Ponty, Kwame Nkrumah, Julius Nyerere, Bertell Ollmann, the Praxis Group in Yugoslavia, Sheila Rowbotham, M. N. Roy, Edward Said, Jean-Paul Sartre, Adam Schaff, Kate Soper, E. P. Thompson, Raymond Williams, etc. can and should inform such a project of intellectual renewal. Given that we live in a type of capitalism, where networked communication plays an important role, we need to critically understand what communication is and what its role is in capitalism. The update of Marxist-humanist theory and politics therefore also needs to be an update of critical communication theory. The works of thinkers such as Sartre can inform the development of a critical, dialectical, humanist theory of communication.

Literature

Althusser, Louis, and Étienne Balibar. 1970/2009. *Reading Capital*. London: Verso

Anderson, Kenneth L. 2002. "Transformations of Subjectivity in Sartre's Critique of Dialectical Reason." *Journal of Philosophical Research 27*: 267–280.

——— 1996 ———. 1996. "Sartre's Early Theory of Language." *American Catholic Philosophical Quarterly 70* (4): 485–505.

Aronson, Ronald. 2010. "Sartre after Marxism." In *New Perspectives on Sartre*, edited by Adrian Mirvish and Adrian van den Hoven, 270–285. Newcastle upon Tyne: Cambridge Scholars Publishing.

Berendzen, J. C. 2006. "Sartre and the Communicative Paradigm in Critical Theory." *Philosophy Today 50* (2): 190–197.

Brecht, Bertolt. 1932/2000. "The Radio as an Apparatus of Communications." In *Brecht on Film & Radio*, edited by Marc Silberman, 41–46. London: Methuen.

Bruhn Jensen, Klaus, and Robert T. Craig, eds. 2016. *The International Encyclopedia of Communication Theory and Philosophy*. Chicester: Wiley.

Busch, Thomas. 2010. "Sartre and Merleau-Ponty on Structuralism, Language, and Communicative Life." In *New Perspectives on Sartre*, edited by Adrian Mirvish and Adrian van den Hoven, 315–328. Newcastle upon Tyne: Cambridge Scholars Publishing.

——— 1999 ———. 1999. *Circulating Being: From Embodiment to Incorporation*. New York: Fordham University Press.

Churchill, Steven, and Jack Reynolds. 2014. "Sartre's Legacy." In *Jean Paul Sartre Key Concepts*, edited by Steven Churchill and Jack Reynolds, 213–228. Abingdon: Routledge.

Clarke, Melissa. 1999. "Merleau-Ponty's Influence on Sartre: On Language, Writing, and Situation." *Journal of the British Society for Phenomenology 30* (3): 291–305.

Cohen-Solal, Annie. 2005. *Jean-Paul Sartre: A Life*. New York: New Press.

Cox, Gary. 2008. *The Sartre Dictionary*. London: Continuum.

De Beauvoir, Simone. 1984. *A Dieux. A Farewell to Sartre*. New York: Pantheon Books.

Enzensberger, Hans Magnus. 1982. *Critical Essays*. New York: Continuum.

Flynn, Thomas R. 2014. *Sartre: A Philosophical Biography*. Cambridge: Cambridge University Press.

Flynn, Thomas R. 2006. *Existentialism: A Very Short Introduction*. Oxford: Oxford University Press.

——— 1997 ———. 1997. *Sartre, Foucault, and Historical Reason. Volume One: Towards an Existentialist Theory of History*. Chicago, IL: The University of Chicago Press.

Fuchs, Christian. 2021. *Social Media: A Critical Introduction.*, 3rd ed. London: Sage.

——— 2020 ———. 2020. *Communication and Capitalism. A Critical Theory*. London: University of Westminster Press.

——— 2016 ———. 2016. *Critical Theory of Communication: New Readings of Lukács,*

Adorno, Marcuse, Honneth and Habermas in the Age of the Internet. London: University of Westminster Press.

Ghavami, Peter. 2020. *Big Data Analytics Methods*. Boston, MA: De Gruyter. Second edition.

Gramsci, Antonio. 1971. *Selections from the Prison Notebooks*. New York: International Publishers.

Horkheimer, Max, & Adorno, Theodor W. 2002. *Dialectic of Enlightenment: Philosophical Fragments*. Stanford, CA: Stanford University Press.

Howells, Christina. 1979. "Sartre and the Language of Literature." *Modern Language Review 74* (3): 572–579.

Hung, Wai-Shun. 2015. "What is Literature? Revisited: Sartre on the Language of Literature." *Journal of the British Society of Phenomenology 46* (1): 1–15.

Jameson, Frederic. 2004. "Foreword." In *Jean-Paul Sartre: Critique of Dialectical Reason. Volume 1: Theory of Practical Ensembles*, xiii–xxxiii. London: Verso.

Jenkins, Henry. 2008. *Convergence Culture: Where Old and New Media Collide*. New York: New York University Press.

Leak, Andy. 2008. "Creation as Non-Communication. Reflections on the Space of Creativity in Sartre and Winnicott." *Sartre Studies International 14* (1): 1–12.

Lévy, Bernard-Henri. 2003. *Sartre: The Philosopher of the Twentieth Century*. Cambridge: Polity.

Littlejohn, Stephen W., and Karen A. Foss, eds. 2009. *Encyclopedia of Communication Theory*. Thousand Oaks, CA: Sage.

Lukács, Georg. 1986. *Zur Ontologie des gesellschaftlichen Seins. 2. Halbband*. Darmstadt: Luchterhand.

——— 1984 ———. 1984. *Zur Ontologie des gesellschaftlichen Seins. 1. Halbband*. Darmstadt: Luchterhand.

——— 1978 ———. 1978. *The Ontology of Social Being. 3: Labour*. London: Merlin.

——— 1971 ———. 1971. *History and Class Consciousness*. London: Merlin.

——— 1949 ———. 1949. "Existentialism." In *Marxism and Human Liberation*, 243–266. New York: Delta Book.

Marcuse, Herbert. 1948. "Existentialism: Remarks on Jean-Paul Sartre's *L'Être et le néant*." *Philosophy and Phenomenological Research 8* (3): 309–336.

Marx, Karl. 1867. *Capital. Volume 1*. London: Penguin.

——— 1847 ———. 1847. "The Poverty of Philosophy." In *Marx & Engels Collected Works (MECW) Volume 6*, 105–212. London: Lawrence & Wishart.

——— 1845 ———. 1845a. "Thesen über Feuerbach." In *Marx Engels Werke (MEW) Band 3*, 5–7. Berlin: Dietz.

——— 1845 ———. 1845b. "Theses on Feuerbach." In *Marx & Engels Collected Works (MECW) Volume 5*, 3–5. London: Lawrence & Wishart.

Mirvish, Adrian, and Adrian van den Hoven, eds. 2010. *New Perspectives on Sartre*. Newcastle upon Tyne: Cambridge Scholars Publishing.

Noudelmann, François, and Gilles Philippe, eds. 2004. *Dictionnaire Sartre*. Paris: Honoré Champion Éditeur.
Peck, Janice. 2006. "Why We Shouldn't Be Bored with the Political Economy versus Cultural Studies Debate." *Cultural Critique 64*: 92–126.
——— 2002 ———. 2002. "The Oprah Effect: Texts, Readers, and the Dialectic of Signification." *The Communication Review 5* (2): 143–178.
Petrović, Gajo. 1967. *Marx in the Mid-Twentieth Century*. Garden City, NY: Anchor.
Rae, Gavin. 2009. "Sartre & the Other. Conflict, Conversion, Language & the We." *Sartre Studies International 15* (2): 54–77.
Sartre, Jean-Paul. 2016. *What Is Subjectivity?* London: Verso.
——— 1993 ———. 1993. *The Family Idiot. Gustave Flaubert 1821-1857. Volume 5*. Chicago, IL: The University of Chicago Press.
——— 1992 ———. 1992. *Notebooks for an Ethics*. Chicago, IL: The University of Chicago Press.
——— 1991 ———. 1991. *Critique of Dialectical Reason. Volume II: The Intelligibility of History*. London: Verso. [CDR2]
——— 1974 ———. 1974/2008. *Between Existentialism and Marxism*. London: Verso.
——— 1968 ———. 1968. *The Ghost of Stalin*. New York: George Braziller.
——— 1963 ———. 1963a. "Preface." In *Frantz Fanon: The Wretched of the Earth*, 7–31. New York: Grove Press.
——— 1963 ———. 1963b. *Search for a Method*. New York: Knopf. [SM]
——— 1963 ———. 1963/2012. *Saint Genet. Actor and Martyr*. Minneapolis, MN: University of Minnesota Press.
——— 1960 ———. 1960/2004. *Critique of Dialectical Reason. Volume 1: Theory of Practical Ensembles*. London: Verso. [CDR1]
Scriven, Michael. 1993. *Sartre and the Media*. London: St. Martin's Press.
Spencer, Robert. 2017. "Postcolonialism is a Humanism." In *For Humanism. Explorations in Theory and Politcs*, edited by David Alderson and Robert Spencer, 120–162. London: Pluto.
Tamassia, Paolo. 2004. "Langue." In *Dictionnaire Sartre*, edited by François Noudelmann and Gilles Philippe, 274–276. Paris: Honoré Champion Éditeur.
Williams, Raymond. 1989. *What I Came to Say*. London: Hutchinson Radius.
——— 1976 ———. 1976. *Communications*. Harmondsworth: Penguin.

Chapter Nine
M. N. Roy, socialist humanism, and the critical analysis of communication

9.1 Introduction
9.2 Humanism
9.3 Technology
9.4 Culture and communication
9.5 Conclusions
Literature

9.1 Introduction

This chapter asks: How can M. N. Roy's radical Marxist humanism inform the critical study of communication, culture, technology, and the human being?

Manabendra Nath (M. N.) Roy (1887–1954) was a Marxist-humanist thinker and politician. As a humanist he opposed Stalinism, Gandhism and the Indian National Congress' and its leader Subhas Chandra Bose's political position towards Hitler and the Nazis, which placed him outside the mainstream of both the communist and the anti-colonial movements, contributing to "the forgetting of M. N. Roy" and his being "lost to the historical record" (Manjapra 2010, xiv). He experienced turmoil, wars and transitions in the 20th century and was a contemporary of Frankfurt School thinkers such as Theodor W. Adorno, Max Horkheimer, and Herbert Marcuse. Coming from India and spending sixteen years (1915–1931) in countries such as the USA, Mexico, Germany, Uzbekistan, France, Luxembourg, and China (see Ray 2016a), he experienced capitalism and colonialism in various parts of the world.

Both Roy and the Frankfurt School were inspired by Marx and humanism and were interested in topics such as the human being, technology, culture, communication, ideology, liberalism, fascism, authoritarianism, and nationalism. Roy wrote his book *Revolution and Counter-Revolution in China* in the late 1920s while connected to the Frankfurt Institute for School Research (Manjapra 2010, xiii, 70, 84, 91 [footnote 27]). In Germany, Roy and August Thalheimer became close friends and the former conversed in communist circles with the likes of Karl Korsch, Georg Lukács, Eduard Fuchs, Willi

Münzberg, Franz Mehring, and Felix Weil (Manjapra 2010, 39–40, 67–70). The latter funded the founding of the Institute for Social Research.

Subhrajit Bhattacharya (2016, 1432) points out that Roy and Horkheimer at the same time in the 1930s "sought to understand the regression of 'civilisation' in the light of philosophy, one in an Indian prison, another in his exile years in America". Both Roy and the Frankfurt School took a critical interdisciplinary approach that combined political economy, philosophy, sociology, psychoanalysis, and cultural criticism. It is interesting to compare the approaches of Roy and the first generation of the Frankfurt School respecting the themes of the human being, technology, culture/communication, ideology, liberalism, fascism, authoritarianism, and nationalism.

As an introduction, some aspects of Roy's biography will now be discussed (for details see Manjapra 2010; Roy, 1997; Tarkunde 1982).

Roy came from a Brahmin family in Bengal. He became a "full-blooded [Indian] nationalist" (Roy 1942, iii) who was convinced that Indian culture was superior to Western culture and determined to organise an armed revolution against the British rule of India. Observers identify three stages in Roy's political development: He "started as an ardent nationalist, became an equally ardent communist and ended as a creatively active Radical Humanist" (Tarkunde 1982, v).

After the first phase in his political development Roy, in the second stage, became a communist when he went abroad during the First World War. Roy was a founder of the Mexican Communist Party in 1917 and the Communist Party of India in the 1920s. While staying abroad in the USA and Mexico he gave up the belief that there was a progressive element in nationalism and embraced aspects of Western culture (Roy, 1987, 1–13). In the 1920s, he was a member of the Communist International (Comintern)'s Presidium.

At the Second Congress of the Comintern in 1920, Lenin (1920) presented *Theses on the National and Colonial Questions*. Lenin argued that the "entire [communist] policy on the national and the colonial questions should rest primarily on a closer union of the proletarians and the working masses of all nations and countries for a joint revolutionary struggle to overthrow the landowners and the bourgeoisie" (1920, 146). Roy (1920) presented *Supplementary Theses on the National and Colonial Question* that were more detailed than Lenin's theses and resulted in Lenin's taking up and agreeing with Roy's inputs. In his theses, Roy (1920) argued that European capitalism "depends on control of extensive colonial markets and a broad field of opportunities for exploitation" in order to counter overproduction, that the "super-profits made in the colonies form one of the main sources of the resources of contemporary capitalism", and that therefore the "Communist International must enter into much closer connection with the revolutionary forces that are at present participating in the overthrow of imperialism in the politically and economically oppressed countries".

Roy was expelled from the Comintern in 1929. He was close to Bukharin, whom Stalin wanted to get rid of, and supported anti-Stalinist Marxist movements such as the Communist Party of Germany (Opposition) (KPO), whose leader August Thalheimer was Roy's friend and ally. Both Thalheimer and Roy were part of the International Communist Opposition. Communists around Thalheimer and Heinrich Brandler opposed the Stalinist position that the social democrats were the main enemy of the working class. Stalinists described social democrats as "social fascists", and did not focus enough on the critique of Nazi-fascism. Members of the Communist opposition movement such as Thalheimer argued for a united front of social democrats and communists against Nazi-fascism. Roy wrote for the KPO's publications and found the notion of the united front of the exploited and oppressed feasible for struggles in the colonies (see Roy 1929a, 1929b). In the late 1920s, Stalin and his followers in the Comintern such as Otto Wille Kuusinen disagreed with Roy's assessment that the "nationalist bourgeoisie" in the colonies was compromising with imperialism but rather claimed that "the Indian bourgeoisie was brutally suppressed by Imperialism" (Roy 1943, 48–49).

Consequently, Stalinists started to oppose Roy, which resulted in his expulsion from the Comintern (see Ray 2016b). The Stalinists accused the likes of Thalheimer, Brandler, and Roy of "Luxemburgism" (Manjapra 2010, 43–44, 70–71, 86–87), which, given Rosa Luxemburg's fusion of socialism, Marxism, and humanism, Roy and his comrades did not take as an insult but as confirmation that they were true communists. Roy (1943, 47) argues that the Communist International's failed assumption that "Social Democracy was a greater enemy of revolution than Fascism" resulted in the Comintern helping "Fascism to capture power in Germany". Roy argues that it was a grave mistake that Soviet Minister of Foreign Affairs Molotov "held British Imperialism responsible for the war and thus, by implication, exonerated Fascism" (Roy 1943, 59–60).

Orthodox Marxists have characterised socialism as the ideology of the working class, which implies the need for dictatorship. They forgot that for Marx the interest of the working class "coincided with the interest of the entire society" (Roy 1943, 72), which is why socialism and Marxism are "the philosophy of the progressive mankind. The world can be reconstructed as a home of freedom and culture only along the lines indicated by Marxism. Therefore, Communism has come to its own. It has become the future of mankind, its heritage" (73). For Roy, the Soviet system wasn't communist. He argued that a true form of communism as radical-democratic humanism remains the important political goal and interest of humanity.

In his third, humanist phase, Roy combined Marxism and humanism. In the 1930s, he joined the Congress Party, where he was active in the socialist faction. He broke with Congress during World World II over the question of how the party should position itself towards Nazi-fascism and the Allied powers. Roy argued that fascism was the world's greatest danger and for the support of the Allies. Others in Congress, such as Gandhi, said that there should only be support on the condition of Indian independence. Gandhi saw Roy as his "enemy number one" (Roy, 1987, 17), while Roy characterised Gandhi as "the patron saint of [Indian] nationalism" (Roy, 1987, 67; Roy 1968, 29).

In 1932, Roy was sentenced to twelve years in prison for having conspired to deprive the King Emperor of his sovereignty in India in the 1920s. The time he served was reduced; he was released in late 1936. He was a vocal critic and opponent of Italian and German fascism. Roy founded the League of Radical Congressmen in 1938, the Radical Democratic Party in 1940, and the Radical Humanist Movement in 1948. The Radical Humanist Movement in 1952, together with other humanist movements, founded the International Humanist and Ethical Union that is today known as Humanists International.

Whereas Roy during his communist phase argued for "[r]evolutionary nationalism" (1922, 177), which he distinguished from "reactionary nationalism" (1922, 166, 216; see the same phrases in Roy 1923, 42, 44), during his humanist phase he opposed "capitalist as well as socialist Nationalism" (Roy 1960/1947, 102) and argued that any nationalism is "a totalitarian cult" (1960/1947, 84) that needs to be replaced by the universal "brotherhood of free individuals" (1960/1947, 102) and the "cosmopolitan commonwealth of free men and women" that is " not compatible with the continuation of National States" (Roy 1953, 35).

Although some attention has been given to Roy's work in India, his philosophy and theory are widely forgotten. Roy's magnum opus *Reason, Romanticism and Revolution*, which has a great deal in common with Horkheimer and Adorno's *Dialectic of*

Enlightenment, is a forgotten and undiscovered work. In September 2019, Roy's main book that was published in two volumes in 1952 (volume 1) and 1955 (volume 2) had just 23 citations on Google Scholar[1]. One of the purposes of this chapter is, therefore, to point critical scholars in the social sciences, humanities, communication and cultural studies towards Roy's works by introducing some of its important aspects.

In order to answer the research question that this chapter poses, it discusses four aspects of Roy's works and assesses their relevance for a critical theory of communication and culture. These themes are humanism (section 2), technology (section 3), culture and communication (section 4). Section 5 draws some conclusions.

9.2 Humanism

Roy was both a humanist and a Marxist. He understood humanism as a romantic movement (section 2.1) and engaged with Marx's works in the context of humanism (section 2.2).

9.2.1 Humanism as romanticism

Roy was a radical humanist and humanist Marxist. Humanism stresses the importance of the capacity of humans to change society. It is based on the insight that "man is the maker of his world" (Roy 1953, 47) and the assumption that the human being is "the archetype of society" (Roy 1960/1947, 94). Marx

> was a passionate Humanist; and, with a burning faith in revolution, he was also a romanticist. The idea of revolution is a romantic idea, because it presupposes man's power to remake the world in which he lives. If purposeful human effort is left out of account, social development becomes a mechanistic evolutionary process, making no room for sudden great changes and occasionally accelerated tempo. As the prophet of revolution, Marx was a romanticist. He proclaimed his faith in the creativeness of man which, accelerating the process of social evolution, brought about revolutions. Marx being a Humanist, the force of his theory of revolution was its powerful moral appeal.
>
> (Roy 1953, 17)

---

1 Data source: https://scholar.google.com/, accessed on 12 September 2019.

For Roy, humanism is built on the insight that the human being "is essentially rational and therefore moral. Morality emanates from the rational desire for harmonious and mutually beneficial social relations" (Roy 1953, 33). Radical humanism "thinks in terms neither of nation nor of class" (1953, 34), but in terms of the human being. Roy foregrounds the role of human activity in society: history "is the record of man's struggle for freedom" (1989, 4). For Roy, romanticism means the "passionate belief in the creativeness and freedom of man. [...] The idea of revolution, therefore, is a romantic idea. [...] The difference between reason and romanticism is that one perceives what is necessary and therefore possible, whereas the other declares impetuously what is desirable, what should be done" (1989, 11).

In society, the human being "is the measure of everything", which implies that "the merit of any pattern of social organisation or political institution is to be judged by the actual measure of freedom it gives to the individual" (Roy 1953, 38). Comparable to Marx, Roy argues that co-operation is the essence of society (Roy 1953, 38). Marx adds that co-operation is a social production process and a work process, which is why the economy is of particular importance in society (see Fuchs 2020a). Roy (1953) says that the experience of conflict results in the alienation of humans from co-operation and a loss of faith of humans in themselves (91) that means a "crisis of the soul of man" so that "man has forgotten what he is" (91).

A free humanist society requires the realisation of the co-operative essence of society: "Freedom is the progressive elimination of all the factors – physical, social, psychological which obstruct the unfolding of man's rational, moral and creative potentialities. The function of social relationships should be to secure for individuals, as individuals, the maximum measure of freedom" (Roy 1953, 38). For Roy, freedom

> is the supreme value of life, because the urge for freedom is the essence of human existence. [...] [The human being's] urge for freedom [...] is undying, eternal. He may not be always conscious of it; often he is not. Nevertheless, it is the basic incentive for him to acquire knowledge and conquer environments by knowing them.
>
> (Roy 1989, 496–497)

In his main philosophical work *Reason, Romanticism and Revolution*, published in two volumes in 1952 and 1955, Roy (1989) describes the history of how humanism, rationality, science, philosophy, art, education, and technology have since the time of the Renaissance challenged religious and supernatural authority and the struggles and contradictions involved in this development. Roy argues that modern science and philosophy were not created by the bourgeoisie, but that later the bourgeoisie "patronised them because they served their purpose" (1989, 46). He stresses that Arab philosophy was important for rescuing reason and the thought of ancient Greece while Europe was stuck in the Middle Ages (1989, 41). Arab thought "ultimately reached Europe to stimulate the age-long struggle for spiritual freedom and search for truth" so that the "examination of social political freedom – modern civilisation – resulted from that struggle" (1989, 74). Roy (1989, 42, 68–69, 74, 128, 314) especially foregrounds the importance of Averroes (1126–1198) and Avicenna (980–1037), who built on Aristotle to establish a rationalist and materialist philosophy.

Roy's stress on Averroes and Avicenna is comparable to the work of Ernst Bloch (2019), who in his book *Avicenna and the Aristotelean Left* stresses the importance of Avicenna and Averroes who "embraced transformation" (67) and advanced a "speculative materialism" (67). Whereas the Right Aristotelians believe in supernatural powers that kept humans from struggling for liberation, Left Aristotelians struggle for humanism.

Humanism is internationalist and cosmopolitan; it wants to organise society as a "cosmopolitan commonwealth of free men and women" combined with "a spiritual community, not limited by the boundaries of National States – capitalist, fascist, communist or of any other kind – which will gradually disappear under the impact of cosmopolitan Humanism" (Roy 1953, 35).

A radical humanist society includes cultural democracy: "Its culture will be based on universal dissemination of knowledge and incentive to scientific and all other kinds of creative activity" (Roy 1953, 46). Roy argues that

> side by side with the efforts to change economic conditions, efforts should be made to create a cultural atmosphere in which the value of freedom will be appreciated by a larger and larger number of people, an atmosphere in which it will be possible to make more and more people feel the urge for freedom, feel that they are human beings and as such capable of experiencing freedom, here and now. (1950a, 188–189)

Freedom requires "economic betterment and [democratic] political institutions" (1950a, 191) as well as a culture of "freedom of thought and judgment" and the advancement of "the spirit of enquiry and the ability to distinguish between right and wrong" (190).

Roy opposes both economic and political forms of dictatorship. He argues for economic, political and cultural democracy: "According to Marx, under Socialism, human reason will overcome irrational forces which now tyrannise the life of man" (1953, 18). Roy argues for a radical humanist society that is a grassroots democracy based on people's committees in politics and co-operatives in the economy. In such a society, local democracy is strengthened (1953, 43). Such committees are also "the school for the political and civic education of the citizen" (1953, 36). For Roy (1989, 474), humanist democracy is "a network of local political schools": "Every citizen will be informed and consulted for his opinion about the affairs of the state, that is, the political administration of his society" (Roy 1949, 939).

The humanist economy produces for human needs (Roy 1953, 46). It consists of

> a network of consumers' and producers' co-operatives, and the economic activities of the society shall be conducted and co-ordinated by the people through these institutions. The co-operative economy shall take full advantage of modern science and technology and effect equitable distribution of social surplus through universal social utility services.
>
> (Roy 1953, 69)

Radical humanist democracy is based on "People's Committees as the primary constituents of the democratic State, and co-operatives as the primary units of the co-operative Commonwealth" (1953, 70): "Economic democracy is no more possible in the absence of political democracy than the latter is in the absence of the former" (1989, 472).

Roy (1989, 355–358) argues that Kant's (1724–1804) idealism is based on a dualism of ideas and the thing-in-itself, subject and object, noumenon and phenomena, appearance and reality, science and philosophy, and nature and mind; and that it, therefore, developed dogmatic ethics that together with the approaches of Herder (1744–1803), Fichte (1762–1814), and Lessing (1729–1781) advanced German nationalism. Roy (1989, Chapter XVIII) writes that Hegel's (1770–1831) dialectical philosophy overcame Kant's dualism, stressing the creativity of the human mind and therefore humanism.

Roy points out that Marx has an "outstanding place in the history of philosophy" because his "materialist monism" questions the dualism of mind and matter by seeing matter "as the ultimate reality capable of producing life" (1989, 417). Roy, again and again, discusses the relationship between Marx and humanism.

9.2.2 Marx and humanism

Roy (1989) argues that Marx's "view of history and social evolution was essentially teleologically fatalistic" (390). This view is disproved by Marx's famous formulation from *The Eighteenth Brumaire of Louis Bonaparte* that humans "make their own history, but they do not make it as they please; they do not make it under circumstances chosen by themselves, but under circumstances directly encountered, given and transmitted from the past" (1852, 103). History is conditioned by society's contradictions so that social struggles and human practices are the sources of freedom that goes beyond and liberates humans from necessity. History is based on a dialectic of structuration and collective agency/struggles.

Roy contradicts his own claim that Marx was a historical fatalist when appreciating Marx's stress on agency and revolution: "The romantic view of life [...] leads to the liberating doctrine that man is the maker of the world, developed during a whole period of history from Vico to Marx. [...] Marxism is an attempted synthesis between the two apparently antithetical views of life – the rationalist and the romantic" (1989, 12).

Roy (1989) argues that the dialectic is for Marx a rational, scientific law, "Hegelianism applied to human history" (408), and that he combined rationalist dialectics with a romanticist theory of revolution (409–410, 412) so that history is for Marx a "contradiction between rationalism and the romantic notion of revolution" (411). Because of his "emphasis on human action" (412) and his "burning faith in revolution" (420), "Marx was a Humanist, and as such a romanticist" (411). Marx's philosophy is a "synthesis of rationalism and romanticism" (413). Roy states that "Marx being a humanist, the force of his theory of revolution was its moral appeal. [...] In the last analysis, *Capital* is a treatise on social ethics – a powerful protest against the servitude of the toiling majority" (420).

Roy argues that Marxism needs to be freed from "the fallacy of economic determinism", which makes it consistent with "Radical Humanism" (421). In the last instance, Roy greatly appreciates Marx as a humanist and revolutionary theorist. But he misinterprets Hegelian dialectics. Dialectics does not just operate at the level of objective contradictions but also at the level of human practices. There is a dialectic of the subjective dialectic and the objective dialectic. And for Marx, class struggle is the subjective dimension of history because the exploited class thereby questions the class relation, by which it is compelled to produce surplus-value that it does not own, and class society. Class struggle as the making and unmaking of class relations between the exploited and the exploited is the subjective dimension of history.

Marx's quote from the *Eighteenth Brumaire* does not have, as Roy assumes, a romantic-revolutionary side (humans make their own history) and a dialectical side (they do so under the dialectical contradictions of class society). It does not combine a non-dialectical and a dialectical aspect of society but expresses society's meta-dialectic of the objective dialectic and the subjective dialectic. Both dimensions of history are dialectical. We cannot say, therefore, as Roy (1989, 491) does, that the "fiery prophet of social justice in Marx was more a Humanist than a Hegelian". Rather, Marx's dialectic is humanist and his humanism dialectical. The problem of economic determinism and breakdown theory is not immanent in Marx's application and development of Hegelian dialectics but was the result of, on the one hand, the Bernstein-tradition of social democratic revision of Marx's theory and, on the other hand, the Stalinist tradition of the vulgarisation of Marx.

Roy says that Marx's insight in the sixth Feuerbach thesis that the individual and the human being's essence are "the ensemble of the social relations" (Marx 1845, 7) was "a great advance in the struggle for freedom" (Roy 1989, 392). Roy claims that Marx ignores that the activities of individuals constitute society (1989, 392). He says Marx omits "mental activity" and "conceptual thought" in society and social evolution (393) and "the human nature which underlies the ensemble of social relations" (395). He writes that by neglecting human nature Marx does not recognise "permanent values" that enable ethics (396). Roy (1989, Chapter IX) here limits his discussion to the *German Ideology* and ignores other works of Marx. In *Capital*, Marx stresses how conceptual thought, mental activities and human will guide human work:

> what distinguishes the worst architect from the best of bees is that the architect builds the cell in his mind before he constructs it in wax. At the end of every labour process, a result emerges which had already been conceived by the worker at the beginning, hence already existed ideally. Man not only effects a change of form in the materials of nature; he also realizes *[verwirklicht]* his own purpose in those materials. And this is a purpose he is conscious of, it determines the mode of his activity with the rigidity of a law, and he must subordinate his will to it.
>
> (Marx 1867, 284)

Roy did not focus on Marx's *Economic and Philosophic Manuscripts* where Marx identifies a dialectic of the individual and social structures as the foundation of society:

> *just as* society itself produces *man as* man, so is society *produced* by him [...] Social activity and social enjoyment exist by no means *only* in the form of some *directly* communal activity and directly *communal* enjoyment [...] that which I make of myself, I make of myself for society and with the consciousness of myself as a social being. [...] Above all we must avoid postulating "society" again as an abstraction *vis-à-vis* the individual. The individual *is the social being*. [...] Man's individual and species-life are not *different*, however much – and this is inevitable – the mode of existence of the individual is a more *particular* or more *general* mode of the life of the species, or the life of the species is a more *particular* or more *general* individual life.
> (Marx 1844, 298–299, emphasis in original)

In the *German Ideology*, the Marxian work Roy (1989, Chapter XIX) is referencing in his discussion, Marx says that the starting point of the analysis of society is "the existence of living human individuals" (Marx and Engels 1845–1846, 31). It is not true that Marx does not assume there is no human nature. His whole concept of alienation is based on the notion of human essence. In the *Economic and Philosophic Manuscripts*, Marx (1844) points out that the human being is, in essence, a natural, social, objective-subjective, conscious, self-conscious, sensual, thinking, active, creative, language-using, working being. He also bases critical humanist ethics on this notion of human essence that advances the insight that class society alienates humans, cripples human nature, and is therefore incompletely human and incompletely social. As a consequence, communism is "practical humanism" and "humanism mediated with itself through the supersession of private property" (Marx 1844, 341).

Written in 1844, the *Economic and Philosophic Manuscripts* were first published in the original German in 1932. Martin Milligan created the first English translation, published in 1959. Roy died in 1954 and was not fluent in German, which means that he could not read the *Manuscripts*. If he had, his judgement of Marx might have been somewhat different. His criticism of Marx can also be read as a self-criticism of his own earlier phase where he relied much more on determinism and economism than in his later stage. Above all, Roy's critique should not be seen as relating to Marx, but to the Stalinists that he opposed by the humanist stress on human agency and democratic socialism.

Since the start of a new world economic crisis in 2008, we have experienced not just a brief spring of progressive movements but also the rise and spread of new nationalisms, new authoritarianism, and new fascism (Fuchs 2018, 2020b). Once again, "[b]ourgeois society stands at the crossroads, either transition to socialism or regression into barbarism" (Luxemburg 1916, 388). Engaging and updating the works of humanist socialists such as Roy, Ernst Bloch, Raya Dunayevskaya, Erich Fromm, Lucien Goldmann, C. L. R. James, Henri Lefebvre, Rosa Luxemburg, Herbert Marcuse, Karl Marx, E. P. Thompson, Raymond Williams, and so on, reminds us that democratic socialism is the strongest weapon against fascism, nationalism, and war.

Humanism shaped how Roy saw various aspects of society, such as technology. The next section discusses his view of the relationship between technology and society.

9.3 Technology

Roy was a critic of technology as a means of exploitation and domination but favoured an alternative, non-capitalist modernity that involves a humanist use of technology. Roy differed in this respect from Gandhi (section 3.1). He provides a dialectical analysis of technology (section 3.2).

9.3.1 Roy and Gandhi

We have already mentioned in the introduction of this chapter that there was no love lost between Roy and Gandhi. Roy questions the identity of anti-imperialism and nationalism (Roy 1942, 3). He says that the disappearance of British imperialism is a precondition for freedom in India, but that this disappearance will not "necessarily mean freedom for India" (1942, 3). He sees nationalism as an unnecessary and dangerous feature of certain anti-imperialist movements, and as having fascist potentials. In the context of India and the Second World War, Roy was particularly critical of "the fact [...] that the sympathies of the average Indian nationalist are all on the side of the Fascist Powers" (1942, 14). Roy believed that the support of the Nazi-fascists by Indians who hated British imperialism would not result in the end of imperialism but in the rise of fascism in India. He opposed any form of nationalism and argued that with the advent of Gandhi's influence, "authoritarianism became the fundamental principle of Indian Nationalism", because Gandhi "demanded submission to a spiritual authority" (Roy 2006/1945, 12): "Gandhism is the accepted ideology of Indian Nationalism" (2006/1945, 26).

Roy argues that Indian nationalists "reject precisely what is 'good' in capitalist civilisation", namely "the tremendous advance of science, in theory and practice" (1950b, 109). Gandhism's focus on "non-violence, poverty, continence" (1960/1947, 19), and "[p]uritanism" (1960/1947, 20) inspires "the capitalist and his employees to work hard and spend little, thus making possible the accumulation of capital", which is why "the Mahatma's teaching has acquired great prestige among the capitalists of India" (1960/1947, 20).

Gandhi had a particular view of what role technologies should play in society. He was critical of industrialisation and modern technologies because he saw them as disruptors of traditional life. Gandhi says in this context:

> I don't believe that industrialization is necessary in any case for any country. It is much less so for India, Indeed I believe that independent India can only discharge her duty towards a groaning world by adopting a simple but ennobled life by developing her thousands of cottages and living at peace with the world. High thinking is inconsistent with a complicated material life, based on high speed imposed on us by Mammon worship. All the graces of life are possible, only when we learn the art of living nobly.
> (Gandhi, in Tendulkar 1953, 224–225)

Gandhi sees machinery as the cause of imperialism, or what he terms the exploitation of one nation by another:

> What is the cause of the present chaos? It is exploitation, I will not say, of the weaker nations by the stronger, but of sister nations by sister nations. And my fundamental objection to machinery rests on the fact that it is machinery that has enabled these nations to exploit others.
> (Gandhi, in Bose 1948, 64–65)

These quotes show that Gandhi equates and conflates modern technology and industry on the one side with capitalism and imperialism on the other side. He does not see the possibility of an alternative, socialist modernisation. He furthermore sees technology as the cause of exploitation. This position is different from techno-optimist determinists such as Marshall McLuhan who see modern technologies as the enablers and causes of a better future. Gandhi is a representative of pessimistic technological determinism that assumes that modern technologies with necessity call forth and are the cause of negative features of society such as commodification and exploitation. Both optimistic and pessimistic technological determinism share the short-sighted assumption that it is the technology that determines society. They disregard how society shapes the character and use of technology and that the relationship between technology and society is dialectical and therefore full of contradictions.

Gandhi favoured the widespread use of manual technologies, especially the spinning-wheel and the handloom. He argued that "[r]estoration [...] of the spinning-wheel solves the economic problem of India at a stroke" (1997, 165): "When as a nation we adopt the spinning-wheel, we not only solve the question of unemployment but we declare that we have no intention of exploiting any nation, and we also end exploitation of the poor by the rich" (1997, 167). Gandhi saw the spinning wheel as "the panacea for the growing pauperism of India" (1983/1948, 441). His view of technology is anti-modern and focused on preserving and advancing manual labour and thereby toil. Gandhi's view of manual technologies is, just like his view of modern technologies, techno-deterministic. He assumes that the spinning wheel and the handloom result in a society without poverty.

Gandhi overlooks that technology is "being looked for and developed with certain purposes and practices already in mind" (Williams 2003/1974, 7). As Williams states: "Technological determinism is an untenable notion because it substitutes for real social, political and economic intention" (2003/1974, 133). Interests and contradictions in society shape the impacts of technology on society. In capitalism, there certainly is an "interlock of military, political and commercial intentions" at play in the design and use of science and technology (Williams 2003/1974, 137). But there is also the potential for shaping science and modern technology by democratic interests (Williams 2003/1974, 146).

Roy (1950b, 124) does not just criticise that Gandhi and his followers want an "ethical capitalism", which means that they overlook how capitalist interests shape science and technology and call forth negative consequences; he also argues that the "core of Gandhism [...] is its hostility to industrialism and the modern world" (1960/1947, 18). For Roy, Gandhi's preaching of the abstention from the use of technology and simple rural life is an ideology that celebrates poverty and thereby supports the profit interests of capitalist organisations: "The spiritualist doctrine of self-control, simple living, voluntary poverty, fits in with the requirements of unsocial capitalism" (1950b, 236).

Roy argues that there is a dialectic of technology and society.

9.3.2 The dialectic of modern technology and society

Roy shared concerns about modern technology but rejected technological determinism. He argued that technology should be seen in the context of society and therefore has potentials to advance both slavery and freedom:

> the emphasis on freedom at this time is called for by a material factor, namely, modern technology. There is a very wide-spread fear that this immense development of technology will bring slavery for mankind, and the fear is not unreasonable. The Nazis were only a little ahead of their time when they tried to set up a single world tyranny, and if such a tyranny is ever established it will be almost impossible to overthrow. Thus this great development of technology puts the problem before us in the form of a choice: world slavery or world freedom.
>
> (Roy 1960/1947, 12)

Roy sees modern technology as standing in a dialectical relationship to society, which means that technology has certain unpredictable dynamics, but is shaped by humans' interests, which means that in principle humans can by practising overcoming domination and exploitation also shape and create technologies that advance freedom, equality and democracy. Roy argued for the creation of humanist technologies as part of the struggle for a humanist society. "Machine should not be the Frankenstein of modem civilisation. Created by men, it must subserve man's purpose – contribute to his freedom" (Roy 1953, 40). He writes that there can be no freedom without humanistic modern technology:

> Technology is capable, in principle, of providing an enjoyable life for all, and there is no good reason why life should not be enjoyed [...] Freedom, equality and democracy are impossible if you reject modern technology.
>
> (Roy 1960/1947, 21)

> Progressive satisfaction of material necessities is the precondition for the individual members of society unfolding their intellectual and other liner human attributes. An economic reorganisation such as will guarantee a progressively rising standard of living will be the foundation of the Radical Democratic State.
>
> (Roy 1953, 46)

While Gandhi was an anti-modernist, Roy argued for alternative modernity, a socialist-humanist modernity that shapes, creates and uses technologies in manners that abolish toil and advance freedom, democracy and sustainability:

> Science not only enables man to conquer nature, but also helps him to understand nature, his relation with it and with other human beings who are integral parts of nature. [...] Modern technological trends threaten to offer mankind at the altar of the Moloch, and create a Frankenstein lusting to devour its creator, because the practical, utilitarian value of scientific knowledge has been allowed to eclipse its ideal value.
>
> (Roy 1947a, iii)

There are strong parallels between Roy's and Herbert Marcuse's analysis of modern technology. Like Roy, Marcuse rejects anti-technological ideology that celebrates toil: "The enemies of technics readily join forces with a terroristic technocracy. The philosophy of the simple life, the struggle against big cities and their culture frequently serves to teach men distrust of the potential instruments that could liberate them" (Marcuse, 1988/1941, 63).

Marcuse, just like Roy, identifies both emancipatory and repressive potentials of modern technology and argues that the actual character and impact of a technology depends on broader societal contexts, interests and struggles: "Technics by itself can promote authoritarianism as well as liberty, scarcity as well as abundance, the extension as well as the abolition of toil" (Marcuse, 1988/1941, 41). Marx and Roy base their analysis on Marx' Hegelian analysis of technology that stresses that there is an antagonism between the essence of modern technology and the actual impacts of technology under capitalist conditions. Marx, for example, argues that

> machinery in itself shortens the hours of labour, but when employed by capital it lengthens them; since in itself it lightens labour, but when employed by capital it heightens its intensity; since in itself it is a victory of man over the forces of nature but in the hands of capital it makes man the slave of those forces; since in itself it increases the wealth of the producers, but in the hands of capital it makes them into paupers.
>
> (Marx 1867, 568–569)

Marcuse, like Roy, argues for socialist modernity where technology is shaped and used in manners that overcome toil and advance freedom and technology is governed in a democratic manner:

> If everyone has become a potential member of the public bureaucracy [...], society will have passed from the stage of hierarchical bureaucratization to the stage of technical self-administration. [...] We have pointed to the possible democratization of functions which technics may promote and which may facilitate complete human development in all branches of work and administration. Moreover, mechanization and standardization may one day help to shift the center of gravity from the necessities of material production to the arena of free human realization. [...] Technological progress would make it possible to decrease the time and energy spent in the production of the necessities of life, and a gradual reduction of scarcity and abolition of competitive pursuits could permit the self to develop from its natural roots. The less time and energy man has to expend in maintaining his life and that of society, the greater the possibility that he can "individualize" the sphere of his human realization.
>
> (Marcuse, 1988/1941, 58–59, 63, 64)

In digital capitalism, we find both techno-optimism and techno-pessimism. In this context, the effects of AI-based automation is a heavily discussed topic.

The futurist Martin Ford (2015) warns in his book *Rise of Robots: Technology and the Threat of a Jobless Future* that AI-based automation "has a dark side of its own, and if it results in widespread unemployment or threatens the economic security of a large fraction of our population" (2015, 283). He writes that

> factory jobs are disappearing across the globe at a rapid clip. Labor-intensive manufacturing as a path to prosperity may begin to evaporate for many developing nations. [...] The greatest risk is that we could face a 'perfect storm' — a situation where technological unemployment and environmental impact unfold roughly in parallel, reinforcing and perhaps even amplifying each other.
>
> (Ford 2015, 283, 284)

Accelerationists such as Srnicek and Williams (2015) and Bastani (2019), in contrast to Martin Ford, point out that AI-based automation should be entirely welcomed. Srnicek and Williams (2015, 179) say that "the automation of mundane labour" forms "the basis for a fully postcapitalist economy, enabling a shift away from scarcity, work and exploitation, and towards the full development of humanity".

Bastani (2019) argues that new technologies will result in a major disruption of society, creating "a world dramatically different from our own" (11): "the old world will transition to the new more quickly than many imagine" (2019, 77); and "within a generation we are set to reach peak human" (2019, 80), ushering in the emergence of fully-automated luxury communism, "a society in which work is eliminated, scarcity replaced by abundance and where labour and leisure blend into one another" (2019, 50). Williams and Srnicek (2013) state that "[w]e want to accelerate the process of technological evolution. [...] the left must take advantage of every technological and scientific advance made possible by capitalist society. We declare that quantification is not an evil to be eliminated, but a tool to be used in the most effective manner possible".

Whereas accelerationists see Artificial Intelligence ushering in communism, neo-liberals see it as a way of accelerating corporate profit-making. The conservative UK government argues in its Industrial Strategy that "[e]mbedding AI across the UK will create thousands of good quality jobs and drive economic growth" (Department for Business, Energy & Industrial Strategy 2019).

While utopian communist optimism and neoliberal optimism expect changes from new technologies that they assess as positive (communism and capitalist growth respectively), pessimists argue that new technologies result in a rise of unemployment, precarity, inequalities, social problems, and so on. The basic problem of all of these approaches is that they do not see modern technology in modern society as a complex, contradictory system but rather inscribe certain societal changes into technology. The actual effects of society depend on the results of class and social struggles that shape the character and use of technology in society.

In the next section, we will discuss aspects of Roy's works that have to do with culture and communication.

9.4 Culture and communication

Roy developed a distinct form of cultural materialism as part of which he discussed the materialist character of society (section 4.1) and the relationship of culture and the economy (section 4.2). He had less to say on communication, but his analysis of culture can inform the critical analysis of communication (section 4.3).

9.4.1 Materialism and society

One basic question for any critical theory is how mind and matter, as well as culture and economy, are related. In Marxist theory, this question is known as the base/superstructure-problem.

For Roy, the entire world is material. Materialism is "the explanation of the world without the assumption of anything super-natural" (Roy 1940, 227). Matter is "a vibratory substance" (Roy 1947a, 86), "the sole existence" (1947a, 99), "the only reality" and "ontologically real" (1947a, 100). Roy argues that in society, both "ideal and physical" (1989, 8–9) realities are material, have "their respective dynamics or dialectics" and are "mutually influenced" (9). Roy advanced a materialist theory of knowledge. "Man's relation with nature has been from the very beginning not of passive contemplation, but of action" (Roy 1940, 249). Therefore, "knowledge is action, not passive contemplation" (249); "whatever is within the ken of human consciousness is material. Because something immaterial (spiritual, in the traditional sense) can never be cogniable to human mind, itself a product of matter in a particular state of organisation" (251).

Roy's philosophy is monistic and materialist. He stresses that the non-human and the human world are material. For Roy, the human being is entirely material because the body and the mind are physical entities developed in the course of evolution. In the realm of humans and their societies, Roy stresses the dialectical interaction of ideas/physical reality, mind/body, nature/society, environment/individual, and economy/culture. All of these realms are expressions of matter as a dynamic, vibratory process. There are no ideas without the human mind's embeddedness into and interact with the body and a natural and social environment.

Roy deals with the question of the means of production in society. He stresses that the brain is humanity's key means of production:

> But may we not ask who created the first means of production? What was there originally? Did the first man appear with hammer and sickle in hand? No. But he did come into the world with another means of production, the most powerful ever created. And that was his brain [...] We are all born with it, and it remains our basic asset, provided that we can appreciate its worth and make proper use of it. If you prefer a crude hammer, or even an electric hammer, or something still better, the most modern technological inventions, to your brain, I wish you luck.
>
> (Roy 1960/1947, 65–66)

> The creation of the first extra-organic means of production was a deed done by an animal with highly developed brain, capable of thought. An idea preceded the creation of the first means of production.
>
> (Roy 1960/1947, 93)
>
> The brain is a means of production, and produces the most revolutionary commodity.
>
> (Roy 1953, 36)

Roy (1989, 17) stresses that conceptual thought is characteristic of humans. Conceptual thought is "thinking stimulated by mental images" (1989, 17). "Conceptual thought depends on language. So, it can be said that man is fully differentiated from his animal ancestry only when he coins words for expressing definite ideas" (17). Animals articulate sounds but this activity is entirely dependent on stimuli from their immediate environment; they lack conceptual thought (17). This means that humans have the capacity to anticipate and reflect on the consequences of their actions, select among different potential actions, make moral judgements that guide their actions, and discuss and communicate their feelings, actual and potential choices, interests, experiences, morals, and actions. Humans are rational, anticipatory, self-conscious, thinking, creative, moral, languaging, social, communicative, societal beings. Roy (1989, 479) argues that the human being is "a thinking animal". But humans are also social, communicative beings.

What needs to be added to Roy's approach is the crucial role of work and production in human existence (see Fuchs 2020a). Based on their capacities as rational, thinking, creative, social beings, humans engage in the social production of ideas, technologies that they use to transform the world, goods that satisfy human needs, collective decisions, worldviews, and culture. They together produce an economy, a political system, and culture, which are forms of sociality and social relations. Work is the process of social production through which humans create something new that satisfies their needs. Social production means that the economy and work are at the heart of all social realms, including the political and cultural life. At the same time, social systems go beyond mere production by having emergent qualities. Once humans produce structures, these structures have specific features and a particular logic that goes beyond economic necessity and are shaped by human interests and their contradictions.

The dialectic of culture and the economy is based on social production, which means that the combination of the human capacities to produce and to be social are at the heart of all realms of society, including the economy and culture. Each social realm is based on social production that forms the material foundation of humans and society.

Each social realm also has particular, emergent dynamics and contradictions that cannot be reduced to production. The capacity for social production is itself a combination of the capacity to form and communicate ideas and the capacity to experience, engage with and transform the environment, that is a dialectic of communication and work. Social production combines the work character of communication and the communicative character of work (Fuchs 2020a).

An important question for any theory of society is that of how culture and the economy are related.

9.4.2 Culture and the economy

Roy challenges the assumption that culture and ideas are reducible to the economy and therefore derive from economic structures, that is productive forces and the relations of production. He stresses that culture has a particular logic that is based on and influences human experiences and events in society:

> The logical development of ideas and the generation of new social forces take place simultaneously, together providing the motive force of history. But in no given period can they be causally connected except in the sense that action is always motivated by ideas. (Roy 1989, 10)

> We do not accept the Marxist doctrine that moral values, cultural patterns, aesthetic tastes, are all ideological super-structures of economic relations […] the so-called ideological super-structure is not hanging in the air; that it too has its own roots. Ideas, undoubtedly, are influenced by social experience, influencing, at the same time, social and historical events. But they have a logic and dynamics of their own.
> (Roy 1960/1947, 70–71)

> Ideation is a physiological process resulting from the awareness of environments. But once they are formed, ideas exist by themselves, governed by their own laws. […] Cultural patterns and ethical values are not mere ideological super-structures of established economic relations. They are also historically determined – by the logic of the history of ideas.
> (Roy 1953, 52)

For Roy, ideologies and ideas are "structures standing by themselves" and not superstructures (1960/1947, 71). Materialism means for Roy that the productive forces do not determine history because they are "the collective expression of the creativeness of man, and the creative man is always a thinking man" (1989, 8). This means that humans, because of their self-consciousness and "the creative role of intelligence" (1989, 8), have the capacity to make choices, to envision the future, to identify and act based on interests, and to organise and act collectively.

In his book *Revolution and Counter-Revolution in China*, Roy (1946/1930, 3, 6–7), following Plekhanov, argues that "social evolution" is determined by "the natural conditions and forces of production" (1946/1930, 3). Roy, therefore, argues, for example, that in ancient China, the "evolution of private property [...] was caused by the development of the means of production", and that the "progressive perfection of tools in the hands of man – the development of the means of production – again is determined by physical conditions" (1946/1930, 17). The problem with this view is that technology, nature and work as aspects of the forces of production do not operate independently but within definite social relations between human beings. The views of Roy and Plekhanov disregard the relations of production and are therefore prone to a naturalistic and technological determinism. Roy's critique of economic determinism during his last, humanist phase of intellectual development was partly also self-criticism of his earlier thought.

Humanism is both a worldview and a political movement. Any movement has a worldview that guides and interacts with its practices. There is a dialectic of ideas and practices. The rise of various humanist movements is not reducible to the economic structure of feudalism but stands in the context of class and social struggles and therefore collective social practices. Humans who oppose a certain social order and organise themselves engage in collective practices and develop collective ideas that guide their collective struggle. Marx's father was a relatively well-situated lawyer. Engels' father owned large textile factories in Salford (UK) and Barmen (Prussia). Rosa Luxemburg's father was a timber trader. George Lukács' mother was the heir of a rich timber trading family and his father was a bank director. These examples show that the class and family backgrounds of those who engage in certain movements do not mechanically determine their political positions and the question of whether they join certain movements. That there is a relative autonomy of ideas so that ideas are socially produced and interact with economy and society means that political position and worldview cannot be read from and are not determined by class background.

Marx points out that once a certain ideology becomes historically attached to a class, this class supports and creates individuals and groups who develop this ideology. He speaks of a "division of mental and material labour" (Marx and Engels 1845–1846, 60) in the ruling class: "inside this class one part appears as the thinkers of the class (its active, conceptive ideologists, who make the formation of the illusions of the class about itself their chief source of livelihood)" (Marx and Engels 1845–1846, 60). The

> individuals composing the ruling class possess among other things consciousness, and therefore think. Insofar, therefore, as they rule as a class and determine the extent and compass of an historical epoch, it is self-evident that they do this in its whole range, hence among other things rule also as thinkers, as producers of ideas, and regulate the production and distribution of the ideas of their age: thus their ideas are the ruling ideas of the epoch.
> (Marx and Engels 1845–1846, 59)

Given a division of labour in the ruling class, one cannot assume that capitalists directly determine the ideas disseminated with the help of books, public debates, business schools, the media, and so on. Intellectuals have their own logic and interests and in the first instance often strive to accumulate reputation and not monetary capital. With the help of funding, donations, consultancy, cultural networks, the support of think tanks, the ownership of media, etc., capital exerts indirect pressure on the realm of the production of ideology. At the same time, ideologues who strive for reputation are also keen on shaping the ideas of members of the ruling class and the political elite in order to increase their own reputation. Similar things can be said about the relationship between intellectuals and politicians who strive to accumulate power.

There is a complex relationship between ideologues, political actors and economic actors in capitalist society. They strive towards accumulating reputation (ideologues), power (political actors) and money capital (capitalists). Insofar as these logics coincide, they enter mutually beneficial relations that can develop their own contradictions and can therefore also break down.

In some, but certainly not all passages of his writings that focus on culture, it seems that Roy sees culture as almost independent from political economy, simply saying that his approach is materialist because everything including ideas is material. The consequence of such an assumption is a materialist dualism where the whole world is material, while within society there are independent material substances, namely culture and the economy. Culture cannot be reduced to political economy; however, it is also not fully independent but grounded in the economy, and at the same time relatively autonomous.

Roy (1947b, 898) argues that Marx's suggestion that being determines consciousness implies that "man's ideals are shaped by the tools with which he works". However, a mode of production does not only consist of the productive forces but also interacts with the relations of production. Marx suggests that consciousness is embedded into society's social relations because humans are ensembles of social relations, which means that technology is not, as assumed by technological determinism, the determining factor of society. Rather, social relations are the determining factor of culture, ideas, politics, and the economy, which means that society only exists in and through humans' social relations.

Marx argues that the mode of production is not simply the "physical existence of the individuals", but "a definite form of activity of these individuals" in which they express their lives (Marx and Engels 1845–1846, 31). It is "a definite *mode of life*" (Marx and Engels 1845–1846, 31): "The production of ideas, of conceptions, of consciousness, is at first directly interwoven with the material activity and the material intercourse of men – the language of real life" (36). Material production includes "[c]onceiving], thinking, the mental intercourse of men" (36), "mental production as expressed in the language of [...] politics, laws, morality, religion, metaphysics, etc." (36). This means that for Marx ideas are material entities and thinking is a material process. And the production of ideas is a social process. Culture as the production and circulation of ideas and meanings takes place within the ensemble of social relations that constitutes the human subject. Marx and Engels stressed that ideas depend on the social relations of the humans who think, create, share, and reproduce them:

> *Ideas* can never lead beyond an old world order but only beyond the ideas of the old world order. Ideas *cannot carry out anything* at all. In order to carry out ideas men are needed who can exert practical force.
> (Marx and Engels 1845, 119)

> Undeterred by this examination, the French Revolution gave rise to ideas which led beyond the *ideas* of the entire old world order.
> (Marx and Engels 1845, 119)

In respect to Marx's (1845–1846) passages from the *German Ideology* mentioned in the preceding paragraph, Roy (1989, 393–394) argues that Marx does not see that consciousness is foundational for human activities. This assessment is flawed: Marx conceives of consciousness as a material because the brain is a material system. And self-consciousness enables human freedom:

free, conscious activity is man's species-character. [...] Conscious life activity distinguishes man immediately from animal life activity. It is just because of this that he is a species-being. Or it is only because he is a species-being that he is a conscious being, that is, that his own life is an object for him. Only because of that is his activity free activity. Estranged labour reverses this relationship, so that it is just because man is a conscious being that he makes his life activity, his *essential being*, a mere means to his *existence*.
(Marx 1844, 276)

The struggle against religious and monarchic authority has expressed itself not just in the realm of politics and the economy but also in realms such as philosophy, science, art, education, and literature, that is in cultural forms. The political-economic and the cultural movements and social forms that challenged the feudal social order that dominated the Dark Ages all shared certain goals and interests but did not originate from the same people and were not organised within one overall unified, consistent movement. The Enlightenment was a political-economic and cultural movement consisting of many strands that challenged the feudal system's economic, political, and cultural structures.

As one example for the relationship of ideas and the economy, Roy discusses the relationship of humanism and the bourgeoisie: "Renaissance Humanism was not the ideology of the rising bourgeoisie" (1989, 79). Humanism rather started and developed as a movement that challenged religious, monarchic, aristocratic, feudal authority and rule. It took on different forms, including liberalism, reactionary romanticism, socialism, and communism, which means that humanism is a contradictory movement.

Liberalism developed in the sixteenth century independently from the economy "according to the logic of the evolution of thought" (1989, 300). Later on, "a particular class" – the bourgeoisie – "accepted it" (300). Roy argues that given this sequence, liberalism is not "the ideology of the bourgeoisie" and the "philosophy of capitalism" (300, see also 303, 318). He writes that liberalism and capitalism developed simultaneously and concomitantly (302) and sees liberalism as going beyond economic philosophy and extending into politics and the ways of life (301–302). For Roy, the origin of liberalism is "the movement for the secularisation of politics" (303). He argues that liberalism did not originate as a capitalist project but was at a certain point of time adopted and shaped by the bourgeois class.

The classical liberal thinkers John Locke (1632–1704) and Thomas Hobbes (1588–1679) predominantly focused on political philosophy. Thinkers such as Adam Smith (1723–1790), Thomas Malthus (1766–1834), David Ricardo (1772–1823), James Mill (1773–1836), and John Stuart Mill (1806–1873) extended classical liberalism from politics to political economy. As a consequence, the classical political economy developed. These thinkers combined economic and moral philosophy. In contrast to Locke and Hobbes, they lived at the time of the decay of feudalism, the emergence of industrial capitalism, the Enlightenment, and the French Revolution. It is certainly true, as Roy argues, that liberalism did not originate as the ideology of capitalism, but as a broader ideology and philosophy that in the 18th and 19th centuries was turned into the ideology of capitalism. This was not an accident but had to do with the search of the rising bourgeoisie for an ideology guiding its practices and justifying its interests.

A certain mode of production or phase of development of the economy does not result in a single dominant idea system or form of culture. Ideas and culture cannot be read off the mode of production. We can learn from Roy that a mode of production influences but does not determine forms of culture. In relation to a particular mode of production, a variety of cultural forms and cultural contradictions exist. In his *Introduction to the Grundrisse*, Marx (1857) speaks in this context of "*the uneven development of material production relative to for example artistic development*" (109, emphasis in original) and stresses that in "the case of the arts, it is well known that certain periods of their flowering are out of all proportion to the general development of society, hence also to the material foundation, the skeletal structure as it were, of its organization". This means that culture can but does not necessarily have to flourish in periods of political-economic crises. A crisis of political economy can but does not have to be accompanied by the demise of dominant cultural forms and the emergence of radical cultural novelties.

Communication is an important theme of cultural theory that the next sub-section addresses.

9.4.3 Communication

For Roy (1950a), culture has to do with the ways we experience the world and with the intellectual and emotional world. Communication is a key feature of culture. Wherever there is communication there is culture, and wherever we communicate we produce and reproduce culture. Marx argues that "neither thoughts nor language in themselves form a realm of their own, that they are only *manifestations* of actual life" (Marx and

Engels 1845–1846, 447). And actual life is the "ensemble of the social relations" of individuals, groups, social systems and society (Marx 1845, 7). Culture and communication exist as social relations in which humans produce meaning in the world. These cultural relations exist in connection to society's ensemble of social relations and the ensemble of social relations that humans engage in.

Roy (1940) argues that "[s]ense-perceptions, human experience, gained not in passive contemplation (it cannot be done that way), but in active functioning of the human organism, and having for their source the material world existing objectively outside our consciousness, independent of it, is the point of departure of all knowledge" (1940, 252). He writes that

> knowledge is derived not in passive contemplation, but in action. 'Philosophers have interpreted the world in various ways, but the real task is to transform it'. Only in the process of transforming the world continuously, does the store of human knowledge endlessly increase; and the knowledge of a given epoch is valuable in so far as it enables man to transform the world, thereby opening a new epoch of progress.
>
> (1940, 268)

Roy states that "[k]nowledge is possible because there is a causal connection between mind and matter" (1947a, 195). Ideas "represent the knowledge of things" (195); they result from mental activities (196); "[k]nowledge results from perception, which is organic reaction to physical contacts" (195). We must add that knowledge is not only formed by humans engaging with physical environments but also with social environments. Humans interact with things when they touch, feel, move, and change them, but things do not talk; they have no language. In the social and societal environment, humans act as languaging, communicating beings so that they interact symbolically with each other, which means that they interpret each other and form meanings of each other.

Living beings react to the world they are part of and that they experience, which is why humans establish a relationship between mind and the world (198). Knowledge is at the same time objective and subjective (198): knowledge is the subjective, mental act of cognising the world (202) that constructs knowledge as an object in the human mind (203). Perception is the process that puts the human subject in relation to the world. Knowing/cognition builds on perception. It is "not a tacit reception or recoding of messages from the external world" (204–205), but an "intelligent reaction" to "messages" that "are stimuli" and sense data (205) gained through experience: "Cognition is an interpretative, denotative, selective, act" (205); "[k]nowledge is a conceptual scheme born out of the insight into the nature of things, gained through critical examination, rational co-ordination and logical deduction of perceptual data" (206).

Roy does not discuss communication in detail, but we can build on his insights. We can apply Roy's ideas to the communication process: in communication, humans establish relations between their minds and thereby between individuals that constitute, produce, and reproduce the social world. They produce and reproduce social relations (Fuchs 2020a). When human beings A and B communicate, then A constructs B as an object in A's mind and B constructs A as an object in B's mind. They sense, perceive, cognise, and experience each other, and react to each other's messages by making meaning of them and creating and externalising symbols as a response. For communicating, humans use their brains as major intellectual means of production, and linguistic and symbolic means of communication through words, grammar, bodily movements, etc. Words are "vehicles for the expression and communication of [...] emotions and ideas" (Roy 1989, 7); "[l]anguages develop to serve the purpose of coordinating disjointed ideas and emotions" (Roy 1989, 7).

Communication is the process through which humans make meaning out of each other. In communication, they mutually reveal ideas, that interprets the world, to each other. Communication is the production of social relations where at least two humans externalise knowledge in symbolic forms, and cognise each other and each other's ideas, such that they interpret the other and their ideas. In communication, humans create messages that reach other humans, beginning a perception and cognition process that results in the construction of mutual knowledge of each other. Communication is the mutual externalisation of knowledge through the human sense organs and the internalisation of externalised knowledge. Given that, for Roy, cognition is an active process, communication is the human production and reproduction of social relations (Fuchs 2020a).

The realm of culture, that is the production and communication of ideas and meanings, is an important aspect of Roy's theory of society.

9.5 Conclusions

This chapter engaged with foundations of M. N. Roy's theory and asked was: How can M. N. Roy's radical, Marxist humanism inform the critical study of communication, culture, technology, and the human being? We can summarise the main findings:

Humanism

- For Roy, humanism is a romantic movement that stresses the transformative capacity of human beings so that they can collectively make their own history.
- For Roy, humanism is a movement for economic, political and cultural democracy, a movement for a participatory democracy that is based on co-operatives and networks of local assemblies.
- Although Roy appreciates Marx's humanism, he argues that there is a fatalistic tendency in Marx's works that sees history as being determined by dialectical economic laws, advances moral relativism, and ignores the importance of human essence for humanism and democracy. Roy's interpretation was not able to take into account some of Marx's important works, especially the *Economic and Philosophic Manuscripts*, where Marx engages with the notions of human essence as social, creative, self-conscious, productive beings and capitalism/class society as alienation from the human essence in order to ground a humanist-socialist philosophy and politics.
- Roy misinterprets Marx's use of Hegelian dialectics. For Marx, dialectics is not simply an objective law but, in society, also operates at the level of the human subject and its social relations, which means that class struggle is an open, dialectical process that has the potential to change society's history. There is a dialectic of the subjective dialectic and the objective dialectic. Class struggle as the making and unmaking of class relations between the exploited and the exploited is the subjective dimension of history. It does not make sense to oppose Marx the humanist and Marx the Hegelian. Marx's dialectic is humanist and his humanism dialectical.

Technology

- Roy opposed Gandhi's nationalism and his vision of ethical capitalism. He argues that Gandhi's politics of a simple life is a form of pessimistic technological determinism, as opposed to industry and modern technologies and thereby celebrating poverty and toil, which support capitalist interests.
- Roy stresses the dialectical character of modern technology; that is, its potential to advance slavery and freedom. The actual effects of science and technology depend on human interests, social relations and human practices in these relations.

- While Gandhi was an anti-modernist, Roy argues for an alternative, socialist-humanist modernity that shapes, creates and uses technologies in manners that abolish toil and advance freedom, democracy and sustainability.
- There are strong parallels between Roy's and Herbert Marcuse's analysis of modern technology. Like Roy, Marcuse rejects anti-technological ideology that celebrates toil; Marcuse, like Roy, identifies both emancipatory and repressive potentials of modern technology and argues that the actual character and impact of technology depends on broader societal contexts, interests and struggles; Marcuse, like Roy, argues for socialist modernity where technology is shaped and used in manners that overcome toil and advance freedom, and technology is governed in a democratic manner.

Communication and culture

- Roy advances a materialist monist position, which states that the entire world is material.
- Roy sees the brain as humans' key means of production and humans as thinking beings capable of conceptual, creative, anticipatory thought. What needs to be added to Roy's approach is the crucial role of work and production in human existence. Humans are thinking, creative, social, producing, communicating beings. Social production combines the work character of communication and the communicative character of work.
- Roy challenges the assumption that culture and ideas are reducible to the economy.
- Roy's critique of economic determinism during his last, humanist phase of intellectual development was partly also self-criticism of his earlier thought that, based on Plekhanov, saw productive forces and especially geography as determining society.
- Society only exists in and through humans' social relations. Culture as the production and circulation of ideas and meanings takes place within the ensemble of social relations that constitutes the human subject.
- Culture cannot be reduced to political economy; however, it is also not fully independent but grounded in the economy, and at the same time relatively autonomous. Ideas and culture cannot be read off the mode of production. We can learn from Roy that a mode of production influences but does not determine forms of culture.

- In the communication process, humans establish relations between their minds and thereby between individuals that constitute, produce, and reproduce the social world. They produce and reproduce social relations.

Roy's approach shows that the claim that Marxian theory, socialism, and humanism are Western- or Euro-centric and therefore cultural imperialist approaches are erroneous. Whereas Dipesh Chakrabarty (2008, 4) argues that Roy was one of the "illustrious members" of the "modern Bengali educated middle classes" that "warmly embraced the themes of rationalism, science, equality, and human rights that the European Enlightenment promulgated", Kris Manjapra (2010) argues in his book about Roy that the latter was not "entrapped in the ideologies attendant to global capital" (xviii), but an "anti-colonial cosmopolitan thinker" (xxi).

Robert Spencer (2017) maintains that post-colonial scholars often tar "all humanisms with the same brush" (121) and "champion difference at the expense of equality" and identity politics over class politics so that to "be a postcolonialist, it seems, is to leave one's humanism at the door" (124). Spencer argues for a humanist postcolonialism that is "exercised above all not by crimes against hybridity but by crimes against humanity" (122), that stresses the human "capacity for self-creation" (128) and that speaks "the language of rights [...] animated by the conviction that there *are* irreducible features of human life" (128) because "it is convinced that only by eradicating the most devastating forms of inhumanity will the human, with all its variability and unpredictableness, come into its own" (129). Humanism means "critical thinking + the ideal of solidarity" (152).

Marxist/socialist humanism allows us to approach the global world as a unity of diverse tendencies. It is an approach that enables the analysis of society in different contexts based on what Vivek Chibber calls the two universalisms, "the universal logic of capital (suitably defined) and social agents' universal interest in their well-being, which impels them to resist capital's expansionary drive" (2013, 291). The first universalism foregrounds the accumulation of economic, political and cultural power that in different contexts and on different levels of organisation of global society creates various inequalities. The second universalism calls for solidarity of the world's oppressed and exploited in their struggles for a better world. One of the "recurring themes" in Roy's works and thought is "the reading of underling unity out of apparent difference" (Manjapra 2010, 168).

Three of the main challenges and global problems that humanity faces today are a) the threats of exploding inequalities, accelerating and deepening political-economic crises, fascism, war, violence and genocide posed by the rise of authoritarian capitalism and new nationalisms, b) the threat posed to humans and the environment by natural disasters, climate change and the global environmental crisis, and c) new forms of control and exploitation in the context of capitalist digital technologies, AI-based automation, and algorithmic politics.

The political-economic crisis, the environmental crisis, and the digital crisis have in common that they are crises that threaten fundamental aspects of human life, namely democracy, the survival of the species and the planet, and self-fulfilment. They are crises of humanity. The three crises together radicalise the alienation of humans from nature, the economy, political systems, and culture to the point that the interaction of these crises can in the future result in a breakdown of humanity and the livelihood of future generations. We need radical alternatives. As Alderson and Spencer state, "The Left [...] requires a compelling vision of the future as *more* just, democratic, ecologically sustainable and subjectively satisfying around which it will be possible to construct a viable counter-hegemony" (2017, 218). Radical humanism is important today because it advances the counter-vision of a humane society against the dystopias the three crises could result in. Radical humanism can thereby inform social struggles. Radical humanism struggles for the strengthening of the political-economic commons (common control of political and economic organisations), the natural commons (common survival in a natural environment that interacts with humans in sustainable manners), and the knowledge and digital commons (knowledge, culture, and digital resources as common goods).

In the age of new nationalisms and authoritarian capitalism, global environmental crises, capitalist crisis, and the digital crisis, socialist-humanist theories such as that of M. N. Roy can inspire struggles for a humanist and socialist society as antidotes to the acceleration and deepening of the three crises. In his *Principles of Radical Democracy*, Roy (1953, 52–62) formulates 22 theses. The final one should be seen as the starting point for contemporary socialist, anti-fascist and anti-nationalist struggles:

> Radicalism starts from the dictum that 'man is the measure of everything' (Protagoras) or 'man is the root of mankind' (Marx), and advocates reconstruction of the world as a commonwealth and fraternity of free [...] [humans], by the collective endeavour of spiritually emancipated moral [...] [humans]. (Roy 1953, 62)

Literature

Alderson, David and Robert Spencer, eds. 2017. *For Humanism: Explorations in Theory and Politics*. London: Pluto Press.

Bastani, Aaron. 2019. *Fully Automated Luxury Communism: A Manifesto*. London: Verso.

Bhattacharya, Subhrajit. 2016. "Perspectives on Fascism: M. N. Roy, Horkheimer and Adorno." In *M. N. Roy Reader: Essential Writings Volume 3*, edited by Bhaskar Sur and R. M. Pal, 1431–1438. Delhi: Aakar Books.

Bloch, Ernst. 2019. *Avicenna and the Aristotelean Left*. New York: Columbia University Press.

Bose, Nirmal Kumar. 1948. *Selections from Gandhi*. Ahmedabad: Navajivan Publishing House.

Chakrabarty, Dipesh. 2008. *Provincializing Europe: Postcolonial Thought and Historical Difference*. Princeton, NJ: Princeton University Press.

Chibber, Vivek. 2013. *Postcolonial Theory and the Specter of Capital*. London: Verso.

Department for Business, Energy & Industrial Strategy. 2019. *The Grand Challenges*. https://www.gov.uk/government/publications/industrial-strategy-the-grand-challenges/industrial-strategy-the-grand-challenges#artificial-intelligence-and-data (version from 22 May 2019).

Ford, Martin. 2015. *Rise of Robots: Technology and the Threat of a Jobless Future*. New York: Basic Books.

Fromm, Erich. 2002/1956. *The Sane Society*. Abingdon: Routledge.

——— 1969 ———. 1969/1941. *Escape from Freedom*. New York: Avon Books.

Fuchs, Christian. 2020a. *Communication and Capitalism. A Critical Theory*. London: University of Westminster Press.

——— 2020 ———. 2020b. *Nationalism on the Internet: Critical Theory and Ideology in the Age of Social Media and Fake News*. New York: Routledge.

——— 2018 ———. 2018. *Digital Demagogue: Authoritarian Capitalism in the Age of Trump and Twitter*. London: Pluto Press.

Gandhi, Mohandas Karamchand. 1997. *"Hind Swaraj" and Other Writings*. Edited by Anthony J. Parel. Cambridge: Cambridge University Press.

——— 1983 ———. 1983/1948. *Autobiography: The Story of My Experiments with Truth*. Mineola, NY: Dover Publications.

Hobsbawm, Eric J. 1992. *Nations and Nationalism since 1780: Programme, Myth, Reality* [second edition]. Cambridge: Cambridge University Press.

——— Hobsbawm 1983 ———. 1983a. "Introduction: Inventing Traditions." In *The Invention of Tradition*, edited by Eric J. Hobsbawm and Terence Ranger, 1–14. Cambridge: Cambridge University Press.

——— Hobsbawm 1983 ———. 1983b. "Mass-Producing Traditions: Europe, 1870-1914." In *The Invention of Tradition*, edited by Eric J. Hobsbawm and Terence Ranger, 263–307. Cambridge: Cambridge University Press.

Lenin, Vladimir I. 1920. "Preliminary Draft Theses on the National and the Colonial Questions.

For the Second Congress of the Communist International." In *Lenin Collected Works Volume 31*, 144–151. Moscow: Progress Publishers.

Luxemburg, Rosa. 1916. "The Junius Pamphlet." In *Rosa Luxemburg Speaks*, edited by Rosa Luxemburg, 371–477. New York: Pathfinder.

Manjapra, Kris. 2010. *M. N. Roy: Marxism and Colonial Cosmopolitanism*. New Delhi: Routledge.

Marcuse, Herbert. 1988/1941. "Some Social Implications of Modern Technology." In *Collected Papers of Herbert Marcuse Volume One: Technology, War and Fascism*, edited by Douglas Kellner, 41–65. London: Routledge.

Marx, Karl. 1867. *Capital Volume One*. London: Penguin.

———— 1857 ————. 1857. *Grundrisse*. London: Penguin.

———— 1852 ————. 1852. "The Eighteenth Brumaire of Louis Bonaparte." In *Marx & Engels Collected Works (MECW) Volume 1*, 99–197. London: Lawrence & Wishart.

———— 1845 ————. 1845. "Theses on Feuerbach." In *Marx & Engels Collected Works (MECW) Volume 5*, 3–8. London: Lawrence & Wishart.

———— 1844 ————. 1844. "Economic and Philosophic Manuscripts of 1844." In *Marx & Engels Collected Works (MECW) Volume 3*, 229–346. London: Lawrence & Wishart.

Marx, Karl, and Friedrich Engels. 1845-1846. *The German Ideology. Marx & Engels Collected Works (MECW) Volume 5*. London: Lawrence & Wishart.

———— 1845 ————. 1845. "The Holy Family, or Critique of Critical Criticism. Against Bruno Bauer and Company." In *Marx & Engels Collected Works (MECW) Volume 4*, 5–211. London: Lawrence & Wishart.

Ray, Sibnarayan. 2016a. "M. N. Roy: A Biographical Chronology." In *M. N. Roy Reader: Essential Writings Volume 3*, edited by Bhaskar Sur and R. M. Pal, 1439–1462. Delhi: Aakar Books.

———— Sur 2016 ————. 2016b. "M. N. Roy in Communist Opposition." In *M. N. Roy Reader: Essential Writings Volume 3*, edited by Bhaskar Sur and R. M. Pal, 1289–1302. Delhi: Aakar Books.

Roy, M. N. 2006/1945. *Problem of Freedom*. Calcutta: Renaissance Publishers.

———— 1989 ————. 1989. *Reason, Romanticism and Revolution*. Delhi: Ajanta Publications.

———— 1968 ————. 1968. *Men I Met*. Bombay: Lalvani Publishing House.

———— 1960 ————. 1960/1947. *Beyond Communism*. Delhi: Ajanta Books.

———— 1953 ————. 1953. *New Humanism: A Manifesto*. 2nd ed. Calcutta: Renaissance Publishers.

———— Bose 1950 ————. 1950a. "Cultural Requisites of Freedom." In *Modern Age & India*, edited by Atindranath Bose, 177–192. Calcutta: Left Book Club.

———— 1950 ————. 1950b. *Fragments of a Prisoner's Diary Volume Two: India's Message*. Calcutta: Renaissance Publishers.

———— Sur 1949 ————. 1949. "A Politics for Our Time." In *M. N. Roy Reader: Essential Writings Volume 2*, edited by Bhaskar Sur and R. M. Pal, 927–941. Delhi: Aakar Books.

——— 1947 ———. 1947a. *Science and Philosophy*. Calcutta: Renaissance Publishers.
——— Sur 1947 ———. 1947b. Since the *Communist Manifesto*. In *M. N. Roy Reader: Essential Writings Volume 2*, edited by Bhaskar Sur and R. M. Pal, 890–913. Delhi: Aakar Books.
——— 1946 ———. 1946/1930. *Revolution and Counter-Revolution in China*. Calcutta: Renaissance Publishers.
——— 1943 ———. 1943. *The Communist International*. Bombay: Radical Democratic Party Publications
——— 1942 ———. 1942. *Nationalism: An Antiquated Cult*. Bombay: Radical Democratic Party
——— 1940 ———. 1940. *Materialism: An Outline of the History of Scientific Thought*. Dehradun: Renaissance Publication.
——— 1938 ———. 1938. *Fascism: Its Philosophy, Professions and Practice*. Calcutta: D.M. Library.
——— 1929 ———. 1929a. "Meine Vebrechen: Offener Brief an die Mitglieder der Kommunistischen Internationale." *Gegen den Strom 37*: 9–11.
——— Sur 1929 ———. 1929b. "My Crime." In *M. N. Roy Reader: Essential Writings Volume 1*, edited by Bhaskar Sur and R. M. Pal, 188–195. Delhi: Aakar Books.
——— 1923 ———. 1923. *India's Problem and its Solution*. Charleston: Nabu Press. Reprint.
——— 1922 ———. 1922. *India in Transition*. Geneva: Edition de la Librairie J.B. Target.
——— 1920 ———. 1920. *Supplementary Theses on the National and Colonial Question*. Presented at the Fourth Session of the Second Congress of the Communist International, July 25. https://www.marxists.org/history/international/comintern/2nd-congress/ch04.htm.
Roy, Samaren. 1997. *M. N. Roy: A Political Biography*. London: Sangam Books.
——— 1987 ———. 1987. *M. N. Roy and Mahatma Gandhi*. Columbia, MO: South Asia Books.
Spencer, Robert. 2017. Postcolonialism is a Humanism. In *For Humanism: Explorations in Theory and Politics*, edited by David Alderson and Robert Spencer, 120–162. London: Pluto Press.
Srnicek, Nick, and Alex Williams. 2015. *Inventing the Future: Postcapitalism and a World Without Work*. London: Verso.
Tarkunde, Vithal Mahaedo. 1982. "Introduction to the Author." In *New Orientation*, edited by M. N. Roy, v–x. Delhi: Ajanta Publications.
Tendulkar, Dinanath Gopal. 1953. *Mahatma: Life of Mohandas Karamchand Gandhi. Vol. VI: 1945-1947*. New Delhi: Publications Division.
Williams, Alex, and Nick Srnicek. 2013. *#Accelerate: Manifesto for An Accelerationist Politics*. https://syntheticedifice.files.wordpress.com/2013/06/accelerate.pdf.
Williams, Raymond. 2003/1974. *Television: Technology and Cultural Form*. London: Routledge.

Chapter Ten
Capitalism, racism, patriarchy

10.1 Introduction
10.2 Housework, reproductive labour, and capitalism
10.3 Capitalism and racism
10.4 Capitalism, racism, patriarchy
10.5 Conclusion
Literature

10.1 Introduction

This chapter asks: How are exploitation and domination related? What is the connection between capitalism, racism, and patriarchy? For providing answers, it engages with and combines Marxist class theory, Marxist feminism, and Black Marxism.

The approach taken engages with and combines Marxist political economy, Marxist feminism, and black Marxism, including works by Vivek Chibber, Mariarosa Dalla Costa, Angela Davis's Marxist black feminism, W. E. B. Du Bois, Zillah Eisenstein, Eric J. Hobsbawm, C. L. R. James, Selma James, Rosa Luxemburg, Karl Marx, Maria Mies, Eve Mitchell, Cedric J. Robinson's, David Roediger's wages of whiteness approach, Marisol Sandoval, Sylvia Walby, Carter Wilson and Audrey Smedley's historical analyses of racism and class, and Cornel West.

One important question that arises in this context is how the economic and the non-economic are related to each other. This question is not just of theoretical relevance but also matters politically. It focuses on how class politics that struggle for redistribution of resources and identity politics that struggle for the recognition of oppressed identities are related (Fraser & Honneth 2003). Reductionist politics privilege either class or identity politics, whereas dualist politics say that both realms and demands are important without relating them (Fuchs 2011, section 2.3).

In Marxist feminism, patriarchy has not just been seen as a form of sexist oppression but as the exploitation of houseworkers in capitalism. In Black Marxism, an inherent connection between capitalism and racism is theorised with the help of the category of racial capitalism.

Section 10.2 discusses the relationship between housework and reproductive labour to capitalism. Section 10.3 analyses the connection between racism and capitalism. Section 10.4 focuses on the relation of capitalism, racism, and patriarchy. Section 10.5 draws conclusions.

10.2 Housework, reproductive labour, and capitalism

Reproductive labour

Women have historically carried out the largest share of reproductive labour, such as child-rearing, care, education, cooking, laundry, shopping, cleaning, etc. In contemporary capitalism, many more women are active in the paid labour force than 100 or 200 years ago. However, housework is still predominantly women's concern, which creates multiple responsibilities and less free time for them.

Friedrich Engels (1892, 131) argues that patriarchy was history's first class relation:

> In an old unpublished manuscript, the work of Marx and myself in 1846, I find the following: 'The first division of labour is that between man and woman for child breeding'. And today I can add: The first class antithesis which appears in history coincides with the development of the antagonism between man and woman in monogamian marriage, and the first class oppression with that of the female sex by the male.
>
> (Engels 1892, 173)

Angela Davis shows that in the USA women slaves' labour was different than white women's labour. Domestic work was the only labour that was not under the slavemaster's control (Davis 1983, 17). There was relative equality in the slaves' quarters, and men and women worked together (Davis 1983, 18). Black women's lives were characterised by "hard work with their men, equality within the family, resistance, floggings and rape" (Davis 1983, 27). In 2017, the white US women's labour force participation rate was 55.6%, whereas it was 58.5% for black women (Bureau of Labor Statistics BLS, 2017, table 3). In 1972, the respective rates were 43.2% and 48.7% (Bureau of Labor Statistics BLS, 2017, table 4). Black American women are to a greater degree both wage- and reproductive-workers than white women. The share of women who are doubly exploited by capital as both wage-workers and houseworkers are larger among blacks than among whites in the USA.

Marxist/socialist feminism version 1

There are two basic positions within socialist feminism on the question of whether or not housework is a form of productive labour. The *first position* can, for example, be found in *The Power of Women and the Subversion of Community* (Dalla Costa & James 1973). Dalla Costa and James (1973, 30–31) maintain that "orthodox Marxism" often assumes that women outside of wage-labour "are also outside of social productivity" and that "women in domestic labor are not productive". Such assumptions would deny "women's potential *social* power" (6). Domestic labour "produces not merely use values, but is essential to the production of surplus value" (31). It produces a commodity "unique to capitalism: the living human being – 'the labourer himself'" (6). The family would be seen not as a superstructure but as a realm of production (33) in which houseworkers perform "social services which capitalist organization transforms into privatized activity, putting them on the backs of housewives" (31). Leopoldina Fortunati (1995) stresses that reproductive labour is productive labour; "it produces and re-produces the individual as a commodity" (70) by "producing and reproducing labor-power" (70) and "the use-value of labor-power" (69). Maria Mies (1986, 37) points out that women face a threefold form of exploitation: "they are exploited [...] by men and they are exploited as housewives by capital. If they are wage-workers they are also exploited as wage-workers".

Marxist/socialist feminism version 2

The *second position* argues that domestic labour is excluded from productive labour and is thereby ideologically rendered as inferior. Roswitha Scholz (2000, 2014) formulated this assumption in the value-dissociation hypothesis (*Wertabspaltungsthese*). Abstract labour would only be possible by dissociating the sphere of reproductive labour, emotions, and sensuality:

> The value-dissociation hypothesis claims [...] a 'dissociation' of the feminine, housework etc. from value, abstract labour and the related forms of rationality that attributes specific qualities such as sensuality, emotionality etc. that are connoted as female to women; the man in contrast stands for intellectual power, strength of character, courage, etc. The man was under

modern development equated with culture, the woman with nature (Scholz 2000, 9, translation from German)[1]

The Endnotes Collective's (2013) argument is comparable to the one made by Scholz:

> The activity of turning the raw materials equivalent to the wage into labour-power takes place *in a separate sphere from the production and circulation of values*. These necessary non-labour activities do not produce value, not because of their concrete characteristics, but rather, because they take place in a sphere of the capitalist mode of production which is not directly mediated by the form of value. [...] There must be an exterior to value in order for value to exist. Similarly, for labour to exist and serve as the measure of value, there must be an exterior to labour. While the autonomist feminists would conclude that every activity which reproduces labour-power produces value, we would say that, for labour-power to have a value, some of these activities have to be cut off or dissociated from the sphere of value production.

Angela Davis shares the second position. For her, housework is dissociated from wage-labour:

> Within capitalism, household labor, generating only the value of utility, is no longer related to the productive apparatus. [...] women experience a double inferiority: They are first prohibited, by virtue of their family standing, from consistently and equally reaching the point of production. Secondly, the labor they continue to monopolize does not measure up to the characteristic labor of capitalist society.
>
> (Davis 1977, 176)

Davis (1977, 176) speaks of the "labor of utility as opposed to that of exchange" and writes that housework is not abstract labour (177). There is "a fundamental *structural* separation between the domestic home economy and the profit-oriented economy of capitalism. Since housework does not generate profit, domestic labor was naturally

---

[1] German original: „Die Wert-Abspaltungsthese behauptet nun [...] eine ‚Abspaltung' des Weiblichen, der Hausarbeit etc. vom Wert, von der abstrakten Arbeit und den damit zusammenhängenden Rationalitätsformen, wobei bestimmte weiblich konnotierte Eigenschaften wie Sinnlichkeit, Emotionalität usw. der Frau zugeschrieben werden; der Mann hingegen steht etwa für Verstandeskraft, charakterliche Stärke, Mut usw. Der Mann wurde in der modernen Entwicklung mit Kultur, die Frau mit Natur gleichgesetzt" (Scholz 2000, 9).

defined as an inferior form of work as compared to capitalist wage labor" (Davis 1983, 228). There is a "structural separation of the public economy of capitalism and the private economy of the home" (229).

One argument against the second position can be found in Marx's works. He argues that the capitalist division of labour resulted in the emergence of the collective labourer (*Gesamtarbeiter*). "In order to work productively, it is no longer necessary for the individual himself to put his hand to the object; it is sufficient for him to be an organ of the collective labourer, and to perform any of its subordinate functions" (Marx 1867, 643–644). This means that in a software company not just the software engineers who produce the software commodity are productive workers, but also the secretaries, cleaners, janitors, accountants, marketers, etc. Productive labour produces surplus-value – "it must appear in surplus produce, that is an *additional increment of a commodity* on behalf of the monopolizer of the means of labour, the capitalist" (1039). The value of labour-power is the time that it takes to reproduce it. "The value of labour-power is determined, as in the case of every other commodity, by the labour-time necessary for the production, and consequently also the reproduction, of this specific article. [...] the value of labour-power is the value of the means of subsistence necessary for the maintenance of its owner" (274).

Wages for housework

Angela Davis is critical of the Wages for Housework movement and its theoretical foundations. "The demand that housewives be paid is based on the assumption that they produce a commodity as important and as valuable as the commodities their husbands produce on the job" (Davis 1983, 233–234). Davis says it cannot be denied that house workers' "procreative, child-rearing and housekeeping roles make it possible for their family members to work – to exchange their labor-power for wages" (234). But house workers would be structurally separated from the capitalist production process. So Davis tends to share the value dissociation hypothesis. Housework

> cannot be defined as an integral component of capitalist production. It is, rather, related to production as a *precondition*. The employer is not concerned in the least about the way labor-power is produced and sustained, he is only concerned about its availability and its ability to generate profit. In other words, the capitalist production process presupposes the existence of a body of exploitable workers.
>
> (Davis 1983, 234)

Wages for housework would not aim at abolishing housework, but could rather reify and keep women tied to the home. The demand would also not question wage-labour as an integral part of capitalism. "The Wages for Housework Movement discourages women from seeking outside jobs" (Davis 1983, 239). "In the United States, women of color – and especially Black women – have been receiving wages for housework for untold decades. [...] Cleaning women, domestic workers, maids – these are the women who know better than anyone else what it means to receive wages for housework" (237). Davis demands the "abolition of housework" and says that "it may well be true that 'slavery to an assembly line' is not in itself 'liberation from the kitchen sink', but the assembly line is doubtlessly the most powerful incentive for women to press for the elimination of their age-old domestic slavery" (243).

Davis is particularly critical of Dalla Costa and James' (1973, 33) formulation that '"[s]lavery to an assembly line is not a liberation from slavery to a kitchen sink". The two socialist feminists argue that wage-labour would not mean the liberation of house workers but another form of slavery: "[W]omen are the slaves of wage slaves' (43). Dalla Costa and James do not uncritically embrace the demand of wages for housework. They say on the one hand that such a demand risks 'to entrench the condition of institutionalized slavery which is produced within the condition of housework" (34) but argue on the other hand that, practically speaking, this demand also helped to radicalise and unify the socialist-feminist movement in Italy (52–53, footnote 16).

Silvia Federici's (1975) *Wages against Housework* manifesto argues that the "unwaged condition of housework has been the most powerful weapon in reinforcing the common assumption that *housework is not work*"(2). "To say that we want money for housework is the first step towards refusing to do it, because the demand for a wage makes our work visible, which is the most indispensable condition to begin to struggle against it [...] To say that we want wages for housework is to expose the fact that housework is already money for capital" (5). The lack of a wage for housework has "also been the primary cause of our [houseworkers'] weakness in the wage labor market" (Federici 2012, 34). The invisibility of housework is also sustained by the fact that it is not included in the calculation of the GDP (Federici 2012, 42). The demand of wages for housework "exposed the enormous amount of unpaid labor that goes on unchallenged and unseen in this society" (Federici 2012, 56). Federici's goal is both the abolition of wage-labour and housework, which is a perspective that Davis shares. They differ on the question of whether or not a wage for housework is a feasible political demand.

The point is to avoid two extremes, namely to focus on political demands and action either solely on the waged workplace or the household. Given that both realms are interlinked, the struggle for the abolishment of wage-labour and housework should also be connected. Demanding wages for housework does not automatically exclude demanding equal pay for equal work. Higher wages in any case weaken capital's power and to find ways to strengthen the autonomy and power of the working class, which includes the power of houseworkers.

A guaranteed basic income funded by capital taxation that guarantees a living wage can both empower wage-workers and houseworkers: wage-workers can refuse to take on jobs that are in any respect precarious, which empowers their position vis-à-vis capital. Houseworkers are strengthened because a basic income that they receive individually makes them independent from wage-workers in the same household and allows them more social and financial autonomy. The total effect of such a version of the basic income guarantee on the labour-capital relationship would be redistribution from the capital to labour that strengthens labour's autonomy vis-à-vis capital. Neither capital nor wage-labour nor housework would thereby automatically cease to exist, but resources, time and spaces that challenge and transcend capitalism could thereby be more easily created.

The main result of this discussion is that the position that reproductive labour is productive labour is feasible. Slave-labour and reproductive labour have in common that they are unwaged, but by being integrated into capitalist society nonetheless they create surplus-value. Racialised labour is partly waged, partly unwaged, but in any case productive and highly exploited labour.

Reproductive labour time

The total production time of capital includes the reproductive labour time that reproduces the labour-power as a commodity. Reproductive labour is productive because it is surplus-labour time unremunerated by capital. Capital not just exploits wage-labour, but also the reproductive labour required for the existence and reproduction of labour-power. Based on Marx's analysis, we can say that the exploitation of labour entails not a dual separation but a dialectic of reproductive labour and wage-labour. If reproductive labour were paid at the average wage, then profits would dwindle and capitalism would not be able to survive. This fact shows on the one hand the importance of reproductive labour in capitalism. On the other hand, it also indicates capitalism's inherent drive and needs to create milieus of unpaid labour to survive.

A very important part of housework is made up of household activities such as food preparation, cleaning, lawn and garden care, and household management. According to statistics, US women in 2019 spent on average 48 minutes more time on such activities than men (men: 1.39 hours per day, women: 2.16 hours per day).[2] Another important activity is caring for and helping others. Whereas US men spent 0.48 hours per day on caring for and helping others, the amount for women was 0.86 hours. Shopping took up 0.61 hours per day for men and 0.87 hours for women. Such data indicate that US women tend to be responsible for, on average, 60% of reproductive labour and men 40%. Reproductive labour is both gendered and racialised. It is predominantly a realm of women, and in the case of paid reproductive labour, low-paid migrant workers and workers of colour form a proportionally very large share of the workforce. Capitalism is inherently connected to patriarchy and racism.

10.3 Capitalism and racism

Ancient and feudal slavery

In the USA, the enslavement of people of colour was the most important historical expression of racism. Although slavery was abolished, racism continued to exist in ideological, political and economic forms of exclusion, discrimination and exploitation.

Audrey Smedley (1998) argues that before the rise of capitalism, kinship, occupation, gender and social position were the crucial features of society that shaped connectedness and identities. In the Middle Ages, religion emerged as another important marker of identity:

> What was absent from these different forms of human identity is what we today would perceive as classifications
> into 'racial' groups, that is, the organization of all peoples into a limited number of unequal or ranked categories theoretically based on differences in their biophysical traits (Smedley 1998, 693)

Slavery as a class phenomenon was, in ancient and feudal society, not essentially based on racism – thus slavery is older than racism. According to Smedley, racism emerged with European colonialism in America, English colonialism in Ireland and the African slave trade in the 16th century. Smedley (1998, 694) maintains: "'Race' developed in the minds of some Europeans as a way to rationalize the conquest and brutal treatment of Native American populations, and especially the retention and perpetuation of slavery for imported Africans". The implication of Smedley's analysis is that there are indications that racism and imperialism have been inherently linked. Racism has provided not just the opportunity for ideological feelings of superiority but also opportunities for justifying exploitation. Modern slavery has, to a significant degree, been racist slavery.

Angela Davis' Black feminist Marxism

Angela Davis acknowledges the importance of labour and capitalism in the analysis of oppression. Her contribution to *The Black Feminist Reader* (James and Sharpley-Whiting, 2000) is the only one of ten chapters that foreground the importance of both labour and capitalism for understanding racism and patriarchy and vice versa. Davis is interested in the role of black women in American slavery and contemporary capitalism. Black women slaves experienced racism by being turned into slaves because of their skin colour. Slave-masters oppressed them as women by raping them. And they were exploited as unpaid workers. The unity of their oppression and exploitation is that they were treated as completely unfree beings, as beings without any rights, who were exploited, oppressed, raped, and killed by slave-masters as they pleased.

Davis (1977, 183) argues that black women worked both outside the home for the slave-master and inside the home, so that they were not, like many white women of the time, defined by the household alone. Slaves were treated as "inorganic conditions of production" (Davis 1977, 171), as means of production, tools and things: "The slave system defined Black people as chattel" (Davis 1983, 5). The majority of slave women were, just like slave men, field workers (Davis 1983, 5). "The slave-holding class expressed its drive for profit by seeking the maximum extraction of surplus labor in utter disregard to the age or sex of the slave" (Davis 1977, 171). Female slaves had to work just like men and were, in addition, raped by white masters and seen as machines to produce new slaves.

> [W]hen it was profitable to exploit them as if they were men, they were regarded, in effect, as genderless, but when they could be exploited, punished and repressed in ways suited only for women, they were locked into their exclusive female roles. [...] They were 'breeders' – animals, whose monetary value could be precisely calculated in terms of their ability to multiply their numbers. [...] Rape, in act, was an uncamouflaged expression of the slaveholder's economic mastery and the overseer's control over Black women as workers.
> (Davis 1983, 6–7)

Slavery

Slavery is the ultimate form of alienation and fetishism: reification and alienation mean for slaves that they are treated purely as a thing and have no rights at all. They are robbed of their humanity, which makes them targets of limitless exploitation and domination. Women slaves can also be subject to rape and theft of the children they give birth to and can be forced to become slave-bearing machines.

C. L. R. James (1989) sees an inherent connection of capitalism and racism. He argues that it is both a mistake to "neglect the racial factor" and to "make it fundamental" (283). "The race question is subsidiary to the class question in politics" (283). Discussing the works of C. L. R. James, Cedric J. Robinson (2000) argues that capitalist class relations have featured both the exploitation of wage-workers and slaves, from which capital yields surplus-value in order to advance accumulation. "Capitalism had produced its social and historical negations in both poles of its expropriation: capitalist accumulation gave birth to the proletariat at the manufacturing core; 'primitive accumulation' deposited the social base for the revolutionary masses in the peripheries" (Robinson 2000, 275). James (1989, 243) writes in this context: "At the same time as the French, the half-savage slaves of San Domingo were showing themselves subject to the same historical laws as the advanced workers of revolutionary Paris".

The implication of James' and Robinson's arguments is that both wage-workers and slaves are part of the working class. Capital is based on the need of exploiting labour. It has the interest to pay no wages at all in order to maximise profits. There is an inherent connection between capitalist interests and violence. Slaves are coerced by physical violence, wage-workers by the dull compulsion of the labour-market. Slavery is capital and exploitation in a pure form that is not limited by forces that compel capital to respect the bare physical life of humans. It denies slaves of all aspects of their humanity.

Robinson (2019) argues that socialism has its foundations in the struggles of the poor. He sees "socialist discourse" as "an irrepressible response to social injustice" (124). "On that score it has been immaterial whether it was generated by peasants or slaves, workers or intellectuals, or whether it took root in the metropole or the periphery" (124). Robinson here certainly is in line with Marx's assumption that history is the history of class struggles (Marx & Engels 1848, 482), which includes the struggles of classes such as wage-workers, peasant workers, slave-workers, houseworkers, etc. Struggles for socialism reflect "the ultimate Marxian objective, the recovery of human life from the spoilage of degradation" (Robinson 2019, 1). Socialism is the struggle for the abolition of alienation.

Writing about the USA, Cornel West (2001, vii) argues that "black people in the United States differ from all other modern people owing to the unprecedented levels of unregulated and unrestrained violence directed at them". "[P]hysical violence" against people of colour has served "the primary purpose of controlling their minds and exploiting their labor for nearly four hundred years. The unique combination of American terrorism – Jim Crow and lynching – as well as American barbarism – slave trade and slave labor – bears witness to the distinctive American assault on black humanity" (West 2001, vii). The exploitation and degradation of people of colour rob them of their humanity. Racism dehumanises and reduces humans to the status of things.

Cedric J. Robinson: racial capitalism

Cedric J. Robinson (2000) argues that feudalism did not end with the rise of capitalism, but was sublated by it, which means that it was preserved in capitalism and has taken on new forms so that violence, slavery, and genocide are inherent potentials and features of capitalism. In this context, Robinson coins the notion of racial capitalism:

> The development, organization, and expansion of capitalist society pursued essentially racial directions, so too did social ideology. As a material force, then, it could be expected that racialism would inevitably permeate the social structures emergent from capitalism.
>
> (Robinson 2000, 2)

There is an inherent connection between capitalism and violence. Violence means physical caused intentionally by a human being (Walby 2020).

Violence does not mean the same as power. Violence is a social relation where humans with intention create physical harm to other human beings who don't consent (Walby 2020). The harm caused is "a physical injury" (Walby et al. 2017, 33). In addition, there can be psychological harm. Violence is the power to turn humans into corpses (Weil 2005, 183). Racism denies the humanity of human groups by declaring them to be subhuman, which is an ideological legitimation of using violence against them and the invitation to enslave them, to exploit them, or to kill them.

Cedric J. Robinson (2000) argues that immigrant and racialised labour has since the start of capitalism in the 16th century been an integral aspect of capitalism's political economy. In the 18th and 19th centuries, Irish workers were important for British capitalism, Polish workers for German capitalism, Polish, Italian and Spanish workers for French capitalism, etc. (Robinson 2000, 24). Racism emerged as ideology that justified the "domination, exploitation, and/or extermination of non-'Europeans' (including Slavs and Jews)" (27). Racism has been connected to the ideology of a superior race, such as Teutonism in Germany, Anglo-Saxonism in England and the United States or Celticism in France, and from the 19th century onwards to nationalism (27).

Building on Robinson's work, Gargi Bhattacharyya (2018, 176) argues that racial capitalism is characterised "by the manner in which powerful actors seek to requisition the means of life and value and to gain benefit from the mobilisation of racialised distinctions". She argues that the term racial capitalism does not "suggest that capitalism is inevitably racialised" (101). That one cannot rule out attempts and actuality of green capitalism, anti-racist capitalism, and feminist capitalism but that history has thus far shown the interaction of capitalism, racism, patriarchy, and environmental destruction.

Racial capitalism "includes […] three interlocking regimes – exploitation, expropriation, expulsion" (Bhattacharyya 2018, 37). "Racial capitalism might be a name for the extraction of additional value from subordinated groups or it might be a name for the racialised expropriation of resources from populations deemed disposable or it might point to processes of expulsion – and it might, most likely, be a name for the world that emerges from these combined processes" (181) – processes that in racial capitalism take place in interaction with racism. Racial capitalism means the use of racism for capitalist development (103).

Eric J. Hobsbawm: nationalism

Eric J. Hobsbawm (1992) points out that nations are not part of human essence. They are not "as old as history" (3). Nations and nationalism came into existence in the 18th century as part of the formation of modern nation-states. Hobsbawm (1992) argues that nationalism started a massive expansion in the 1980s. Integral to nationalism is the focus on linguistic, cultural and "racial" differences. Along with it comes biological and/or cultural racism that claims that certain groups are biologically and/or culturally superior and others inferior. Hobsbawm (1983) speaks about nationalism as an invented tradition, by which he means that the formation of nation-states requires the systematic invention of traditions, including nationalism. Nationalism and racism require each other. Whereas the first focuses on the glorification of the nation and a national people, the second constructs differences between the nation and perceive inferior cultures and/or "races".

From the 16th to the 19th centuries, the transatlantic slave trade was the major form of slavery and the major source of slave labour. Ideologically, Africans were seen not as humans but as "Negros", which ideologically supported their political-economic exploitation as slave-labourers working in the sugar-, tobacco-, cotton-, mining-, etc. industries. 'The invention of the Negro was proceeding apace with the growth of slave labor" (Robinson 2000, 119). Estimations of the number of individuals transported from Africa in the transatlantic slave trade range between ten and fifty million (Robinson 2000, 112).

Marx on slavery

Slavery has been part of the formation and development of capitalism. Marx argues in this context:

> direct slavery, the slavery of the Blacks in Surinam, in Brazil, in the southern regions of North America [...] is as much the pivot upon which our present-day industrialism turns as are machinery, credit, etc. Without slavery there would be no cotton, without cotton there would be no modern industry. It is slavery which has given value to the colonies, it is the colonies which have created world trade, and world trade is the necessary condition for large-scale machine industry. [...] Slavery is therefore an economic category of paramount importance. Without slavery, North America, the most progressive nation, would be transformed into a patriarchal country.
>
> (Marx 1846, 102)

Cedric Robinson argues that "African labor power as slave labor was integrated into the organic composition of nineteenth-century manufacturing and industrial capitalism, thus sustaining the emergence of an extra-European world market within which the accumulation of capital was garnered for the further development of industrial production" (Robinson 2000, 113).

After the American Civil War, the United States formally abolished slavery in 1865. But this in no way meant that equality was established. Up until today, black Americans face discriminatory forms of domination and expression. As the Black Lives Matter movement has shown, one of the most extreme racist forms is that blacks are much more likely to be killed by state power than whites, either in the form of police killings or the death penalty.

Carter Wilson: dimensions of racism

Carter Wilson (1996) argues that racism has economic, political and cultural dimensions:

> [R]acial oppression is sustained within an exploitative and oppressive economic structure. This structure shapes the formation of a racist culture that functions to reinforce patterns of racial oppression. The state, operating within this economic and cultural context, generally supports and legitimizes oppressive relations. ... Whereas racial oppression is grounded in oppressive and exploitative economic arrangements and maintained by the state, culture plays a role in sustaining racism. That is, culture structures the way people think about and behave toward race in ways that perpetuate racial oppression.
>
> (Wilson 1996, 16, 24)

Wilson shows that racism in North America subsequently took on the forms of the slave mode of production and dominative racism (1787–1865), debt peonage and dominative aversive racism (1865–1965), and meta-racism (since 1970). Forms of aversive racism continue to exist, especially racial discrimination in the labour market, urban racial segregation, and housing segregation. Affirmative action programmes brought some improvements. Advanced capitalism features the increasing importance of knowledge and service work, financial capital, capital export, monopolisation, and automation. Capital mobility and global communications extended the international division of labour.

Wilson argues that in advanced capitalism high black poverty in urban centres is the most distinctive feature of racism in the USA. The black middle class was undermined. Meta-racism has been accompanied by particular racist images: "Today's images include those of the black under-class: crazed, uncontrollable, powerful, violent, drug-addicted black men; promiscuous black women; and black welfare queens" (Wilson 1996, 224).

Working conditions of Afro-Americans

Angela Davis (1983, 87–88) cites data from the 1890 US census that shows that 38.7% of black women employees worked in agriculture, 30.8% in domestic households, 15.6% in laundry work, and 2.8% in manufacturing. Black people had the lowest-paid, most precarious jobs and a system of de facto peonage emerged. Table 10.1 and Table 10.2 show that racist discrimination continues to exist in the US economy today.

1 = management, business and financial occupations,

2 = professional occupations (computing, architecture, scientists, community and social service, legal occupations, education, training, libraries, arts, design, entertainment, sports, media, healthcare practitioners and technicians),

3 = service occupations (healthcare support, protective services, food preparation and serving, cleaning, personal care),

4 = sales occupations,

5 = office and administrative occupations,

6 = agricultural occupations (farming, fishing, forestry occupations),

7 = manufacturing and transport occupations,

8 = construction and extraction,

9 = installation, maintenance, and repair.

The two tables show the reality of economic discrimination in contemporary America. In the USA, the median income of a black household in 1968 was 59.0% that of a white household. In 2018, the situation had not much improved: The figure was 61.8%. Black women and men have a much higher unemployment rate than white women and men. Among young people, blacks have an unemployment rate that is almost twice as large as whites. Black men and women are also more affected by precarious labour than white men and women. Whereas a larger share of black Americans than white Americans work in service labour, office labour, manufacturing and transport, white Americans are more represented in management and professional occupations. Given that management and professional jobs tend to be highly paid, racist wage and salary discrimination is built into the US occupational structure. One of the features of what Wilson (1996) terms the era of meta-racism is that American blacks tend to be more affected by unemployment than whites. And their jobs are much more likely to be precarious, low-paid service jobs such as waiters, cleaners, fast food workers, or clerks. For example: While in 2018 18.6% of white US men worked as managers or in financial or business services, just 10.8% of black US men had the same occupation (data source: BLS). In contrast, while 15.9% of US whites work in lower skill services such as security services, food serving, cleaning and care, 24.4% of US blacks conduct such labour (data source: BLS).

Racialised groups often face higher unemployment and higher underemployment, are concentrated in undesirable economic sectors and occupations, are more likely to be precariously self-employed, face high levels of discrimination at work, are more likely to lose their jobs in crises (Bhattacharyya 2018, 107–108).

The prison-industrial complex

Davis (2003, 2005, 2012, 2016) is also a critic of the prison-industrial complex. The privatisation of prisons turns these institutions into for-profit companies that make inmates labour to create profit. Racism makes people of colour more likely to be imprisoned, which is why there is not just a racist practice of imprisonment but also racist exploitation in the prison-industrial complex. "The institution of the prison tells us that the nightmare of slavery continues to haunt us" (Davis 2012, 138). "[B]lack bodies are considered dispensable within the 'free world' but as a major source of profit in the prison world" (Davis 2003, 95).

Through the prison-industrial complex, "racism generates enormous profits for private corporations" (Davis 2012, 174). Davis speaks of the "imprisonment binge" (Davis 2005, 37). Instead of tackling the causes of social problems, the homeless, illiterate, poor, black and unemployed are imprisoned. "According to this logic the prison becomes a way of disappearing people in the false hope of disappearing the underlying social problems they represent" (Davis 2005, 38). Mass imprisonment "is supposed to make people feel better [and safer], but what it really does is divert their attention away from those threats to security that come from the military, police, profit-seeking corporations, and sometimes from one's own intimate partners" (Davis 2005, 39–40). The prison

> functions ideologically as an abstract site into which undesirables are deposited, relieving us of the responsibility of thinking about the real issues afflicting those communities from which prisoners are drawn in such

TABLE 10.1 Income, unemployment and involuntary part-time work in the USA

	Median household income, 1968	Median household income, 2018	Unemployment rate, August 2016	Part-time for economic reasons 2015	Unemployment rate, June 2020
Data source	US Census Bureau	US Census Bureau	BLS	BLS	BLS
All	46,245	63,179	4.9%	4.4%	11.1%
White	48,151	66,943	4.4%	4.2%	10.1%
Black	28,394	41,361	8.1%	6.1%	15.4%
White women			3.9%	4.6%	10.3%
Black women			7.1%	6.2%	14.0%
White men			4.1%	3.9%	9.0%
Black men			7.6%	5.9%	16.3%
16–19 year olds, white			14.0%		23.3%
16–19 year olds, black			26.1%		34.9%
Men			5.0%	4.1%	10.2%
Women			4.9%	4.8%	11.2%

disproportionate numbers. This is the ideological work that the prison performs – it relieves us of the responsibility of seriously engaging with the problems of our society, especially those produced by racism and, increasingly, global capitalism.

(Davis 2003, 16)

Angela Davis analyses the unfreedom of blacks in America as it was instituted by slavery. Women slaves not just faced exploitation like male slaves but in addition were sexually oppressed and exploited by being raped and forced to bear slaves in an industrial manner. In contemporary America, black people face multiple forms of discrimination and domination. In the prison-industrial complex, state-violence forces them to work for profit-generating corporations.

> Although Black individuals have entered economic, social, and political hierarchies (the most dramatic example being the 2008 election of Barack Obama), the overwhelming number of Black people are subject to economic,

TABLE 10.2 Occupational structure in the USA, 2018 annual averages

Source	1 BLS	2 BLS	3 BLS	4 BLS	5 BLS	6 BLS	7 BLS	8 BLS	9 BLS
All	16.6%	23.5%	17.2%	10.1%	11.3%	0.7%	11.9%	5.4%	3.2%
White	17.5%	23.3%	15.9%	10.4%	10.4%	0.8%	11.4%	6.0%	3.4%
Black	11.1%	20.2%	24.4%	9.1%	9.1%	0.2%	16.1%	3.1%	2.5%
White women	16.3%	28.9%	19.6%	10.9%	17.8%	0.4%	5.4%	0.4%	0.2%
Black women	11.4%	24.8%	28.0%	9.8%	17.2%	0.1%	8.1%	0.2%	0.3%
White men	18.6%	18.5%	12.8%	10.0%	5.6%	1.2%	16.4%	10.7%	6.2%
Black men	10.8%	15.1%	20.3%	8.3%	9.0%	0.3%	25.0%	6.3%	4.9%
Men	17.5%	19.1%	13.8%	9.7%	6.1%	1.0%	17.2%	9.7%	5.8%
Women	15.6%	28.4%	21.1%	10.7%	17.3%	0.4%	5.9%	0.4%	0.3%

educational, and carceral racism to a far greater extent than during the pre-civil rights era. In many ways, the demands of the BPP's Ten-Point Program are just as relevant – or perhaps even more relevant – as during the 1960s, when they were first formulated.

(Davis 2016, 2)

The Black Panther Party's programme demanded, for example: "We Want An End To The Robbery By The Capitalists Of Our Black Community. [...] We Want An Immediate End To Police Brutality And Murder Of Black People" (Black Panther Party 1966).

By analysing the role of black women and men in American capitalism, Davis shows that capitalism requires gender-based and racist forms of exploitation. Sexism and racism are furthermore ideologies that reduce women to "sexual, childbearing, natural" beings (Davis 1977, 163) and people of colour to their skin in order to justify discriminatory and exclusionary practices and distract attention from the real causes of society's problems. The analysis shows that racism continues to play an important ideological and economic role in capitalism and sustains exclusion and exploitation.

10.4 Capitalism, racism, patriarchy

Intersectionality theory

The question arises as to how we can make sense of the relationship of capitalism, patriarchy and racism today. One argument underlying this article is that we have to go beyond the intersectionality theory. Intersectionality theory is one of the most widely adopted approaches for understanding the relationship between forms of oppression. In the 1970s, the black-feminist Combahee River Collective (1977, 261) argued that "the major systems of oppression are interlocking". These forms of domination are "racial, sexual, heterosexual, and class oppression" (261). Based on such influences, intersectionality theory developed as an "analysis claiming that systems of race, social class, gender, sexuality, ethnicity, nation, and age form mutually constructing features of social organization" (Hill Collins 2000, 299). Inequality and power are

> being shaped not by a single axis of social division, be it race or gender or class, but by many axes that work together and influence each other. [...] Intersectionality as an analytic tool examines how power relations are intertwined and mutually constructing. Race, class, gender, sexuality, dis/ability, ethnicity, nation, religion, and age are categories of analysis, terms that reference important social divisions.
>
> (Hill Collins and Bilge 2016, 2, 7)

Critiques of intersectionality theory

Eve Mitchell (2013) criticises intersectionality theory from a Marxist-feminist perspective. She writes that the intersectionality approach to identity politics is a form of individualistic, naturalising "bourgeois politics" (21). Intersectionality theory would neglect the material commonalities of the oppressed, namely the importance of labour and that all oppressed groups and individuals are human. "Identity politics argues, 'I am a black man', or 'I am a woman', without filling out the other side of the contradiction '…and I am human'" (15–16). Mitchell points out that intersectionality theory provides an analysis of interlocking dimensions of oppression. It is incomplete because it does not reflect on how these dimensions are grounded. The result is a relativist theory of oppression.

Vivek Chibber's (2013) critique of Subaltern Studies is comparable to Mitchell's critique of intersectionality theory. Chibber questions the assumption that the Global South is so fundamentally different from the West that theories hoping to understand it has to be radically different from any theory originating in the West, including Marxism. He argues that there is a universalising drive of capitalism that affects people worldwide in different ways, but also makes their oppression and struggles common. Marxism's critique of capitalism would allow a critique that is "cross-cultural, common to East as well as West" (Chibber 2013, 285). Both the East and the West would see two forces of universalism – "the universal logic of capital [...] and social agents' universal interest in their well-being, which impels them to resist capital's expansionary drive" (291). One can say that Chibber stresses, just like Mitchell, that their quest for a humane society unites the world's oppressed. The struggle for such a society can best be termed socialism.

How can we think systematically about the relationship of capitalism, patriarchy and racism and avoid both reductionism (as in economic reductionism and identity politics-reductionism) and dualism (as in intersectionality theory)? How can one go beyond post-colonialism's and intersectionality theory's relativism?

Alienation

Alienation is a key category of Marxist humanist theory. The basic meaning of alienation is that certain relations rob humans of influence on the conditions that shape their lives. For Marx, economic alienation means class relations where workers are exploited. But he extended alienation also into the realms of politics and culture. Political alienation means dictatorial control. Cultural alienation means ideology and disrespect. In capitalism, the three forms of alienation have in common that they aim at advancing accumulation. The logic of accumulation stems from the capitalist economy but extends into other realms of capitalist society, where it takes on its particular forms that have a relative autonomy and are interacting with the economy. Economic alienation results in the ruling class accumulation of economic power (capital in capitalist societies). Political alienation results in domination and dictators or elites' accumulation of decision-making power. Cultural alienation advances influencers' accumulation of reputation and status.

Racism and patriarchy are integral aspects of capitalist society. Economic, political and cultural alienation therefore not just exist in respect to workers, citizens, and humans, but in specific forms in respect to particular workers, citizens, and humans such as racialised and gender-defined groups and workers, who suffer from racist and gender-related forms of exploitation, domination, and ideology/disrespect. Table 10.3 presents a model that relates alienation to capitalism, racism, and patriarchy. Table 10.4 shows further details of the information presented in Table 10.3.

Table 10.4 Alienation denies human beings their full humanity. It denies them a good life. It reserves the good life for some humans and restricts it for alienated groups and individuals who are forced to lead damaged lives. Workers, racialised groups, gender-structured groups such as women, etc. suffer from capitalist society's structures of alienation. Class, racism, and gender oppression are the three main forms of power relations that advance alienation and thereby deny humans their humanity.

Zillah Eisenstein on alienation

Zillah Eisenstein (1979) argues that alienation is related to the dialectic of potentiality and actuality and between essence and existence of the human species-being. She writes that alienation means the denial of the realisation of possibilities.

> Woman is structured by what she is today-and this defines real possibilities for tomorrow; but what she is today does not determine the outer limits of her capacities or potentialities. This is of course true for the alienated worker. While a worker is cut off from his/her creative abilities s/he is still potentially a creative being. This contradiction between existence and essence lies, therefore, at the base of the revolutionary proletariat as well as the revolutionary woman. [...] By locating revolutionary potential as it reflects conflicts between people's real conditions (existence) and possibilities (essence), we can understand how patriarchal relations inhibit the development of human essence.
> (Eisenstein 1979, 9)

Generalising Eisenstein's argument, we can say that class, racism, and gender oppression and their interactions deny human's status as humans by inhibiting the development and realisation of certain groups' and individuals' human potentials.

Table 10.5 shows a typology of the interaction of class, racism, and gender oppression. Of course, there is also the interaction of all three forms at once in the form of the dehumanisation of individuals and groups because of their class, ascribed race, and gender. The materialist aspects of such interactions are that (a) power differences are processes of production, (b) racism and gender oppression always have a class dimension, (c) the economic logic of accumulation shapes the interaction of class/racism/gender oppression.

Communication in the context of class, racism, and gender-related oppression

Table 10.6 outlines economic, political and cultural forms of communication in respect to class, racism, and gender-related oppression. Economic structures communicate to humans the denial of the full humanity of workers, racialised workers, and gender-structured workers (such as house workers) via the creation of the unequal distribution of wealth. It is an indirect form of communication, where the differences in wealth communicate economic inhumanity. The rich person driving in his Ferrari past a homeless person who carries their few belongings around in a shopping trolley signifies this form of economic communication. Political structures such as the state and bureaucracy communicate the denial of full humanity to groups of citizens by unequal treatment so that they have fewer practical rights and political influence in comparison to others. An example is the police killing of George Floyd in 2020. Racism led to a state institution's denial of Floyd's right to life. That certain individuals or groups are treated in an exclusory or discriminatory manner by state institutions or other bureaucracies is not always known to the public. The denial of rights is in the first instance an act of communication from a political actor to their victim that might not be known to the public. In the case of surveillance, individuals often do not know that they are monitored. This shows that alienation can try to remain hidden, unacknowledged, and uncommunicated. That white police officer Derek Chauvin killed Floyd by kneeling on his neck for around eight minutes was the communication of racism from the officer to his victim. George Floyd tried to alarm the public by screaming "I cannot breathe". He was gasping for air and help. He communicated the denial of his humanity. But without success. He was killed. Videos recorded by witnesses and CCTV cameras were made public, which resulted in large protests of the Black Lives Matter movements all across the USA and the world. These videos documented the killing and communicated what had happened to the public. The protests that followed communicated resistance to racism. Practices of resistance such as protests and strikes communicate counter-power. Ideology is the form of alienation that communicates most directly not just via structures but via language and images. Think for example of a racist newspaper article that scapegoats immigrants for the poor status of the health care system. It distracts attention from the more complex political-economic causes of the health care crisis such as the neoliberal destruction of the welfare state. But ideology also operates in hidden forms such as commodity fetishism and in the unconscious so that it remains uncommunicated.

Commodity fetishism makes capitalism and wage-labour appear as natural properties of society, which tends to sustain both capitalism and class ideologically. Racism is an ideology that often justifies slavery and discriminatory labour practices. Sexism is an ideology that tries to chain women to the household and to create a gender pay gap. In housework, there is inverse commodity fetishism (Fuchs 2014, chapter 11; 2015,

TABLE 10.3 Alienation in the context of capitalism, racism, and patriarchy

	Alienation	Capitalism, racism, patriarchy	Capitalism, racism, patriarchy
Economy	Exploitation	Exploitation of workers results in the accumulation of capital	The exploitation of racialised workers, reproductive labour, and gender-defined groups advances the accumulation of capital
Politics	Domination, dictatorship	The political domination of citizens results in elites or dictators' accumulation of political decision power	The political domination of racialised individuals/groups and gender-defined individuals/groups, including forms of domination such as bureaucratic discrimination, surveillance, state violence such as police violence and police killings, physical violence, wars, genocide, rape, etc.) advances the accumulation of dominant groups' political power
Culture	Ideology that results in disrespect	The ideological scapegoating and disrespect of certain groups results in the accumulation of influencers' reputation and status	The ideological scapegoating and disrespect of racialised and gender-defined individuals/groups results in the accumulation of influencers' reputation and statu

Capitalism, racism, patriarchy

TABLE 10.4 The economic, political and cultural-ideological dimensions of capitalism, racism, and patriarchy

	Capitalism	Racism	Patriarchy
Economic dimension	the exploitation of the working class	the exploitation and super-exploitation of racialised groups	the exploitation and super-exploitation of gender-defined groups, including houseworkers, female care workers, and female wage-workers
Political dimension	bureaucratic discrimination of, surveillance of, state control of, and violence directed against dominated classes (such as wage-workers, slave-workers, particular types of workers, etc.)	bureaucratic discrimination of, surveillance of, state control of, and violence directed against racialised groups	bureaucratic discrimination of, surveillance of, state control of, and violence directed against gender-defined groups
Cultural-ideological dimension	denial of voice, respect, recognition, attention and visibility of the working class, ideological scapegoating of the working class	denial of voice, respect, recognition, attention and visibility of racialised groups, ideological scapegoating of racialised groups	denial of voice, respect, recognition, attention and visibility of gender-defined groups, ideological scapegoating of gender-defined groups

chapter 5). The workers' immediate experience is not the production of commodities but the creation of social relations.

David R. Roediger: *Wages of whiteness*

David R. Roediger (2007) in his book *Wages of Whiteness* says that the racism practised by a proportion of white workers is not a form of dopiness but a form of strategic agency. Based on W. E. B. Du Bois, Roediger argues that "the pleasures of whiteness could function as a 'wage' for white workers. That is, status and privileges conferred by race could be used to make up for alienating and exploitative class relationships" (Roediger 2007, 13). Wages of whiteness are for Angela Davis (2005, 93) "the privileges of those who benefit from the persistence of racism". Roediger does not give much attention to the circumstance that not all white people are part of the working class because there are also white (as well as non-white) capitalists. He also does not so much focus on white anti-racists, non-white racists and nationalists, and the "relationship between the struggle against male supremacism and white supremacism" (Allen 2001).

However, Roediger's wages of whiteness approach is nonetheless an important approach in how to think about the relationship of class, gender and racism. It can be

TABLE 10.5 The interaction of class, racism, gender oppression

	Class	Racism	Gender-related oppression, patriarchy
Class	Exploitation	Racist exploitation	Gender-structured exploitation
Racism	Racist exploitation	Racism	Discrimination of racialised individuals or groups of a particular gender
Gender-related oppression, patriarchy	Gender-structured exploitation	Discrimination of racialised individuals or groups of a particular gender	Gender discrimination

generalised: whiteness can be understood in a Bourdieuian sense as a form of cultural or ideological capital that allows white workers to distinguish themselves from blacks. Masculinity is a form of ideological capital that makes men distinguish themselves from women and LGBT people. Whiteness and masculinity as ideologies help to accumulate reputation, status, and social distinction, that is cultural capital. As ideologies, they are produced in social relations, that is there is the labour of producing and reproducing whiteness and masculinity. Masculinity and whiteness are as patriarchal and racist ideology forms of bio-politics as they are grounded in making the human body a terrain of politics that acts as a field of the accumulation of cultural power. The motivation for masculinity, whiteness, racism, nationalism, etc., is often, as Roediger shows, the feeling of having to make up for alienation and exploitation by producing and reproducing oppression. The effect is then a distraction of energy and struggles from the "real" enemies. The pleasure derived from oppression and exploitation can be seen as a cultural "wage". Political advantages derived from oppression and exploitation form a political "wage". But there is a dimension beyond social distinction. Another wage of whiteness, nationalism and masculinity can in racist, nationalist and sexist societies and organisations, be that ideological power is used for attaining economic capital and/or political power, that is better economic positions, wages, salaries, income and more political influence. In these cases, whiteness, nationalism, masculinity and other ideologies also take on the role of economic and political wages. Racism, nationalism, sexism and other ideologies can create an economic, political and cultural surplus-"wages" or, better expressed, economic, political and cultural power. The combination of capitalism, whiteness, nationalism and masculinity is not just wide-spread today but has with Donald Trump become a directly ruling force that advances an authoritarian form of capitalism in the USA and world politics (Fuchs 2017).

TABLE 10.6 Economic, political and cultural communication in the context of class, racism, and gender-related oppression

	Class	Racism	Patriarchy, gender-related oppression
Economic communication	Structural inequality of wealth between classes as economic communication	Structural inequalities that racialised workers face in the economy as economic communication	Structural inequalities that women or other gender-defined groups face in the economy as economic communication
Political communication	Bureaucratic and state discrimination of workers as political communication	Political communication in the form of bureaucratic, state and other forms of discrimination exerted against racialised individuals	Bureaucratic and state discrimination of women or other gender-defined groups as political communication
Cultural communication	Ideological scapegoating of workers, commodity fetishism as cultural communication	Ideological scapegoating of racialised individuals as cultural communication	Ideological scapegoating of women or other gender-defined groups as cultural communication

Desan (2013) argues that Bourdieu has a limited understanding of capital and does not sufficiently theorise economic capital. The "notion of economic capital remains largely undertheorized" (337). By capital, "Bourdieu seems to mean simply any resource insofar as it yields power [...] In the end, what Bourdieu's notion of capital lacks is not only an idea of capitalism as a particular historical formation but more fundamentally an idea of exploitation as a particular operation of power" (332). Although "Bourdieu is sensitive to class conflict, he does not in fact have a theory of exploitation in the sense of appropriating surplus-labor" (335).

Economical, political and ideological surpluses

Desan does not conclude that Marx and Bourdieu cannot be combined but instead implies that such a combination must be guided by Marxist theory. Erik Olin Wright (1997) has attempted such a combination. He grounds the concept of class on the notion of exploitation and adds to it the concepts of skills and authority that are close to Bourdieu's concepts of cultural and political/social capital. Both Wright and Bourdieu stress the importance of property, skill, and authority in-class analysis. The difference is that there are two different rankings in these approaches: "*property, skill, authority* for Marxist class analysis; *skill, property, authority* for Bourdieu's culturally grounded class analysis" (Wright 1997, 173). For Wright, class exploitation remains the dominant aspect of capitalism, but he maintains that skill and authority can result in "skill exploitation" (17) and "loyalty rent" (21). Relating this argument back to Roediger, we can say that within the capitalist economy, authority, culture and ideology can result in a monetary surplus-wage. And within the political and cultural system, exploitation and oppression can result in certain individuals and groups' social advantages at the expense of others, or what could, in a metaphorical sense, be termed an ideological wage (a surplus of pleasure, enjoyment and status) and a political wage (a surplus of political influence). One aspect that Bourdieu's and Marx's analysis shares is the stress on how the logic of accumulation shapes capitalist society and brings about inequalities. Wright and Roediger extend this analysis in a Marxist manner by arguing that a) ideology, culture and authority result in capital accumulation, profit, and surplus-wages in the economy and b) ideology and politics in modern society are systems of accumulation, in which political and cultural surpluses are accumulated.

W. E. B. Du Bois

The surplus that ideology can produce is not just surplus pleasure and enjoyment in the suffering of others, but it can also be economic, political and cultural in character. W. E. B. Du Bois argued in this context:

> It must be remembered that the white group of laborers, while they received a low wage, were compensated in part by a sort of public and psychological wage. They were given public deference and tides of courtesy because they were white. They were admitted freely with all classes of white people to public functions, public parks, and the best schools. The police were drawn from their ranks, and the courts, dependent upon their votes, treated them with such leniency as to encourage lawlessness. Their vote selected public officials, and while this had small effect upon the economic situation, it had great effect upon their personal treatment and the deference shown them. White schoolhouses were the best in the community, and conspicuously placed, and they cost anywhere from twice to ten times as much per capita as the colored schools. The newspapers specialized on news that flattered the poor whites and almost utterly ignored the Negro except in crime and ridicule
>
> (Du Bois, 1935, 700–701)

The economic dimension of the interrelation of different forms of labour is that capitalism requires and creates milieus of exploitation in order to sustain profitability. It strives to maximise capital accumulation by minimising labour costs. The diversification of labour is a result of the profit imperative. Non-standard forms of labour, such as slavery, precarious labour, freelancing, unpaid user labour, or housework, are an expression of this diversification.

The normalisation of overexploitation

Capitalism is based on the capitalist class's appropriation of surplus-labour and surplus-value. Given that the working day consists of two parts, necessary labour and surplus-labour, that is paid labour and unpaid labour, all labour in capitalism contains unpaid labour. It is in the capitalist class's interest to maximise unpaid labour time. Étienne Balibar (2013) argues in this context that "what characterizes capitalism is a *normalization of overexploitation*. The reverse side of this is a class struggle that tends to impose limits". The sustenance and creation of forms of labour that are completely unpaid or have a high degree of unpaid labour time should therefore be understood as being part of this capitalist tendency to normalise over-exploitation. Unpaid labour is one of the newest manifestations of this tendency. Balibar concludes that "we should question the axiom" of "the distinction of *productive and unproductive labor*".

A typology of wage labour, slave labour, reproductive labour, and racialised labour based on Marisol Sandoval's work

Marisol Sandoval (2013) provides a typology with 14 dimensions that are relevant for a systematic analysis of labour in capitalism. These dimensions can be grouped into the categories of means of production, workforce, relations of production, production process, results of production, and the role of the state. Table 10.7 builds on Sandoval's typology. It uses a compressed version of her typology and adds to it the dimension of ideology that focuses on how justifications for the exploitation of specific forms of labour appear and are presented in public. The typology used in Table 10.7 focuses on economic, political, and cultural/ideological dimensions of labour. It outlines these dimensions for wage-labour, slave-labour, reproductive labour, and racialised labour. It summarises the discussion of this article.

The control and coercion of labour work with both political-economic and ideological means. Political-economic means include physical violence, sexual power, monopoly power, social power, and the labour market's structural power. Ideological repression takes on specific forms in the international division of digital labour.

New racism justifies the exploitation, exclusion, domination, or annihilation of an outgroup. One can draw a "distinction between a racism of extermination or elimination ('exclusive' racism) and a racism of oppression or exploitation ('inclusive' racism)" (Balibar & Wallerstein 1991, 39). In the international division of labour, one can both find the exclusive and the exploitative type of racism.

One of the most important differences between wage-labour, slave-labour, and reproductive labour concerns their legal status and what makes the workers conduct labour. Slave-workers' bodies and minds are a private property that the slave-master owns at all time. Slavery is the most reified form of labour, which means that slaves have no rights so that the slave-master can treat them as he pleases and is legally allowed to kill them. So what makes the slave work is in the final instance the fear of being killed or experiencing physical violence. In slavery, "the worker is distinguishable only as *instrumentum vocale* [vocal instrument] from an animal, which is *instrumentum semi-vocale* [semi-vocal instrument], and from a lifeless implement, which is *instrumentum mutum* [silent instrument]" (Marx 1867, 303, footnote 18).

Whereas the slave constantly faces the threat of death, wage-labour only does so in particular cases, for example when workers are being asked to conduct life-threatening work, such as cleaning up nuclear waste. Other than the slave, the wage-worker owns him-/herself. In *Capital* (Volume 1, chapter 6) Marx (1867) formulates the unfreedom of wage-labour as the double freedom of labour. Modern labour is free because it is better off than slaves (although slavery has continued to exist in global capitalism), but it is also unfree because it is compelled to be exploited by capital and to have to enter class relations in order to be able to survive. Proletarians' minds and bodies are not the private property of the dominant class, as slaves are, they are rather compelled by the "silent compulsion of economic relations" (Marx 1867, 899), the repression of the market that makes ordinary people die if they do not obtain the money that allows them to buy commodities, which compels many to become wage-workers.

A specific share of women experiences domestic violence and economic dependence that forces them to conduct reproductive labour against their will and creates their fear to leave their partner. So, direct violence can be a means of coercion in the case of housework. But also commitment, solidarity and love are important driving forces of reproductive labour. Housework can frequently involve hybrids of love and hatred, pain and pleasure, play and toil, care and violence, feelings of self-fulfilment and alienation.

It would be a mistake to assume that the rise of capitalism and wage-labour has brought an end to slavery. Although slavery is older than wage-labour, it continues to exist in specific forms in capitalism. According to estimates, in the year 2018, there were 40 slaves in the world (Walk Free Foundation 2018), including high numbers in India, China, Pakistan, North Korea, Nigeria, Iran, Indonesia, Democratic Republic of Congo, Russia, and the Philippines (Walk Free Foundation 2018). The Walk Free Foundation gives a concise definition of slavery as "situations of exploitation that a person cannot refuse or leave because of threats, violence, coercion, abuse of power or deception, with treatment akin to a farm animal" (Walk Free Foundation 2016, 158).

Slavery can be used as a more restrictive or more expansive term. Marx did both at once. He on the one hand saw the differences between slave-labour and wage-labour by stressing that slavery is the most unfree and life-threatening form of labour. He however also stressed certain parallels between pure slavery and other class relations. So, for example, he characterised patriarchy as a system in which "the wife and children are the slaves of the husband" (Marx & Engels 1845, 52) and spoke of capitalism's "two poles of Capital and Wage-slavery" (Marx 1871, 335). Every class relation at least bears traces and has certain features of slavery because it always entails some form of unfreedom and coercion. There are historical dialectics of slavery.

But there are also reasons for not expanding the term slavery to every form of exploitation. There is a difference in respect to the difficulty of refusing labour, that is in respect to the political dimension of political economy that governs human activity, labour-power and labour-time. Regular wage-workers because of their double freedom can leave their employer's factory or office at the end of the working day. They have to return in order to earn a wage, but they can also choose to search for another job, which is relative freedom within unfreedom. In contrast to the wage-worker, the slave-worker cannot leave the job without being shot. Nonetheless, all labour and all class relations have certain dimensions of slavery because they are all coerced into labour in particular ways. The exploitation of the wage-worker, the slave, and the houseworker are in certain respects different as well as in certain other respects comparable. Only the collective revolt of slaves and other workers exploited by transnational corporations, their collective refusal to labour and search for alternatives, can put an end to capitalism and slavery.

Slaves do not have political and social rights. Wage-workers have specific social rights with respect to wages, social security, and trade union representation. Houseworkers only have limited social rights with respect to, for example, child benefits. Whereas the wage-worker has a contractual and legally enforceable right to be paid a wage for the performed labour, slaves and house workers do not have such a right, which enables their

TABLE 10.7 Characteristics of four types of labour

Dimen-sion	Aspect	Wage-labour	Slave-labour	Reproductive labour	Racialised labour
1. Economy	Means of production	Brain, body, tools	Brain, body, uterus and genitals (women slaves), tools	Brain, body, uterus (women), genitals, tools	Brain, body, tools, uterus, genitals
	Product of labour	Use-values and commodities owned by capitalist	Use-values and commodities owned by the slave-master, slaves (women slaves), workforce/labour-power (house slaves)	Commodity/use-value for capital: workforce and labour-power; use-value: affects, social relations, means of subsistence	Use-values, commodities, labour-power, affects, social relations, means of subsistence
	Spaces of labour	Factory, office, social factory	Plantation (including contemporary plantations such as for-profit prisons)	Household, social factory	Factory, office, social factory, plantation, household
	Labour-time	Legal division between labour time and leisure time, necessary labour-time (paid) and surplus labour-time (unpaid)	Slave-master controls all time and can turn all life-time of slaves into labour-time, all labour-time is unpaid, slave-master has the legal power to end a slave's life-time by killing her/him	a) All labour-time is unpaid; wages of the household's wage labourers are used for buying the household's means of consumption as means of production;b) Paid reproductive workers are freelancers or work for the state or for-profit companies	Because of racism, workers of colour are more highly exploited, discriminated and repressed, which includes that they conduct more unpaid labour-time and create more surplus-value than other workers who conduct the same labour
2. Politics	Wages and benefits	Wages and salary, legally guaranteed social benefits (unemployment insurance, health insurance, pension system)	No wages/salary, unpaid labour,no legally guaranteed social benefits	a) No wages/salary, unpaid labour, limited legally guaranteed social benefits (child benefits);b) low-paid	Oorkers of colour tend to have lower wages and fewer benefits than other workers. They tend to be overrepresented in low-skill,

(Continued)

Capitalism, racism, patriarchy

TABLE 10.7 (Cont.)

Dimen-sion	Aspect	Wage-labour	Slave-labour	Reproductive labour (paid cleaners, babysitters and carers)	Racialised labour
	Legal aspects of labour	Double free labour: Labour-contract and labour legislation, freedom of the person, 'wage-slave'	Double unfree labour: no labour-contract and legislation, no human rights, no freedom of the person: slave's body is owned by the slave-master	Unfree labour: no labour-contract and no labour legislation, family law, full or partial or no freedom of the person	Racialised labour low-wage, low prestige and pecarious/insecure jobs and underrepresented in high-skill, high-wage, high-prestige and secure jobs Double free labour or double unfree labour or unfree labour, in racist state systems, workers of colour tend to have fewer legal protections, to be discriminated by the state, and to face threats such as police violence and police killings (such as the police killing of George Floyd)
	Political representation of labour	Trade unions, labour parties	Abolition movement, anti-racist movement,	Feminist movement	Anti-racist movements
	Labour struggles and demands	Strikes, sabotage, occupations, worker co-operatives;wage-demands, shortening of the working day, better working conditions	Slave rebellions,political freedom, equality	Protests,equality, wages for housework, equal pay for equal work, abolishment and socialisation of housework	Protests, rebellions, strikes, sabotage, occupations, demand of better working conditions for workers of colour
	Coercion and control of labour	Dull compulsion and structural power of the labour-market	Physical violence, death threats, rape	Physical and sexual violence, social commitment (social repression)	Racist discrimination, racist wage repression, racist violence, racist repression
3. Culture and Ideology	**Ideology of labour repression**	Commodity fetishism, wage-labour fetishism	Racism	Sexism, inverse commodity fetishism	Racism

exploitation as unpaid workers. But not all housework is unpaid. Parts of it are conducted as contractual labour. Paid carers and cleaners are an example. These are typically low-paid types of labour, often conducted by migrants and women. The intersection of reproductive labour and wage-labour tends to have a racialised and patriarchal character.

Racialised labour is labour that faces high levels of exploitation, discrimination, and repression motivated by racism. The classic example is the transatlantic slave-trade in the 16th, 17th and 18th, and 19th centuries, where millions of Africans were transported over the Atlantic and turned into slaves in Europe, the Americas and the Caribbean, especially by Denmark, France, Great Britain, the Netherlands, Portugal, and Spain. Historically, slavery has often been motivated by racism. In such cases, private property owners and their governments do not see people of colour as humans. They denied people of colour their humanity. As a consequence, they treat them like things, which entails the denial of human rights, the use of violence, and murder. Slaves are unfree and extremely highly exploited. Slavery is often, but not necessarily racialised labour. Racialised labour is not necessarily slave-labour, also wage-labour, reproductive labour and diverse forms of precarious and unpaid labour can be racialised. For example, black workers who earn less than white workers for the same job conduct racialised labour.

Enikö Vincze provides a characterisation of racialised labour and stresses that it is a form of labour where workers of colour are considered less than:

> Racialised labour "is created as an inferior labour or a labour performed by people considered less than persons or less human than their fellow citizens. Racialized labour is precarious, that is unsecure, underpaid, and dehumanizing, and most importantly is conceived as expropriable. Racialized labour includes different types of labour that are considered less valuable labour, or not labour at all, such as: informal labour, labour performed for the 'guaranteed minimum income' of the 'socially assisted', exploited day or seasonal labour, and underpaid labour on stigmatized domains" (Vincze 2019, 85–86).

10.5 Conclusion

This chapter has studied the connection between capitalism, patriarchy, and racism. Capitalism is inherently patriarchal and racist in character and uses ideology and discrimination for deepening exploitation and domination. Unpaid labour is not unproductive, but rather constitutes a super-exploited form of productive labour that generates surplus-value without a wage. Racism, nationalism, sexism and other ideologies can create an economic, political and cultural surplus, or, better expressed, forms of economic, political and cultural power for dominant groups.

Rosa Luxemburg: Milieus of primitive accumulation

Capitalism requires what Rosa Luxemburg (1913/2003) termed milieus of primitive accumulation in order to survive. Capital wants to "mobilise world labour power without restriction in order to utilise all productive forces of the globe" (Luxemburg 1913/2003, 343). Milieus of ongoing primitive accumulation are "indispensable for accumulation" (363). Capital accumulates "by eating [...] up" the labour conducted in such milieus (363). Forms of unpaid labour constitute such territories. Housework has traditionally been such a milieu of exploitation that has sustained capitalism and wage-labour. Housework means "super-exploitation of non-wage labourers [...] upon which wage labour exploitation then is possible" (Mies 1986, 48) because it involves the "externalization, or ex-territorialization of costs which otherwise would have to be covered by the capitalists" (110). Housewifisation means the extension of super-exploitation and unpaid labour into realms beyond housework so that work or labour is transformed in such ways that it shows some parallels with the conditions of housework (Mies, Bennholdt-Thomsen, and Werlhof 1988; Mies 1986; Fuchs 2014). Housewifised labour "bears the characteristics of housework" (Maria, Bennholdt-Thomsen, and Werlhof 1988, 10). Neoliberalism has extended housewifisation to realms such as precarious labour (e.g. temporary work, part-time work, contract labour, freelancers, etc.). Digital capitalism has extended housewifised labour to precarious and unremunerated digital labour (Fuchs 2021). Racial capitalism means that housewifisation interacts with racism so that racialised groups face exploitation, expropriation, and expulsion (Bhattacharyya 2018).

Summary

We can summarise this chapter's main findings:

- Capitalism, racism, and patriarchy/gender-related oppression are inherently connected and interacting. The economy plays a particular role in this interaction because these power relations are relations of production and accumulation of power.
- The capitalist economy creates forms of highly exploited, insecure, precarious labour, including racialised labour, unpaid labour, reproductive labour, and gender-defined labour, in order to maximise profits.

- Racism and patriarchy have economic, political, and ideological dimensions. In capitalism, these dimensions are united by the logic of accumulation.
- Class, racism, and gender oppression are the three main forms of power relations that advance alienation, deny humans their humanity, and create damaged lives.
- Ideology, culture and authority result in capital accumulation, profit, and surplus-wages in the economy. Ideology and politics in modern society are systems of accumulation, in which political and cultural surpluses are accumulated.
- Structural inequality, discrimination, and ideology are forms of communication. They communicate dehumanisation to alienated groups and individuals. Communication is not just a direct form of mutual symbolic interaction mediated by language, but also a structural and more indirect relation where power relations communicate the superiority of certain groups such as capitalists, managers, groups who see themselves as culturally or biologically superior, etc.

Literature

Allen, Theodor W. 2001. "On Roediger's Wages of Whiteness." *Cultural Logic* 4(2), DOI: https://doi.org/10.14288/clogic.v8i0.191856.

Balibar, Étienne. 2013. "Exploitation." *Political Concepts* 3(3). Accessed July 30, 2020. http://www.politicalconcepts.org/balibar-exploitation/.

Balibar, Étienne, and Immanuel Wallerstein. 1991. *Race, Nation, Class*. London: Verso.

Bhattacharyya, Gargi. 2018. *Rethinking Racial Capitalism. Questions of Reproduction and Survival*. London: Rowman & Littlefield.

Black Panther Party. 2010. *The Ten-Point Programme*. Accessed on July 30, 2020. https://www.marxists.org/history/usa/workers/black-panthers/1966/10/15.htm.

Bureau of Labor Statistics (BLS). 2017. *Labor Force Characteristics by Race and Ethnicity*. Accessed July 30, 2020. https://www.bls.gov/opub/reports/race-and-ethnicity/2017/pdf/home.pdf.

Chibber, Vivek. 2013. *Postcolonial Theory and the Spectre of Capital*. London: Verso.

Combahee River Collective. 1977. "A Black Feminist Statement." In *The Black Feminist Reader*, edited by James Joy and T. Denean Sharpley-Whiting, 261–270. Malden, MA: Blackwell.

Dalla Costa, Mariarosa, and Selma James. 1973. *The Power of Women and the Subversion of Community*. Bristol: Falling Wall Press. Second edition.

Davis, Angela Y. 2016. *Freedom Is a Constant Struggle: Ferguson, Palestine, and the Foundations of a Movement*. Chicago, IL: Ferguson.

———. 2012. *The Meaning of Freedom*. San Francisco, CA: City Lights.

---. 2005. *Abolition Democracy*. New York, NY: Seven Stories.

---. 2003. *Are Prisons Obsolete?* New York, NY: Seven Stories.

---. 1983. *Women, Race & Class*. New York, NY: Vintage.

---. 1977. "Women and Capitalism: Dialectics of Oppression and Liberation." In *The Angela Y. Davis Reader*, edited by Joy James, 161–192. Malden, MA: Blackwell.

Desan, Mathieu Hikaru. 2013. "Bourdieu, Marx, and Capital: A Critique of the Extension Model." *Sociological Theory 31* (4): 318–342.

Du Bois, W. E. B. 1935. *Black Reconstruction: An Essay Toward a History of the Part which Black Folk Played in the Attempt to Reconstruct Democracy in America, 1860–1880*. New York, NY: Harcourt, Brace & Co.

Eisenstein, Zillah. 1979. "Developing a Theory of Capitalist Patriarchy and Socialist Feminism." In *Capitalist Patriarchy and the Case for Socialist Feminism*, edited by Zillah Eisenstein, 5–40. New York: Monthly Review Press.

Endnotes Collective. 2013. *The Logic of Gender: On the Separation of Spheres and the Process of Abjection. Endnotes 3*. Accessed July30, 2020). https://endnotes.org.uk/issues/3/en/endnotes-the-logic-of-gender.

Engels, Friedrich. 1892. "The Origin of the Family, Private Property and the State. In the Light of the Researches by Lewis H. Morgan." In *Marx & Engels Collected Works (MECW) Volume 26*, 129–276. London: Lawrence & Wishart.

Federici, Silvia. 2012. *Revolution at Point Zero: Housework, Reproduction and Feminist Struggle*. Oakland, CA: PM Press.

---. 1975. *Wages Against Housework*. Bristol: Falling Wall Press.

Fortunati, Leopoldina. 1995. *The Arcane of Reproduction: Housework, Prostitution, Labor and Capital*. New York, NY: Autonomedia.

Fraser, Nancy, and Axel Honneth. 2003. *Redistribution or Recognition?* London: Verso.

Fuchs, Christian. 2021. *Social Media: A Critical Introduction*. London: Sage. Third edition.

---. 2017. "Donald Trump: A Critical Theory-Perspective on Authoritarian Capitalism." *tripleC: Communication, Capitalism & Critique 15* (1): 1–72.

---. 2015. *Culture and Economy in the Age of Social Media*. New York, NY: Routledge.

---. 2014. *Digital Labour and Karl Marx*. New York, NY: Routledge.

---. 2011. *Foundations of Critical Media and Information Studies*. London: Routledge.

Hill Collins, Patricia. 2000. *Black Feminist Thought: Knowledge, Consciousness, and the Politics of Empowerment*. New York, NY: Routledge. 2nd edition.

Hill Collins, Patricia, and Sirma Bilge. 2016. *Intersectionality*. Cambridge: Polity.

Hobsbawm, Eric J. 1992. *Nations and Nationalism since 1780. Programme, Myth, Reality*. Cambridge: Cambridge University Press. Second edition.

---. 1983. "Mass-Producing Traditions: Europe, 1870-1914." In *The Invention of Tradition*, edited by Eric J. Hobsbawm and Terence Ranger, 263–307. Cambridge: Cambridge University Press.

James, C. L. R. 1989. *The Black Jacobins. Toussaint L'Ouverture and the San Domingo Revolution.* New York: Vintage Books.

James, Joy, and T. Denean Sharpley-Whiting, eds. 2000. *The Black Feminist Reader.* Malden, MA: Blackwell.

Luxemburg, Rosa. 1913/2003. *The Accumulation of Capital.* New York: Routledge.

Marx, Karl. 1871. "The Civil War in France." In *Marx & Engels Collected Works (MECW) Volume 22*, 307–359. London: Lawrence & Wishart.

———. 1867. *Capital. Volume 1.* London: Penguin.

———. 1846. "Marx to Pavel Vasilyevich Annenov, 28 December 1846." In *Marx & Engels Collected Works (MECW) Volume 38*, 95–106. London: Lawrence & Wishart.

Marx, Karl, and Friedrich Engels. 1848. "The Manifesto of the Communist Party." In *Marx & Engels Collected Works (MECW) Volume 6*, 477–519. London: Lawrence & Wishart.

———. 1845. *The German Ideology.* Amherst, NY: Prometheus.

Mies, Maria. 1986. *Patriarchy & Accumulation on a World Scale: Women in the International Division of Labour.* London: Zed Books.

Mies, Maria, Veronika Bennholdt-Thomsen, and Claudia Von Werlhof. 1988. *Women: The Last Colony.* London: Zed Books.

Mitchell, Eve. 2013. *I Am a Woman and a Human: A Marxist-Feminist Critique of intersectionality Theory.* Accessed December 25, 2016. https://libcom.org/files/intersectionality-pamphlet.pdf.

Robinson, Cedric J. 2019. *An Anthropology of Marxism.* 2nd ed. Chapel Hill, NC: The University of North Carolina Press.

———. 2000. *Black Marxism. The Making of the Black Radical Tradition.* New ed. Chapel Hill, NC: The University of North Carolina Press.

Roediger, David R. 2007. *The Wages of Whiteness: Race and the Making of the American Working Class, rev. edn.* London: Verso.

Sandoval, Marisol. 2013. "Foxconned Labour as the Dark Side of the Information Age: Working Conditions at Apple's Contract Manufacturers in China." *tripleC: Communication, Capitalism & Critique 11* (2): 318–347.

Scholz, Roswitha. 2000. *Das Geschlecht des Kapitalismus. Feministische Theorien und die postmoderne Metamorphose des Patriarchats.* Bad Honnef: Horlemann.

———. 2014. "Patriarchy and Commodity Society: Gender Without the Body." In *Marxism and the Critique of Value*, edited by Neil Larsen, Mathias Nilges, Josh Robinson, and Nicholas Brown, 132–142. Chicago, IL: MCM.

Smedley, Audrey. 1998. ""Race" and the Construction of Human Identity." *American Anthropologist 100* (3): 690–702.

Vincze, Enikö. 2019. "Ghettoization: The Production of Marginal Spaces of Housing and the Reproduction of Racialized Labour." In *Racialized Labour in Romania: Spaces of Marginality at* the Periphery of Global Capitalism, edted by Enikö Vincze, Norbert Petrovici, Cristina Rat, and Giovanni Picker, 63–96. Cham: Palgrave Macmillan.

Walby, Sylvia. 2020. *Theorizing Violence*. Cambridge: Polity

Walby, Sylvia et al. 2017. *The Concept and Measurement of Violence against Women and Men*. Bristol: Policy Press.

Walk Free Foundation. 2018. *Global Slavery Index 2018*. Accessed July31, 2020. https://www.globalslaveryindex.org/.

———. 2016. *The Global Slavery Index 2016*. Accessed December25, 2016. http://www.globalslaveryindex.org.

Weil, Simone. 2005. *An Anthology*. London: Penguin.

West, Cornel. 2001. *Race Matters*. Boston, MA: Beacon Press.

Wilson, Carter A. 1996. *Racism: From Slavery to Advanced Capitalism*. Thousand Oaks, CA: Sage.

Wright, Erik Olin. 1997. *Class Counts*. Cambridge: Cambridge University Press.

Chapter Eleven
Conclusion

11.1 Capitalism, racism, patriarchy
11.2 The base/superstructure-problem
11.3 Theorising communication
11.4 The political economy of communication
11.5 Ideology critique
11.6 Communication/struggles/alternatives
11.7 Communication and alienation
11.8 Humanism

The task of the book at hand is to provide readings of and engage with selected Marxist humanist theoretical approaches in order to identify and create elements for the foundations of a critical theory of communication. It is now time to summarise some of the findings.

11.1 Capitalism, racism, patriarchy

Capitalist society is a society that is shaped by the logic of accumulation and instrumental reason. In the economy, accumulation means the accumulation of capital. In the political system, accumulation means the accumulation of decision-power. In the cultural system, accumulation means the accumulation of reputation and attention.

Instrumental reason is a logic that instrumentalizes humans in order to realise the partial interests of the ruling class and dominant groups. Through exploitation, domination and ideology, instrumental reason turns humans into instruments that advance partial interests of classes and groups that dominate society. In a capitalist society, instrumental reason takes on the form of accumulation and results in inequalities. Instrumental reason undermines human equality. Exploitation, domination, and ideology deny humans their humanity. They are forms of alienation. Alienation means anti-humanism.

Table 11.1 provides an overview of the types of alienation introduced in the introduction of this book (see also Chapter 1).

Capitalism, racism, and patriarchy are three modes of power relations that each combine economic alienation, political alienation, and cultural alienation. Capitalism, racism, and patriarchy involve specific forms of exploitation, domination, and ideology. The three forms of alienation are interacting in particular forms of power relations.

Table 11.2 shows the economic, political and cultural dimensions of capitalism, racism, and patriachy.

Capitalism, racism, and patriarchy/gender-related oppression are inherently connected and interacting. The economy plays a particular role in this interaction because these

TABLE 11.1 Alienation processes and the main actors in an alienated and humanist society

	Alienation process	Alienated society	Humanist society
Economy	Exploitation	Exploiter	Socialist
Politics	Domination	Dictator	Democrat
Culture	Ideology	Ideologue, demagogue	Friend

TABLE 11.2 The economic, political and cultural-ideological dimensions of capitalism, racism, and patriarchy

	Capitalism	Racism	Patriarchy
Economic dimension	the exploitation of the working class	the exploitation and super-exploitation of racialised groups	the exploitation and super-exploitation of gender-defined groups, including houseworkers, female care workers, and female wage-workers
Political dimension	bureaucratic discrimination of, surveillance of, state control of, and violence directed against dominated classes (such as wage-workers, slave-workers, particular types of workers, etc.)	bureaucratic discrimination of, surveillance of, state control of, and violence directed against racialised groups	bureaucratic discrimination of, surveillance of, state control of, and violence directed against gender-defined groups
Cultural-ideological dimension	denial of voice, respect, recognition, attention and visibility of the working class, ideological scapegoating of the working class	denial of voice, respect, recognition, attention and visibility of racialised groups, ideological scapegoating of racialised groups	denial of voice, respect, recognition, attention and visibility of gender-defined groups, ideological scapegoating of gender-defined groups

TABLE 11.3 The interaction of class, racism, gender oppression

	Class	Racism	Gender-related oppression, patriarchy
Class	Exploitation	Racist exploitation	Gender-structured exploitation
Racism	Racist exploitation	Racism	Discrimination of racialised individuals or groups of a particular gender
Gender-related oppression, patriarchy	Gender-structured exploitation	Discrimination of racialised individuals or groups of a particular gender	Gender discrimination

power relations are relations of production and accumulation of power. Table 11.3 provides an overview of the interactions of capitalism, racism, and patriarchy.

The capitalist economy creates forms of highly exploited, insecure, precarious labour, including racialised labour, unpaid labour, reproductive labour, and gender-defined labour, in order to maximise profits. Racism and patriarchy have economic, political, and ideological dimensions. In capitalism, these dimensions are united by the logic of accumulation. Class, racism, and gender oppression/patriarchy are the three main forms of power relations that advance alienation, deny humans their humanity, and create damaged lives.

Ideology, culture and authority result in capital accumulation, profit, and surplus-wages in the economy. Ideology and politics in modern society are systems of accumulation, in which political and cultural surpluses are accumulated.

The approaches analysed in this book contribute to the following dimensions of a critical theory of communication:

1) The base/superstructure-problem
2) Theorising communication
3) The political economy of communication
4) Ideology critique
5) Communication/struggles/alternatives
6) Communication and alienation
7) Humanism

11.2 The base/superstructure-problem

Concepts of culture and communication that see the economy, the means of production, and work as forming the "base" and politics and culture as forming the "superstructure", advance a dualist and idealist understanding where culture, ideas, and communication are immaterial and separate from the economy. Raymond Williams argues against such approaches that culture, ideas, and communication are material and part of material production. For example, the existence of the cultural industry, cultural labour, and cultural commodities shows that we cannot neatly separate the economy and culture.

A dialectical solution of the base/superstructure-problem is that social production is the foundation of society and forms the economic moment that operates in all social relations and all realms of society. Communication is the mediation process in social production. Humans not just produce economic goods but also political decisions, rules, ideas, meanings, etc. Social production is economical but also operates inside non-economic realms such as politics and culture. Politics and culture are at the same time economic and non-economic. Their structures are produced and reproduced in and through social practices. Once produced, they take on emergent qualities that cannot be reduced to the moment of social production. Politics and culture are economical because there are political and cultural workers who produce and reproduce political and economic structures that have relative autonomy from the economy.

In *Die Eigenart des Ästhetischen(The Specificity of the Aesthetic)*, Lukács describes everyday life metaphorically as a river that produces new qualities. Production is for him a flow, from which emergent qualities and novelty arise. The metaphor of society as a river is much more dynamic than the one of a building. In a building, there is a basement and there are floors that sit on top of the basement. The river in contrast is a productive flow that constantly produces something new through which the flow and the river as a system reproduce themselves.

Culture cannot be reduced to political economy; however, it is also not fully independent but grounded in the economy, and at the same time relatively autonomous. Ideas and culture cannot be read off the mode of production. We can learn from M. N. Roy that a mode of production influences but does not determine forms of culture.

11.3 Theorising communication

Erich Fromm's approach can inform a critical theory of communication in multiple respects. For example, his notion of the social character allows underpinning such a theory with foundations from critical psychology. The social character is a socio-psychological mediation. It mediates between the levels of the individual psyche and society. Fromm's distinction between the authoritarian and the humanistic character can be used for discerning among authoritarian and humanistic communication as two forms of communication. These two types can exist in relation to the economy, politics, and culture.

E. P. Thompson stresses that experience mediates between structures and individuals in society. Further developing Thompson's approach, we can argue that communication is the social experience and process that mediates between the individual and structures in society.

The human being is a natural, social, co-operating and self-conscious being. These characteristics are only possible through social relations that humans produce in society. There is a dialectic of communication and production. *Communication is productive*, and *production is communicative*. Communication is the process of the production of sociality, which includes the production and reproduction of social relations, social structures, social systems, and society as a totality. Production is a social process where communication is the mediation process.

Georg Lukács argues that work and production are the foundations of human existence and society. In his book *Zur Ontologie des gesellschaftlichen Seins* (*Ontology of Society's Being*), he characterises work and production as teleological positing. They are oriented on a goal (a telos), namely, to produce something that helps humans achieve certain purposes. What Lukács terms teleological positing, is seen as practices by Jean-Paul Sartre. Communication is a specific form of teleological positing, a symbolic process of human interaction through which humans realise the purpose of understanding each other and (re)producing social relations. This means that communication is work.

But not just is communication work, also work is communicative: For attaining certain purposes in processes of teleological positing, humans do normally not act as lone wolves but must communicate with others, coordinate actions, and to a specific degree co-operate. In Die Eigenart des Ästhetischen (*The Specificity of the Aesthetic*), Lukács argues that human information processes make use of three signal systems: signal system 1 coordinates instincts, signal system 1' thought, and signal system 2 communication. Lukács argues that humans think and communicate in order to form concepts for work in the work process.

Sartre points out that communication is not just a relation between two humans who symbolically interact with each other, but a ternary relation where the relation between two becomes possible through a third party. The third moment that mediates the social relation between two humans can be a third human, a social system, a techno-social system, a subsystem as society, or society. Sartre stresses the human aspect of mediation. Mediation does not simply involve machines, tools, and technologies, but is a human-made and human-led process that often involves techno-social systems. The communication process is a productive practice that produces and reproduces a group, that is sociality.

Henri Lefebvre argues that humans socially produce space. Social space is a bounded collection of interacting humans, social structures, social systems, and institutions. There is a dialectic of social space and human action. Humans produce and reproduce social relations. A multitude of social relations together forms social spaces. The implication is that humans also produce and reproduce social spaces that condition, that enables and constrains, human practices. Communication is a mediation process of humans' social production. Communication is the human production process of sociality, including social spaces. Communication takes place in and creates social space.

11.4 The political economy of communication

Modern society is a generalised form of accumulation, in which classes and social groups strive for the accumulation of economic power (money-capital), political power (influence on decision-making), and cultural power (reputation). Capitalism is not just an economic mode of production, but a societal mode of production, a societal formation that is based on the principle of accumulation.

Information faces a contradiction between commodification and commonification. The movement of information becoming a commons undercuts the commodification of information. Examples are creative commons, file-sharing platforms, open access publishing, open wireless communities, free software, Wikipedia, etc

There are two basic forms of social relations. One is shaped by alienation, the other one by individual and social self-management. Sartre speaks of the series in opposition to the fused group. The first is characterised by instrumentality, impersonality, domination, imitation, separation, isolation, massification, and interchangeability; the second is characterised by reciprocity, freedom, co-operation, fraternity, community, synthesis, and union. At the level of society, these differences translate into the opposition between class societies/dominative societies and socialism. Socialism is a humanist society, a society that guarantees a good life for all humans. Class societies, dominative societies, and capitalist societies are anti-humanist societies.

The two types of social relations translate into two basic types of communication:

a) Alienated, capitalist, authoritarian, anti-humanist, ideological communication;
b) Unalienated, socialist, democratic, humanist communication.

11.5 Ideology critique

Ideology tries to reduce human thought and action to automatic reflexes of signal system 1 that lack reflection and communicative encounter. This is just another formulation for saying that ideology tries to create instrumentally thinking humans who act and think like programmable machines. Ideology wants to deny human freedom of thought by trying to impose dominant interests that require exploitation and domination. Ideology tries to turn thought and consciousness into things that are robbed of universal human interests, freedom, and creativity. Ideology is what Lukács in his book *History and Class Consciousness* terms reified consciousness.

In *Die Antiquiertheit des Menschen 2(The Antiquatedness of the Human Being 2)*, Günther Anders writes that false consciousness is just the immediate goal that ideologues want to achieve. For Anders, ideology is an apparatus for the creation of a false will and false action. For Anders, commercial media's ideological manufacturing of reality entails banalisation, unilateralism, di-vidualism, sensationalism, and anti-sensationalism.

Erich Fromm's work can inform ideology critique: The ideology of having shapes life, thought, language and social action in capitalism. In capitalism, technology (including computing) is fetishized and the logic of quantification shapes social relations. A typical example is the digital positivism and fetishism of quantification advanced by big data analytics and computational social science. Fromm's quest for humanist technology and participatory computing can inform contemporary debates about digital capitalism and its alternatives. Fromm's critique of the ideology of having corresponded to Georg Lukács critique of reified consciousness, Max Horkheimer's and Theodor W. Adorno's critique of instrumental reason, and Jean-Paul Sartre's critique of analytical reason. At the level of ideology, the ideology of having, reified consciousness, instrumental reason, and analytical reason try to turn human consciousness into an instrument that assesses exploitation and domination positively. To the extent that ideology succeeds, the interest of the ruling class and dominative groups are legitimated and reproduced.

Günther Anders introduced the notions of the Promethean gap and Promethean shame as contributions to ideology critique in the context of technologies. He argues that many modern and capitalist technologies have an aura of greatness that produces a gap between production and imagination, a kind of technological fetishism. On the one hand, such technologies can under the conditions of class society and domination have alienating effects so that humans are not in control of technologies. Marx argues in this context that technologies become capital and means of control that mediate turning the human being into a machine and instrument that serves the interests of capital and bureaucracy. Anders argues that technological alienation is often accompanied by technological fetishism, humans feel ashamed of being human and imagine the machine as perfect and God-like. They blindly trust the capacities of machines and believe in technological solutions and fixes to society's problems. The resulting technocracy often makes things worse. Instead of solutions to society's problems, existing problems are exacerbated, and new ones created.

11.6 Communication/struggles/alternatives

The term communication in modern language is derived from the Latin verb *communicare*. *Communicare* means to share and to make something common. Struggles for the commons aim at overcoming class and heteronomy and to make society a realm of common control.

The humanistic shaping and design of computer technology and society has the potential to advance participatory democracy. A truly communicative society is a society, in which the original meaning of communication as making something common is the organising principle. A true communication society is a society of the commons, where the means of production, political decision-making, and collective meaning-making are controlled by humans in common. Society and therefore also communication's existence then correspond to communication's essence.

11.7 Communication and alienation

Structural inequality, discrimination, and ideology are forms of communication. They communicate dehumanisation to alienated groups and individuals. Communication is not just a direct form of mutual symbolic interaction mediated by language, but also a structural and more indirect relation where power relations communicate the superiority of certain groups such as capitalists, managers, groups who see themselves as culturally or biologically superior, etc.

Communication is a human process of symbolic interaction. Communications are communication systems, means of communication that humans use in the communication process. In alienated societies, communication and communications tend to take on an alienated character. This is not an absolute and total process. It depends on the presence and results of social struggle Table 11.4 gives an overview of forms of alienation communication(s)

Capitalism, racism, and patriarchy have aspects of economic communication, political communication, and ideological/cultural communication. These aspects are summarised in Table 11.5.

Table 11.6 applies Table 11.4 to the realm of digital media. It identifies three forms of digital alienation and identifies ten examples.

Table 11.7 describes the three forms of digital alienation as the antagonism between ruling and ruled subjects.

TABLE 11.4 Types of alienated communication(s)

Type of alienated communication(s)	Alienated communication	Alienated means of communication (= communications)
Alienated economic communication(s)	exploitation of communication workers; humans are economically disabled from or limited in producing, disseminating, or consuming information	private ownership of the means of communication
Alienated political communication(s)	exclusion of humans and their voices from political communication that influences political decisions	dictatorial governance of the means of communication
Alienated cultural communication(s)	the production and dissemination of ideology and the (re)production of asymmetries of attention and visibility of communication	ideological means of communication that advance malrecognition

TABLE 11.5 Economic, political and cultural communication in the context of class, racism, and gender-related oppression

	Class	Racism	Patriarchy, gender-related oppression
Economic communication	Structural inequality of wealth between classes as economic communication	Structural inequalities that racialised workers face in the economy as economic communication	Structural inequalities that women or other gender-defined groups face in the economy as economic communication
Political communication	Bureaucratic and state discrimination of workers as political communication	Political communication in the form of bureaucratic, state and other forms of discrimination exerted against racialised individuals	Bureaucratic and state discrimination of women or other gender-defined groups as political communication
Cultural communication	Ideological scapegoating of workers, commodity fetishism as cultural communication	ideological scapegoating of racialised individuals as cultural communication	Ideological scapegoating of women or other gender-defined groups as cultural communication

TABLE 11.6 Three forms of digital alienation

Economic digital alienation: digital exploitation	(1) Digital class relations, digital monopolies, (2) digital individualism, digital accumulation, digital competition
Political digital alienation: digital domination	(3) Digital surveillance, (4) anti-social social media, digital authoritarianism, (5) algorithmic politics, (6) online filter bubbles
Cultural digital alienation: digital ideology	(7) Digital boulevard, digital cultural industry, (8) influencer capitalism, (9) digital acceleration, (10) online false news

TABLE 11.7 Three antagonisms of digital alienation

Type of Alienation	Dominant subject(s)	Dominated subjects
Economic digital alienation:digital exploitation	Digital capital	Digital labour
Political digital alienation:digital domination	Digital dictators	Digital citizens
Cultural digital alienation:digital ideology	Digital ideologues	Digital humans

The capitalist economy, positivism, capitalist machinery/technologies, dehumanising bureaucracy, advertising, ideologies such as racism and neoliberalism, and the culture industry are examples of alienation. In the context of digital capitalist society and digital alienation, such phenomena take on forms such as digital capitalism, digital/big data positivism, digital machines, e-government, online and mobile ads, ideologies online (including online racism, online neoliberalism, etc.).

For M. N. Roy, humanism is a movement for economic, political and cultural democracy, a movement for a participatory democracy that is based on co-operatives and networks of local assemblies. Humanism questions alienation in general. Digital humanism challenges digital alienation. Humanism and socialism belong together. In the age of digital technologies, we need a digital humanism combined with digital socialism.

11.8 Humanism

A humanist society is a just, democratic, free and fair society. Table 11.8 provides an overview of the humanist organisation of society's various realms.

Table 11.9 provides an overview of forms of humanist communication and media.

Humanist, just communication means socialist media/communication in the economy, democratic media/communication in politics, and respectful communication and media that are a source of the recognition of everyone. Humanist, just communication stands in an antagonism to class-based, exploitative media/communication, dictatorial media/communication, and ideological media/communication that advance malrecognition and asymmetries of voice.

Table 11.10 provides an overview of just, humanist digital communication(s).

Communication is a central aspect of humans and society. It is not a superstructural or idealist phenomenon, but an aspect of the materiality of society and humans. Communication is the process of the production of human sociality. It is the social production process that produces sociality. Class and dominative societies are

TABLE 11.8 Dimensions of a humanist society

Realm of society	Dimension of humanism	Meaning of humanism
Economy: economic justice	Socialism	self-managed economic organisations where the means of production are collectively owned and controlled, wealth for all
Politics: political justice	Participatory democracy	All humans are enabled to participate in the decision-making processes that concern their lives
Culture: cultural justice	Respect, recognition	Human beings and groups are welcomed and their interests, identities, worldviews, and lifestyles are recognised; there is unity in diversity of identities, worldviews, interests, and lifestyles

TABLE 11.9 Forms of humanist and just communication/media

Dimension of humanism	Humanist, just communication	Humanist, just media/means of communication
Economic justice	Socialist communication: worker self-management of communication companies; enablement of humans to produce, disseminate, and consume information	Socialist media: collective ownership of means of communication (public service media, citizen media); information and information technologies as common and public goods
Political justice	Democratic communication: participation of humans in political communication so that their voices are heard and make a collective difference	Democratic media: democratic governance of the means of communication
Cultural justice	Respectful communication: the production and dissemination of respect and an inclusive culture that enables everyone to be visible in the public sphere; unity in diversity of voices; education in how to argue in complex and intelligent ways and make one's critical voice heard; respectful, complex, controversial, critical debate, and constructive disagreement	Media of recognition: friendly and inclusive means of communication that make humans' interests and voices heard and respected by others

TABLE 11.10 A typology of just, humanist digital communication(s)

Realm of society	Type of humanist, digital justice	Meaning of humanist, digital justice
Economy	Digital socialism	Network access for everyone, community is in control of technology, digital resources as common goods, green computing/ICTs
Politics	Digital democracy	Digital technologies support participatory and deliberative democracy and inclusive political communication in the public sphere
Culture	Digital recognition	Digital media/communication support making the voices of all heard, recognition of all; the unity of diversity of identities, lifestyles and worldviews; education in obtaining digital skills that help practicing unity in diversity, socialism, and democracy

alienated societies. In such societies, communication is alienated communication. The alternative to alienation is humanism. Humanism includes socialism, participatory democracy, and recognition. Overcoming alienated communication requires overcoming alienated society. Socialist communication, democratic communication, and respectful communication are the aspects of humanism. Democratic socialism is a humanism. True humanism is democratic socialism.

Index

abstract space 114
abstract thought 113
acclerationists 221–222
accumulation 16, 72
The Accumulation of Capital (Luxemburg) 12
Actor Network Theory (Bruno Latour's) 6, 201
Adorno, Theodor W. 4, 5, 40, 105, 147, 191, 196, 201, 205, 286
advertising 35, 197–198; as an ideology 94–95; propaganda and 37
Advertising: The Magic System (Williams) 94, 95
Afro-Americans 11; working conditioned of 254–256
After Dark 170
Age of Capital 8
The Age of Capital: Europe 1848–1875 (Hobsbawm) 12
The Age of Empire: Europe 1875–1914 (Hobsbawm) 12
The Age of Revolution: Europe 1789–1848 (Hobsbawm) 12
Alderson, David 236
algorithms 159
alienation 2, 4, 154, 190, 194–195, 284; capitalism and 13–14, 16; class, race and gender oppression in 261; communication and 287–290; forms of and antagonisms 16, 16t; in humanistic society 17t; as important concept in Marxist humanism 13–16; meaning of 260; political and ideological 13; racism and patriarchy in 260–261; slavery as ultimate form of 250–251; of social in capitalism 57; universality of 14–16
Althusser, Louis 4, 7, 10, 49, 50, 53, 54–56, 61, 67, 74, 92, 103, 182
Althusser/E. P. Thompson-controversy 49

Althusserian concept of articulation 57, 61, 64, 117
analytical reason 196
The Anatomy of Human Destructiveness (Fromm) 10, 19
Anders, Günther 4, 9, 10, 151–174, 201, 285, 286
Anderson, Kevin 4, 201
Anderson, Perry 61, 63, 65
Anthropocene 6, 8, 201
Die Antiquiertheit des Menschen (The Outdatedness/Antiquatedness of the Human Being) (Anders) 10, 151–152, 161, 162, 169
Die Antiquiertheit des Menschen 2 (The Outdatedness/Antiquatedness of the Human Being 2) (Anders) 285
anti-social media 42
Arbeit und Interaktion (Work and Interaction) (Habermas) 139
Arendt, Hannah 151
Are Prisons Obsolete (Davis) 11
articulation 67
artificial intelligence (AI) 41, 221, 222
The Art of Loving (Fromm) 19
Assembly (Hardt & Negri) 107
assimilation 23, 24
audience and consumer labour 162–164
authoritarian capitalism 5, 42, 236
authoritarian communication 80
authoritarianism 5, 216; exploitation and 29–30; as opposite of humanism 22
authoritarian statism 4
autonomous Marxism 107
Averroes 211
Avicenna 211
Avicenna and Aristotelean Left (Bloch) 211

Badiou, Alain 50
Balibar, Étienne 50, 57, 58, 61, 67, 268
banalisation 164–165, 168
Barthes, Roland 53, 108
base and superstructure 50, 54–55, 79, 86–89, 109–110, 118, 223, 282
Base and Superstructure (Williams) 88
Bastani, Aaron 221, 222
Being and Nothingness (Sartre) 11, 178, 179, 186
Benjamin, Walter 151, 191
Bennholdt-Thomsen, Veronika 12
Bhattacharya, Gargi 252
Bhattacharya, Subhrajit 206
big data capitalism 163
big data fetishism 156–160
big data studies 40–41
The Black Feminist Reader (Joy James & Sharpley-Whiting) 249
The Black Jacobins: Toussaint L'Ouverture and the San Domingo Revolution (James) 12
Black Lives Matter movement 5, 253–254
Black Marxism 241
Black Marxism: The Making of the Black Radical Tradition (Robinson) 12
Black Panther Party 258
Black Prophetic Fire (West) 13
Black Reconstruction in America: An Essay Toward a History of the Part Which Black Folk Played in the Attempt to Reconstruct Democracy in America (Du Bois) 11
Bloch, Ernst 4, 201, 211, 216
Bolsheviks 63
Bose, Subhas Chandra 205
Bourdieu, Pierre 264, 265, 266, 267
Brandler, Heinrich 207
Brecht, Bertold 191, 192
Brezhnev, Leonid 62
Bukharin, Nikolai 63, 64, 207
Butler, Judith 50

Capital (Marx) 13, 14, 57, 68, 155, 214
capitalism: focus on having compared to being 34; information and communication technologies in 107, 115–116, 123–124; inherently connected with racism and patriarchy 274–275, 279–281; overexploitation in 268; typology for analysis of labour in 268–269
Capitalist Patriarchy and the Case for Socialist Feminism (Eisenstein) 12
Capitalocene 8
Cassirer, Ernst 151
Castells, Manuel 50, 117
Chakrabarty, Dipesh 235
Chibber, Vivek 11, 235, 241, 259
class, role of 2; in capital and labour 14; as historical and human relationship 65; slavery and 248–249
class experience 64–65
class struggle 4, 6
class theory 241
Club 2.0 43, 44f, 170–173, 173f
cognitive capitalism 107
Cohen-Sola, Annie 177
colonialism 205
Combahee River Collective 259
commercial communication 80–81
commodification of information 123–124
Commonwealth (Hardt & Negri) 107
communication: alienation and 287–290; alternative 82, 83; authoritarian compared to humanistic 30–32; class, racism and gender-related oppression in 261–264; compared to communications 52, 80; compared to culture 51; critical theory of 283–284; culture and 222–233, 234–236; democratic and capitalist forms of 191–192; dialectic of economy and culture in 26–27; digital 79; direct and indirect 188–189; human 52; importance of form and content in 70; of love 24; Marxist theory of 49–53, 67–70, 75; materialist theory of 80–82, 104; materiality of 79; as a means of social production 70–71; mediation and 184–185; in modern language 74; political economy of 284–285; power and 190–191; purpose of 80–81; role of in society 49–50; as social process 20, 24–26; types 80–81
Communication and Capitalism: A Critical Theory (Fuchs) 1
Communications (Williams) 79, 80, 83
communicative materialism 54, 91–92, 97, 99
communism 11, 206
Communist International (Comintern)'s Presidium 206, 207
Communist Party of Great Britain (CPGB) 62
conceptual thought 224
consciousness as a material 229
consumer capitalism 197–198
consumption 35
Contribution to the Critique of Hegel's Philosophy of Law (Marx) 13
Coole, Maeve 120
co-operative media 81
critical ethics 4
Critique of Dialectical Reason (CDR) (Sartre) 11, 177, 179, 180, 182, 185, 186, 195, 200, 201
Critique of Everyday Life (Lefebvre) 10, 115, 123
Crutzen, Paul J. 8
Cultural Creation in Modern Society (Goldmann) 10, 132, 141

culturalism 51
cultural materialism 84, 91, 126
cultural studies 106
culture: communication and 222–232, 234–236; economy and 225–230; newspapers as cultural artifacts 88–89; participatory online 97; as system in itself 85; as system of meaning-making 51; as a whole way of life 80
Culture & Society (Williams) 88, 90

Dalla Costa, Mariarosa 11, 241, 246
Davis, Angela 4, 11, 201, 241, 242, 244, 245, 249, 254, 256, 257, 258, 264
death-affirmative societies 28, 29
de Beauvoir, Simone 4, 11, 201
Debray, Régis 50
deep ecology 201
Deleuze, Gilles 178
deliberative and participatory democracy 41–42
democratic communication 80, 81
democratic socialism 4
Derrida, Jacques 50, 108, 178
Desan, Mathieu Hikaru 265, 266
de Saussure, Ferdinand 53, 108
Dialectical Materialism (Lefebvre) 108
dialectical philosophy 2, 6
Dialectic of Enlightenment (Horkheimer & Adorno) 196
dictatorship 212
Dictionnaire Sartre (Noudelmann & Philippe) 179
digital alienation 288*t*
digital capitalism 104, 197, 221
digital democracy 41
digital labour 49
digital media world 83
Du Bois, W. E. B. 11, 241, 264, 267–268
Dunayevskaya, Raya 4, 56, 201, 216

Ecofeminism (Mies & Shiva) 12
Economic and Philosophic Manuscripts of 1884 (Marx) 4, 13, 33, 108, 215
economic determinism 213
The Economist 156, 157, 159
Die Eigenart des Ästhetischen (The Specificity of the Aesthetic) (Lukács) 129, 131, 132, 134, 135, 146, 282, 283
1844 Economic and Philosophic Manuscripts (Marx) 56
The Eighteenth Brumaire of Louis Bonaparte (Marx) 213, 214
Eisenstein, Zillah 4, 11, 12, 201, 241, 261
Elden, Stuart 103
Empire (Hardt & Negri) 107
Encoding/Decoding (Hall) 98

Encyclopedia of Communication Theory (Littlejohn & Foss) 178
Endnotes Collective 244
Engels, Friedrich 22, 53, 63, 93, 104, 228, 242
environmentalism 6, 8–9
Enzensberger, Hans Magnus 191, 192, 193
Epicurus 13
epistemological break (in Marx's works) 4
Epstein, Barbara 4, 201
E. P. Thompson and the Making of the New Left (ed. Winslow) 50
Erdoğan, Recep 42
Escape from Freedom (Fromm) 9, 19
Essays on Method in the Sociology of Literature (Goldman) 132, 141
essence of human beings 2
The Ethical Dimensions of Marxist Thought (West) 13
e-waste 91
existentialism 103
exploitation 29
Extinction Rebellion movement 8

fake news 42, 43
false consciousness 35–36
Fanon, Frantz 4, 198, 201
Farage, Nigel 42
fascism 4, 5, 207, 216, 236
Fascism: Its Philosophy, Professions and Practice (Roy) 11
Federici, Silvia 246
feminism 6, 11, 241, 242, 249–249
fetishism 57, 72, 104, 114, 122, 143, 262; big data 156–160; commodity 155, 168; slavery as ultimate form of 250; technological 154–156, 286
fetishism of difference 7
Feuerbach, Ludwig 56, 69
Fichte, Johann Gottlieb 212
Floyd, George 5, 262
Ford, Martin 221
For Marx (Althusser) 50, 56
Foucault, Michel 5, 50, 53, 178
Frankfurt School 9, 94, 95, 105, 129, 143, 147, 151, 164, 205
Fraser, Nancy 9
Freud, Sigmund 23
Freundlich, Elisabeth 151
Fridays For Future movement 8
From Corporate to Social Media: Critical Perspectives on Corporate Social Responsibility in media and Communication Industries (Sandoval) 12
Fromm, Erich 4–5, 9, 19–56, 201, 216, 283, 285

Fuchs, Christian 1
Fuchs, Eduard 205

Gandhi, Mahatma 208, 216–218, 234
Gandhism 205
German Ideology (Marx) 82, 214, 228
Giddens, Anthony 68
globalisation 104, 114–115, 123
Goldmann, Lucien 5, 7, 9, 10, 56, 129, 130, 131, 132, 141–146, 201, 216
Gorz, André 5, 201
Gramsci, Antonio 89, 90, 105, 181
Grundrisse (Marx) 13, 14, 98, 230
guaranteed basic income 247

Habermas, Jürgen 49, 105, 129–130, 139
Hall, Stuart 50, 51, 52, 53, 97, 98, 99, 105, 106
Hardt, Michael 107
Harvey, David 5, 14, 15, 201
Hegel, Georg Wilhelm Friedrich 2, 13, 137, 138, 139, 141, 212, 233
Hegelian Marxism 2, 104, 180, 213
hegemony, concept (Gramsci's) 89, 90
Heidigger, Martin 141, 151, 173
Von Herder, Johann Gottfried 212
Hesiod 153
heteronomous societies 72, 73, 74
historicist humanism 182
History and Class Consciousness (Lukács) 10, 93, 105, 131, 195, 285
Hitler, Adolf 19, 151
Hobbes, Thomas 242
Hobsbawm, Eric J. 11, 12, 241, 252, 253
Hoggart, Richard 51
Honneth, Axel 9
Horkheimer, Max 5, 19, 40, 105, 191, 196, 201, 205, 286
housework as productive labour 243–245, 247–248
human being 20–21; as co-operating beings 21; as dialectic of body and mind 21; as measure of everything in society 210; as social being 56; social production as essence of 24–25
humanism 3, 50, 106, 207, 208, 233; economy and 211, 212; freedom as essence of 210, 211; morality in 210; as opposite of authoritarianism 22; as romanticism 209–212; as socialism 3; and structuralism 107–110, 116–119; as theory movement 56; as world view and political movement 226–227
humanistic character 28–29
humanist modernity 219, 220
Humanists International 208
The Human Sciences and Philosophy (Goldmann) 10

Hungarian revolution (1956) 56, 62
Husserl, Edmund 151

I Am a Women and a Human: A Marxist-Feminist Critique of Intersectionality Theory (Mitchell) 12
idealism 212
idealistic mystification 179
ideation 225
ideological state apparatus (ISA) 57
ideology 195–196; advertising as 94–95; authoritarian 42, 43; class 227; concept of 92–93; critique 285–286; as false consciousness 93, 164; as form of communication 20, 66; and instrumental reason 140–141; Marxist understandings of 93–94; and the media 164–169; mode of having compared to mode of being 33–35; racism as 252; as social unconscious 32–33
Ideology and Ideological State Apparatuses (Althusser) 50, 55
ideology critique 3–4
individualism 11, 142, 144
information society 49, 91
Information Technology and Daily Life (Lefebvre) 116, 125
In Search of Method (SM) (Sartre) 177, 180
Institute of Social Research 19
instrumental media 81
instrumental reason 105; ideologies and 140–141
international division of digital labour (IDDL) 91–92
The International Encyclopedia of Communication theory and Philosophy (Jensen & Craig) 178
Internet 83, 201; ideologies of and on 96–97; instrumental logic of society and 83; and surveillance capitalism 163–164; YouTube 192–194
intersectionality theory 258–260

James, C. L. R. 5, 11, 12, 56, 201, 216, 241, 250
James, Selma 11, 12, 241, 243, 246
Jameson, Frederic 178
Janeism 144
Jena philosophy (of Hegel) 139
The Jewish Question (Marx) 13

Kant, Emmanuel 141, 144, 212
Korsch, Karl 5, 201, 205
Kosik, Karel 5, 56, 201
Kristeva, Julia 108

Krushchev, Nikita 62
Kurzweil, Raymond 160, 161
Kuusinen, Otto Willie 207

labour in commercial media 162–164
Lacan, Jacques 23
Lacanian theory 7
Laclau, Ernesto 50, 51, 106
language as refection of material reality 84
Lasswell's formula 95
Latour, Bruno 6
Lefebvre, Henri 5, 9, 10, 56, 103–126, 201, 216, 284
Lenin, Vladimir 11, 206
Lenin and Philosophy and Other Essays (Althusser) 57
Le Pen, Marine 42
Lessing, Gotthold Ephraim 212
Lévy, Bernard-Henri 180
liberalism 229–230
life-affirmative societies 28, 29
Locke, John 230
Long Revolution (Williams) 54
The Long Revolution (Williams) 90
Lukács, Georg/György 5, 9, 10, 36, 56, 69, 71, 93, 94, 95, 105, 129–147, 154, 164, 180, 183, 185, 195, 196, 201, 205, 282, 283, 286
Lukács and Heidegger: Towards a New Philosophy (Goldmann) 10, 144
Luxemburg, Rosa 11, 12, 216, 226, 241, 274
Luxemburgism 207
Lyotard, Jean-François 178

The Making of the English Working Class (Thompson) 10, 50, 66
Malthus, Thomas 230
Man for Himself (Fromm) 19
Manjapra, Kris 235
Mao, Tse Tung 54, 62, 64
Maoism 63
Marcuse, Herbert 5, 23, 56, 105, 151, 165, 167, 191, 201, 205, 216, 220, 234
Marx, Capital and the Madness of Economic Reason (Harvey) 15
Marx, Karl 4, 5, 6, 11, 13, 14, 16, 33, 51, 53, 68, 69, 81, 93, 98, 104, 106, 129, 139, 154, 181, 196, 213, 216, 228, 233, 241, 243, 286
Marxism and Literature, Communications (Williams) 10, 84, 87, 92
Marxism and the Philosophy of Language (Vološinov) 84
Marxism and the Problems of Linguistics (Stalin) 62
Marxist communication theory 104–105

Marxist humanism 103, 104; alienation as central category of 2, 13–16; decline of 5; definition 1–2; dialectical philosophy in 2; as form of open Marxism 3; and quest for socialism 19–21; reasons for need for renewal of 5–8
Marx's Concept of Man (Fromm) 9–10
masculinity 264, 265
materialism 223–224, 226
materialist theory of communication 80–82, 86, 997
McArthur, Douglas 154
McGuigan, Jim 79
Means of Communication as Means of Production (Williams) 85
mechanistic conceptions of society 63, 64
mediation, concept of 69, 88
Mehring, Franz 22, 206
Merleau-Ponty, Maurice 5, 178, 201
meta-racism 254
Mies, Maria 11, 12, 241, 243
Mill, James 230
Mill, John Stuart 230
Milligan, Martin 215
Mitchell, Eve 11, 12, 241, 259
Modern Politics, and World Revolution, 1917–1936: The Rise and Fall of the Communist International (James) 12
Modern World System (Wallerstein) 122
Modi, Narendra 42
Molotov, Yvacheslav 207
monopoly capitalism 145
Moore, Jason W. 8
Moore's Law 40
Mouffe, Chantalle 106
Multitude (Hardt & Negri) 107
Münzberg, Willi 205–206

National Association for the Advancement of Colored People (NAACP) 11
nationalism 216, 236, 253
Nazi Germany 31, 151, 207
Negri, Antonio 50, 107
neoliberalism 96, 106, 274
New Humanism: A Manifesto (Roy) 11
new materialism 6, 201
nihilism 11
Nkrumah, Kwame 5, 201
Notes on Dialectics: Hegel, Marx and Lenin (James) 12
Nyerere, Julius 5, 201

occasional philosophy 152
Ollman, Bertell 5, 201

Zur Ontologie des gesellschaftlichen Seins (On the Ontology of Social Being) (Lukács) 10, 131, 132, 180, 283
open access journals and media 83
Orbán, Viktor 42
orientalism 6

Paris protests, May 1968 7
Parti communiste français (PCF) 62, 103, 177
Pascal, Blaise 144
paternal communication 80, 81
patriarchy 11, 265; alienation and 260–261; inherently connected with racism and capitalism 274–275, 279–281
Patriarchy and Accumulation on a World Scale: Women in the International Division of Labour (Mies) 12
Patriarchy at Work: Patriarchal and Capitalist Relations in Employment, 1800–1984 (Walby) 12–13
Peck, Janice 178
Phenomenology of Mind (Hegel) 137
Piaget, Jean 141
Policing the Crisis (Hall) 52
post-colonial theory 6
Postcolonial Theory and the Specter of Capital (Chibber) 11
post-humanism 56, 160–161, 201
post-Marxism 53
postmodernism 5–6, 7, 106
poststructuralism 5, 7, 53, 201
Poulantzas, Nicos 50
The Poverty of Theory and Other Essays (Thompson) 10, 50, 59, 61
The Power of Women and the Subversion of the Community (Dalla Costa & S. James) 11, 243
practico-inert 185–188
Prague Spring (1968) 56
praxis 2, 4, 7, 104, 181, 182, 183
Praxis Group, Yugoslavia 5, 56, 181, 201
Principles of Radical Democracy (Roy) 236
prison-industrial complex 256–257
Production of Space (Lefebvre) 103
The Production of Space and the Critique of Everyday Life (Lefebvre) 10, 104, 110, 111, 116, 117, 133
Promethean Gap 153, 154, 286
Prometheus 153–154, 160
propaganda 37
Putin, Vladimir 42

Race in North America: Origin and Evolution of a Worldview (Smedley) 12
Race Matters (West) 13
racial capitalism 251–252
racialised labour 273
Racine, Jean 144
racism 5, 198, 248–249; alienation and 260–261; dimensions of 254; as ideology 252; inherently connected with capitalism and patriarchy 274–275, 279–281; in prison-industrial complex 256–257
Racism: From Slavery to Advanced Capitalism (Wilson) 13
radical humanism 213, 236
The Ragged-Trousered Philanthropists (Tressell) 94
Ranciére, Jacques 50
rationalism 57, 81
Reading Capital (Althusser & Balibar) 50, 56, 58
Reason, Romanticism and Revolution (Roy) 11, 208, 210
The Reasoner: A Quarterly Journal of Socialist Humanism 62
red-green socialism 9
reification 105, 194–195, 250
reified consciousness 36
Representation (Hall) 53
reproductive labour 242–245
Revolution and Counter-Revolution in China (Roy) 11, 205, 226
revolutionary humanism 16
Ricardo, David 230
Rise of Robots: Technology and the Threat of a Jobless Future (Ford) 221
Robinson, Cedric J. 11, 12, 241, 250, 251, 252, 253
Roediger, David 11, 12, 241, 264, 266
Rowbotham, Sheila 5, 201
Roy, Manabendra Nath (a.k.a. M. N. Roy) 5, 9, 11, 201, 205–237, 282, 290

Said, Edward 5, 201
Sandoval, Marisol 11, 12, 241, 268–269
Sane Society (Fromm) 19
The Sane Society (Fromm) 9
Sartre, Jean-Paul 5, 9, 56, 103, 177–200, 201, 283, 284, 286
Sartre Dictionary (Cox) 179
Saville, John 62
Schaff, Adam 5, 201
Scholz, Roswitha 243
Science and Philosophy (Roy) 11
Science of Logic (Hegel) 139
semiotics 53, 105
Seventeen Contradictions and the End of Capitalism (Harvey) 15

Shiva, Vandana 12
signal systems 135–136, 141
slavery 248–249, 250–251; compared to wage-labour and reproductive-labour 269–270; expansion or restrictive usage of term 270–273; as part of formulation and development of capitalism 253–254
Smedley, Audrey 11, 12, 241, 248
Smith, Adam 230
Smythe, Dallas 162
Snowden, Edward 83, 123
social beings 56–57
social character types 29–30, 29*t*
socialisation 23, 24
socialism: as humanism 3; as ideology of the working class 207–208; quest for an Marxist humanism 19–21
socialist humanism 20–21, 62
Socialist Humanism (Thompson) 53
Socialist Humanism: An International Symposium (ed. Fromm) 10
social media 166–168, 172
social production 224–225
social production of space 107, 109, 110–115, 119–123
social relations 19–20, 67–68; basic forms of 284–285; communication inherently involved in 84–85; as mediator between economy and culture 22–23; socialisation and assimilation in 23–24
Sohn-Rethel, Alfred 113
Soper, Kate 5, 201
The Souls of Black Folk (Du Bois) 11
Soviet socialism 62
Spencer, Robert 235, 236
Srnicek, Nick 221, 222
Stalin, Joseph V. 62, 63, 64, 199, 207
Stalinism 3, 4, 61, 62, 82, 103, 108, 198–200, 205, 207
State Capitalism and World Revolution (James) 12
Stencilled Occasional Papers-Series (Hall) 98
Strache, H. C. 42
structuralist Marxism 50, 53, 74, 103, 104–105, 142; humanism and 107–110, 116–119
The Structural Transformation of the Public Sphere (Habermas) 105
structure/agency problem 49–50
structures of feeling 90
Das System der spekulativen Philosophie (System of Speculative Philosophy) (Hegel) 139

technological determinism 96, 155–156, 219
technological fetishism 154–156, 286

technology 216–222, 233–234; in dialectical relationship to society 219–220; grounding principles of 38; humanised 38–39; to obtain goals 19; philosophy of 173–174; potentials of modern 219, 220–221; rise of in capitalist society 37; use of alternative 39
teleological positing 71
Television, Technology and Cultural Form (Williams) 10, 96
Thalheimer, August 205, 207
Thatcherism 96
Theogony (Hesiod) 153
Theorizing Patriarchy (Walby) 12
Theorizing Violence (Walby) 13
theory of communication (Jürgen Habernas) 49
Theses on the National and Colonial Questions (Lenin) 11, 206
Thompson, E. P. 5, 9, 10, 49–66, 74, 106, 107, 201, 216, 283
Thorez, Maurice 62
To Have Or To Be? (Fromm) 19
Tressell, Robert 94
Trotsky, Leon 63, 64
Trump, Donald 42, 83, 92, 265
truth, societal 3

unilateralism 165, 168
Universal Alienation (Harvey) 14

Vincze, Enikö 273
Vološinov, Valentin 84
Von Werlhof, Claudia 12

wages for housework 245–247
The Wages of Whiteness: Race and the Making of the American Working Class (Roediger) 12, 264
Walby, Sylvia 11, 12, 241
The Walk Free Foundation 270
Wallerstein 122
Weber, Max 68
Weil, Felix 206
West, Cornel 11, 13, 241, 251
Wiggershaus, Rolf 129
Wikipedia 83
Wilders, Geert 42
William Morris: Romantic to Revolutionary (Thompson) 10, 50
Williams, Alex 221, 222
Williams, Raymond 5, 9, 10, 25, 26, 51, 52, 54, 70, 79–96, 105, 106, 107, 118, 123, 126, 141, 201, 216
Wilson, Carter 11, 13, 241, 254
Winslow, Carl 50

Wired Magazine 156, 157, 159
Women, Race & Class (Davis) 11
Women: The Last Colony (Mies, Bennholdt-Thomsen & Von Werlhof) 12
work as model of social production 183

The Wretched of the Earth (Fanon) 198
Wright, Erik Olin 266

Žižek, Slavoj 50

For Product Safety Concerns and Information please contact our EU
representative GPSR@taylorandfrancis.com
Taylor & Francis Verlag GmbH, Kaufingerstraße 24, 80331 München, Germany

www.ingramcontent.com/pod-product-compliance
Lightning Source LLC
Chambersburg PA
CBHW070746020526
44116CB00032B/1994